AVATĀRA

Antonio T. de Nicolás

AVATĀRA

THE HUMANIZATION OF PHILOSOPHY THROUGH THE BHAGAVAD GĪTĀ

A philosophical journey through Greek Philosophy, contemporary philosophy the *Bhagavad Gītā* on Ortega y Gasset's intercultural theme: Man and Circumstance

Including a new translation with critical notes of the *Bhagavad Gītā*

With Prologue by Raimundo Panikkar

NICOLAS HAYS, Ltd.

Published in cooperation with
The Institute for Advanced Studies of World Religions
New York, N.Y.

Library of Congress Cataloging in Publication Data

de Nicolás, Antonio T.
Avatāra, the humanization of philosophy through the Bhagavad Gītā.

Includes bibliographical references and index.
I. Mahābhārata. Bhagavadgītā. 2. Philosophy—History. I. Mahābhārata. Bhagavadgītā. II. Title.
BL1130.D46 294.5′924 76-152
ISBN 0-89254-001-X

Nicolas Hays Ltd.
40 East 20 St.
New York, N.Y. 10003

Library of Congress Catalog Card Number 76-152
International Standard Book Number 0-89254-001-X Hardbound
0-89254-002-8 Softbound
Printed in the United States of America

For Susie, who wanted to know.

Acknowledgements

My very special thanks to Ernest McClain who, with his constant enthusiasm, friendship, and positive suggestions on the structure of music as implied in my previous book, *Four-Dimensional Man,* made it so easy for me to write Chapter Six of this book and venture other interpretations I might, without him, have kept to myself, and lived the rest of my life the victim of their weight. Now they are scattered to the four winds and their echoes might open new human spaces for all of us. I thank him also for the musical charts he drew for Chapter Six.

I am also deeply grateful to Dr. Christopher George. He has not only pain-stakingly seen to every Sanskrit word in the text, but has also helped me with major editorial suggestions in the rearrangement of the English text so that the whole book would be more bearable for the reader. But above all, I am grateful for one of the first fringe benefits of this book: our friendship.

My very special thanks to the editors of *Main Currents in Modern Thought,* especially Emily Sellon and Patrick Milburn, who read through this manuscript several times and encouraged me by publishing abstracts of some of the chapters in their magazine.

My thanks to my colleagues Donn Welton, Dick Howard, Chung-ying Cheng, Kenneth Inada and Thomas Berry, who read through some parts of the manuscript and helped me, with their criticisms, to make my own philosophical activity more clear to myself and, hopefully, to the reader.

The efforts of my friends and colleagues, and even my own, would have been almost impossible without the unselfish dedication to every one of the words in this book by Linda Wallace. She typed the manuscript several times, at odd hours, under great pressure and sacrifices, without a single complaint. To her I am deeply grateful.

And last, but not least, my thanks to this "world in transition" of the State University of New York at Stony Brook. It is through this concrete world of great faith, narrow perspectives and struggling to gain vision, that this book was conceived and delivered.

Prologue

Spain, India and North America

In our times of all too often superficial attempts to compare East and West on practically every level, from politics to religion, it is refreshing to find a study which takes seriously, even incorporates 'bodily,' the encounter and mutual fecundation of these two great branches of human experience. It is not by 'comparing' the twain that they shall meet, but rather by a new and yet primordial incest—but now is not the moment to propound my own ideas (India).

In our times of little philosophical awareness in which authentic philosophy is replaced by analyses from the sciences or questionnaires by sociologists—important as these are, and honorable exceptions though there be—it is encouraging to meet a daring effort at genuine philosophical reflection on the only thing with which philosophy really ever deals, namely life and the ever elusive, ever evolving reality . . . rather than with 'ideas,' 'concepts' or facts from the past or even from the present. It is not by thinking *about* others and *about* data that we can genuinely philosophize. Rather, by thinking *with* others and *through* past experiences, we may indeed contribute to the *doing* of one of the highest and most effective human activities—but again, I should restrain myself from elaborating further (Spain).

In our times of 'academic' self-consciousness, 'critical' awareness and 'scientific' approaches to just about everything, especially in academia, it is a positive sign to find an ambitious study of the sort many of us had intended when we first began to stick our necks out in the intellectual 'arena' and which we shelved for lack of time, or courage, or security or perhaps real human *pathos*. It is not by creating perfect works that perfection is achieved—only Allah is perfect, as any muslim carpet weaver knows—but it is by risking error and accepting correction that we can contribute to enhancing the quality of all life under the sun—but once again, it is not my task now to criticize the book I am introducing (North America).

Now a book dealing with the Kṣatriya spirit, Spanish philosophy and the North American environment, i.e., touching upon almost my entire 'circumstance' and moreover coming from a friend I have seen in those three worlds under much different conditions than those he finds himself in now, and for whose inner urge and *daimon* I can vouch, seems to call to me, to conjure my *karma,* my *gana* and my *pleasure* to write a *pro-logos* or, quoting Ortega, a "pre-translation" of what is the case. For Don José (as he remained for some of us) that "into which being is translated is precisely language, the *logos."* Language is nothing but the translation, the very revelation or the simple manifestation of being. For this reason being and truth have the same root and often the same name in Sanskrit: *sat, satya.*

But to speak of being, to translate it into language is the business of the author, of the *logos*. My *dharma* here is simply that of a 'pro-loger,' i.e., that of putting in a word both *for* and *before* the logos of the author. I shall try to dispatch these two functions, albeit in an overcondensed manner.

If being or reality could be totally translated into logos, there would be no room for any prologue; the logos would exhaust reality, blanket it, and leave no place for anything else. There could be no-thing *before* the logos. If the author of a logos could say everything—even everything he wants to say—there would equally be no reason for any other logos *for* him.

My *pro-logue* will then, first of all, be to say a word *for* the author, to underscore the importance of Antonio de Nicolás' attempt here. As I have already hinted, this man authentically philosophizes; he is engaged in real thinking and tries to draw his experience from the vast field of the western world. His incursions into the development of western man may be debatable, but they show the workings of a mind coming to grips with real problems and in close contact with all of western history. His attempt is to decipher the mystery outside and within himself. He does not, further, remain at the level of spare generalities, but takes his inspiration from the important and neglected Ortega y Gasset. Equipped with some of Ortega's fundamental philosophical insights, the author takes a giant step—like one of the traditional strides of Viṣṇu—and reinterprets for us a major document of an ancient time: the Bhagavad Gītā.

Even if the reader should not agree with some or many of his visions, his very daring in undertaking such a formidable task situates de Nicolás in a prominent place, both as an interpreter of the Gītā and as a cross-cultural thinker. His is more than a mere essay. It is a study in depth of a sacred book with hermeneutical tools quite different from those a classical mimāmšaka or a traditional biblicist might employ. He would probably agree with me that any authentic reading of a text is as much a reading *into* as a reading *from.* And a sacred document is always a text which allows this liberal reading without screams of betrayal. The Gītā is certainly a happy choice for many reasons, which I need not go into now, except for the obvious fact that today she has become one of the bridges between the wisdom of the East and that of the West.

Antonio de Nicolás' effort to bring together these three afore-mentioned worlds is an enterprise which surely merits our putting in a word *for* it. And this is my pro-logue.

And now my word *before* his. If I am rightly understood when I say that the logos is only the translation, the incarnation, revelation, expression . . . of being or reality, then my prologue here is not to say something about the logos of the book, or even something 'else' by way of criticism or compliment. It should rather be an essay to make room for a special awareness, an awareness of the unsaid, of the unthought, of that reality which is impermeable to the logos, above all because any trans-lation would kill it outright. It can no more thrive in foreign soil than it can live in an alien body. This is the *mythos,* the other component of the real; it is also the *pneuma,* the *brahman,* the Spirit irreducible to *logos,* to *ātman,* to *Word.*

The way to proceed towards this sphere of the real is not a method of mere rationality. It could be one of inspiring like the Spirit, or suggesting like the Delphic oracle, or breathing like only brahman. *"La musica callada, la soledad sonora,"* the 'silent music and sonorous solitude' of St. John of the Cross, mentioned by de Nicolás, could perhaps introduce us into this new realm.

Here there is of course nothing to say. It remains for us only to direct our attention and intention to that realm where East and West do not need to meet, because they have never parted; where the human, the cosmic and the divine are neither dialectically opposed nor existentially severed, because they are not 'three' but one reality. Is this not the realm into which Kṛṣṇa tries to lead Arjuna? Is this not the hidden kingdom, the living myth? Is the author not urging us to 'do' philosophy, to 'embody' the mental, to 'real-ize' the primacy of life?

Once upon a time, i.e., once, viz. at a time which can only occur once, for it is not repeatable . . . it happens upon the time, not just in time, let alone on time; once upon a time—at that primordial time which we can all re-enact if we do not let ourselves be exhausted by and drowned in time—there were Yama, the Man, the God, Culture, the West, and Yamī, the Woman, the Goddess, Nature, the East. They were alone in all Universe. What else could there be? Yama felt barren and despondent, full of power, weapons, riches, technologies and yet on the brink of despair. Yamī felt powerless, anarchic, hungry, dirty, poor, forlorn and on the verge of paroxysm. And for all that, they were twins, they wanted to be together and eventually to bear an offspring which would belie all the unhappy *kalpas* of exploitation, injustice and suffering. At the same time they knew that a merely sentimental embrace would kill them both, would uproot them, would be forbidden by the universal *dharma*. Yamī yearned for the embrace—she wanted technology, riches, all the gadgets of science, all the know-how, all the while knowing that this would be her death. Yama was convinced that he did not have the answer—that he would kill perhaps the only remaining hope in the universe, the first innocence, the free care in the carefree attitude toward life. Incest would solve nothing because the estrangement was too enormous. One cannot have it both ways. Nobody can serve two masters. Freedom and justice, riches and happiness, know-how and know-why, science and wisdom . . . where are they in harmonious 'convivencia'—as Ortega would say—in our world? The universe has been able to subsist only because the Gods retired to their mansions and left room for Man on earth. Then apartheid politics began. Let the East develop its idiosyncracy and the West follow its destiny. What is all this clamor for a new incarnation? Has it not cost us millenia of effort to disentangle matter from spirit, body from soul, the human from the divine, human beings from all other animals and terrestrial beings? The 'circumstance' is the 'man,' the earth is not man's body nor the divine another dimension of the real of which Man is the epistemic but not the ontic, not even the ontological, center. Why this desire now to blur all the careful distinctions that Man has so painfully elaborated? Such refrains are familiar enough nowadays; the dialectical quandary. Yama and Yamī want to be together and yet they sense that the new original sin that will ensue would only make the following *kalpa* worse than the previous one.

Once upon a time, the Ṛg Veda tells us, the future of the entire human race depended on whether Yama and Yamī would come together, transgressing the *dharma* of the Gods that forbids 'morals' to perpetrate incest, an act fitting only for divine beings. If they do come together, their affront to the *dharma* is worse than Arjuna killing kith and kin. If they do not, this spells the end of the human race. And the two famous hymns of the Ṛg Veda keep silent about the denouement of the dilemma, apparently because they did not want us to fall into the dialectical trap. The incest was not perpetrated, nor was the human race stillborn. And this overcoming of dialectics simply lets the miracle of life be, it leaves room for the unsaid, the unthought and the unthinkable without despising the dialectical rules, or the place and the proper function of the logos. The myth cannot be reduced to logos, just as the spirit is in no way subordinate to the word.

I am not going to explain, to translate this myth. It is only a word *before* the authentic word that the reader is now invited to enjoy in the pages which I have the honor to present.

Raimundo Panikkar
Santa Barbara
Univesity of California
August 1975

Contents

Part I

The Forest

This book you are holding in your hands was originally conceived in several forests: *Mount Abu* and *Mahabaleshuar*, in India; *La Herrería,* in El Escorial, Spain; and finally in Setauket, in the forest surrounding my own home in America. The writing of this book was done in a single breath of inspiration when I realized that my American forest contained all of the others, or to be more nearly accurate, when I realized that in the American forest where I now live, the other forests are as present to me as they were separately years ago.

The text of the book, its thoughts, are divided into two parts. The first part (Part II) concentrates on the radical origin of these thoughts in the ground on which they rest, the human ground of Europe and America. The second part (Parts III and IV) deals with India and concretely with the Bhagavad Gītā. The whole text of this book—its thoughts—deals not only with thoughts but also with the actions they justify, as diverse and legitimate as one may wish to find or avoid in one's life or one's dreams.

The book has several introductions to the Eastern and Western cultural examples it examines. The whole book in fact is an introduction. The total unity of the book, however, could be missed if one paid too much attention to the trees, the thoughts, and isolated them from the total forest of the book. The unity of the book is "The Forest": the meditation, a special kind of activity, which links the whole book together. It is this activity that orders thoughts and actions to form the ground upon which men set their human foot to take every human and authentic step that this book focuses upon. Since the book, however, does not describe or define how this is done and simply goes ahead and does it, it has been considered convenient to add Part I here.

What constitutes a human ground? On which soil do I stand as a human to take my steps forward or backward? What makes a human way, and how do I go about discovering it by myself, without gurus, soothsayers, priests, prophets, or psychiatrists? On what solid ground does my human life, to be mine and to be human, stand?

Part I will not attempt to give an answer. Instead it will offer a series of images—not yet meditations—leading to a path, or a way. An invitation to a journey which no one can undertake unless he or she first discovers the need to do so. To discover the need is to already discover the untravelled dark corridors of one's own biographical life upon which one's thoughts and actions rest, like so many tired bats waiting for the dusk to roam blindly.

They have just killed another bull, a *toro.* A *toro,* a Spanish fighting bull, has hardly any similarities at all with the bull the English language designates by that name. The *toro* is a compact fury of life, thrust, power, legs, and horns. At least this is how they were before I stopped seeing bull-fights.

The Spanish *toro de lidia* is a special breed, wild and fierce, and is kept that way for one very special purpose, to die face to face with a man in a bull-ring in front of thousands of people. The sight of the fierce and powerful animal next to the man in the ring is almost ridiculous. Any move of the bull, or even the wind, and one would suspect the man had no chance at all. Yet the bull is killed. He almost always dies, sometimes killing, but almost always in vain.

The *toro de lidia,* the wild bull, has two weaknesses. First, he is an animal "on the spot" because he has only one spot, *la querencia,* and second, his fury can be enticed, with instant needs and desires, away from his spot or *querencia* just by moving the flaming cape in front of his horns. Away from his one spot, the wild bull is lost, his fury controlled, his power reduced, his death imminent.

The first thing the bull does when charging into the bull-ring is to give away his spot to the bullfighter by returning to it, again and again. In the lonely moment before the fight starts, all eyes are on the bullfighter and the bull. The bull is looking for his own security, his spot, as the air smells of danger and blood. This is the bull's moment; the one moment he has been prepared by generations of breeding before him. Yet against man, a trained man who knows the fighting, and whose feet "know" all the spots in the ring as his own, one spot to live in danger is not enough. The bull must die. He must almost always die, always frightened, almost always in vain. They have just killed another bull.

They have just *zombied* another student. To the north side of the campus of my university there is a flat two-story building heralded by a lonesome, naked, tall, dead tree. Some call them the totem pole and the slaughter house. Actually they are a lonesome, naked, tall, dead tree and the Infirmary. They are in the dead center of the campus. I have known students of mine to come out of there transformed into perfect zombies.

Someone in the seventeenth century said that *having thoughts* was all there was to thinking. Later, someone added that *having thoughts* could be read as behaving in a certain manner. Others linked having thoughts and behavior to the brain; others determined the behavior to be had; others invented the pills, electric shocks, lobotomies, etc., which would guarantee the uniformity of behavior, and therefore, the death of anxiety. Again there is man, beyond freedom and dignity, reduced to the one spot where fighting bulls die.

What Descartes started in the seventeenth century is now systematically being executed in jails, hospitals, on psychiatric couches, and campus infirmaries. The totem pole is dead, yet aims for the skies, and the slaughter houses are as active as the bull-rings. Where is the human soil? Where are the live trees, the shadows, the leaves? The bulldozer took them away!

Julián Marías, that perfect disciple of Ortega y Gasset, and his own master, told me last May, "Go to *La Herrería*! Recover Ortega!"

La Herrería is a forest in El Escorial, so near Madrid that you can take your secretary to lunch in the Felipe II Hotel and be back at the office in time for the afternoon shift. In our younger days we all knew the route by heart, having to escape Madrid in the heat of summer, girlfriends on Sundays, or the boredom of Holy Week when all entertainment was closed by Ministerial Order. Few, however, knew *La Herrería,* the forest. None knew it as Ortega knew it.

I find it an anachronism that Ortega discovered this

forest in 1914 to be the "radical reality of human life." Hinduism and Buddhism knew about the forest in the same sense; they both were born in the forest. Judaism, however, was expelled from the forest the moment Adam and Eve decided to roam about and ask the apple and the tree for knowledge. An angel has stood at the door ever since with a flaming sword to prevent anyone from entering. The external, hard, direct way of the law was the reply man gave to himself in view of the failure of his pretended autonomy.

Christendom was born in the desert, away from the world, because it could not allow itself to belong to the world. Christianity was born in the village, in the city, when the "word became flesh." It foresaw the possibility of the transformation of the world through the paths of knowledge opened by The Word. Christianity believed that the humanization of the world could come only through the salvation of community. The Greeks populated the forest, but Moira, destiny, made knowledge in the forest almost trivial.

Ortega agrees with Hinduism and Buddhism that the forest and the world are inseparable and both need to be lived, if not simultaneously—this is only for the most proficient—at least successively, for the present is the compact presence of the past and their mutual projection, the future. Even more, Ortega agrees with Hinduism and Buddhism that the forest is the humanization of the world; that thoughts and actions have a common ground: meditation, the forest. So, by the hand of Ortega, let us enter the Forest.

> The monastery of the Escorial rises on a hill. The south side of this hill slopes down under the covering of a grove which is simultaneously of both oak and ash trees. The site is called "La Herrería." The character of the exemplary gray mass of the building changes with the seasons, for the thick blanket of vegetation spread out at its feet is copper-hued in winter, golden in autumn, and dark green in summer. Spring passes through here swiftly, instantaneously and exuberantly—like an erotic image through the steely soul of a monk. The trees are rapidly covered with luxuriant masses of leaves of a bright fresh green; the ground disappears under an emerald grass which, in its turn, is one day dressed up with the yellow of daisies, another day with the purple of

lavender. There are places of a wonderful silence—which is never absolute silence. When all things around are completely quiet, the noiseless void they leave demands that it be filled by something, and then we hear the pounding of our own hearts, the throbbing of the blood in our temples, the flow of air which floods into our lungs and then hurriedly rushes out. All this is disturbing because it has too concrete a meaning. Each heart beat sounds as if it were to be our last. The following beat which saves us always seems to come accidentally and does not guarantee the next one. That is why it is preferable to have a silence in which purely decorative, inconcrete sounds are heard. This place is like that. It is crisscrossed by clear murmuring streams, and small birds sing amid its verdure—greenfinches, linnets, orioles, and an occasional sublime nightingale.

Is this the forest? Not yet. It has to be *my forest* before proceeding any further. I have to feel it as mine, with its hills, meadows, birds, the passing of the seasons, sounds, and anxious silences. It has to be a forest where I hear the pounding of my own heart, the throbbing of my own blood in my temples, the flow of air rushing through my own lungs and out of me. It must have the flow of my biographical rivers running through it to be mine, to be *the* forest.

The forest has to be a place like this to me for in a forest like this I have been *thrown in* to make my life. My forest and I make each other necessary; without the forest there is no reference to me; without me there is no forest. Which forest? This one or that one? None and each one! It is that ubiquitous bull-ring where I find myself immersed in the immense drama of living. Without the forest I cannot make my life. Without me the forest is a bundle of mute things, senseless, like my life without the forest. My possibilities, in the face of the forest, in the face of this concrete portion of circumstance in front of me, constitute the inner meaning, the being, the reason for being of the forest. I, like a new born tree, am one of the things I find in the forest. While I, the true I, and the forest will start right now looking for each other, to unravel the mystery. "I am myself plus my circumstance" says Ortega, and "unless I save it I cannot save myself." Myself-plus-my-circumstance is what I find in my forest. In saving them in their mutual relations and dependences I save the first I, the I which like the forest escapes me-and-my-circumstance as I approach.

The dramatic hero advances like a projected arrow towards the goal of self-discovery by giving meaning to his own life, his own self. But which self? Mine of course! The one I find in front of me, around me, above me, like I find a tree or a landscape? Yes, and no. When can I rest in the quest for my own meaning? When I start looking at it!

How many trees make up a forest? How many houses a city?

As the peasant of Poitiers used to sing,

> *La hauteur des maisons*
> *empêche de voir la ville,*
>
> (The height of the buildings
> does not allow one to see the city)

or, as the German proverb goes, one cannot see the forest for the trees. Forest and city are two things essentially deep, and depth is fatally condemned to become a surface (superficial) if it is to be visible.

Right now I have around me as many as two dozen grave oaks and graceful ashes. Is this a forest? Certainly not. These are the trees I see of a forest. The real forest is made up of the trees which I do not see. The forest is an invisible nature——hence the halo of mystery its name preserves in all languages.

I could now get up and take one of these blurred trails ahead of me, criss-crossed by the blackbirds. The trees I saw before will be replaced by similar trees. The forest will be breaking up into a series of successively visible portions, but I shall never find it where I am. The forest flees from one's eyes.

When we arrive at one of these small clearings in the verdure, it seems as if a man had been sitting there on a stone, his elbows on his knees, his hands on his temples, and that just as we were about to arrive he had stood up and left. We suspect that this man, taking a short roundabout path, has gone to take up the same position not far from us. If we yield to the desire to surprise him—to that power of attraction which the center of forests exerts on those who enter them, the scene would repeat itself indefinitely.

The forest is always a little beyond where we are. It has just gone away from where we are and all that remains is its still fresh footprint. The ancients, who projected their emotions into corporeal and living forms, peopled the forest with ever fugitive nymphs. Nothing could be more exact and expressive. As you walk along, glance quickly at a clearing in the bush and you will notice a quivering of the air as if it were hastening to fill the void left by the sudden departure of a slender, naked form.

From any spot within its borders the forest is strictly a possibility. It is a path along which we could proceed, a spring from which a gentle murmur is brought to us in the arms of silence and which we might discover a few steps away, snatches of song sung in the distance by birds perched on branches under which we could pass. The forest is the collection of possible acts of ours which, when carried out, would lose their genuine value. What of the forest lies immediately before us is only a pretext for the rest of it to lie hidden and distant."

As soon as we have dared to confront our own circumstance, the first few trees in front of us, the first few bushes still quivering with the thoughts of others searching and proclaiming the meaning of the forest, we find ourselves lost. Which way to go? Which paths to follow? The one the others took? The markings of others on the quivering branches? Which is my path? The one I must find, or forever run other peoples' paths and be lost. From all the possibilities that lie in front of me I have to find my own impulse, my own concrete way, the path I have to follow or be lost in the trees forever. I must draw a map! I am beginning to make the possible appear in the visible trees. I have to start by interpreting.

The trees do not allow the forest to be seen, and it is thanks to the fact that this is the case, that the forest exists. The mission of the patent trees is to make the rest of them latent, and only when we fully realize that the visible landscape is concealing other invisible landscapes do we feel ourselves to be in a forest.

This invisibility, this being hidden, is not a merely

negative quality, but a positive one which when focused on a thing, transforms the thing it hides, making a new thing of it. It is absurd, in this sense, to try to see the forest. The forest is the latent as such . . .

There are things which, when revealed openly, succumb or lose their value and, on the other hand, reach their fullness when they are hidden or overlooked . . .

Some men refuse to recognize the depth of something because they demand that the profound should manifest itself in the same way as the superficial. Not accepting the fact that there may be several kinds of clarity, they pay exclusive attention to the clarity peculiar to surfaces. They do not realize that what is essential to depth is that it hides under the surface, merely appearing through it, throbbing underneath it.

To ignore the fact that each thing has a character of its own and not what we wish to demand of it is, in my opinion, the real capital sin, which I call a sin of the heart because it originates from lack of love. There is nothing so illicit as to dwarf the world by means of our manias and blindness, to minimize reality, to imagine the suppression of fragments of what exists.

This happens when one demands that what is deep should appear in the same way as what is superficial. No, there are things which present only that part of themselves which is strictly necessary to enable us to realize that they lie concealed behind it . . .

This truth is all too obvious, but it is not completely useless, because there are still some people who demand that we make them see everything as clearly as they see an orange before their eyes. But if seeing is understood, as they do, as a merely perceptible function, then neither they nor anyone else has ever seen an orange in their terms. The latter is a spherical body, therefore with an obverse and a reverse. Can anyone claim to have the obverse and the reverse of an orange in front of him at the same time? With our eyes we see one part of the orange, but the entire fruit is never presented to us in a perceptible form; the larger portion of the orange is concealed from our eyes . . .

What is seen is not the only thing that is clear. The third dimension of a body is offered to us with as much clarity as the other two dimensions and yet things or certain of their qualities would not exist for us if there were no *other method of seeing* than the passive method of vision in the strict sense.

The fact of the matter is that even things have not always been. There is nothing passive or neutral about man and his contact with the forest. What he calls things is a spacio-temporal variation of multiple structures which make them appear and disappear in its invisible net. Without the general overview—the map—and the invisible structures, things are neither things nor no-thing. From meaning, to structure, to context, the path of man moves on in the invisible and latent forest.

Our thought is now a dialectical fawn pursuing the essence of the forest as if it were chasing a fleeing nymph. In touch with the naked body of an idea, it experiences a sort of amorous delight.

Having found in the forest its fleeting nature, always absent always concealed—a bundle of possibilities—our idea of the forest is not yet complete. If the deep and latent is to exist for us it must manifest itself to us, and do so in such a form that it does not lose its depth or its latency.

As I said before, depth suffers the inevitable fate of showing itself through superficial features. Let us see how it does so.

This water which is flowing at my feet complains gently as it strikes the pebbles and forms a curved arm of crystal around the root of this oak tree. Just now an oriole has entered the oak tree as a king's daughter enters her palace. From the oriole's throat comes a deep warble, so musical that it seems a note snatched from the nightingale's song, a short sudden shrill which fills the visible area of the forest completely for an instant, just as a pang of sorrow suddenly fills the area of our consciousness.

Now I have two sounds before me, but they are not alone. They are merely lines or dots of sound which stand out above a multitude of other murmurs and sounds interwoven with them because of their genuine fullness and their peculiar brilliance.

If from the song of an oriole perched over my head and

the sound of the water which flows at my feet I let my attention wander to other sounds, I hear again an oriole's song and a murmuring of water as it struggles along in its stony bed. But what happens to these new sounds? I recognize one of them without hesitation as the oriole's song, but it lacks sharpness, intensity. Its piercing sound does not strike the air with the same energy, it does not fill the atmosphere in the same way as the first one but, rather, it slips by surreptitiously, timidly. I recognize also this second sound of water, but, alas, what a pitiful sound it is! Is it an ailing spring? It is a sound like the previous one, but more halting, more like a sniffle, less rich in inner resonance, somewhat muffled, blurred, and sometimes not strong enough to reach my ear; it is a poor, weak murmur that stumbles along on its way.

Such is the presence of these new sounds, such they are as mere impressions. But I, on hearing them, did not stop to describe their mere presence, as I have done here. Without having to think, as soon as I hear them I wrap them up in an act of ideal interpretation and throw them away from me. I hear them as distant . . . It is I, then, by an act of mine, who keeps them virtually separated: if this act were lacking, the distance would disappear and everything would occupy one and the same plane without distinction.

It follows from this that distance is a virtual quality of certain present things, a quality which they only acquire by virtue of an act of the subject. The sound is not distant, I make it distant.

One can make similar reflections on the visual distance of the trees, on the paths which set out in search of the heart of the forest. All this depth of distance exists because of my collaboration, it comes from a structure of relations which my mind interposes between some sensations and others . . . We need, it is true, to open something more than our eyes and to perform more strenuous acts in order to make this superior world exist for us, but the measure of this effort neither adds to nor detracts from the reality of that world. The deep world is as clear as the superficial one, but it demands more of us.

Human life is just this kind of doing. Much of what is called its secret lies in the discovery of precisely *what* this *doing* entails. Who has drawn these imaginary lines? Who established the dividing lines between interiors and exteriors? Who has perceived them? Why do I follow these markings in the forest? Which is the interior of the forest? The trees, the springs, the sounds, the silence, my body, the air I breathe, the throbbing of my own heart, my thoughts are all exterior from the forest viewpoint. Who made me believe my thoughts were mine, inside myself? Which is my inside? All I see, hear, and think is outside myself. What is below and what is above, what inside and what outside? The markings I cannot see, touch, or hear in the forest. They are not in the forest, much less the forest itself. Let us proceed, however, on the paths of the forest.

> This beneficent forest, which annoints my body with health, has provided a great lesson for my spirit. It is a magisterial forest; old, as teachers should be, serene and complex. In addition it practices the pedagogy of suggestion, the only delicate and profound pedagogy. He who wishes to teach us a truth should not tell it to us, but simply suggest it with a brief gesture, a gesture which starts an ideal trajectory in the air along which we glide until we find ourselves at the feet of the new truth . . .
>
> This forest has taught me that there is a first plane of realities which imposes itself upon me in a violent way: they are the colors, the sounds, the pleasure and pain of the senses . . . But behind those realities there appear others, as the outlines of the higher mountains appear in a sierra when we have reached the first foothills. Some, rising over the tops of others, like new planes of reality, ever more profound, more suggestive, wait for us to ascend them, to reach them. But these higher realities are rather bashful and so do not seize us as their victims. On the contrary, they make themselves apparent to us only on one condition: that we desire their existence and that we strive towards them. In a way, then, they depend on our will for their existence. Science, art, justice, manners, religion, are orbits of reality which do not overwhelm our persons in a brutal way as hunger or cold does; they exist only for him who wills them to exist.

> When the man of great faith says that he sees God in the flowery fields and in the arch of the night sky, he does not express himself more metaphorically than if he should speak of having seen an orange. If there were only a passive way of seeing, the world would be reduced to a chaos of luminous dots. But the human way of seeing is an active seeing which interprets by seeing and sees by interpreting, a seeing which is observing . . . Hence, the third dimension of an orange is no more than an *idea*; God, thus, being the countryside's final dimension.

This observing is a doing, a constant creating of my own life held together by the forest. If I have in mind the forest as my map to orient my life, then my actions follow each other like neon signs illuminating the dark countryside. If I have in mind less than that, if I am content with just being the owl in the countryside, a perspective only, a viewpoint to take the place of the forest, then I am condemned to witness my own ruin.

> There is no more mysticism in this than when we say we are seeing a faded color. What color do we see when we see a faded color? The blue which we see before us we see as *having been* a more intense blue, and this seeing the present color along with its past color, through what it was formerly, is an active vision which is not like a reflection in a mirror; it is an *idea*. The fading or dulling of a color is a new virtual quality which comes over it, giving it something like a temporal depth. Without the need of reasoning, in a single, momentary vision, we discover the color and its history, its hour of splendor and its present ruin. And something within us echoes, instantly, that same process of decline, of decay; hence the somewhat depressing effect a faded color has on us.

Vision-of-surface-depth is made possible by being able to reconstruct constantly our original map of the forest which sets us in motion along one of its paths. By resketching this profile we constantly refocus on the receding limits of things and perspectives, whereby, simple insights lead to effective and authentic visions. These are embodied visions through which I rescue the forest and myself, through our structures and contexts, from the everlasting danger of remaining forever mute things and a mutilated forest. But this path demands the sacrifices of perspectives: time is strewn with unwilling corpses.

We are still in the forest. The sawed stump of an old oak tree provides my tired muscles with momentary rest. I am now sitting at the top of a mild hill. Through the clearings in the foliage and over the branches I am now able to see a larger portion of this forest. I not only see a larger portion of this forest but also of the maps people like me had previously drawn and executed of this forest. The forest is in part devastated; the trees uprooted, the thickness gone. In places it is transparent. I see a farmer's house. It makes itself present to me by projecting its white and red structure against the landscape. The forest around it has been scratched into a red surface in places. A plow, resting against the stomach of a well, must have been the one to pierce the forest into many such paths, furrows, and waving seas of tall wheat. The farmer has executed his own map; his own idea of the forest on the forest, on what is not the forest. This is his vision, his perspective of the forest.

This stump of an old deceased oak tree I am sitting on is the victim of archeologists and geologists. These men need for the execution of their idea of the forest on the forest the accuracy demanded by their scientific vision or perspective of the forest. They need a dendrochronological (tree-ring) dating technique for dating the carbon-14 calendar of trees. By decapitating old and young trees around the same area of the forest, scientists are able to measure carbon-14 and estimate the age of trees, as far back as 5,600 years.

Radioactive carbon-14 is produced in the atmosphere by cosmic rays and absorbed by living plants and animals until they die. After plants and animals die, the carbon-14 left in the tissues breaks down steadily into stable carbon-12 at a known rate. By decapitating old and young trees around the same area in the forest the scientists execute their own map of the forest.

Mythology peopled the forest with genies, fawns, nymphs, gods, and heroes: other vision-perspectives of itself, without the need to execute their visions on the forest. They simply just let it be protected by its own guardians, the Foresters.

Which one of these perspectives is the forest? Are all the forest? Is the sum of perspectives the forest? How many perspectives make up a forest? Here I am sitting on an old oak tree stump and on the ideas of others about the forest. The forest and the ideas of the forest both came to me in the net of structures I webbed in my walk. The forest still stands, mysterious and untouched all around me. What I see is the execution of ideas about the forest. What I see is the structure proclaimed god: a myth of the forest and a myth executed on the forest. Can the lobotomizers of mice and men execute forever the human forest?

The sun is high now and on the unprotected hill top it beats mercilessly on my head. Beyond the fringes of the visible forest, near the furrows besieging the farm house, I can see the sun's devastation. The land is dry, parched. The blades of grass, not so long ago moist and brilliant, are now dry, bristling in the breeze, flacid straws bending anguishingly for moisture. The sun is like that. Too much of it, too near it, and it destroys. Is that what happened to the forest when forced to become just a perspective?

I have meandered down the hill for a while avoiding the cruelty of the sun. My feet—holding a cooler head—play now with the green grass and fallen twigs. An irresistible urge, like a cramp, snuggles in my stomach and my eyes shoot, perilously adventurous, into the dark openings in the forest beckoning with unknown—maybe forbidden?—paths. The forest is like that. It is suggestive, absorbing, bewitching. There are a thousand fingers pulling one down, to the moisture and the softness; a thousand thighs quivering amidst the tall grass; a thousand stomachs heaving with sensuous anticipation. One is easily drawn into the forest. One is easily lost embraced to its creatures. One can get lost looking for refuge from the sun, under a little shade, a grove of trees, a murmuring spring. Suddenly, hopping through the leaves, the sounds of a guitar and of human voices take me away from my own risky trance. I shake the twigs from the seat of my pants and follow, jumping down the hill, the direction of the human stirrings. A ring of carts, a few horses, clothes hanging from trees, naked children, women with colorfully patched long wide skirts, dark, unshaven men: a gypsy caravan.

I am welcomed by the barking of dogs and the laughter of naked children. By the hand of their barking and their laughter I am led to a group of about fifty adults, men, and women, standing around in a wide circle. They look at me from the corner of their eyes, as if not wanting to acknowledge my presence. Their adult hands clap chasing the flowing and intense rhythm of a *flamenco* tune, while their eyes, reassured of my non-intromission, turn intently on the figures in the center of the circle. The children and the dogs have abandoned me and have been reabsorbed by the human rhythmic wave.

A male voice sings. Its sound comes as from the tree tops, melancholic and joyful, high and deep, breathless. At times it stops suddenly as if fighting with the air to find a path down from the trees, but then it re-emerges from the depths, as a trained hawk, menacing and wide, chasing fugitive stirrings in the highest branches. It pours down the audience, tired, breaking, with the crackling of broken reeds. Another voice takes over, but faintly for a guitar is tuning its strings ready to sound.

The guitar has now taken over where the voices left. Its sound, in contrast, appears to come from below, down below, from the guts of the forest. It is a deep and flowing whimper, almost a human voice, so close that it appears at times as if the forest had found her own voice. (If the forest had a voice, it would sound like a Spanish guitar in the eager and expert hands of a gypsy.)

Four dancers—two male, two female—in the center of the human ring blend their fiery rhythms with those of the whimpering guitar. They are tall, slender figures, silhouetted against the verdure over their heads. They look almost aethereal when, with their arms, they reach for the heights, but they suddenly transform their mood and with a decisive and broken gesture they bear their arms and bodies down beating fiercely with their feet the crust of the earth. Their eyes are now thin rays of coal piercing the footsteps of their heels, as if by some magic the witching-sticks of their legs would be able to break open the earth and force out its mysteries. The four dancers finally recede into the wave of hand-clappers around them. There is a moment of almost silence, filled with echoes. There is expectation in the crowd which begins again, first softly, then decidedly, a new rhythm.

One single dancer, a woman, breaks into the human and floral ring. She is young, very young. Her ear is cocked trying to follow the tentative timings her audience throws at her. She listens to the chords of the guitar, tries some hieroglyphics on the dust with her feet. She slowly picks up the tempo. She raises her hands in the air. She poses there for a while feeling the current of her own imaginary waves. Her face, beautiful, sensitive, sensuous and trembling, wipes out any human messages and becomes deadly serious. Suddenly, her eyes are fixed on the earth. She makes a sudden break with her shoulders, like a mare when it is being broken, and her whole body descends on the earth with a fierce clipping of the feet. The woman is now transfixed. She is a dancer, not a human. She is a creator, not a follower. She does not smile, she can no longer feign. She is not a divided self: a soul and a body. She is the earth. Her hips shake and vibrate and undulate and thrust. Her face does not smile. The earth is shaking, vibrating, undulating, thrusting. Her wide long skirt fans the air in a futile gesture to swallow the forest. The air recedes against the chorus round her and eyes follow her long, dark, shivering flesh as her feet struggle to plant themselves at the center of the earth: to be split wide open, to become fertile. What desire drives those feet down? What visions are appearing to those closed gypsy eyes? What worlds are being created by the dust of her feet? Gyrating herself into frenzy, the fury of life in her body, the gypsy woman bends over the earth, whole and exhausted. The sudden roar of the audience breaks the forest like a new child a mother's womb. Slowly the dance picks up again, like a ritual: variations of structure, but the eternal gypsy perspective of the forest unchanging.

Meanwhile, between the sun and the earth straw dogs are burning in the forest. It is dusk.

In a forest of India a mere child is splitting fig seeds. It is easily done even for such soft fingers. The child, however, finds *nothing* inside the seed and wonders how out of such *nothing* the whole forest was born.

Many years before him, the men of the Ṛg Veda, the seers, chanted:

This forest (altar) is the limit of the Earth.
This dance (sacrifice) is the center of the Universe.
This drink (Soma) is the semen of the Cosmic Horse.
This man (Brahmā) is the ultimate house of Language.

Ṛg Veda 1.164.35

Three thousand five hundred years later when men had thought many thoughts and were parched by the light of the sun, dry and impotent, the *Hevajra Tantra* said:

The whole of existence arises in me (this body)
In me arise the three worlds.
By me is all this pervaded.
Of nothing else does the world consist.

Eight hundred years before Christ in an *Upaniṣadic* forest of India, Indra and Virocana had propped themselves up against the bank of a limpid pool and watched their reflections in the waters. Virocana saw what he wanted in the mirror: himself, smiling, with lotus garlands around his neck. He needed no more. This image on the limpid waters would be *him* forever.

Indra was lost in his own image. If it was only an image, where was Indra? The more he looked at the image in the mirror, the more he saw the image to be an image of another previous image in the mirror! But where was Indra? Beyond the image on the mirror were also trees, and clouds, and sky. Only the sky was not a sky, it was below, a pool, in the image of the mirror. The tops of the trees were not up, but down, resting on the sky, and the roots were not down, but up, striving for the hidden sun. For one hundred and one years Indra looked at the mirror until the mirage was transformed into a vision. The mirror was full of emptiness.

It has also been said before by the seers of the *Ṛg Veda* (1.24.7) when looking at the living "peepal" tree:

The tree of the Universe remains erect
Its stem in the groundless region.
The sun-baked top craves for the hidden roots;
The roots hanker for the sun.

It has always been the same story: the story of the forest; the story of the emptiness we share; the emptiness of which all these worlds of man have been created. It is frightening and avoided when unknown, loved and searched for when acknowledged. To know it makes all the difference, but once known, perhaps, it makes no difference at all.

Marbella, June 15, 1975

Part II

The Problem of Philosophy

Chapter One

Philosophy and Method as Dependent on Context, Structure and Meaning

INTRODUCTION

The goal of our present project is the *Bhagavad Gītā*. In general terms, we must agree from the start that we do not yet *know*, or we should not in any way presuppose that we *know* anything of human relevance concerning the *Bhagavad Gītā*. Our first step in our project's journey is to orient ourselves to precisely what it is that such an encounter as this, between us and the *Bhagavad Gītā,* will necessarily and sufficiently entail. It is, to say the least, problematic at the level at which we propose this authentic encounter to occur as to just what the result will be. We cannot imagine the view from the top of the mountain before we even start climbing it. We are used to encountering other lives by comparing ideas of our lives with those of others and thinking that in this way our lives are enriched. It makes us feel more comfortable among the chaos we see in ourselves and the world around us. We have chosen, among all the possible choices we make ourselves, to settle and live comfortably with problems, especially the problem of man-making. Man, however, is not ideas, nor is man made up only of ideas. Man is *flesh,* and unless we discover the way (path, method) by which man becomes himself through the embodiment of his own actualized possibilities, he will forever remain a stranger unto himself and others, and therefore his tasks will mostly be in vain.

In setting for ourselves the project of interpreting the *Bhagavad Gītā,* we are in fact asking ourselves to see other men as *they saw themselves;* not as we see them—through the determination of our own history—nor as they reveal themselves to us in view of our expectations of them—the determination of our politico-educational system and methods. The *Bhagavad Gītā,* as an example, has been a victim of both biases. We have used the text of the *Bhagavad Gītā* to reflect what we already know of ourselves. Even Indian scholars trying to do our task for us had no other alternatives than to fulfill our expectations by repeating to us what we expect and what was academically understandable on our own terms. We have been calling these kinds of studies of others comparative: comparative literature, comparative philosophy, comparative religion, comparative linguistics.

Thus we have not succeeded in encountering the other, but rather we have pushed through this method the possibilities of other men and ours to the verge of almost human triviality. It is true that the preparatory work of some of these comparative disciplines was necessary if man had to encounter man, face to face, on man's own terms. It is also true, however, that what had been offered as a genuine encounter between man and man was not sufficient for him to understand himself as man: a bundle of possibilities realized in concrete and multiple historical domains of space and time.

There is no absolute man, like there is no universal man, nor is there an absolute individual man. Human life is in the flesh: an experience of man living together with other men. Man and other men, the life of a community, is not, again, a universal situation. Man lives with men in the flesh in concrete situations, within concrete historical circumstances. Man's life is circumscribed by concrete historical horizons, finite interpretations of what human life is, and finite possibilities as realized within those human and partial horizons. For man to know man, he has no other alternative but to know man in his own circumstantial situation, neither universalizing one situation, nor particularizing man's circumstantial possibilities by exclusion of others on some arbitrary, moral, political or imperialistic design. If man is to discover himself, he must acknowledge all men as equal: they are his own possibilities. This acknowledgement demands, however, that he consider man and the knowledge of man to be the condition—necessary and sufficient—for the human project of making his own human life. Thus, for man to know man, he has to face man constantly; man is his own circumstance. The method of man discovering man can be the only method by which he constitutes himself as man circumstantially, seeing himself in concrete historical situations, in the face of his problems and in the light of the projects or tasks through which he defines himself as circumstantial man. Thus, the only common element we can apply to methodological man is the fact that he acts, performs tasks constantly, and that his acting is in view of his own particular circumstance, known by himself or dictated by others. There is no way we can discover man by trying to agree among ourselves about the *ideas*—aetherial or disembodied—which make him up. Man in the flesh is man and circumstance.

Man and circumstance, therefore, is the theme of this book. This theme, however, cannot be actualized unless it becomes our own "flesh" in the form of a decision to make this theme our joint project in view of our mutual ends: to resurrect the *Bhagavad Gītā* from the ashes of its own concrete circumstantial situation and to give meaning to ourselves while giving meaning to the *Bhagavad Gītā*.

This task we have decided to commit ourselves to is set from the start with a multiplicity of difficulties. It is a task set in the future under the urgent need to uncover and justify our present possibilities, and at the same time it is determined by the past as dogmatized possibilities already realized by others. Fate and freedom stare us straight in the face from the start. The past is man's only moment of identity, what man has been. Our present task is precisely the liberation of man from what man has been, the liberation of man from "going on being" by giving him the freedom to invent himself anew: to live again. Yet this fundamental project that we have undertaken absolutely decides the path which will save the past through us, and through the action of writing/reading this book will also decide its meaning. Thus, in the midst of the pressure, urgency, and demands of the present and the past, we choose by the very projection of our present/future ends the path to be followed. This path runs through man and circumstance and we identify it as what Ortega y Gasset called historic reason.

Though we are now about to exemplify our method by following the path Western philosophy has marked for us, chronology—the history of philosophy—cannot determine our course; time cannot be time measured as the calendar pages turn. Man and circumstance, as theme and project, demand us to look for time as lived: life as interpreted historically. Our steps on this path of historic reason will be a step-by-step circumstantial discovery and actualization of man's historical steps within the limits of his own situation historically realized. We are in no way looking for principles that apply to all men, but on the contrary, we are looking for man made flesh resurrected from the ashes of his own historical circumstance. We understand man, therefore, to be the possibilities of man as actualized by man; and circumstance (circum-stance: what surrounds me) as the constitutive and radical condition of human life. We further establish philosophy to be the activity that actualizes man in his circumstantial situations as he becomes aware of them through their actualization and modification.

It is almost a triviality to affirm that man's possibilities are lost to man because he has not been able to discover them in other men, other cultures, other human worlds, other circumstantial situations. It is not a triviality, however, to affirm that where man has not been able to discover his own possibilities in other men, in other cultures, in the flesh of man, he has excused himself from the need to know—of making truth—with foggy words like "the mystery of life," "mysticism," "metaphysics," or by dressing other cultures to look like one of ours.

We do not know what life is, nor is there an absolute life. What we find instead is a plurality of life-forms, interpretations of life, with us in them. Man is man in a concrete life-world. We find ourselves in it, suddenly and without knowing how. Thus, life is never ready-made; and we find ourselves trying to make it for ourselves, each one our own. Life is always a task to be performed at every step of our human way. We must decide for ourselves and at our own risk what we are going to do. A decision which would be impossible unless we already "counted on" something previous to our own decisions: beliefs and convictions concerning the world, the nature of things around us, man, ourselves. Only in the light of these beliefs can we choose and live. It follows that man is always swimming in an ocean of beliefs on which he counts in order to swim, and that the structure of what he calls his life depends originally on the beliefs he counts on. These beliefs are the air of our breath, the water of our swim, the ground beneath our feet: the human ground. This is what we "count on" in order to live. This is what we "count on" to guide us in our conduct, in performing our tasks. These beliefs, however, do not come in universal packages for the whole of the human race. On the contrary, they appear as discreet circumstantial situations—concrete *quanta*—in discreet human situations of space and time. To diagnose any human existence, ours or the *Bhagavad Gītā's,* we must begin by establishing the repertory of convictions, of beliefs, which will determine not only the structure of a particular life but also its meaning. Thus we are methodologically condemned to take our steps, one at a time, and wait for the result—the total picture—at the end of the journey.

Our choice of Ortega's theme is also a choice concerning his philosophical method: historic reason. To understand our position we need to take account of Ortega's own warning that,

> A statement is a kind of act, or doing . . . [and this doing] is the act and habit of choosing [to do] from among many things precisely the one that demands to be done.

Ortega made this very explicit by suggesting that what demands to be done is:

> . . . the possibility that what we are now beginning to engage in under the traditional aegis of philosophy is not another philosophy but something new and different,

Namely,

> . . . to take the philosophic activity itself, the doing of philosophy itself, and submit it radically to an analysis.

Ortega's whole philosophical endeavor is summed up in his prophetic words:

> . . . If we are unable to find lodging among the philosophies of the past, we have no choice but to attempt to construct one of our own. The history of the philosophical past catapults us into the still empty spaces of the future, toward a philosophy yet to come. . .

Ortega's invitation is to jump from the Eleatic identification with the being of the past into the nonidentifiable, non-Eleatic action of the present to save both the *past* and the future: a new creation. What this means is that although Ortega might have had a clear vision of his own philosophy, the cycle of its actualization could not be closed in a system. It is a philosophy in the making, knowing "at a glance" what to do, and how to execute one's visons. Ortega's way is a decisive step in a radical phenomenology of focusing on the problem of what philosophy is—its essential active unity—and that this unity can only be exercised —actualized—through the retrospective contemplation of historic reason as it reveals the dramatic situation of its origin in the total past and its dramatic encounter by the philosopher in view of his total future. The philosopher's interpretation of the world is also a transformation of the world: the dramatic excitement of infusing meaning to the world.

Thus, what "demands to be done" becomes clear: *the doing of philosophy,* an occupation which though radically linked to the life of men, has been a permanent one for humanity; a legacy, in our culture, from the Greeks with no guarantee, however, of its continuation. On the other hand, where this activity should take place, in Ortega's case, is also revealed by Ortega's own concrete, historical, and contextual situation in the world. What Ortega, therefore, tried to do for philosophy was for philosophy to find its own justification as philosophy. It is not sufficient to have recourse to the past as past, for this would only explain why philosophy exists—namely, the giving of some analysis of philosophy's own historical motives. This, of course, can justify neither philosophy nor the task of the philosopher as a philosopher. Ortega's justification of philosophy is grounded on present "human needs" as determined by the past and prelived in the future—namely, human possibilities realized through an activity which constitutes itself—philosophy—as it interprets and makes its own life, and that of man. Thus, while we may have an ocean of retrospective glances at the past, we can only have one kind of activity that can save human life, present and future, as human, in terms of man's own discovery of his present circumstantial needs and possibilities.

As the reader will have immediately understood, Ortega's path (method) of philosophy is capable of leading the philosopher not only into his own philosophical past—as part of his own actual human ground and possibilities—but also to that of any other culture with which it might be confronted—again as the same condition of his own human ground and possibilities, or into the life of any other man, sane or insane—for all men are equal under these conditions—with whom he might be confronted. This is our task, our philosophical past and present, and that of the *Bhagavad Gītā*. If our journey through Greek and contemporary philosophy is necessary, it is for the sake of clarifying the method while exercising it and to become aware of its aims and biases. We have not only a multiplicity of views of the philosophical past, but also of what philosophy is, of what the *Bhagavad Gītā* is, and also of the tradition from which it comes. If skepticism and triviality are to be avoided, then a method (way) is needed which is capable of making human life (past–future) while it interprets it (present). This is the method we call in Ortega's tradition historic reason.

Ortega y Gasset summarized the project of philosophy as a task of salvation. His own coined expression is that, "I am I and my circumstance; unless I save it I cannot save myself." This could be translated as *I* (the ground of all human possibilities and projects) *am I* (the actual reflexive I as already found within realized possibilities) *and my circumstance* (the interpretations within which my life moves from a present which comprehends and is determined by the past and which prelives the future). This is in fact my life. My life, however, to be mine, to save myself, consists in the possession of the reflexive I-am-I-being-I as it reveals itself through the circumstance, as it makes its meaning.

It is obvious, therefore, that Ortega's program of human salvation is not a monastic ideal. Man is condemned to save himself through the other, to go through others to encounter himself; man has to save his worlds. These worlds are the human circumstance, and their discovery is human salvation and renewal. This circumstance, however, as we have already indicated is rigorously made up of a multiplicity of beliefs, each with a concrete form or structure, and their actualization is meaning. We shall, for simplicity sake, identify these elements of circumstance as context, structure and meaning.

It is therefore obvious that our encounter with others is a comparative study of some sort. We already find however, a whole field of comparative studies born from different positions than ours, with their concrete and tidy conclusions as to what others—the *Bhagavad Gītā* for example—are. We find that our need for questioning the method of comparative studies—linguistics, religion, philosophy—is, to say the least, urgent, before skepticism and triviality become institutionalized. We are not, however, offering a new method instead of the method now in use. We may state our aims as follows:

- There is a need in comparative studies for radically questioning their presuppositions.
- This radical (from its roots) questioning is a philosophical enterprise.
- Philosophy, however, is not defined, but focused upon as it culturally constitutes itself or interprets life-forms.
- The clarifying elements of these life interpretations (circumstance) are *context, structure* and *meaning.*

We also claim that this method not only contains its self-justification, but is also the method contemporary philosophy leads to and apparently demands for its justification.

Before, however, some eyebrows are raised in our sweeping demands for reform in the disciplines of comparative studies, let me clarify my position further. What those disciplines have done within linguistics, religion and even philosophy was a necessary task. It was done because it was needed. We needed to look at others as objects, as past, as capable of labels, in order to proceed further in understanding them, or dominating them, or reducing them, or even understanding our own possibilities. Yet we remained in the past as past and took our conclusions as final. We sacrificed the present at the expense of saving the past as past; we remained unchanged while discovering others. Our methods determined our own lack of human growth.

Since the turn of the century there has been a great proliferation of comparative studies. While the effort of scholars comparing East and West has been more than remarkable in carrying out these studies, the results of such an enterprise have been disappointing. We have voluminous catalogues of odd practices and sayings from different cultures and peoples, but we lack the understanding or justification that made those customs and sayings meaningful to those people and cultures in the first place. In short, we know almost everything about everybody but understand almost nothing. The root of the problem, it seems to me, lies in the fact that these comparative studies have not been understood as radically problematic; a problem which has been avoided by proliferating new problems and settling peacefully among them. Scholars comparing East and West and trying to synthesize them have forgotten the original dramatic force which the situation under study acquired when it became *problematic,* that is, when the people living it could no longer *remain* in it, and a solution was therefore *urgently* needed. A problem is a real obstacle, a *problema,* or *aporía* of the Greeks, the lack of any pore or hole through which to escape a situation. Scholars delving into East and West and writing about comparative religion or philosophy have done so by ignoring this fundamental fact, grounding thus their understanding of other cultures and their own on the unquestioned premises of their disciplines. By doing so, misinformation and misunderstanding has been disseminated on an international scale. Any possible efficient synthesis or embodiment in the understanding of the human condition has not only become impossible, but what has been offered as such is trivial.

It is obvious that I am not claiming that what those comparative studies have achieved is completely useless. They were a necessary task, though they were not sufficient. I am only questioning their efficiency as a method to understanding and thus, embodying the human condition, either in our culture or in others. What is philosophically necessarily done does not mean that it is philosophically sufficient.

The problem, therefore, we have to go through is one of *method* (way). We will fail if our method (way) does not coincide with the method (way) of the people we study. In no way can our method, though contemporary in its realization, be any of the contemporary methods of the American or Western philosophical or religious "scene." Our only solution to the problem of method is to proclaim from the start our knowledge or ignorance that despite the many definitions and talk about religion, philosophy, reason, truth, language, and knowledge, all these terms remain as problematic today as they were to the people who first *had* to use them. Furthermore, no one religion, school of philosophy, theory of reason, truth, language, and knowledge can justify itself without presupposing itself. We have therefore, no other alternative but to surprise man as he historically constitutes himself as man through his radical *interpretation* of his life-world. Man, in any historical situation *had* to make this radical interpretation of a life-world so that he could live. Or, in other words, man could not be man and function as such unless he interpreted and therefore oriented his life. Man has no other alternative to be man than to *verify* life *(verum facere):* "to make truth." The truth that man makes when he verifies life is that he does not passively wait for life to distill its truth, but it is man himself who makes the truth happen. Truth is not what is said to man by life, oracles, priests, prophets, seers and gurus, but rather it is what man does with his world or worlds, his interpretation of life, and the oracles, priests, prophets, seers and gurus. It is through the multitude of such life interpretations that man has been able to make his own biographical history. This systematic, historical, diverse and plural life-interpretation by man has taken many forms from the gods of Homer and Hesiod to the measurements of quantum mechanics, through the history of philosophy in our culture. An identical activity has taken place, though with different names, in every other culture. The underlying unity of all these *forms of life* is that they are all interpretations which men needed in concrete situations of time and space—therefore historical—to cope with experience. The underlying disunity of these *forms of life* is that they are as many as there are concrete historical and cultural human needs. This means

- that philosophy has to contend with the plurality of its own repeated activity of interpretation. Thus the problem of philosophy lies in remaining always a new frontier, an unfinished task, something to be done again and again if we are to know what religion, reason, truth, language, and knowledge are; and
- that the philosophical method, which demands its own justification to be philosophical, can only justify itself if it uncovers this multiple activity of interpretation as it constitutes itself historically.

What we propose, therefore, in this book is that, for the moment, we forget the talk, definitions or ideas about philosophy that has pervaded Western tradition for about twenty-five centuries and focus rather on what philosophy *has done* to constitute itself as philosophy; i.e., as a radical interpretation of a life-world in different historical domains. With this initial step taken we propose to show how this radical interpretation, which is philosophy, can be clarified by showing that what Ortega calls circumstance is further and systematically analysable as "context, structure, and meaning," and that these three elements of circumstance constitute the necessary and sufficient philosophical conditions for: (a) the conceptual and empirical justification of any "form of life," "field" or "language" under inquiry; and (b) the justification of a method (philosophy's way) which justifies the activity itself of doing philosophy.

To further clarify our method, the main presuppositions on which it is based will be brought out through some examples of Greek philosophy. Furthermore, in order to become more aware of the problem and justify its contemporary need, we will suggest an application of the method, even though schematically, to contemporary American philosophy in chapter two. Finally, the method will be followed in interpreting the *Bhagavad Gītā* with its implications of a possible theory of embodiment.

THE BIRTH OF PHILOSOPHY

The face of Truth is covered by the sun (a golden vase)
Iśopaniṣad. 15.

To understand what the doing of philosophy is, and *a fortiori,* what philosophy is, we find little help from the word "philosophy" itself, except for the fact that it thrusts us onto the shores of a tradition: the Western and, in particular, the Greek tradition. Even here, however, we do not derive much light. The words the Greeks used to designate science include *historía, exétasis,* and *philosophía,* meaning a "learning by inquiry, a searching out," and "a systematic treatment of a subject."

The name *philo-sophía* appeared comparatively late in Greece, as can be seen from Cicero's astonishment in *Tusculan Disputation,* V. 3. The term appeared to be novel and so did the activity, an activity which was *not to be learned,* but which was primarily concerned with *seeking knowledge;* an activity closer to what the word *episteme* refers to in the bundle of meanings included in our words "knowledge" and "understanding."

The task of understanding what philosophy is, is even further complicated by the fact that philosophy stands in general for what philosophers like Plato, Aristotle, Descartes, or Kant did in Western Tradition. Were these philosophers to return to Harvard, Princeton, Oxford, or the Sorbonne today they would encounter very few familiar road signs: not only the topics that engage philosophers but even the ways of "doing" philosophy are so different from theirs that the question of philosophy appears even more problematic.

If philosophy has been "done" in the past or needs to be "done" in the present, in our civilization or in any other, philosophy will have to be discovered in its roots and its reasons, in concrete human needs such that human life would have been impossible without it. Man, historical man, has always needed to know what to be guided by with regard to what is radical in reality. He has always needed to know something without which what he understood as human life could not be lived. In other words, when we know what people living in different historical domains had to know in order to know what to be guided by—what to know in order to deal with the things about them, in order to know what to do—then we know at a radical level (at the root level of what constitutes human life) what is really and necessarily done when philosophy is done. This task turns out to be in every case a radical interpretation by man of what, for him, life consists of, in such a way that the original need which prompted that concrete interpretation of what life consists of is at least temporarily satisfied.

We, therefore, have the following sequence: First, human life is radically such because it consists primarily of a multitude of intrinsic theories of itself. Second, these theories which constitute human life are not self-evident, but have to be accounted for; in fact, they have always been so accounted for by *somebody*. Finally, this intrinsic theory of life and its reasons or justification have always taken place in the history of mankind for man himself.

These three elements of what human life consists of—intrinsic theory, justification, and existence *for somebody*—correspond to the three elements of our methodology which we consider necessary and sufficient, both for the discovery of what philosophy is, and for its justification, i.e., context, structure and meaning.

It might be objected to that my idea of philosophy is not what most philosophers do today when they "do" philosophy. My answer is simple. To call philosophy only what philosophers do today begs the question. It lacks self-justification; it cannot prove itself without taking itself for granted, and this is the problem of philosophy. The answer demands that philosophy be done so that the historical roots upon which the doing of philosophy is based today emerge in order to clarify the present problem and therefore go beyond it. It is not, therefore, philosophical to hide behind some academically fashionable idea of philosophy and renounce knowledge by declaring certain ways of knowledge inaccessible, impossible, or uninteresting. This attitude of renunciation in relation to knowledge is of course contrary to the essence of philosophy, and therefore human life—for human life consists of such intrinsic theories about itself—and human life cannot be rid of itself without self-amputation.

Philosopy in History: a sketchy outline

We must remember that human life is such because of its accumulative historical nature. The reason philosophy has to be done again and again is because we encounter it in our tradition, because what carries over from the past does not serve our changing needs, and because we feel the need to make a new interpretation to serve the present needs, precisely our own. If we did not have to make *another* philosophy, we would not find philosophy necessary at all. We would be making what has already been made. We would be designating theories of philosophy, designating what others needed, what is dead: the past, as past. Philosophy, to do philosophy, demands that it be done radically: i.e., within the multitude of historical domains within which human life gains meaning. Only thus can the doing of philosophy discover its own necessary and sufficient conditions for its own justification.

PHILOSOPHY IN HISTORY: a sketchy outline

Philosophy understood as a radical form of human life, or the interpretation of life-forms at a radical level which people had in order to live a meaningful human life, goes beyond the narrow understanding of academic philosophy. We cannot focus, in order to discover philosophy, on the present academic models of what philosophy is determined to be, but rather we should focus on "philosophy as a radical form of birth" which all humans have to go through in order to live a human life. I do not imply by this that all humans have "done" philosophy. We all know many people live a borrowed life. I simply want to focus on the simple fact that any form of human life requires the seizure and possession of a certain vision of itself, plus the giving account of that form of life and its connections and try to surprise this activity historically together with the need to do so.

Since the word philosophy thrusts us into the shores of Greek life, it will help to bring out what we have in mind if we surprise the activity of "doing" philosophy in the origins of this same tradition with some examples from this tradition.

THE GREEK WAY

It would be ridiculous to claim that the Greeks had nothing to "guide themselves by" until the Presocratics appeared on the scene. If the Presocratics appeared on the scene it was precisely *because* there was already present an interpretation of life, a life-form which came to be considered insufficient for "knowing" what to be guided by, for knowing what to do.

Hesiod speaks in the *Theogony* (volumes 27–28) of the Muses as:

> We know how to speak many lies similar to true things;
> but we know, when we want to, how to proclaim truths.

Similar to *(pseúda)* is opposed to authentic, true, genuine *(étyma),* to distinguish things which are true from those which are only apparently so; *alethéa,* signifies truths which are spoken or declared, *revealed* or discovered. Similarly the *Odyssey* (XIX, 203) through Ulysses speaks of "many lies similar to true things," referring also to the Muses as "truthful" or "inclined to the exact word"; that is, they speak in a way that is precise and adequate for us to know what to be guided by.

A further clue to what the men of the Odyssey, of Hesiod and of Herodotus had to know in order to know what to be guided by was the meaning of the word "*Moira*" (as in *Herodotus* I,91). Sacrifices, knowledge and the word of the oracles, plus "*Moira*" are the elements of the context and structure of what was real for those men. Reality consisted of "knowing" through the oracles (by divinations) the ultimate reality out of which everybody's life was shaped. That ultimate, immutable latent origin and ultimate reason of things apparent was the *Moira.* This is the presupposition of the oracles. People trusted it with their own lives because they believed life was constituted by such inexorable structure. This was their "theory" of life, their "vision"; this was the way things were necessarily, and therefore what happened had of necessity to be so. To the degree that a man had faith in the flashing revelations of the real (through oracles, divinations, etc.) he was oriented, and he knew what to be guided by.

The moment the oracles begin to be questioned (see for example Herodotus and the examination of the oracles by Croesus, and the conflict of Xenophon in the *Anabasis* between the evidence of reason and man's orientation by means of sacrifices), a new model of "knowing" is born in Greece. Man no longer waits passively for revelation through the oracle in order to know his share of *Moira,* a situation beyond the will of the gods. He now holds reality in his own hand, addresses it directly and forces it to respond. The heavens empty themselves of gods, and man becomes the measure of all things. There is not only a new method *(hodós, methodós),* or a new path, but more significantly, this method will historically consist in systematically narrowing down the possibilities of what "knowing" really consists of so that it handles only that which it truly knows. Our historical reflection on philosophy in this book will show the proclivity of philosophy to force this reductionism of knowledge in our tradition.

THE PRESOCRATICS

The early life-interpretation by the Greeks is held together by the all-embracing image of *Moira,* as destiny, one's life's destiny which could only be made manifest through the structure of divinations and the word of oracles. The path from the hidden to the manifest was a one-way trip only. Man could only wait passively for reality to reveal itself. But this one-way trip was considered insufficient for those men of early Greek-known civilization. They needed what Heraclitus would call later a method, a path which would include also the possibility of return, "the road up and the road down," *(hodós áno kaĩ káto).* In one direction it would arrive at *natural things;* on the other at the *nature of things. Nature* dethrones *Moira* as the image of reality and becomes the new general outline, or guiding image of the interpretation of the real; things are *reduced* to a primary basis from which they emerge. *Arkhé,* source or beginning, stands for these early Greeks for this interpretation of Nature. The Milesians emphasized the element of *generation* in reality and made a *physiología,* while the Pythagorians affirmed that all "things are by imitation" *(mimesis),* that is, they insisted on "consistency" or invarience, for "only" numbers are consistent.

Nature stands for and is both: generation and imitation. Parmenides exaggerated the invarient aspect of things and affirmed that things consist *(ón)* in consisting. What he called the *éon* and was later called *ón* (being) became the *consistent.* Things (consistencies) are dissipated when they confront the "consistent," and become irrelevant; from the point of view of the *ón,* of Being, or the "Entity" they *do not count.* It is not the case for Parmenides that they (things) do not exist, but they are only "names men give to things"; they are opinions "*doxa,*" "seemings" of variation, change, movement and plurality. Parmenides claims that exactly the opposite is the case: what really is, is *alétheia,* manifestation, and *ón,* Being.

Unfortunately *phýsis* dissolves in the face of Being, and reality as "things" was abandoned literally in the streets under the names of "matters, tasks," *(prágmata, Khrémata)* and a new turn in philosophy took place. Sophistry's own justification consisted in its willingness to deal with practical matters by elevating *doxa* to the skies and attempting to guide men's lives thereby; but sophism forgot truth *(alétheia)* and therefore was incapable of collecting these matters into a comprehensible unity, i.e., the Sophists were unable to develop *logos* (from *légein,* in its primary meaning of collecting what is dispersed). This led to the "vertigo" of which Plato speaks in his letter VII, and the crisis of Greece and Athens. Crisis about what? The men of Greece, and of Athens in particular, did not know what to hold to in their lives. They were in the same predicament as the Presocratics. They did not know what to do in relation to things, because they could not find a way to go to them and away from them. Philosophy had become in the hands of the Sophists a dialectical and lucrative game but it did not give the Greeks what they needed to know in order to live.

SOCRATES AND PLATO

Socrates put the Sophists in their proper place by declaring that the path of what they claimed wisdom was radically grounded on ignorance. To know one-self truly ignorant was true wisdom. Socrates' first move consisted in showing the Sophists that wisdom or knowledge was not something already possessed (a *sophía*) but something to be sought for its own sake (a *philo-sophía*): an activity which consisted radically not in the possession of a doctrine but in the exercise of its own repetition: a search.

Socrates reproaches his contemporary *sophoí* that despite their great theories, notwithstanding their mutual contradictions, they are unable to know from Nature what is most necessary for man: how he may predict and handle the events of his life. Furthermore, Socrates tries to destroy the pretentions to knowledge of the *sophoí* by cornering them on the *tí*, the *what* of things, or the correlate of a definition to make knowledge precise. Ignorance thus becomes in the hands of Socrates not a state, but a method of self-reflection to find within oneself the "concept" of what is being sought, and thus arrive at the definition of what was being ignored. This, for Socrates, leads to a happy life, for it is born out of one's own self and therefore confers self-autonomy on the man who follows it even unto death.

Plato, bred in the school of Socrates, carried this path to its ultimate limit. That is, Socrates' precision of knowledge could be possible only in the light of the *eĩdos,* or *ídeá* (ideas), which can only be apprehended in a mental vision which he named the *nous*. This vision is what makes it possible with exactness and rigor to separate the being of one thing from that of another, and to discover in the idea the internal relations of its notes and its relations with others: that is, its definition. The Socratic ignorance thus turns into dialectics. Plato's dialectic divides by genera in order not to confuse one idea with another—so that a single vision appears of "a single idea through many" *(mían idéan diá pollõn):* an idea which does not lose its unity in the multitude of separate and solitary possible ideas (communities of ideas) *(koinoníai)*. It is a matter of arriving at ideas through speeches, *logoí,* which on occasion may be an "ocean of speaches," *(pélagos logon)*.

For Plato to do philosophy is an *acquisition* of knowledge, it is a *use* of this knowledge and it is also a habit which guarantees the proper and continued use of this acquired knowledge and the acquisition of it. Plato insists on the dialogue as the form of this transaction of knowledge rather than in writing, for philosophy, not yet a science, is above all a personal matter. Furthermore, it is important to notice that for Plato the definition of the *ousía* or *logos* does not exhaust the reality about which a dialogue is held; it only demarcates its limits and makes sure everyone is talking about the same thing. Plato does not believe that reality can in any way be exhausted intellectually. Plato assures us this is a divine task, not human. He makes sure we understand it so by placing myth after his definitions, as when talking about the soul in *Faedrus* 245 c.e., the myth of the cave at the beginning of Book VII of *The Republic* and following the conceptual definitions of Book VI, the clowns and musicians breaking up the ontological "demarcations" of the *Symposium,* and in many other instances. For a moment in Greek tradition it would appear there was a method, a path, from things to *eĩdos* and back. Dialogue would make it possible to traverse this path by focusing in different areas of reality and making them the proper object of knowledge. Through Plato the gods became alive again, and so does Nature, and virtue, rhetoric, mathematics, physics, politics,in a word, the Hellenic world. Dialectics makes it possible (or could make it possible) to embody the culture up to one's own time by being able to follow the path of a philosophy which moves in jumps of visions, or Ideas, and is never frozen by preconception of what philosophy ought to be.

ARISTOTLE

According to Aristotle there had been many philosophies before him, but not philosophy, because up to his time philosophy had not become strictly a science. This was, first, because it was not an apodictic, demonstrative science, and second, because it was not "a" knowledge since it lacked its own proper, rigorous, formal object. This object of philosophy as a science had to be, according to Aristotle, strictly universal, not in the trivial sense of the universality of concepts, but in the strict sense of the totality of all things *(kathólou),* where the totality *(hólon)* is a totality of *being* and everything is a part of the whole in as far as it *is*. The formal object of philosophy will be for Aristotle being *qua* being.

Aristotle dedicates two chapters of his *tà metá tà physiká* (Metaphysics) to tell us what he understands by philosophy. The word metaphysics was, of course, not his; his editor Andronicus of Rhodes invented it when he published some of Aristotles' articles. Aristotle named "what comes after physics," First Philosophy, a searched science *(dzetouméne epistéme)* grounded on the first causes and reasons *(tá prõta)* of being and therefore the supreme knowledge *(prõte philosophía)*.

Looking over his shoulder at the previous tradition Aristotle claims to have at last found the searched wisdom the whole tradition was looking for. Aristotle rests his case mostly on these four criteria:

1. Philosophy is a new way of knowledge. What we call experience is knowledge organized by memory and all men (even animals) share in this way of knowing. Aristotle claims his philosophy to be more, however. It is a *tékhne:* a *knowledge* of how to do things and at this level of knowing this knowledge can be taught *(máthema)*. It is also a *phrónesis:* a knowledge of how to deal with the good and the bad. It is a practical way of being *(prãxis)* in action *(énérgeia)*. It is an *épistéme* in the strict sense of a science which causes that what a thing is *(tí),* be shown *(deĩxis)* from its own self *(ápo)* the reason why *(dióti)* it is necessarily so and not otherwise. This demonstration of the thing is nothing else than the necessary internal structure which the thing is, in order to be such a thing and not another. To be more exact, it is to be able to demonstrate that what a thing is, is necessarily so and not otherwise. For Aristotle, what a thing is is a *substance* knowable through the four necessary causes. The method which Aristotle chooses for his demonstrations is the *logos.* The mental structure leading to this logos is called logic. However, philosophy cannot do like other sciences: act on unquestioned premises. Philosophy must make a question of its own principles (reasons and causes) until what is, is demonstratable from these first principles: *epistéme* and *Nous* join together in such a way that philosophy as a science performs the intellectual function of a *philosophía,* wisdom.
2. Philosophy is for Aristotle an intellectual activity in the sense that to know *(eidénai)* is to possess intellectually the truth of things. In the first line of the Metaphysics he writes, "All men by nature have the desire to know *(Pántes ánthropoi toũ eidénai orégontai physei)*." Where the criterion of this desire *(órexis)* is the sign *(semeĩon)* of the pleasure, we experience *(he tõn aisthéseos ágápesis)*

when we feel its exercise. However, since Aristotle is looking for a science he is not content with descriptions, but looks for explanation. Nature is in the first place generation and birth. By virtue of this, two things are fundamentally the same thing, one comes (or is reduced) to the other. This is the nucleous of interpretation: from the immediate and manifest we appeal to the mediate and hidden. From the two things I saw before me a while ago I pass to the one thing which the two are fundamentally; immediately one thinks that this fundament or ground is in fact Nature. It is this ground from which things issue and to which they are reduced that is seen through philosophy as more important and radical. Consequently Nature is *principle, arkhé,* in the double sense of origin or starting point and of command and power. From this point of view the unity or identity of Nature is essential. Things, fundamentally, in their Nature are the same: this requirement of identity arises above all from the fact that principle is also power or command, something which imposes an order *(kósmos, táxis)* by virtue of which a man may know what to hold to amid the changing variations of the immediate. Homer used to say and Aristotle liked to repeat

> The rule of many is not good; let the one be the ruler *(Ouk agathón polykoiranín eĩs koíranos ésto).*

However, principle as Nature, or origin, or *arkhé,* suffers at the hand of Aristotle a subtle and decisive change. It is no longer the nature of a thing, always latent and therefore always present, but became the nature of things; a principle of explanation. Logic or analytic is for Aristotle a reduction to elements, a movement of substituting things for logic. Aristotle turns around the original meaning and intention of *arkhé* and from its root meaning of (knowing) the radical origin of things it becomes (a knowing) of the first principles of logic. This is the task of the *epistéme* and the Nous.

3. Philosophy for Aristotle is a mode of action. Aristotle held philosophy as a supreme mode of theory. But theory is not for him a once in a while activity but rather a being-in-activity. The sum of the vital activities of man is life *(bíos).* The streams of vital activities of philosophy are *bíos theoretikhós:* contemplative life.

4. However, since action is nothing unless it is exercised and life is being-in-constant-action, life as a whole can only be exercised if it is self-fulfilling: a happy life *(eudaimonía)*. The most self-fulfilling activity of man is philosophy, the most pleasurable, the most self-sufficient, the only activity exercised for its own sake, the only thing the gods, to be gods, could do.

Aristotle was convinced that through his philosophy he had achieved the goals of Heraclitus, Parmenides, Socrates and Plato. But, while he said in many words what his doing of philosophy consisted of, he became unaware of what he had really done when he did philosophy within his own tradition. For one thing he grounded his whole philosophy in what he called a substance:

> And thus, what has from earlier times and now been looked for, and what has always remained in difficulty, namely, what is being *(tí to ón)*. [I say] it is nothing other than substance *(tís he ousía)*

We will have to wait till the following generation of stoics, cinics, hedonists, etc., to find out the results of this move. These people, the stoics in particular, rejected the substances of life with a lot of philosophy. They did not think theoretic life to be the most divine of all lives, nor that in order to possess a self-sufficient life one must be a philosopher as described by Aristotle. Aristotle himself in his old age wrote: "The more I am by myself, and alone, the fonder I have become of myths." This is not to intimate that Aristotle gave up his idea of philosophy in his old age, only that in this expression to Antipater his idea of philosophy as the most divine life of man appeared to him no doubt a bit awesome. In fact what Aristotle really did with his doing of philosophy was to cut his own culture from many of its other possibilities and reduce it to the one possibility his philosophy permitted: the knowledge of principles of logic, and what this knowledge could organize. In fact, he elevated his own idea of knowledge to the realms of myth and, once more we have a philosopher proving the dramatic point of philosophy developing between these two possible paths: *the myths of a culture which have not yet become knowledge, and a form of knowledge elevated to the realms of myth for the whole culture to accept.* As a clarification of Aristotle and the points we are trying to make it will be convenient here to suggest what followed Aristotle in his own culture.

THE STOICS, HEDONISTS, CYNICS, SKEPTICS

For the Stoics, and to the same degree the others following Aristotle, wisdom or knowledge was also the science of things human and divine and philosophy the exercise of an art whose project was wisdom. This supreme task was divided into the traditional three branches of Logic: regarding discourse; Physics: regarding the world; and Ethics: regarding human life. Wisdom is thus primarily directed towards *practical action* (Cicero and Seneca) opposing Aristotle's primacy of contemplation.

The practical action of the Stoics was principally directed to the consolidation of Law as a norm of behavior between individuals and peoples. The Stoics were critical of the Law yet adhered to its norm as the people of old to the sayings of the oracles. The Law, however, was not established or accepted as a norm to guide one's life by or as an ontological ground for man's own inquiry about his own life. It became rather a form of absolutized morality whereby all law is a form of obligation (rationality) binding not just the entire people, but each of them individually (thus atomizing persons and actions and ontologically identifying them), while the body of law (the Constitution) secured the nation in a network of legally enforceable, mutually dependent rights and responsibilities. Thus, with the Stoics principally, the Law which is well organized and knowable is forcefully separated from Nature which is chaotic and unknowable. But this step meant the giving up of the idea that knowledge was possible, that is, searched knowledge as wisdom *(philo-sophía),* which the previous traditions had so laboriously searched for. Greek thought is permeated during the period following Aristotle, and in many senses even from its beginning, with an almost radical pessimism. This pessimism reappears almost with a vengeance with the Stoics, Hedonists, Skeptics, and Cynics. This is the absolute pessimism about knowledge, or that the needed knowledge to guide one's life by is possible. Thus with the tradition which followed Aristotle we have a "*quasi desperata cognitioni certi,*" people posessed with the despair of not being able to know. Philosophy, at the hands of the Stoics, Hedonists, Cynics, Skeptics becomes a sort of therapy. In what sense? What these schools got from the previous tradition was the fact that being a "man of substance" (*Ousía*: substance) brought along many emotional and moral problems: attachment to things, intranquillity, greediness, etc., etc. Also that the phenomena of Nature, earthquakes, thunder, rains, disasters, etc., produced in peoples fears, dependences, disorientation. Well, philosophy's task then would be to calm peoples fears, to liberate them from attachment to things, to provide them with tranquillity, imperturbability, in one word with *"ataraxía"* which means all the above things and we would today translate as learning how to "keep cool" under the adverse conditions which an abundant or a poor life brings, or a benevolent or contrary Nature provides. Epicureanism in particular is very apt at giving explanations of natural phenomena, thunder, etc., not for the sake of knowledge but in order to explain them away: since all these happenings have an explanation and are not the wrath of the gods, they should not disturb anyone even when their reasons are ignored. In relation to personal substance, or property one should again avoid anxiety by becoming adept at *"ataraxía."* In its more technical sense *ataraxía* is an invitation to inaction in relation to knowledge *(philosophía)*; it is an in-action, an *apathía*, apathy and abstention *(epokhé)*: a position of the mind whereby we neither affirm nor deny anything. From Zeno and Chysippus to Cicero, Seneca and Marcus Aurelius, Nature coincides with what is rational in the double sense of that which can be explained away and that *that* which they had proclaimed rational (Law) was natural. The important thing would be to behave in accordance with this reason, come what may; (of course they should have *known* better). Things, man and life—if one wanted to be happy—should become indifferent *(adiáphora),* though certain social pressure may, from time to time, force us to prefer some things to others. Not being moved by things Seneca proclaimed it to be a state close to the condition of a god. This is what they called *Ataraxía* or tranquillity.

In sum we could write the epitaph of these philosophies as: "Hold on, the times are bad, but they will be worse if you do not give up delusions of knowledge *(philosophía)*."

However, contrary to the previous philosophies of searched knowledge, which had been the exclusive problem and property of a small minority of the population, Stoicism principally became a very popular philosophy; so popular that it is the easiest to recognize in our popular philosophies of today. Christian philosophy will try to use this popular philosophy's appeal and integrate Stoic moral endurance and its respect for the Law, with the traditional searched science of the previous Greek generation through a symbiotic reconciliation in the new concept of Natural Law. This integration would not have been possible without a simultaneous and larger integration of Destiny *(Moira)* and Fate *(fatum,* the saying of the law) within the theoretical umbrella of Providence. Above all, these syntheses would have been impossible without the Medieaval exaggeration of individuality restricted to the limited confines of the physicobiological body. This is, however, another project.

THE PROBLEM OF PHILOSOPHY RESTATED

Ortega y Gasset summarized the project of philosophy, saying, "I am I and my circumstance; unless I save it I cannot save myself." We found that this project was something man had to do, and has been calling it, at its radical origin, philosophy. We did not define philosophy but tried to surprise or focus on it as different people executed it in different historical domains to interpret—give meaning—to a concrete form of life. This radical interpretation of a life form we found was necessary for certain men in concrete historical domains so that they could act in a world. We further discovered that man is not an abstract entity, a faceless digit, but a man in the flesh facing constantly a world, or worlds as concrete bundles of human possibilities which he can only realize in the face of another. This "other" we discovered was his own circumstance—what surrounds him—the life-interpretations he must possess in facing others—peoples, cultures, worlds—to execute his own possibilities. Thus, we found out that "circumstance" could more accurately, systematically and concretely be identified as: context, structure and meaning. The activity of philosophy, therefore, is again nothing abstract nor one more task among the many tasks man performs, but rather the one task man must of necessity perform, every step of his human way, to stay human. In this sense we established that the concrete project of philosophy—or philosophy's way or method, or path—is dependent for its execution on context, structure and meaning: philosophy is what man must necessarily and sufficiently do to save himself through his circumstance. There are many tasks man performs necessarily and sufficiently for man to be man and that is philosophy as here identified.

The previous sketch of part of the philosophical life of Greece is just a small and suggestive effort at such an active possession of life and its interpretations both as focusing on the activity of doing philosophy in our tradition and also as uncovering the ground on which we stand today and from which we face others—people, cultures, worlds—because of that early philosophical activity in our tradition. The journey has a few pointed suggestions:

- Man finds himself in a world, or a multiplicity of worlds—a multiplicity of life-interpretations, realities—which he not only encounters but "counts on" in order to live.
- These realities which he counts on are more absent than present; they are possibilities the culture, world, people, offer him, which man must realize, seize (know) in order to live with them, in order to act in them, to make his life by going beyond them (by knowing them).
- This implies that human life is such because intrinsic to such life is its self-interpretation. Human life is theory laden; it is at its roots interpretation. The face of truth will forever be covered by the golden face of the sun.
- Man, therefore, is condemned to make himself through others; others are man's own possibilities. No doing of philosophy, therefore, is born out of nothing; it arises in the midst of interpretation, of our own life, or of other peoples lives. No philosophy is presuppositionless, but the task of philosophy is primarily to become aware of its presuppositions: to see the world, feel, touch, listen to the world from inside the skin of others, not as others but as selves. We have no other alternative but to possess other peoples' circumstance as ours, for theirs is also our circumstance as the necessary and sufficient condition for our lives.
- Since a culture defines itself, however, according to some arbitrary temporary interpretation of itself, in order to solve some particular pressing problem, to satisfy some communal interests, philosophy must keep itself open to the plurality of its own activity as constituting a plurality of life interpretations within the culture, and not

only of the interests defined by a momentary arbitrariness of power, or principles. Philosophy's activity is *anonymous* and can not be reduced to fashionable, interested or imperialistic manipulations rationalized by criteria alien to the action of philosophy though dressed in philosophical garb. Philosophy is not just giving reasons, reasons are given because there is already a "philosophy."

In order to summarize in more detail what we have already done and in order to anticipate what we are about to do in the next chapter, we need to further clarify what we call our methodology—what steps to take, what to do. This method or way we have identified as the discovery of what constitutes the *circumstance* and which we have identified as *context, structure* and *meaning*. For, we have established, it is only through the recovery of such concrete elements that philosophy constitutes itself radically—necessarily and sufficiently—when interpreting ourselves in our circumstance or that of others in their/our circumstance.

Context

In the most general terms we may identify context as a latent, all-embracing image which organizes human experience in a certain definite way. That is, it makes it possible for man to act in a world. In its more technical sense context would be the horizon of all horizons within a particular historical, social, scientific or human domain in the sense that the latent image, or ultimate horizon, helps organize and give meaning to all the other ideas, isolated or systematic within each one of those fields. Thus we must be cautious to distinguish context in the above sense from the notions of "leading idea," *(Leitfaden),* "guiding motif," "a horizon to be known," etc., which may at times be arbitrarily assigned the role of absolute context yet differ from our radical context in the sense that our notion of radical context functions always in a way which is latent—it is grounded on a "consciousness I count on" in order to act—while the notion of leading idea, or guiding motif, or horizon is always explicit and grounded on the "consciousness of" in order to act. Context in our sense is always a radical belief—an idea people count on, believe in, in order to act. Or rather, a system of beliefs, mutually connected, related in a hierarchical order of priorities, with the absolute power of organizing the whole system or systems of conscious ideas within a particular domain of a culture or a period within a culture, a field, a human endeavour. Context is the ultimate ground on which man stands in order to act.

Thus we must have seen how in Greek philosophy *Moira* as Destiny, The Elements, Nature, *Physis, Arkhé,* Being, *Doxa* (Opinion), *Alétheia,* Definition, Wisdom, *Eĩdos,* Ideas, Substance, Principles of Logic, *Ataraxía,* etc., are the organizing images of certain particular human experiences and actions. Whether these images are the ultimate context of our Greek tradition is to say the least problematic. The fact is that men acted on them to organize their lives in a certain definite way, and that these images determined in a certain definite way the paths philosophy followed up to our times.

Structure

In the most general terms structure may be identified as "conscious order plus things." In practical terms we find that what we call reality and things *consist in structure:* a conscious ordering or mapping for the sake of another: i.e. context, in the ultimate, radical sense; or in the particular sense of a horizon, a theory, a leading idea, etc. Thus we find in the history of philosophy—our own—that structure has as many definitions as particular contexts determine it: (a) Objects have structure in the sense that they are known to us through concepts. (b) Objects have structure in the sense that they have a configuration independent of all knowing minds. (c) Two objects have the same structure in the sense in which they participate in the same type. (d) Two objects have the same structure in the sense that we speak of them with a word that has a univocal meaning. (e) Two objects have the same structure in the sense that there is an image that unifies them. (f) Structure is not a function of objects but of facts. These and other definitions of structure point out the main claim of our method that structure is always for the sake of another. Structure is context dependent. The History of Philosophy is a clear example of how philosophers, oblivious of this dependence, have tirelessly tried to freeze structures into absolute form with the demand that it be applicable to all men. The individual biography of every man is also another example of how this obliviousness of dependence has not only frozen for many their own rationality but has also reduced their possibilities to absolutizing objects, again as ultimate and radical ground of their lives.

Meaning

In its radical form meaning can only be identified as an activity of "making truth": the verification of a life form, the salvation of the human circumstance the discovery of the other as one's own possibilities, what people—philosophers included—had to do in order to necessarily and sufficiently effectively act in a world. Meaning is therefore context and structure dependent. It is the capacity and a habit to judge—act—by being able to, so to speak at a glance, size up a circumstantial situation—past, present, future—and infuse it with a renewed life. Meaning, however, is also dependent on context and structure and the different meanings of meaning have to be discovered circumstantially. In every case, even in the case of the claim of meaning being the meaning of words independent of subjects, meaning is context and structure dependent.

It is obvious from the above that what philosophy is cannot be defined, that is, limited to some particular use. What philosophy is can only be discovered as philosophy constitutes itself historically and problematically. Nor can the activity of philosophy be reduced to being one among the many activities men perform. No activity of man is possible without a conscious or unconscious acceptance of a radical interpretation of a life form: this is the activity philosophy performs.

We have seen from the examples of Greek philosophy how the men of those days moved between the demands for philosophy to justify a world which would be universal, i.e., universal principles—unification through method and ideas—which would be universally applied and accepted; and, on the other hand, the demand to reduce knowledge—unification through method and communal though partial agreement—to only that which, in its particular form, knowledge could handle. Once this method and agreement about knowledge was accepted by the part of the population that counted—had the power to execute this vision—then it became an established form of knowledge for the culture to accept. A particular form of knowledge became thus myth, devaluating both knowledge and the world. Medieval philosophy will follow the trend by requiring through philosophy that there be only *one* universal world, derived and rationalized through such metaphysical principles. The following period of science will exemplify the demands for only one form of knowledge, again in the form of a universal myth, i.e., that the method of science as explanation, prediction and the implied possibilities of the control of phenomena should be necessary and sufficient conditions for the organization of human life. The temptation exists for philosophers to elevate structure to the heights of context, demanding simultaneously that their interpretative and *public*—not universal—condition be forgotten. Whichever way the culture and men move philosophy can always open both to their own plurality of interpretations and possibilities avoiding thus any form of conceptual imperialism and human reductionism.

I doubt, however, that anyone will follow the way of philosophy unless he loves *(philé)* his own culture enough not to settle for imitations of life. The doing of philosophy is not a task of duty, but of love—to keep life living. Philosophy like love is an activity whose only and radical verification is the execution of its own repetition. We *make* philosophy like we *make* love, on equal and anonymous terms; the rest is interpretation. It is a curious repetition of many cultures that the seat of the mind is located in the heart. Is philosophy possible without the love of the culture—the human circumstance? The Greeks would, of course, have answered no. In our american situation the question and the answer are more pressing. Democracy, at a radical level, presupposes the acceptance on equal terms of every human circumstance, and not only the already established and institutionalized affaires of the culture. But the diversity cannot be recognized and embodied unless it is first discovered, unless democracy is really made up of people in the flesh and not of ideas of people. Looking for the origins—the circumstance—is a democratic enterprise: it is the philosophical enterprise of a democracy.

The Problem of Contemporary Philosophy

Chapter Two

INTRODUCTION

The interpretation of other cultures is in many ways *determined* by a host of philosophical presuppositions of which the interpreters seem to be unaware. This statement applies equally to philologists, theologians, and those dealing in comparative literature, religion, and philosophy. Since the methods of these interpreters and the presuppositions on which these methods are grounded are opaque to them, we deem it necessary to unveil in this chapter the radical presuppositions from which *others* are interpreted or to which *others* are systematically reduced. In order to make this difficult journey more bearable to the reader, we shall concentrate in the body of this chapter with general and critical remarks while relegating to an Appendix the concrete examples which will empirically confirm our generalizations and critical remarks. The reader, or scholar, will thus, at his leisure, complete a task we are just initiating.

Interpretation is ultimately grounded on some philosophical presuppositions. The freedom of the interpreter lies ultimately in being able to seize them, and know them, so that he can get rid of them and not be determined by them in his own interpretations of others. Since interpreters of other cultures are the product of western academic methods, our current task is to seize the philosophical tradition on which these methods are grounded. Thus, we are forced to deal with the contemporary philosophical scene as determined by its immediate historical past and as determining and theoretically colonializing the future if this determination is not philosophically checked in time.

When we view the contemporary scene of philosophy, there is no doubt that the predominant interest of contemporary philosophy is language, and its analysis and understanding. It was through the interest in language that comtemporary philosophy hoped to bypass, at the turn of the century, the problems of nineteenth-century philosophy. Thus, we may see two main moves within contemporary philosophy in its dealings with language. (Language, of course, will be understood to refer to life indirectly, or it will be presupposed or demanded that reality or human life conform with the requirements of a particular and strict logic applied to language.) These moves are historically sequential, within contemporary philosophy's interests, i.e., (a) the study of language, on the demand that it be grounded on logic, independent of people's uses of language; language is thus understood as being one, universal, an image of reality or isomorphic with reality; (b) the study of language not as one but as many, or dependent of peoples uses of language; that is, not grounded on logic but on rhetoric. While knowledge is very precise and clear in the first instance, in the second it is only a vague project which our suggested methodology could bridge. In either case we shall try to show that context, structure and meaning embody both moves of the philosophical activity of contemporary philosophy, making knowledge not only precise but also possible in relation to overarching contexts.

Thus, if we view contemporary philosophy against the background of the birth of philosophy in Greece, certain features make themselves self-evident.

- Philosophy has become a problem-solving human action which takes its own activity for granted: it is concerned with solving the problems of one model of what knowing is.
- Philosophy in trying to solve these problems is oblivious that these problems are a dictate of the immediate philosophical past, rather than a need for understanding and making human life possible: of uncovering the present models of knowledge constituting our present circumstance.
- When contemporary philosophy is viewed in relation to its radical presuppositions—the things it counts on to do

philosophy—two main contexts are presupposed on which the *structure* and *meaning* of things philosophical are grounded: logic and rhetoric. These two contexts, however, work on the same metaphysical presuppositions of the universality of the one world, and its explanation and/or description according to a philosophical method which lacks self-awareness to be efficient. It is a method which stops either at therapy or some form of vague subjectivism.

- The hope is that the philosophical method here proposed is capable, by making itself present to its own radical activity, of leading to a possible possession of knowledge embodied in the multiple variations in which it appears through the multiple contexts, structures, and meanings which make human life possible, i.e., as an activity capable of embodying other models of knowledge as historically constituting the worlds of present-day man.

THE DETERMINATION OF THE PAST

Contemporary phillsophy found itself by the turn of the century under a double-barreled gun. On the one hand it was threatened with extinction by being lumped with "psychologism" and therefore unnecessary, and on the other hand it found itself, as philosophy, condemned to proceed to its own justification by carrying over the previous historical determinism of the sort of problems Descartes and later on Kant dictated for philosophy.

Since 1781, after Kant's *Critique of Pure Reason* and echoing the Cartesian dualism of the previous century, philosophy wavered within a metaphysical and an epistemological dualism which claimed two sorts of entities in the world: minds and material objects. A mind knows objects and other minds by means of mental states, also called ideas, representations, impressions, phantasms, which are caused by these objects and which resemble them. Despite minor differences, the followers of Descartes and Locke agreed that the mind is only acquainted with its own states. Hume showed the difficulty of this view by pointing out that if the mind knows its own states only, its own states are all the mind knows. Hume, of course, believed in the existence of other minds and of an external world. But, these beliefs he held to be incompatible with any kind of proof: they are merely the expression of a "blind and powerful instinct of nature." It is not reason, or logic, or knowledge (ruled by reason and logic), but only "custom" or "opinion" that is "the great guide of human life."

What most pre-Kantian philosophers held in common was the presupposition that the mind was a passive receptor of impression from the outside. Despite their agreement that the mind could combine, in accordance with the laws of association, the materials received from the outside, they held that the mind in its essence was passive, in Locke's phrase *tamquam tabula rasa,* an empty blackboard. Kant proposed what he termed a Copernican revolution. Just as Copernicus had shifted the frame of reference from the earth to the sun, Kant shifted the frame of reference from the objects to the mind. That is, he proposed that instead of holding the view that the mind passively registered what was already-out-there-now-real, it should instead be viewed on the hypotheses that the mind in turn selects and structures what is out there. This led him to suppose that the mind in turn contains selecting and structuring principles and that it is possible to know what those principles are. If this could be verified, as Kant believed, it would follow that certain and absolute knowledge of nature could be had. This, of course, would not be an absolute and certain knowledge of particular facts but of the basic structure of nature as far as we can experience it. The basic structure of nature, of course, would be the product of the mind's activity, not something independent of that activity. In this view the mind would no longer be a Cartesian substance contemplating other Cartesian substances from a distance; the mind would not be equally a "thing" at all but an activity, a sequence of "transcendental syntheses." What followed from this epistemological shift was a metaphysical one. The so-called objective world, the object of the mind's experience, not the object of the things-in-themselves, is a construct, a product of the synthesizing activity of the mind organizing the material of the "sensuous manifold." Kant believed that the mind's organizing and synthesizing activities were sufficient to justify the fundamental principles of Newtonian physics, above all the principle of the uniformity of nature, which Hume had maintained was the product of blind instinct and opinion, rather than logic or evidence.

Kant's prerequisite for knowledge was that particular causal laws such as "all bodies gravitate," "friction causes heat," are only probable since they depend on empirical observation and are arrived at *a posteriori,* but, the basic law on which the whole of physics rests, i.e., that every event has a cause is *certain,* since it is *a priori,* for the human mind structures its experience in a cause-effect way. The human mind within the range of its own structure can be sure of its own ground.

Contrary to what Copernicus had done in astronomy by removing the earth and man from the center of the periphery, what Kant did with his epistemological Copernican revolution was to prepare the way for man to reoccupy that center, thus opening the way to idealism.

Idealism is philosophically interesting not so much for what it proclaimed about the subject or consciousness but, rather for what it denied of the *a prioricity* of the mind. While Kant needed to conceive his twelve categories as timeless features of all minds' activities universally valid, Hegel argued that mind had a history, therefore was time bound. According to Hegel the mind passes through a series of stages, each stage holding a particular level or form of experience. Each level of experience, of course, would succeed the other according to a dialectical pattern such that a later level of experience would include the earliest ones and transcend them. Thus Kant's *a priori* was preceeded by another *a priori:* the sequential pattern of dialectical development that the history of culture reveals. But, while Hegel argued that this dialectical flight of the mind was a *spiritual* journey, Marx counter argued that the various sequences of world experiences rather than revealing a pattern of *spiritual* development reflected instead their dependence on a *material* dialectics: they were relative to the changing modes of economic production and exchange. Thus the two *a priori* of historic spiritual and material reason cancel the Kantian *a priori* while turning history into a battlefield of two substances—spiritual and material—fighting for supremacy.

Nietzsche, echoing the old stoics, summed up the period as in "despair of truth," of "crumbling skepticism and relativism," lost in a kind of "involuntary and unaware memoirs" a task he claimed had been the thinking of philosophers of the past and even of science, which according to him was not better than philosophy: "Physics too is only an interpretation of the universe, an arrangement of it (to suit us, if I may be so bold!), rather than a clarification."

Bradley's *Appearance and Reality* was published in 1893. He was not so much concerned with saving objectivity by keeping at a minimum the role the mind plays in constructing the world-of-experience, but in saving the things-in-themselves which Kant had abandoned in the streets for the phenomena. For if these things-in-themselves are unknowable, Bradley pointed out, then there is no evidence that they exist at all. This "unknowable" was transformed by Bradley into the Absolute: The all-inclusive, the One: a system. But, he confessed that this idea, "true as far as it goes" inevitably remains "abstract and incomplete" all we can hope for is to "gain some idea of its main features."

So, by the end of the 19th century the Kantian strategy of establishing a mind center instead of the old external and objective center was floundering. The Kantian transcendentalism rooted in the universal and necessary characteristics of the human mind lacked above all the awareness of its own presupposition-condition and, it also lacked empirical evidence, for who is there to know all the human minds.

Thus, by the end of the 19th century philosophy was caught in a multitude of disputes over method. There were those who favored the deductive method against the inductive one, or the transcendental against both, or the dialectic as a synthesis of them all. The significant point, however, and on which all of these methods agree is that *man* is neutral in regards to them all: either in respect to the forms of knowing assumed by transcendentalists, or in respect to the forms of the objects known, assumed by rationalists, or in respect to a dialectic reason which in order to be dialectical had to be assumed to be a-historical. This assumption of neutrality explains away the substitution of *man* for the I and the reduction of the vital activities of man to the intellectual—mind only. Defenders of the purely *deductive* method assumed a human power attributable only to the creative intellect; defenders of the purely *inductive* method assumed human impotence attributable only to man's complete dependence on the givenness of objective events; defenders of the *transcendental* method, assumed that the receptive-categorizing mind and its data are the measure of the real; defenders of the *dialectical* method, spirit or matter, assumed an imperialist form of historic reason to which man had of necessity to succumb. It is the latter method which has more chances of success for it has at least read carefully the determined trajectory of a model of reason, which since Aristotle has dominated the idea of rationality in the West, with exclusion of other possibilities within Western culture.

LOGIC AND RHETORIC AS CONTEXTS

The American circumstances in philosophy are a repetition and in many ways a mimicry of the European situation at the turn of the century. In many ways American philosophy is still laboriously trying to demarcate its own domain, distinct from the domains of natural science and psychology. Europe lived through the same problem around 1900–1913, a period which gave birth to the new philosophies of phenomenology, language analysis, and their many variations. What American philosophers have missed, however, is the pangs of giving birth to those philosophies as they were needed to justify the "life" of their times, and have settled instead into a kind of philosophy by inertia. What is needed is a systematic integration of the activity itself of philosophizing as it constructs itself in its contextual domain, at the risk, as Ortega puts it, that "once each (doctrine) is constructed it is beheaded by its successor, and that time is strewn with corpses." The systematic integration of the activity itself of philosophizing needs, as a first step, that we clarify the presupposed context upon which interpreters from the various Western disciplines, philosophers in particular, have labored to ground "meaning." This context or contexts we call logic and rhetoric in the sense that they organize the activity of philosophers and interpreters.

In a broad sense, logic studies how to put together the words of a language in acceptable phrases and also how to modify those words as required by their position in the phrases. Logic expects that a language-user will be able to recognize when an expression or a sequence of expressions is absurd or contradictory. The key point for our analysis lies in the fact that logic, in a broad sense, studies the absurdities and contradictions of language and proceeds formally, presenting its rules in terms of the expressions themselves *without reference to the time or place or circumstances of their use.*

The study of discourse as rhetoric, on the other hand, has concentrated its attention on the more subtle features of public speech and of literature and on the classification of styles. Rhetoric has included within its domain the discussion of the proper use of contradictory statements, such as the logical absurdities that occur in metaphors. Rhetoric is thus not a matter of pure form, but has to do with the relation of language to the world through the relation of linguistic expressions *to the specific circumstances in which their use makes sense.* Thus, rhetoric implicitly claims a kind of priority over logic.

The very fact that logic and rhetoric both have to do with the use and interpretation of signs not only points to us different styles of doing philosophy today, but above all, leaves an unanswered question as to the justification of those different styles of doing philosophy: How can there be two independent grounds for the theory of meaning?

It is obvious to anyone who is even superficially acquainted with contemporary philosophy and the different disciplines in the social sciences that our Western history has been systematically reduced to its philosophy of language. As it turned out, the philosophy of language in the Western tradition—including a great deal of its metaphysics—has almost invariably been based on logic rather than rhetoric. This is certainly true of Aristotle's doctrine of predication, of the medieval controversy over universals, of Leibniz' project for a universal symbolism, and of rationalism and idealism in general. But this is indeed a grave amputation of the *History of Philosophy.* It is also true, though less obviously so, of empiricist philosophy from Hobbes and Locke through Brentano and James to Russell; for the empiricists have taken it for granted that the ideas represented by our linguistic signs already stand in logical relations to one another *before* we have signs to represent them. There are of course exceptions, but the exceptions that come to mind are on the fringe of the tradition.

By the turn of the century it was apparent that the dominant theme was to be an increasing submission of philosophy in general, and of philosophy of language in particular, to the sovereignty of logic. This movement was due primarily to the work of five great men: Russell, Frege, Husserl, Whitehead and Wittgenstein. All five of these powerful figures were logicians, all five associated the problem of logic in some way or other with the problems of mathematics, and the five, together gave an irresistible impetus to the view that language is basically and primarily logical in character and that the fundamental essential features of language can be determined on the basis of *requirements* of logic. This first initial move will lead to other interests as can be seen from the later work of Husserl and Wittgenstein.

This first move to ground language on logic gave rise to the countermove to ground language on rhetoric or use. Under this flag rallied many phenomenologists, existentialists, and analytic philosophers following the leads of Heidegger, Sartre and the later Wittgenstein. In order to avoid overgeneralizations and help the reader progress in this critical journey here undertaken, we refer him to Appendix I where he will find concrete expositions of the way some of these philosophers did philosophy. Since we presuppose here that the reader has done his homework and is therefore familiar with his own historical tradition, we shall offer some general critical remarks under the general contexts of Logic (I) and Rhetoric (II) to guide us in our journey. In a most important sense these critical remarks are not against anybody but are offered as a model of rationality which needs the other in order to continue being rational. As the reader will notice, these critical remarks are not even wholly original in the sense that they, as remarks, have not been made before by some philosopher or another. In fact, we refer the reader to the work of Jacques Derrida, *Speech and Phenomena and Other Essays on Husserl's Theory of Signs* (Northwestern University Press, Evanston, Illinois, 1973) translated by David B. Allison and in particular to the preface to the book by Newton Garver. The reader will be able to discover in that book and the preface many of the points here made. Yet, we are doing something different and, therefore, saying something else. Our main purpose in this book is to focus on the activity itself of doing philosophy critically in such a way that by systematically integrating such an activity as what philosophy of necessity radically does we may transcend "critical statements" for a way of doing philosophy which justifies and constitutes itself through the other; "critical statements" being only the clue of such radical and grounding human action. In this sense we emphatically affirm, through our way of doing philosophy, our own culture, or whatever culture surrounds us, while we emphatically negate any one *method* that affirms itself at the expense of culture.

LOGIC AS CONTEXT or THE DEMAND FOR ONE MODEL OF REASON

In order to radically question the intelligibility of the tradition that takes logic as the ground of meaning and hence understand the cogency of the methods of doing philosophy based upon it, it is necessary to try to get a general picture of the presuppositions common to this way of doing philosophy. We are, of course, aware of the risk involved in such generalization. Those who have learned to regard the differences, for example, between empiricism and rationalism as more fundamental than their common agreement with a philosophical method that uses logic rather than rhetoric as the ultimate criterion for meaning, might find these generalzations dangerous. What rationalists and empiricists disagree about, however, is the origin of ideas; what they have in common is the view that signs represent ideas and that an idea is something that stands in semantic contrast or contradiction to another idea—and can be seen to stand in such contrast or contradiction without reference to contexts of communication. And it is precisely this common logical ground, based on the common view that the primary purpose of language is epistemological (early Wittgenstein) that is in question. In which case our generalization turns out to be a critical re-examination of the radical presuppositions upon which a particular method of doing philosophy is based.

The first important consequence of the above presupposition is that signs stand for ideas and that these ideas are timeless; namely, they are not to be located and identified in space and time. In this respect they are to be distinguished from the acts of communication, or actual utterances that occur in the course of our activities as language-users. This presupposition, however, that signs represent timeless ideas, carries with it inevitable conclusions:

The first of these is that a sign in at least one prominent sense of that term, is something with physical characteristics that occurs in a spatial-temporal context and therefore a distinction must be made, at least in kind, between signs and what they signify. In other words, on this presupposition a view of reality is dogmatically claimed to consist of some sort of ideas or things which can stand in logical relations to one another and that *this* is the ultimately real. But, this view of the world implies that the logical distinction between signs and ideas is also a metaphysical distinction between reality (thus metaphysically conceived) and signs. Thus a certain metaphysical conception of the world is imposed upon reality not because reality appears to be so, but because the philosophical method used demands that reality be so.

The second consequence of taking the timelessness of ideas as a foundation of language is that a certain amount of reductionism is inevitable in that the actual is explained in terms of the ideal. How is the speaker's meaning (what he means in a concrete context of time and place) to be explained? In Frege's terminology, the sense *(Sinn)* or in Husserl's terminology, the meaning *(Bedeutung)* of the sentence he utters must be explicated by means of the ideas that are represented by the constituent words of that sentence. But, this account of language (meaning) makes language impossible. For how can language (meaning) ever be used in reference to objects and circumstances which are not permanent, but transient, given that language is established and constituted independent of those transient objects and circumstances? Wittgenstein seems to be aware of the same problem when he asks himself in the *Tractatus:*

> The "experience" that we need in order to understand logic is not that something or other is the state of things, but that something *is:* that, however, is *not* an experience.
>
> Logic is *prior* to every experience—that something *is* so.
>
> It is prior to the question 'How?,' not prior to the question "What?."
>
> And, if this were not so, how could we apply logic? We might put it in this way: if there would be a logic even if there were no world, how then could there be a logic given that there is a world?"

A third consequence of the above method is that there must be a radical distinction between what Frege called sense and reference, or between what Husserl called expression and indication. These distinctions are not exactly the same, but they share the same purpose; namely, to distinguish as two separate and independent domains the timeless, (context-free) semantic relations of signs to one another and the (time-dependent, contextual variant) semantic relations of signs to the world. It is now commonplace among British and American philosophers to suppose that the theory of meaning must be divided into at least two parts, a theory of sense and a theory of reference. The underlying assumption is that what linguistic expressions *mean* is one sort of question and that how and when they are to be *applied* is a separate and independent question. But, to the extent that this assumption is part and parcel of the logical conception of the foundation of language, one challenges it when one denies that these two domains of meaning can really be kept separate. The later work of Wittgenstein is a striking example of such a denial.

A curious feature of the philosophy of language based on logic and just as much a curious escapism, is the commitment to what Wittgenstein called a "private language." This is the belief that there is some form of private understanding or inner speech such that it is possible for linguistic expressions to have meaning for us in "private mental life," quite independent of *any* reference to public objects or external circumstances. Such a commitment to private language or to private understanding cannot be renounced once the criterion for linguistic meaning has been set within the domain of logic. For logical truths and logical considerations are formal and do not vary according to circumstances. What is independent of circumstance in this way I cannot learn by example or by teaching. If I learn it at all, it must be within a realm that lies entirely within me, in my private mental life. This kind of commitment is obvious throughout modern philosophy, from Descartes through Locke to Husserl and Russell. One of the rewarding efforts of going through Wittgenstein's *Philosophical Investigations* (243–315) is to come across his vigorous rejection of the possibility of private understanding in his famous "private-language argument." It would seem ironical that a method based on the absolute need for absolute intelligibility had to end up in denying its own intelligibility by making its origins inaccessible to public scrutiny.

Methodologically, this early and positivistic stage of language analysis demands that "doing philosophy" be reduced to the function of shielding philosophy from its own self-reflection about the conditions and meaning of the knowledge thus achieved. Knowledge is thus identified with the form of knowledge science produces (a *method*) remaining *philosophical* only in the sense that it is used for the single purpose of its necessity to exorcize philosophical self-reflection from the body of science. Language grounded on logic starts from a type of knowledge—mathematical and physical—which is prototypical of science, and undertakes to investigate the organization of the obviously reliable capacity for knowledge which it has. This method posits without reservation the *normative* validity of a distinct and particular category of knowledge and demands that it be the only true one and universally applicable. The *decision* to do so, however, remains itself outside the possibility of its own critique. For the sake of a form of knowledge (scientific, defined mostly through achievements), a normative value is imposed on philosophy alien to mathematical or scientific knowledge, oblivious of the fact that this is a historical mediation of how philosophical activity is thus presently constituted. Methodologically, therefore, this demand of grounding philosophy on logic though demanding a commitment for philosophy (not philosophically grounded), is *in fact* doing something else which is philosophically grounded and thus able to surrender its rationality to the critical philosopher: it emerges as a philosophy constituting itself as philosophy and exhibiting to us its own formation as philosophy in-the-making. A method is thus turned into a culture, a regional ontology, and cleansed from its absolutistic and imperialistic demand to reduce the whole culture to itself.

RHETORIC AS CONTEXT

The second movement of the twentieth century philosophy of language is an effort at grounding meaning of discourse on rhetoric. There have been philosophers who have emphasized this aspect of meaning, either as one part of a semantic dualism or as a primary sense of meaning within which the logical aspects of meaning must find a specialized and restricted niche. This group philosophizes in many ways as a criticism of the previous demands for a logical context, in some cases made by themselves.

In Britain and America semantic dualism undoubtedly rests most prominently on the work of Frege and his distinction between sense and reference. Within the framework of that general distinction or some variation on it, there have developed the ideas of operational definitions and coordinating definitions in science and of recursive definitions in mathematics. It is characteristic of these definitions that they do not really explain the meaning (*Bedeutung,* in Husserl's sense) or the sense (*Sinn,* in Frege's sense) of the expressions they are used to define but serve instead to present *effective criteria* for the use of those expressions. It may seem obvious that definitions of this sort present rhetorical rather than logical considerations as governing the "meaning" of words.

Philosophers who have given some impetus to the view that discourse, language-as-used or rhetoric rather than logic provides the foundation for linguistic meaning include, among others, Peirce and Royce, Ortega y Gasset, Heidegger, Sartre, Wittgenstein, Wisdom, Austin, Ryle, Strawson, Quine, etc. Ortega y Gasset has been mostly ignored. Peirce was undoubtedly one of the first to advocate operational definitions; but his more general philosophy of language is difficult to interpret. Nonetheless, his emphasis on *interpretation* suggests that meanings are to be explained ultimately in terms of the human context in which they are interpreted. The same insight is prevalent in Dilthey, who like Peirce emphatically demanded the self-reflection of the sciences from their positivism to the point where knowledge becomes visible by grounding it in the life relationships of instrumental and communicative behaviour of the scientific community. But both fell short in their effort because they lacked the conceptual intentionality of a historic reason which constitutes itself as it reflects on its own formation. This last statement is, however, premature at this point. We shall proceed by illustrating our insights through some historical examples. The reader will find in Appendix I some notes on Heidegger and Sartre. We shall here concentrate on Wittgenstein's own criticism of the tradition he helped to form.

PHILOSOPHICAL INVESTIGATIONS AND THE FALL OUT

Wittgenstein's *Tractatus* appeared in 1921 and became the major influence in positivist thinking. In 1953, two years after his death, Wittgenstein's *Philosophical Investigations* appeared devastatingly criticizing the 'picture theory' of language which constituted the central feature of the *Tractatus.*

Section 107 of the *Philosophical Investigations* presents as clearly as one could wish the trend of his later thinking about the foundation for the pure logical grammar of his earlier work:

> The more narrowly we examine actual language, the sharper becomes the conflict between it and our requirement. (For the crystalline purity of logic was, of course, not a *result of investigation:* it was a requirement.) The conflict becomes intolerable; the requirement is now in danger of becoming empty. . . . We have got on to slippery ice, where there is no friction, and so in a certain sense the conditions are ideal; but also, just because of that, we are back to the rough ground.

Wittgenstein did not think that the picture theory of language as presented in the *Tractatus* was mistaken and that therefore a better focused picture should be offered. He maintained radically that the picture of *language as a picture* was a required distortion of reality for the sake of logical simplicity and clarity.

Wittgenstein noted in the *Tractatus,* "The general form of propositions is: This is how things stand . . . A proposition has one and only one complete analysis."

> That is the kind of proposition that one repeats to oneself countless times. One thinks that one is tracing the outline of the thing's nature over and over again, and one is merely tracing round the frame through which we look at it.

The picture which holds us captive, of course, is the picture of language as a picture. This picture, however, is not wholly false. In fact, it is appropriate within its own limits; that is, only in certain cases but not covering the immense variety of language uses, which no theory, or description can do. But what does such a general description amount to?

> Think of the tools in a tool-box: there is a hammer, pliers, a saw, a screw-driver, a rule, a glue-pot, glue, nails and screws—The function of words are as diverse as the function of these objects. (And in both cases there are similarities.) . . .

> When we say: "Every word in language signifies something" we have so far said nothing whatever; unless we have explained exactly what distinction we wish to make . . .
>
> Imagine someone's saying: "All tools serve to modify something. Thus the hammer modifies the position of the nail, the saw the shape of the board, and so on."—And what is modified by the rule, the glue-pot, the nails?—"Our knowledge of a thing's length, the temperature of the glue, and the solidity of the box." Would anything be gained by this assimilation of expressions.

This passage shows the new technique of philosophizing. Wittgenstein does not argue; he just produces counter examples to generalizations and shows what in other situations might not be the case.

Overgeneralization is made to cover what to the overgeneralizer is important. But to someone else, in a different situation, other cases will seem equally, or more, important. Not only that but generalizations are possible only by stretching language artificially, thus making generalization sound plausible. Hiding behind the generalizations of philosophers is their desire for certainty. But such rules for the satisfaction of such desire by classifying particular objects in certain definite ways are only for this purpose: to satisfy such needs. Wittgenstein came to the conclusion that concepts were instruments, and that only those whose view was distorted by their neurotic need for certainty would fail to see it so. What one sees in the world is not universals but "family resemblances," or "language games" where language is instrumental to a goal-directed activity and where language is effective (a "good" language) if it furthers that activity. Family resemblance is what we see when we actually look. No neurotic problems about essenses, universals, knowledge, being, object, I, proposition, name. What we have to look for is how each one of these words is originally used in the language game which is its original home.

Under the same attack is the logician's claim that there can be no vagueness in logic. The crystalline purity they find in logic is but a requirement that is but the reflection of the logician's quest for certainty. As to the "ideal language": the mathematical calculi of the logicians are useful for special purposes, but to call them ideal,

> is liable to mislead, for it sounds as if these languages were better, more perfect, than our everyday language; and as if it took the logician to show people at last what a proper sentence looked like.

In the end Wittgenstein's correction of philosophy is to take it away from the neurotic passion of saying the unsayable. We are bewitched by language because we suffer from "deep disquietudes,"—among them the passion of metaphysics.

When Wittgenstein turned from explanation to description—for his later philosophy is based firmly on the conviction that a philosopher has to look and see what happens and that he can only describe and in no way impose requirements—what he saw was that linguistic expressions are everywhere embedded in contexts of human activity. In order to conclude that they are in fact intrinsically and inextricably embedded in such activity, he had to present two sorts of considerations:

- to break down the seeming necessity for metaphysical foundations, by showing that the metaphysical demands and hypotheses are ultimately incoherent; and
- to show how both the familiar and the problematic features of language and language use can be accounted for within a theory of language which takes Rhetoric rather than word meaning as the foundations for language.

It is very easy to overemphasize the importance of Wittgenstein's rejection of his earlier position, since such an overemphasis quickly leads us to overlook the remaining similarities. But there is nonetheless a strong negative component in Wittgenstein's presentation of his new position, a component consisting of at least four sorts of argument:

- against the primacy of names;
- against the possibility, or even the conceivability of objects that are absolutely or metaphysically simple;
- against both the coherence and cogency of the demand of absolute exactness, which Frege had earlier persuaded him was essential if there is to be any conceptual meaning at all;
- and against the possibility of private language or private

understandings or private meanings, such as seems to be presupposed by any theory which begins by associating words with ideas or by taking names to be signs for ideas in the mind of the person that uses them.

These negative arguments of Wittgenstein's against his former views (and against other philosophies which take logic as constituting the essence of language) are set firmly in an alternative constructive conception of language according to which the meaning of linguistic expressions is based ultimately on the role that they play in human activities. The central notions in terms of which Wittgenstein elaborates this new view of language are those of *language-games,* of *rules and practices,* and of *forms of life.* To understand a linguistic expression, one has to know the "game" being played with it. This in turn often depends largely (never wholly) on knowing the "rules of the game" and always depends in part on being able (knowing how) to follow the rules. Being able to follow the rules depends, in turn, on practice and training, on being initiated into a "form of life" and this is what is ultimately "given" as the basis of language. Thus language and logic (which are ideal) are founded on training (which is empirical and contextual)—a starting point for philosophical inquiry which "seems to abolish logic, but does not do so." The relationship between language and logic in this context is a different one from the relationship between logic and reality as it appeared in the previous context of trying to ground meaning in logic. In this latter sense the meaning of any sentence could only be read if it conformed to a previously accepted picture (metaphysics) of the world which was claimed to be "scientific," "true," and in "accord with reality." But by grounding meaning a "a form of life" which is contextual, neither reality nor logic give language meaning. What is real in a contextual domain and what is unreal shows itself *in* the meaning that language has within that contextual domain. Meaning, structure and context, however, appear and must be taken together; that is, simultaneously, for it is thus that a form of life has found its own justification, and therefore constituted itself as human life.

Wittgenstein's reasons appeared to many too powerful to be ignored. In his wake a procession of other language-philosophers did philosophy around his themes and problems, the same way some phenomenologists and existentialists did philosophy around the themes and problems of Husserl, Heidegger and Sartre.

John Wisdom followed the therapeutic theme further. J. L. Austin attacked philosophical usage of individual terms. Gilbert Ryle showed that philosophical problems arise because terms belonging to different "categories" are mistakenly grouped together: "We must rectify the logical geography of the knowledge which we already possess." Ryle's argument is that philosophical criticism does not operate in terms of an ideal standard such as Wittgenstein attacked, it only uncovers the correlations implicit in ordinary, everyday languages. If we determine the correlations that actually obtain among the concepts we all use all the time, philosophers will stop confusing themselves and other people.

P. F. Strawson, in the heart of ordinary-language, does what he calls "descriptive metaphysics." He opposes this kind of metaphysics to revisionary metaphysics which was concerned with providing a better structure for our thought. What descriptive metaphysics is content to do is to describe the actual structure of our thought. Language games and Ryle's "galaxies" of ideas are too near the surface. Let's look for the common foundations. This task should be a human, not an objective one, in contrast to Kant.

Agreement about the nature of time, about values, about the structure of the world is easier to reach within a particular form of life, but what about other forms of life? Linguists like Chomsky and anthropologists like Levi–Strauss believe in a "universal" deep structure, for if there are as many houses as there are languages, still all these houses must have a common architectural plan. Quine is one of the few to have considered this question. And he has reached the opposite conclusion. "We can never free ourselves from all theories and face the facts themselves in their purity. We can never do better than occupy the standpoint of some theory or other, the best we can muster at the time."

This over emphasis on *theory* was carried over by analytic philosophers into moral philosophy. Moral discourse from any culture was thus subject to total revisionism. This could only be accomplished by analytic moral philosophy by taking from the positivists the doctrine that the logical category of fact is totally distinct from that of value, and that no knowledge of value can be derived from knowledge of fact. It was agreed that "what is" is wholly distinct from "what ought to be," and that statements about "what ought to be" can be neither true nor false. Ethics was thus radically vanished from the realm of knowledge and metaethics was born. Metaethics is concerned not with the study of the good and the right but with the study of statements *about* the good and the right. A wholly theoretical, ethically neutral activity conducted at a higher level of abstraction than moral judgement itself.

Thus by the routes of phenomenology and language analysis we find philosophy cornered against the wall of its own self-reflective constitution struggling for its own radical orientation. To justify itself philosophy has now to recognize the power of its own emancipatory state, renounce being anyone's slave and acknowledge itself as the constitutive and radical activity of human acting, theorizing and communicating.

The activity of philosophy, in the hands of Heidegger and Sartre, though necessary in its role as critic of the previous generation of philosophers, is not *sufficient* for the justification of their own doing of philosophy. Agreement about Being or about the absurd passion of man's life is not sufficient justification for philosophy. Both philosophers are oblivious of the one thing they are both unwilling to reflect upon: the *decision* that it be so. This decision is not part of the reflective consciousness-of on which the reasons for the agreement are given, but rather it is the consciousness the philosopher himself "counts on" in order to do philosophy: to orient his life-knowledge, to communicate, to act. Nor is it sufficient to justify philosophy by gathering agreement about an event like death, or by defining man as being a situation. In both cases there is also the knowledge that it is so, the ability to communicate it so and the decision that it be so. These three elements are not a part of the event death, nor of the situation. They are the constitutive elements of the activity itself of interpreting the life of man as man constitutes it. They are the *historical mediation* on which philosophy is radically grounded.

The conception of language as a plurality of language games is not justifiable in terms of the *conception* itself. When we say that the meaning of a word is its use in a certain language game, that the relation of language games is just family resemblance and deny the possibility of *knowing* overarching contexts, we still have to justify what is being said against the theory of meaning making such claims. This theory of meaning has to exhibit its possibility as a theory of meaning. When the philosopher, however, talks about language games as different forms of life, his talk is an interpretative talk. The talking the philosopher does in this manner is not a move in any one language game. His talk, therefore, is not meaningful according to his own theory of meaning. If, however, his talk about the problem of meaning is only a talk, let's say, within the language game of philosophy, then his general theory of meaning is no theory of meaning at all: a move in a language game is not talk about language games. Thus, once again, philosophers are thrown against the wall of their own self-reflective activity, as the activity they "count on" to do philosophy. What the philosophers *do* is therefore constitutive of philosophy as much as *theory* and *communication.* A critical self-reflection on this *doing* is therefore also necessary for philosophy's rationality to emerge. Thus our analysis of logic and rhetoric as context has led us into the necessity of justifying philosophy on its own constitutive activity as it theorizes, communicates and acts while constituting and reproducing itself as the radical ground of man.

To summarize: What the philosophers we have seen here did with their philosophies was, on the one hand, a reduction of knowledge to one form of knowledge. We would call this reduction, in our terminology, the demand that one structure of human knowing be accepted as a universal context of knowing; and on the other hand the demand that *meaning* be also reduced to an agreement about *meaning* as exemplified by the accepted theory of knowledge. In both cases the *doing* of philosophy by these philosophers was guaranteed by an activity—a decision on a radical orientation—outside the critical domain of their method of doing philosophy and previous to their philosophies. Thus the *activity*—at its radical level—of doing philosophy was leading the doing of philosophy to deeper and more critical areas in need and search of its own justification.

PHILOSOPHY'S SOCIAL PRACTICE

Underlying the social practices of contemporary man, from a job in the streets to the teaching in the university, there are those philosophical presuppositions we have just gone through. They either determine man's social acting or reproduce social acting by the power of their own self-reproducing drive without in any way contributing to man's emancipation from the controls surrounding him. The professional in the University or the man in the street cannot hide behind the protection of his own discipline or job and claim neutrality to what goes on "around him." He is definitely the creator of what goes on around him in precisely the degree in which he is able to seize the presuppositions on which his acting is grounded; i.e., insofar as he can turn himself from a natural into a cultural man. In this sense all the actions of man, and particularly the ones we are directly concerned with here, comparative studies and philosophy, share with philosophy the problem of their own social practice; i.e., the problem that what is done—comparative studies, philosophy, is necessarily the way it is actually being done. The problem, therefore, we are focusing on is primarily the distinction between grounding rationality on a method universally applicable, or grounding rationality on cultural man. It is in this context that the specific methods of the disciplines, including philosophy, fail to gain emancipation and self-sufficiency because they lack originally the ability to reflect on what their social practice, their actions, imply and actually *do* when what what they *do*—philosophy, philology, comparative studies—is self-sufficiently conceived. In other words, when philosophers, or for that matter psychologists, philologists, etc., systematically conceal from themselves and others the public and social dimension of their way of doing philosophy, or whatever they are doing, then the disciplines, including philosophy, turn into ideologies. Ideology being a radical and systematic misunderstanding which demands that society be rational in a certain way, while the actual and possible rationality of society remains opaque to the members of society. When rationality is thus concealed, the members of a society, philosophers included, are at the mercy of social powers. These social powers become, to the unknowing subject, causal and natural laws, on the same ideological footing as philosophy deprived of the self-critical awareness of its own constitutive power as a radical activity of human intentions. On the other hand, the social sciences, deprived of a critical philosophy which renounces systematically to constitute itself critically, can only confirm the existing social conditions by concealing the historicity of man and isolating man from his own rationality.

The philosopher teaching philosophy—and for that matter the philologist, or psychologist, or cultural expert—cannot absolve himself from the responsibilities of his teaching and even less claim neutrality or innocence in relation to his teaching. The philosopher, in teaching, is by that activity guilty: what he does while teaching is a tacit claim that his philosophy as taught is necessarily the way it is being taught. In other words, philosophers teaching philosophy either *demand* through the activity implied in their teaching that their practice of philosophy leaves society in its barbarian natural raw state or if they became aware—and critical—of their own *practice,* they can seriously struggle for the recovery of the multi-form rationality that surrounds them radically constituting the rational ground on which society rests.

There are very few instances in the teaching of philosophy where philosophy is taught as a *practice* —methodic and systematic—of being multi-reasonable. Being a *practice,* philosophy cannot be taught at the expense or ignorance of the full rationality of the present. Being a *method,* it cannot ignore any areas of the past and present in their influences on the constitution of the future. Being a *system,* it cannot blindly let itself fall, like any ideology, on the fatal hands of naturally created interests which arise naturally out of the natural compulsion toward the reproduction of social action.

It is common knowledge today that man is not a being of nature but of culture. But the making of a cultural man has been a laborious process—at least in our culture—to such a degree that cultural man, as opposed to natural man, is still programmatic and to a great extent a stranger in the University. The main reason for this impasse is that philosophy has not been understood as the *activity* it is—self-forming, while self-reflecting—but rather as an uncritical recitation of other peoples' reason, i.e., the study of reason from the outside or the reduction of other reasons to one, not realizing that this approach is unphilosophical in the sense that the only reason studied was reason modeled on scientific knowledge and therefore a reason which was incapable of knowing itself even while conscious of itself. In a philosophical, strict sense it is knowledge without reason.

The "theory of knowledge" first appeared in the nineteenth century as the question of the possibility of reliable knowledge. Kant posed it first in this transcendental form and thus helped the theory of knowledge become conscious of itself. He started with a type of knowledge—mathematical and physical—which appeared to him prototypical for science, and undertakes to investigate the organization of the obviously reliable capacity for knowledge which it obviously has. But that means that Kant's criticism is not as critical as it appears: he posits without reservation the normative validity of a particular category of knowledge and wants to model all other areas on it. The critique of knowledge, even at birth, already chose a particular kind of knowledge as the only true one, and thus renounced making that *decision* itself the object of criticism. The theory of knowledge to be critical, however, lays claim to nothing but its pure critical consciousness: a whole process of formation or constitution at a level of reflection to which it does not admit and therefore also cannot legitimate.

Thus what the critique of knowledge has to start with is the presuppositions on which this early critique started: the presupposition of the normative concept of science; the presupposition of an equally normative subject of knowledge and the rigid separation between theoretical (i.e., the ability to produce sciences of the understanding) and practical reason (i.e., the ability to set norms and determine the will).

Hegel fell in the same error of Kant by making a particular concept of knowledge, i.e., the concept of science, the only authoritative one: he ends his *Phenomenology* by identifying the critical theory of the theory of knowledge with "absolute knowledge."

Marx's formulation of the theory of knowledge fails again in the identification of all reality with a concrete human activity and the instruments of that activity. Human activity is conceived as a transcendental achievement grounded in the real process of human labor. The reduction through identification of the act of human self-formation to labor finally opened the door for all the positivistic claims about knowledge. For as in Kant and Hegel it led to establishing a particular category of knowledge as normative.

The positivistic project as regards philosophy followed in order to immunize science against philosophy. The concrete misunderstanding of this project being the demand that man's behaviour, like nature, must remain static and invariant while the instruments for its explanation, control and prediction become more and more sophisticated. But this view of life, like all others, must contend with its own justification, factually satisfying the claims to justification without recourse to the demand that men must conform to a limited and controlled discussion, i.e., linguistic uniformity.

The philosopher teaching philosophy must therefore be aware of what he does when he gives up the "searched knowledge" needed to orient man's social and individual life at a radical level, in the face of present radical needs and future aims of the cultural life around him. He must realize in his teaching that reason is *practical* and that the kind of social practice he is engaged in—when teaching philosophy in a noncritical vain—is that social practice should not renew itself in any significant human way. We are all familiar with the *descriptions* of phenomenologists and even more familiar with the habit of language analysis philosophers who end any discussion of morals, religion, politics, aesthetics, etc., in logic. But this only confirms the social world that already is, it does not *do* anything to it. Besides, the world is not made only of these kind of things. The world that surrounds the philosopher—the circumstance—is full of rationality; different reasons. The philosopher's task is to make reason by uncovering the preconditions for the possibility of any reason surrounding him. And if these reasons need to be discovered, it is because they are there, facing the philosopher when he does philosophy, regardless of whether he sees them or not.

To teach philosophy is radically different from teaching any other subject in the natural sciences. Philosophy's language—action—is within a lived world and presupposes a radical orientation and involvement towards this world, a public language and the particular kind of action which philosophy does in this world. Neither explanation, nor prediction, nor control of the educational processes of philosophy are compatible with the essense of philosophy. Philosophy's task is precisely the liberation of man from these social—natural—controls.

Philosophy's relation to the essense of philosophy is that of inter-rationality. Philosophy is done between bodies. A bodiless philosophy is impossible. This means that for philosophy's rationality to be possible the philosopher has to encounter the "other" not as a thing, an object, not even a subject: but as an equal interpreter. The rationality that emerges while teaching philosophy is that both professor and student are engaged in an equal task of mutual interpretation, where what is interpreted is not the "other" but the "other" is only the occasion for one's own rational emergence and its interpretation. Rationality is possible only on equal terms. It is this equality, also, which makes rationality—that of others—our own possibilities. It is philosophy's task to constitute itself rationally through the other by methodically and persistently discovering its own possibilities in the other co-interpreters with whom the rational constitution of man is taking place in the present in view of the future social action. Through the teaching of philosophy intersubjectivity is claimed, but not realized. Through the teaching of philosophy our own needs can be identified as the discovery in the other of his own rationality—our own possibilities—as a possibility to realize uncontrolled communication. Through the teaching of philosophy we are able to anticipate the possibility of embodying plural subjects at a radical equal base with our own interpretive activity which is not yet realized. Through the teaching of philosophy we may attempt to restore the self-formation process of social man through a process of self-reflection which will enable social man to reinterpret the legitimacy of existing control systems. Insofar as these controls are able to repress dimensions of historical rationality of individual and collective self-forming processes, man may be liberated. The teaching of philosophy should be capable, if critically oriented, to remove the conditions needed to perpetuate unnecessary behavioral orientations in the systematic and methodic de-humanization of man. To put it dramatically in G. Radnitzsky's terminology, we must overcome the view that humans are "a cross-breed of computer and rat." Philosophy as social practice cannot be an instrument of information or of social control only. Philosophy must liberate and constitute man as man through the discovering constitution of the multiform reasons of man.

SUMMARY AND CONCLUSIONS

We started our journey through Greek and contemporary philosophy in the hope of clarifying Ortega y Gasset's theme Man and Circumstance. The path we followed was that of Historic Reason; i.e., the activity itself of doing philosophy, in different historical domains, for the particular people of those domains. We tried to show that this has been the implicit path of philosophy from its beginning and the path contemporary philosophy leads to for its own grounding and justification.

If our analysis of *man* and *circumstance* is at least in general terms, functionally possible, it is obvious that the biases of interpretation of our own life or of other peoples' rest mostly on the exaggerated inflation of "structure" to the heights of context, and the reduction of meaning to agreement about generalized structural elements. As we have seen, Aristotle started the trend in Western philosophy by elevating one particular structure (the knowledge of logical causes and reasons) to the heights of context (a universal knowledge for all about all that there is). Thus a particular model of knowledge was accepted and universalized for a whole culture to follow. Contemporary philosophy, as we have seen, made the same move on the wake of the Kantian critic by identifying philosophy with a particular rationality or by grounding philosophy on logic and rhetoric. In both cases *structure* takes the form of myth—organizes and controls or claims organization of the whole of human life in a total and sufficient way—while *context*—other models of knowledge, other present reasons—and *meaning* are both claimed to be less than the human circumstance demands. The human circumstance is always concrete and varied. Man is always man in a concrete *situation.* Man's search for his own meaning can be distinguished but not separated from his situation, for it is the concrete situation that forms him and his possibilities. Nor can structure be inflated to such a gigantic size as to push out of the skies of philosophy the actual knowledge men of different times and cultures had to invent for themselves to make their lives possible. One model of knowledge does not know itself. Man deprived from his own circumstantial *situation* is not a man, but an abstraction. A philosophy that does not recognize these totalitarian tendencies of its own history is not only blind, it is short of being a philosophy; it is rather an ideology. It neither reveals knowledge—it just repeats empty, dead forms—nor acknowledges the present empirical condition of man in his own situation as equal possibilities for man's rationality to constitute itself as human. Thus no philosophy can justify itself unless it is capable of and able to save the human circumstance; unless any contextual, structural domain can be reconstructed as historically justified, as man discovered the meaning of his own circumstantial situation. Otherwise philosophical method, for lack of critical self-awareness, proceeds to universalize principles of thought or action, or in weak moments of generosity and guilt abrogates tolerance for other peoples' views. But in the process philosophy has lost sight of the concrete social synthesis with which history—historic reason—confronts its own activity daily. Knowledge and man are both reduced to one single example of the universal traits which make up an isolated structure.

If meaning is grounded on human contexts, man—the philosopher—has to recognize that he is simultaneously multi-lingual. That is, he moves simultaneously within many languages, natural and artificial, many language-games, many forms of life. He has also to recognize that this multiplicity-condition is what makes his human experiencing humanly possible. Each language man uses is the condition for man's self-expression: his self-choosing, creation, growth. The real philosophical enterprise is not only constitution, but also the renovation of human life. It is up to every man to decide for himself the language he chooses as the source of his creativity as a human and it is senseless for anyone to teach him which is the "proper" language to use for such creativity. However, no renovation, or recreation of the human experience is possible if man is not given or is not allowed a philosophical method which will guarantee for him the possible reconstitution of human living as it is self-constituted in its multiple contextual and social domains. In this sense it is as philosophically interesting and vitally needed to study Indian, Chinese, or Japanese thought, as it is to study "Black" or "Puerto Rican–American" thought. It is as philosophically interesting and vitally needed to study the language of the "hard sciences" as it is to study the language of "poetry." What no institution, education or political—least of all philosophy departments—can afford to do, without risking becoming trivial or superfluous, is to encourage or justify the substitution of human creativity for human conformism by trying to reduce all men to linguistic uniformity.

When analyzing ours and other cultures as they both meet in our present situational circumstance, the empirical material which the philosopher counts on is language and linguistic behavior; but, language and linguistic behavior comes to the philosopher in concrete contexts and structures. Neither language, contexts or structures are universal. They are, however, *public*; that is, the meaning of any language or statements of a language are always verifiable within the contextual domains, set of rules and criteria of identification provided by the context and structures of each language and applicable only to the language under analysis.

Philosophical method cannot, therefore, justify itself fully by universalizing the criteria for meaning of one particular language to apply to all the others, but can only justify itself if it is capable of accounting for the particular criteria for meaning within each language.

It is in this sense that philosophical method depends for its own life on being able to uncover other contexts and other structures which make human life possible and different for the people of those different contexts and structures. It is in this sense that philosophical method is dependent for its full justification on context, structure and meaning. To know other cultures, other languages, as they knew themselves, as they are present in our own needs or possibilities, and in such a way that we recognize them, is the necessary and sufficient condition for philosophy's own justification. For it is only because they knew themselves as they did, because they are our present need and possibilities, because they are recognizable by us, that they and we are able to create and recreate ourselves through them in our mutual equality and communicative intersubjectivity.

A further note of methodological interest is that the saving of the human circumstantial situation demands a complete detachment or nonidentification with our own philosophical methods. The whole circumstance has to be saved whole, or what we have instead is a repetition of our own forms. For example, language analysis alone will not do: parts do not make a whole. Phenomenology will not do either in the following sense. Phenomenology and "historic reason"—saving the human circumstance—advocated here, both agree that human experience is anonymous and that the subsequent candidates one finds for it (experience) are merely a function of self-commitments, of decisions made independent of the experience itself. Now, whereas phenomenological reduction proceeds by 'bracketing out' categories of things to preserve the immediate appearances (phenomena) of experience, historic reason or the saving of the human circumstance demands a broader reduction than just phenomenological reduction. It demands an *ontological reduction* which is capable of saving such human circumstance as one encounters. Ontological reduction is grounded on the realization of nonexistence of reference for language, perception or experience in general. Or that immediate experience is not the reference of language or perception. Experience's origin is only possible in its own anyonymity. Names and forms, ontological and ontic commitments are decisions of self-commitment, but there is nothing whatsoever to which commitment can be attached to except on a self-decision and for self-identification. Neither ideas nor things have an ultimate substance, unless we decide for them to have it. Saving the human circumstance in its complexity of context, structure and meaning presupposes this ontological reduction for it is in such 'human wholes' that any particular form of life is presented or appears. Philosophy understood as "historic reason" is the only experience of man capable, through its own critical constitution, of guaranteeing both its own anonymity and its non-identification.

Philosophy's own life depends, therefore, in avoiding these two extremes: *archaic parochialism*—the repetition of accepted forms without empirical content—and *universalism* or conceptual colonialism—the genocide of other peoples' experiences by reducing all meaning to only the formal criteria for meaning of one language, or by reducing the multilinguistic condition of man to only one language which might appear to some at a certain historical time to be the only meaningful one for all men.

It is in the hope of leading philosophical method to an embodied vision of itself—to feed one model of knowing through other models of knowing—and of human life—our present vital needs to be executed—by making man aware of the radical need and interpretative condition of both these possibilities—man's contemporary circumstance—that our journey through the *Bhagavad Gītā* is here undertaken. Not because the *Gītā* needs to measure up to our rationality, but because we need the *Gītā*'s rationality for our own rational survival.

Part III

Bhagavad Gītā: The Song of Embodied-Vision

Chapter Three

Translation and Critical Notes by
Antonio T. de Nicolás

Chapter I
THE YOGA OF ARJUNA'S CRISIS

Dhṛtarāṣṭra said:

1. My sons and those of Pāṇḍu, what did they do,
Saṃjaya, when, eager to fight, they assembled
On the field of the Kurus, the field of *dharma*?

Saṃjaya said:

2. Having looked over
The Pāṇḍava troop drawn up in battle order, then
Prince Duryodhana approached his teacher (Droṇa) and spoke these words:

3. Behold, O Teacher, this great army of the sons of Pāṇḍu,
Gathered by an intelligent pupil of yours,
The son of Drupada.

4. Here are great archers who are equal in battle
To Bhīma and Arjuna, heroes like Yuyudhāna and Virāta, and Drupada,
A great chariot-warrior;

5. Together with Dhṛṣṭaketu, Cekitāna, and the courageous King of Kāśi;
Then, too, Purujit, Kuntibhoja, and Śaibya,
The best of men.

6. And then there is Yudhāmanyu the strong, and Uttamaujas the brave,
And the son of Subhadrā and the sons of Draupadī,
All of them mighty chariot-warriors.

7. O Highest of the Twice-Born,
Know also the most distinguished of our men, leaders in my army.
Let me name them for your recognition.

8. There is yourself (Droṇa), and Bhīṣma and Karṇa,
And Kṛpa victorious in battle,
Aśvatthāman and Vikarṇa, and also the son of Somadatta.

9. Many other heroes are also willing to risk their lives for my sake,
And all of them are skilled in war
And armed with many kinds of weapons.

10. Our force, however, commanded by Bhīṣma,
Appears to be unlimited
While theirs, commanded by Bhīma, appears to be small.

11. Therefore above all let all you lords,
Posted in all directions,
Support Bhīṣma.

12. To bring him (Duryodhana) joy,
The oldest grandson of the Kurus (Bhīṣma) roared loudly like a lion,
And blew his conch shell.

13. Then conches and kettledrums, cymbals and drums and horns,
All were suddenly sounded,
And the noise was tumultuous.

14. Then Mādhava (Kṛṣṇa) and the son of Pāṇḍu (Arjuna),
Both stationed in a great chariot yoked to white horses,
Blew their wondrous conches.

15. The Lord-of-the-Senses (Kṛṣṇa) blew Pāñcajanya,

Wealth-Winner (Arjuna), Devadatta,
And Bhīma, voracious, of terrible deeds, blew his great conch, Pauṇḍra.

16. Soon Prince Yudhiṣṭhira, son of Kuntī,
Was blowing Anantavijaya,
Nakula and Sahadeva were blowing Sughoṣa and Maṇipuṣpaka.

17. They were joined by the supreme archer of Kāśi,
And the great warrior Śikhaṇḍin, and Dhṛṣṭadyumna,
Virāṭa, and the invincible Sātyaki;

18. Drupada, the sons of Draupadī,
And the strong-armed son of Subhadrā:
O Lord of Earth, all these also blew their conches.

19. The tumultuous noise, resounding through heaven and earth,
Rent open the hearts of the sons of Dhṛtarāṣṭra.

20. Then, Lord of Earth, with the fighting about to begin,
The ape-bannered son of Pāṇḍu (Arjuna) seeing Dhṛtarāṣṭra's sons
Stationed in battle order, took up his bow.

21. And to Hṛṣīkeśa (Kṛṣṇa), then, O Lord of Earth,
He spoke these words:
Stop my chariot in the middle of the two armies, Unshaken one,

22. That I may behold these men standing there eager to fight,
With whom I am to engage in this war.

23. I want to see those who, about to fight, are assembled here
Desirous of accomplishing in battle
What is dear to the evil-minded son of Dhṛtarāṣṭra.

24. Thus addressed by Guḍākeśa (Arjuna), O Descendant of Bhārata (Dhṛtarāṣṭra),

Hṛṣīkeśa (Kṛṣṇa) placed the best of chariots in the middle of the two armies.

25. And when they were placed facing Bhīṣma, Droṇa and all the princes,
He said: O Son of Pṛthā (Arjuna),
Behold the assembled Kurus!

26. Arjuna saw standing there fathers and grandfathers,
Teachers, uncles, brothers, sons, grandsons, companions,

27. Fathers-in-law and friends, belonging to both armies.
And having looked closely at all these relations standing there,
The son of Kuntī (Arjuna)

28. Filled with the utmost sadness,
And weighed down by his sorrow, he said:
Kṛṣṇa, seeing my own kin on hand and eager to fight,

29. My limbs become weak, my mouth dries up,
My body trembles, and my hair stands on end.

30. Gāṇḍīva (the bow) slips from my hand;
My skin is also burning, I can scarcely remain standing;
My mind is reeling.

31. And I see bad omens, O Keśava (Kṛṣṇa),
And I forsee no good that could come from having slain my own kin in war.

32. I do not crave victory for myself, Kṛṣṇa, nor kingdom nor pleasures.
Of what use is kingdom to us, O Govinda (Kṛṣṇa)
Of what use pleasure, or even life?

33. Those for whose sake kingdom and enjoyments and pleasures we desire,
Are entering the fight
Relinquishing their lives and riches.

34. Teachers, fathers, sons, grandfathers, uncles,
Fathers-in-law, grandsons, brothers-in-law, and (other) relations:

35. Though I am slain, I do not desire to slay them. O Madhusūdana (Kṛṣṇa),
Even for the kingship of the three worlds.
Why, then, for the sake of the earth?

36. What pleasure would there be for us in slaying Dhṛtarāṣṭra's sons,
O Janārdana (Kṛṣṇa), Exciter-of-Men?
Only evil would attach to us if we slayed these (our would be) murderers.

37. Hence we ought not slay Dhṛtarāṣṭra's sons, our kinsmen;
For having slain our own kin,
How will we be happy, O Mādhava?

38. Even if they, whose minds are afflicted with greed,
Do not see the evil caused by destruction of a family
And the crime incurred in the harming of a friend;

39. Why is it not wise for us, O Janārdana (Kṛṣṇa),
Who see this evil of causing the destruction of a family,
To hold back from this sin?

40. In the ruin of a family, the ancient family *dharma* disappears,
And with the destruction of *dharma,*
Adharma overcomes the whole family.

41. When *adharma* conquers, O Kṛṣṇa,
The women in a family become corrupt;
And among fallen women, O Vārṣṇeya (Kṛṣṇa), caste-mixture arises.

42. This mixing brings both the family and its destroyers to hell,
For the spirits of their ancestors fall
When deprived of their offerings of rice and water.

43. By these evils of those who destroy a family
And create caste mixtures,
The immemorial *dharmas* of caste and family are destroyed.

44. We have heard, O Janārdana,
That a place in hell is reserved
For men of a family whose *dharmas* are destroyed.

45. Alas, we have resolved to commit a great sin
By undertaking to slay our own kin
Out of greed for the joys of kingship.

46. It would be better for me if Dhṛtarāṣṭra's sons,
Would slay me, weapons in hand,
Unarmed and unresisting, in battle.

47. Having spoken thus in the battle field,
Arjuna threw down his bow and arrow and sank down upon his chariot seat,
His mind overcome by grief.

This is the end of the first chapter, entitled "The Yoga of Arjuna's Crisis" *(arjunaviṣādayoga)*.

Chapter II
THE YOGA OF UNDERSTANDING

Saṃjaya said:

1. To him who was thus burdened with sadness,
His eyes filled with tears and confused, who was sinking into depression,
Madhusūdana (Kṛṣṇa) spoke these words:

The Blessed One said:

2. Whence came to you this weakness in this (moment of) crisis?
It is ignoble, O Arjuna,
And neither leads to heaven nor brings glory.

3. Yield not to such unmanliness, Son of Pṛthā,
It does not befit you!
Having relinquished this petty faintheartedness, stand up, O Foe-Destroyer!

Arjuna said:

4. O Madhusūdana (Kṛṣṇa), how am I to fight with arrows

Against Bhīṣma and Droṇa,
Both worthy of reverence?

5. Surely it would be better to be even a beggar in this world
Than to have slain those mighty teachers.
For having slain them, wealth-desiring though they are,
I would enjoy only blood-smeared pleasures here on earth.

6. We know not which is better for us,
To conquer them or that they should conquer us.
For having slain those sons of Dhṛtarāṣṭra standing there before us,
We would not desire to live.

7. My inmost being is stricken by this flaw of pity,
For my mind is confused about *dharma,* I ask you which would be better?
Tell me decisively, I am your pupil;
Instruct me who have come to you.

8. For I do not myself see what would take from me this grief
Which dries up my senses,
Even if I gained sole rule over a thriving kingdom on earth,
Or even sovereignty over the gods.

Saṃjaya said:

9. Having so spoken to Hṛṣīkeśa (Kṛṣṇa),
And having said to Govinda, 'I will not fight!'
Guḍākeśa became silent.

10. Then, O Bhārata (Dhṛtarāṣṭra), Hṛṣīkeśa (Kṛṣṇa), as it were smiling,
Spoke these words to him who was sinking into depression
In the middle of the two armies:

The Blessed One said:

11. You grieve for those who are not to be grieved for,
Yet you speak words that sound like wisdom.
The wise do not grieve for the dead or for the living.

12. Never was there a time when I was not,
Nor you nor these rulers of men;
And never hereafter shall there be a time when any of us will not be.

13. For just as the embodied (one) comes to childhood, youth and old age in this body,
So he comes to another body (after departure from this body form):
The intelligent man is not deluded by this.

14. It is contact with objects of the senses, O Son of Kuntī (Arjuna),
That yield pleasure and pain, cold and heat,
These conditions are not lasting,
They come and go. Endure them, O Bhārata (Arjuna).

15. For he whom these do not disturb, O Bull among men,
The intelligent man who remains the same amidst pleasure and pain,
He is fit for immortality.

16. Of what-is-not there is no coming to be;
Of what-is there is no ceasing to be.
The final truth of these is also known to those who see the truth.

17. Know that that by which all this is pervaded, is indestructible;
Nothing can work the destruction of this which is imperishable.

18. These bodies, it is said, come to an end,
(But they belong) to an embodied one who is eternal, indestructible, immeasurable.
Therefore, fight, O Bhārata!

19. Both he who considers this to be slayer
And he who considers this to be slain,
Fail to understand: this neither slays nor is slain.

20. Nor is it ever born, nor dies,
Nor having come to be will it not be once again.

Unborn, eternal, everlasting,
This primeval one is not slain when the body is slain.

21. He who knows this which is indestructible, eternal, unborn, changeless,
How and whom does this man slay or cause another to slay, O Son of Pṛthā (Arjuna)?

22. Just as a man, casts off clothes and takes on new ones,
So the embodied one, casts off worn-out bodies
And takes on others that are new.

23. Weapons do not cut it, fire does not burn it,
Water does not wet it, winds do not dry it.

24. It is not able to be cleaved in two, burned, wetted, dried;
It is eternal, all-pervasive, unchanging, and immovable.

25. This is said to be unmanifest, unthinkable, invariable.
Therefore, knowing it as such, you should not grieve.

26. And likewise, even if you think this is perpetually born and perpetually dying,
Even so, O Strong-Armed, you should not grieve for this.

27. For to one born, death is certain,
And to one dying, birth is certain.
Therefore you must not grieve over what is unavoidable.

28. Beings are unmanifested in their beginnings, apparent in their middles,
And unmanifested in their ends:
What in this is to be lamented, O Bhārata?

29. Some take this for a marvel, others speak of this as a marvel,
And others hear of this as a marvel;
But even having heard of this, no one knows it yet.

30. This embodied one in the body of each, is eternal and invulnerable:
Therefore, O Bhārata, you must not grieve for any being!

31. Moreover, having regard to your own *dharma,* you must not falter.
There is no higher good for a *kṣatriya*
Than to fight accordant with *dharma.*

32. Happy is the *kṣatriya,* Son of Pṛthā,
Who meets with such a fight which, falling to his lot by chance,
Throws open the door of heaven.

33. But if you will not engage in this righteous battle,
Then having forsaken your own particular *dharma* as well as glory,
You will incur sin.

34. Besides, men will recount your unalterable dishonor;
And for one who has been held in honor,
Dishonor is worse than death.

35. Great warriors will think you withdrew from battle out of fear,
And you, having been highly thought of by them,
Will be made light of.

36. Your enemies will speak many unseemly words,
Scorning your courage.
What could be more painful than that?

37. Either, slain you will gain heaven,
Or victorious, you will enjoy the earth.
Therefore, stand up, Son of Kuntī, resolved to fight.

38. Treating pleasure and pain, gain and loss, victory and defeat as all alike,
Become readied for battle.
Thus you will not incur sin.

39. This (preceding) wisdom declared to you is the (wisdom of) *Sāṃkhya;*
But listen to the following wisdom of Yoga, O son of Pṛthā;
When disciplined with it, son of Pṛthā, you will leave behind the bondage of *karma.*

40. In this path, there is no unsuccessful effort,
No reversal is known;
Even a little of this *dharma* rescues one from great fear.

41. In this, O Joy-of-the-Kurus, understanding is resolute and unitary;
Many-branched, indeed, and endless is the understanding of him who is not resolute.

42. The undiscerning who delight in flowery words,
Who rejoice in the letter of the Veda, O son of Pṛthā,
Saying that there is nothing else,

43. Whose selves are made of desire, whose highest goal is heaven,
Who are full of ritual acts for the sake of enjoyment and power,
They only gather rebirth as the fruit of these actions *(karman)*.

44. The intellect of those men devoted to enjoyment and power,
Robbed of insight by these (words) is not established in meditation *(samādhi)*.

45. The Vedas deal with three *guṇas;* but you, Arjuna, become free of the three *guṇas*
Constantly take your stand in *sattva:* (light, wisdom)
Free of dualities, free of acquisition-and-possession, self-possessed.

46. For a *brāhman* who understands, (who knows what stands-under)
There is as much use in all the Vedas
As there is in a well when there is a flood of water on all sides.

47. Your interest is in action *(karman)* alone, never in its fruits:
Let not the fruit of action *(karman)* be what impels you,
But do not let yourself be attached to in-action *(akarman)* either.

48. Taking your stand in yoga, be active, O Winner of Wealth,
Having relinquished attachment and having gained equilibrium amidst success and failure.
Serenity of mind is called yoga.

49. Action *(karman)* is inferior by far indeed to the disciplined-intellect *(buddhiyoga),* O Winner of Wealth;
Seek refuge in *buddhi.*
Pitiful are those who are impelled by the fruit of action *(karman).*

50. One whose intellect is disciplined leaves behind good and evil while on earth.
Therefore become readied for yoga,
For yoga is skill in action *(karman).*

51. Having relinquished the fruit born of action *(karman),*
Having disciplined their understanding,
The wise are free from the bondage of birth,
And arrive at a state which is beyond delusion.

52. When your intellect shall cross over the tangle of delusion,
Then you will become unattached
To what has been or will be heard (from the Veda).

53. When your intellect, turned this way and that from what you have heard (the Veda),
Shall stand in meditation *(samādhi),* immovable,
Then you will attain yoga.

Arjuna said:
54. What is the mark of the man of firm wisdom,
Of the one who is centered in meditation *(samādhi),* O Keśava?
How might the man of steady wisdom speak?
How might he walk, how sit?

The Blessed One said:
55. When a man forsakes all the desires of his mind, O Son of Pṛthā (Arjuna),

And through himself becomes content in his self alone,
Then, he is said to be of firm wisdom.

56. He whose mind is not troubled in the midst of sorrows,
Is free from desire in the midst of pleasures,
From whom passion, fear, and anger have departed,
He is said to be a sage of steady-wisdom.

57. He who has no attachment to anything,
And who neither rejoices nor is upset when he obtains good or evil,
His wisdom is firmly established.

58. When he, like a tortoise drawing in his limbs,
Withdraws his senses altogether from sense objects,
His wisdom is firmly established.

59. The objects of sense recede from the embodied one who abstains from feeding on them,
But a taste for such things persists.
Even that taste recedes, however, when the highest has been seen.

60. But, O Son of Kuntī, even the excited senses of a wise man
Endeavoring to make his way toward fulfillment,
Forcibly carry away his mind.

61. Having held all these in check, he should sit disciplined,
Intent on me; for he whose senses are submissive,
His intelligence is firmly established.

62. When a man dwells upon objects of sense,
Attachment to them is born.
From attachment, desire is born,
And from such desire anger arises.

63. From anger arises delusion, and from delusion loss of memory.
From loss of memory the destruction of intelligence,
And from this destruction, he perishes.

64. But that man finds clarity of mind,

Who moves among things of sense with his senses under control,
Free from desire and aversion
And who is thus self-controlled.

65. And in that clarity, the cessation of all his sorrows is born.
For the intelligence of a calm mind is quickly re-established.

66. For the one uncontrolled, there is no intelligence,
Nor is there realization;
And without realization there is no peace,
And how can there be happiness without peace?

67. Verily, the mind which yields to the roving senses,
Carries away man's understanding,
Like a wind carrying away a ship on the waters.

68. Therefore, O Mighty-Armed (Arjuna),
His intelligence is firmly established
Whose senses do not have sense-objects as an end.

69. When it is night for all beings, then the man of self-discipline is awake;
When beings are awake, then is night for the sage who sees.

70. He attains peace into whom all desires flow like waters entering the sea,
Though he is always being filled, he is always unaffected,
And not one who cherishes desires.

71. The man who abandons all desires, and acts without yearning,
Without possessiveness, without ego (not making himself to be the doer),
He finds peace.

72. O Son of Pṛthā, having reached this eternal state,
One does not again become bewildered and deluded.

Fixed in it up to the end of his time
He attains Brahman–Nirvāṇa.

This is the end of Chapter II, called "The Yoga of Understanding" *(sāṃkhyayoga)*.

Chapter III
THE YOGA OF ACTION

Arjuna said:

1. If to your mind (the discipline of) understanding is superior to (the discipline of) action, O Janārdana,
Then why, O Keśava (Kṛṣṇa), do you enjoin me to the dreadful deed?

2. You are bewildering my understanding with these apparently confused propositions.
Therefore, tell me unequivocally
The one way by which I may gain what is good.

The Blessed One said:

3. Long ago, Blameless-One, I proclaimed a two-fold path of (living in) this world;
The path of knowledge *(jñānayoga)* for men of discrimination *(sāṃkhya)*
And the path of action *(karmayoga)* for men of action (yogins).

4. No man attains freedom from the bondage of action *(naiṣkarmya)*
Simply by not undertaking actions:
Nor by mere renunciation does one attain perfection.

5. For no one can remain absolutely inactive even for a moment.
Everyone is made to engage in action, however unwillingly,
By way of the *guṇas* born of *prakṛti*.

6. He who controls his powers of action, but continues to remember sense objects with his mind,
Is deluded and is to be called a hypocrite.

7. But he who controls his senses by his mind, O Arjuna,
And, without attachment, engages the action-senses in *karmayoga,*
He excels.

8. Do your allotted action,
For action is superior to inaction.
Even the maintenance of your body cannot be accomplished without action.

9. Except for the action engaged in as sacrifice,
This world is subject to the bondage of action.
For the sake of that, Son of Kuntī,
Perform action free from attachment as a sacrifice.

10. Long ago, Prajāpati created creatures together with sacrifice, and said:
By this shall you prosper,
Let this be the milch-cow for your desires.

11. By this, nourish the gods, and may the gods nourish you;
Thus nourishing each other, you will attain to the supreme good.

12. For the gods, nourished by the sacrifice,
Will give you the enjoyments you desire.
He who enjoys their gifts without giving to them in return,
Is nothing but a thief.

13. Good men, eating of the remains of the sacrifice,
Are free from all sins,
But wicked men who prepare food for their own sake alone (not sharing with the gods and others),
Eat sin.

14. Beings arise from food;
Food is produced from rain;
Rain arises from the sacrifice,
And sacrifice is born of action.

15. Know that action has its origin in Brahman (the Veda),
And the Brahman has its origin in the imperishable.

Therefore, Brahman, the all-pervading,
Is always grounded in sacrifice.

16. He who on earth does not contribute
To the continued movement of the wheel thus set in motion, is evil, O Son of Pṛthā;
Delighting in the senses, he lives in vain.

17. The man, however, who can be delighted in his self alone,
Who is pleased with the self and content only with the self,
For him there is no work to be done.

18. He has no interest in this world
To gain by what is done or by what is not done.
He is not dependent on any of these beings for any advantage.

19. Therefore, perform the action that has to be done,
Continually free from attachment,
For by performing action without attachment,
A man reaches the supreme.

20. For by action alone, it was,
That Janaka and others ascended to perfection.
And also you must act,
Attending to no less than the holding together of the world.

21. For whatever the superior man does,
That other people also do.
He sets the standard which the world follows.

22. For me, O Son of Pṛthā,
There is no work whatever to be done in the three worlds,
Nothing unobtained which is to be obtained;
Yet without fail, I continue in action.

23. For if I were not ever unweariedly engaged in action, Son of Pṛthā,
Men everywhere would follow my path.

24. These worlds would be destroyed if I did not perform action
And I would be the author of confusion,
And would destroy these people.

25. As those who are ignorant *(avidyā)* act from attachment to action;
The wise should also act, O Bhārata,
But without attachment,
Desiring to act so as to hold the world together.

26. Let no wise man shake the minds of the ignorant who are attached to action;
Acting with yoga-wisdom, let the wise make all action attractive.

27. Actions are engaged in by way of the *guṇas* of *prakṛti* alone;
Yet he who is deluded by the sense of I thinks "I am the doer."

28. But O Strong-Armed, he who knows the truth
About the differentiation from *guṇas* and action, thinks (and knows that):
Guṇas act upon *guṇas,*
He is not attached.

29. Those who are deluded by the *guṇas* of *prakṛti*
Are attached to the workings of the *guṇas.*
But let not him who knows the whole,
Unsettle the sluggish, who know only a part.

30. With your mind on the supreme self,
Surrendering all action to me,
And being free of desire and selfishness,
Your (mental) fever vanished, fight.

31. Men who constantly follow out this teaching of mine,
Uncomplaining and full of faith,
They too are released from (the bondage of) their actions.

32. But those who murmur against my teaching,
Who do not follow it out,

Know those mindless ones, deluded in all understanding,
To be lost.

33. Even the wise man functions in conformity with *prakṛti.*
Beings follow *prakṛti,*
What will suppression accomplish?

34. Attraction and repulsion for the objects of sense
Are seated in the senses.
Let no one come under the control of these two;
They are his worse enemies.

35. One's own *dharma,* even when not done perfectly,
Is better than someone else's *dharma,* even though well performed;
Indeed, death in one's own *dharma* is better,
For another's is perilous.

Arjuna said:

36. Then what, O Descendant of Vṛṣṇi,
Is that by which a man who performs evil, is bidden,
Even against his will,
Impelled so-to-speak by force?

The Blessed One said:

37. Desire it is, anger it is,
Produced from the *guṇa* of passion *(rajas),*
All-consuming and greatly sinful.
Know this to be the enemy here.

38. For just as fire is concealed by smoke,
A mirror by dust, and an embryo by the womb,
So is this (knowledge) concealed by that (passion).

39. Knowledge, O Son of Kuntī,
Is concealed by that constant enemy of the wise,
That insatiable flame of desire.

40. The senses, the mind *(manas),* the *buddhi,*
Are said to be its seat.
Having concealed knowledge through these,
It deludes the embodied one.

41. Therefore, having controlled the senses to begin with, O Best of the Bhāratas,
Slay this evil which brings loss of knowledge and understanding.

42. The senses are great, they say;
But the mind is above the senses, and *buddhi* above mind.
And above *buddhi* is He.

43. Thus having become aware of that which is greater than *buddhi,*
Having strengthened yourself through yourself,
Slay the enemy, Strong-Armed, which is so hard to get at,
And has the form of desire.

This is the third chapter, entitled "The Yoga of Action" *(karmayoga).*

Chapter IV
THE YOGA OF KNOWLEDGE

The Blessed One said:

1. I proclaimed this imperishable discipline (yoga) to Vivasvān,
He told it to Manu, and he, to Ikṣvāku.

2. Handed down in this way from one to another,
This yoga was known by the sage-kings,
But, Foe-Destroyer, it became lost on earth with the lapse of time.

3. This very yoga of old
Is being proclaimed by me to you today.
For you are devoted to me, and my friend,
And this yoga is, indeed, the supreme secret.

Arjuna said:

4. Later was your birth, earlier was the birth of Vivasvān:
How am I to understand this,

That you proclaimed this discipline (to him) in the beginning?

The Blessed One said:

5. Many are my past lives and yours, Arjuna;
I know them all, you do not, Foe–Destroyer.

6. Though I am unborn and of changeless self,
Though I am Lord of beings, having taken my stand over my own *prakṛti*
I am born by my own self's power *(māyā).*

7. For whenever there is a decrease in *dharma,* O Bhārata,
And a rise in *adharma,*
Then I send forth myself.

8. For the protection of the good and the destruction of evil,
For the purpose of the establishment of *dharma,*
I am born from age to age.

9. He who knows in truth this, my divine birth and actions,
Having relinquished his body,
He goes not to rebirth but to me, Arjuna.

10. With passion, fear, and anger gone,
Taking refuge in me,
Being filled with me,
Many, purified by the exercise of wisdom,
Attain my state *(bhāva).*

11. In whatever way men approach me,
In the same way they receive their reward;
Men follow my path in every case, Son of Pṛthā.

12. Those desiring fulfillment of their actions on earth,
Sacrifice to the gods.
Quickly, indeed, comes fulfillment in the world of men from such actions.

13. I created the four classes by the differentiation of *guṇa* and *karma.*
Although I made them,
Know me as the imperishable non-doer.

14. Actions do not pollute me,
I do not covet their fruit.
He who knows me thus, is not bound by actions.

15. So knowing, the ancients who desired release were active.
You be active, therefore,
Just as the ancients were long ago.

16. What is action? What is inaction?
Even the wise are confused on this point.
I will declare to you that action which, if you know it,
You will be released from evil.

17. You must understand not only action, however,
But improper action *(vikarman)* and inaction *(akarman):*
The way of action is difficult to fathom.

18. He who can see action in inaction,
And inaction in action,
Is a wise man;
He does action in a disciplined way.

19. He whose every undertaking is free of compulsive desire,
Whose actions are burned up by the fire of knowledge,
Him the wise call learned.

20. Having relinquished attachment to the fruit of action,
(karmaphalāsaṇgaṃ, literally, "identification with the fruit of action")
Being constantly satisfied and without dependence.
He does nothing whatever,
Even though he is engaged in action.

21. Without craving, with mind restrained and relinquishing all possessions,
Being active with body alone,
He does not incur sin.

22. Content with what he happens to find,
Himself beyond the dualities, free from envy,

And the same in success and failure,
He is not bound even though he is acting.

23. The action of the unattached man is free,
Whose understanding is firmly rooted in knowledge,
And who acts as a sacrifice, is wholly dissolved.

24. The act of offering is Brahman, the oblation (offered) is Brahman,
It is poured by Brahman in the fire of Brahman.
Brahman becomes he whose actions are centered on Brahman.

25. Some yogins offer sacrifice to the gods only,
While others make sacrifice by sacrificing the sacrifice itself.

26. There are others who offer hearing and their other senses
Into the fires of equanimity;
Others sacrifice sense objects, into the fire of the senses.

27. Others offer up all the actions of all the senses
And of the vital-breath
Into the fire of the disciplined concentration (yoga) of self-restraint
Which is kindled by knowledge.

28. Others offer as sacrifice their possessions, their austerity,
Or their yogic exercises;
While still others of firmly restrained minds and austere vows,
Offer their scriptural study (Veda) and their knowledge (of it).

29. Others, likewise, having controlled the course of their inbreathing and outbreathing *(prāṇāpānagatī ruddhvā)*,
Wholly devoted to breath control *(praṇāyāmaparāyaṇāḥ)*
Sacrifice the one breath into the other *(apāne juhvati prāṇaṃ)*.

30. And others, the abstemious in food,
Offer as sacrifice their life breaths in life breaths.
All these are knowers of sacrifice,
And by sacrifice their sins are destroyed.

31. Those who eat the food of immortality left after the sacrifice,
Attain the primeval Brahman.
Not even this world is for one who does not sacrifice,
How then the next world, Highest of the Kurus?

32. Thus manifold sacrifices are spread out in the face of Brahman.
Know them all to be born of action.
Knowing this, you will be freed.

33. The sacrifice of knowledge is better, Foe–Destroyer,
Than the sacrifice of material things.
All action without exception is completely terminated in knowledge, O Son of Pṛthā.

34. Know this by obeisance, by inquiry, and by service to them.
Men of wisdom, the seers of truth,
Will explain to you this knowledge.

35. You will never be deluded again, Son of Pāṇḍu,
When you have learned this:
For by this you will see all beings without exception in yourself and in me.

36. Even if you were among sinners the worse of sinners,
You will cross beyond all evil
By the boat of knowledge alone.

37. Just as a kindled fire reduces its fuel to ashes, Arjuna,
So the fire of knowledge reduces all action to ashes.

38. For no equal to wisdom as a purifier is known on earth.
This, the one reaching his own ultimate fulfillment in yoga
Finds in himself with time.

39. He who has faith, who is committed to it, whose senses are controlled,
Gains knowledge, and having obtained it,
He quickly attains supreme peace.

40. But he who is without insight and is without faith,
His very self being doubt,
He is lost:
For the doubting one, there is neither this world nor the next,
Nor is there happiness.

41. Actions do not blind him, O Wealth-Winner,
Who has renounced all actions in yoga,
Who has cut out doubt by knowledge,
And who is self-possessed.

42. Therefore, having cut out with your self's own sword of knowledge,
This doubt in your heart which is born of ignorance,
Get into yoga and raise yourself up, O Bhārata.

This is the fourth chapter, entitled "The Yoga of Knowledge," *(jñānayoga)*.

Chapter V
THE YOGA OF RENUNCIATION OF ACTIONS

Arjuna said:

1. Kṛṣṇa, you praise the renunciation of actions,
And then again, their disciplined undertaking.
Which one of these is the better one:
Tell me quite decisively.

The Blessed One said:

2. The renunciation and the yoga of action
Both bring the ultimate good,
But of the two, the yoga of action is better than the renunciation of action.

3. He who neither hates nor desires,

Is to be known as one who constantly renounces.
For free from dualities, O Strong-Armed,
He is easily released from bondage.

4. It is the childish, not the men of learning,
Who declare *Sāṃkhya* and Yoga to be diverse.
He who takes his stand in either one properly,
Obtains the fruit of both.

5. That place and standing which is attained by (the men of) *Sāṃkhya,*
Is reached also by Yoga.
Sāṃkhya and Yoga are one:
He who sees this sees truly.

6. Renunciation, O Strong-Armed, is difficult to attain without yoga.
The sage who is disciplined in yoga
Attains to Brahman quickly.

7. Committed to yoga, himself pure in mind,
His senses conquered, his self conquered
And his self having become the self of all beings,
He is not polluted even when he acts.

8. "I am doing nothing at all."
So the disciplined one who knows the truth thinks:
Seeing, hearing, touching, smelling, tasting,
Walking, sleeping, breathing,

9. Talking, grasping and letting go,
Opening and closing his eyes,
He keeps present that in these, only the senses are active among sense-objects.

10. Having placed his actions in Brahman,
Having relinquished attachment,
One who acts is not touched by sin,
Just as the lotus leaf is not wet by water.

11. For self-purification, men of disciplined effort (yogins)
Are active only by way of the body, mind, understanding or the senses,
Without attachment.

12. The disciplined man, having relinquished the fruit of action,
Attains perfect peace.
The undisciplined man, impelled by desire,
Is attached to the fruit and is bound.

13. Having renounced with his mind all actions,
The embodied one sits at ease,
In the city of nine gates (the body),
Neither acting nor causing action.

14. That one stands over what is born,
Neither creates agency of the world, nor actions, nor the conjunction of action with the fruit
Rather, this is a natural power *(svabhāvaḥ).*

15. This pervasive one does not take on anyone's sin
Nor his good deeds either.
Knowledge is concealed by ignorance:
With this, creatures are deluded.

16. But for those in whom ignorance is destroyed by knowledge,
For them knowledge brightens the highest (in them) like the sun.

17. Fixed on that (highest vision), the self open to that,
With commitment to that,
They attain a condition from where there is no return;
Their sins removed by knowledge.

18. Men of learning view with equal eye a Brāhman of knowledge and good learning,
A cow, an elephant, and even a dog and an outcaste.

19. Creation is overcome, even here on earth,
By those whose minds are established in equality.
For Brahman is the same, without defect to all.
Therefore they are firm and abiding in Brahman.

20. One should not exult on gaining the pleasant,
Nor should one be dismayed on meeting the unpleasant.
His understanding steady, undeluded,
The knower of Brahman is centered on Brahman.

21. The self which is unattached to external contacts
Finds happiness in himself.
Being joined by yoga to Brahman
He obtains undecaying happiness.

22. For those pleasures which are born of contact
Are merely sources of sorrow, possessing a beginning and an end.
The man who is awake takes no delight in them, O Son of Kuntī.

23. The man who here on earth, before giving up his body,
Is able to hold out against the force born of desire and anger,
He is disciplined, he is happy.

24. He who is happy within, whose joy is within,
And whose light is within,
He becomes Brahman and goes on to the happiness of Brahman.

25. Those sages whose sins are destroyed,
Whose indecisions are dispelled, whose selves are disciplined,
And who rejoice in the welfare of every being,
Attain to the happiness of Brahman.

26. To those wise men who have destroyed desire and anger,
Who have controlled their minds, and realized the self,
The happiness of Brahman is near.

27. Having shut out external contacts
And fixed the eye in the middle between the two brows,
Having equalized the two breaths moving within the nostrils,

28. Having controlled the senses, mind and intelligence,
The sage who has freedom as his goal,
Who has cast away desire, fear and anger,
Is freed forever.

29. Knowing me as the enjoyer of sacrifices and austerities,
As the great lord of all the worlds,

A friend of all beings,
One attains peace.

This is the fifth chapter, entitled "The Yoga of Renunciation of Action"
(karmasaṃnyāsayoga).

Chapter VI
THE YOGA OF MEDITATION

The Blessed One said:

1. He who does the action that has to be done
But without resting on its fruit,
Is a man of disciplined engagement in action,
He is a yogin, a man of renunciation,
And not he who is without sacrificial fire and without ritual actions.

2. What is called renunciation,
Know it to be the disciplined engagement in action, O Son of Pāṇḍu.
For no one becomes a yogin
Who has not renounced compulsive purpose.

3. Action is the medium for the sage who desires to ascend to yoga;
Tranquillity is the medium of him who has already ascended to such yoga.

4. For when one has renounced all compulsive purpose and
Is attached neither to actions nor to sense-objects,
He is then said to have ascended to yoga.

5. Let a man lift his self by his own self;
Let him not lower himself;
One's self alone is one's own self's friend and foe.

6. One's self is friend of one's self when self-conquered;
But the self of one not so self-possessed,
Becomes hostile like an enemy.

7. The higher self of one who is self-conquered and at peace,

Is composed amidst cold and heat, pleasure and pain, honor and dishonor.

8. The yogin who is satisfied with wisdom and understanding,
Who is unshaken, with his senses conquered,
To whom gold, a stone, a clod of earth are the same,
Is said to be disciplined.

9. He excels whose understanding is the same,
Amidst the well-disposed, the friendly, the neutral arbiter and hostile,
Amidst enemies and allies,
Amidst the righteous and the sinful.

10. Let the yogin always concentrate his mind,
Living alone in solitude, his mind and self restrained,
Without cravings and (longing for) possessions.

11. Let him fix for himself on a clean place a firm seat,
Which is neither too high nor too low,
Made of Kuśa grass, a deerskin, and a cloth,
One over the other.

12. Sitting on that seat, making his mind one-pointed,
Controlling the activity of his mind and senses,
Let him engage in yoga for the purification of the self.

13. Let him hold his body, neck, and head erect and motionless,
Looking fixedly at the tip of his nose,
Not looking in any direction.

14. And having his thoughts on me, absorbed in me,
With the self calm and free from fear
And keeping his vow of celibacy,
Let him sit disciplined.

15. Thus continually disciplining himself and with his mind controlled,
He attains peace, the supreme bliss,
That which exists in me.

16. Yoga is not for one who eats too much or not at all.
It is not for him, Arjuna, who sleeps too much or too little.

17. For one whose enjoyment of food and pleasure is disciplined,
Whose engagement in actions is disciplined,
Whose sleeping and waking are disciplined,
Yoga becomes a destroyer of sorrow.

18. When one's controlled mind abides in one's self alone,
Freed from yearning,
Then one is said to be disciplined.

19. Unflickering, like a lamp in a sheltered place:
So the man of disciplined thought
Practicing yoga of the self.

20. That in which thought ceases,
Stopped by the practice of disciplined concentration,
And in which, seeing himself through himself,
One is content in himself;

21. That in which he knows that which is boundless happiness,
Beyond the senses but perceivable by understanding,
And in which, established,
He knows this and swerves not from the truth;

22. That which, having obtained it,
One thinks there is no further gain beyond it,
And in which he is established,
By no sorrow, however heavy, is he shaken;

23. Let this disengagement of the connection with sorrow
Be known as yoga.
This yoga is to be practiced with determination,
With a mind free from depression.

24. Abandoning entirely all desires originating in compulsive purpose,
Having exercised restraint on every side
Over all the senses by the mind,

25. Let him be stilled little by little,
Through understanding firmly grounded;
And fixing his mind on the self,
Let him not set his thoughts on anything else.

26. Having restrained the mind, restless, unsteady,
From whatever it goes out to,
Let him bring it into the control of his self alone.

27. Indeed, the highest happiness comes to the yogin
Whose mind is peaceful,
In whom passions are at rest, who is sinless, has become Brahman.

28. Continually exercising himself in disciplined-concentration in this way,
The yogin free from his sin,
Easily attains to the boundless happiness in touch with Brahman.

29. The one whose self is disciplined by yoga,
Sees the self abiding in every being
And sees every being in the self;
He sees the same in all beings.

30. He who sees me everywhere, and sees all in me,
I am not lost to him, and he is not lost to me.

31. He who standing in oneness,
Worships me abiding in all beings,
Exists in me, whatever happens.

32. When one sees the pleasure or pain of others
To be equal to one's own, O Arjuna,
He is considered the highest yogin.

Arjuna said:

33. You have proclaimed yoga of sameness, O Madhusūdana,
But I do not see a firm grounding of this yoga
Because of man's restlessness.

34. Restless, indeed, is the mind, O Kṛṣṇa,
It is turbulent, strong and hard.

Its restraint, I think, would be as difficult to accomplish
as controlling the wind.

The Blessed One said:

35. Doubtless, Strong-Armed, the mind is restless and hard
to restrain,
But by practice and nonattachment,
It can be held, Son of Kuntī.

36. Yoga is impossible to attain with an unrestrained self:
So I think.
But it can be attained with a controlled self
In skillful ways.

Arjuna said:

37. What way does one go, O Kṛṣṇa,
Who is undisciplined but possesses faith,
And whose mind swerves away from yoga
Before he has obtained the ultimate fulfillment in yoga?

38. Fallen from both, not having become firm,
And bewildered over the path to Brahman,
Does he not perish, O Strong-Armed,
Like a severed rain cloud?

39. You must cut off completely this doubt of mine, O Kṛṣṇa,
For there is no remover of this doubt
Other than you to be found.

The Blessed One said:

40. Son of Pṛthā, neither in this world nor the next does
such a one know destruction.
For, my dear one, no one who does good goes to an evil
end.

41. Having attained the worlds of the meritorious,
Having dwelled there many years,
The one who has fallen from yoga
Is born in a house of the pure and prosperous.

42. Or else he is born in a family of wise yogins:
Of course, such a birth in the world is more difficult to
obtain.

43. There, he gains the mental traits of his previous embodiment,
And once more from that point
He strives for fulfillment, O Joy of the Kurus.

44. By his previous practise alone,
He is carried onward,
Even without willing this.
He who desires the knowledge of yoga is beyond the Vedic rule.

45. But the yogin who strives with perseverence,
Who is purified of sin,
And is perfected through many lives
Goes to the highest goal.

46. The yogin is greater than the ascetic,
He is considered greater than the men of knowledge;
He is greater than doers of ritual works:
Therefore, become a yogin, O Arjuna.

47. Of all yogins, the one who full of faith,
Worships me with his inner self given over to me,
I consider him to be nearest to my vision.

This ends the sixth chapter, entitled "The Yoga of Meditation" *(dhyānayoga)*

Chapter VII
THE YOGA OF WISDOM AND UNDERSTANDING

The Blessed One said:

1. Hear this, O Son of Pṛthā, by fastening your mind on me,
By practicing yoga, relying on me,
You will gain knowledge of me fully, without doubt.

2. I will tell you the whole of this wisdom
Accompanied by knowledge which, when known,
There remains nothing more on earth to be known.

3. Scarcely one man in thousands strives for perfection,
And of those who strive and are successful,
Perhaps one knows me in essence.

4. Earth, water, fire, air, ether, mind, understanding, and the sense of I:
This is my *prakṛti* which is divided eight-fold.

5. This is my lower *prakṛti*.
But know now, O Strong-Armed, my other *prakṛti*,
Supreme and the source of life,
By which the world is supported.

6. Know that all beings have this for their womb.
I am the origin of the world
And also its dissolution.

7. There is nothing whatever above me, O Wealth-Winner.
All this (world) is strung on me
Like jewels on a string.

8. I am the taste in the waters, O Son of Kuntī,
I am the radiance in the sun and moon;
The sacred syllable *(Oṃ)* in all the Vedas,
The sound in ether, and manliness in men.

9. I am the pleasant fragrance in earth,
The glowing brightness in fire,
The life in all beings,
The austerity in ascetics.

10. Know me to be the seed of all beings, O Son of Pṛthā.
I am the understanding of the wise,
The splendor of the splendid.

11. I am the strength of the strong, O Master of the Bhāratas,
Devoid of desire and passion.
I am that desire in all beings which is not incompatible with *dharma*.

12. And know also that whatever conditions (in beings) are

sattvic (lucid) *rajasic* (active) or even *tamasic* (indolent),
Are from me alone.
But I am not in them,
They are in me.

13. Deluded by these conditions composed of the three *guṇas,*
This whole world does not recognize me,
Changeless and above them.

14. For this divine *māyā* (elusive power) of mine composed of the *guṇas,*
Is difficult to transcend.
Only those who resort to me,
Cross beyond this deluding power *(māyā).*

15. Foolish evil-doers, lowest of men,
Whose understanding is carried away by this deluding power *(māyā)*
And whose essence is bound (to their actions),
Do not resort to me.

16. Men of good deeds who worship me, O Arjuna,
Are of four kinds:
The afflicted, the seekers of knowledge, the seeker of wealth,
And also, O Bull of the Bhāratas, the wise.

17 Of these, the wise, always whole,
And whose committment is to the One, excels.
Indeed, I am exceedingly dear to the wise,
And he is dear to me.

18. Noble are all these without exception,
But to my mind, the wise is my very self.
For he with disciplined self-effort *(yuktātmā)*
Is firmly grounded in me alone as the highest goal.

19. At the end of many births,
The man of wisdom comes to me
Aware that Vāsudeva is all.
Such a man of great self is very hard to find.

20. Those whose understanding has been carried away by one desire or another,
Flee to other gods,
Having carried out one or another observance,
Led by their own (bound) *prakṛti.*

21. I make unshakeable the faith of any devotee
Who wishes to worship with faith any form whatever.

22. Disciplined with that faith,
He seeks the propitiation of such a manifestation (god),
And from it he gains his desires.
Indeed, it is I who ordains (the benefits) of those desires.

23. But transient is that fruit of those of little intelligence.
Those who sacrifice to the gods, go to the gods;
But those who are dedicated to me, go to me.

24. Those without understanding think me, the nonapparent,
To have appeared,
Not being cognizant of my supreme nature, changeless and unsurpassed.

25. Covered by my elusive power *(yoga-māyā),*
I do not appear to all.
The world is deluded and does not recognize me, unborn, imperishable.

26. I know the beings of the past, present and yet to be, O Arjuna,
But no one verily knows me.

27. All beings at birth are subject to delusion, O Descendant of Bhārata,
By the illusion arising from the pairs of opposites,
Desire and aversion, O Conqueror of the Foe.

28. But those men of meritorious deeds in whom sin has come to an end,
Who are thus released from the illusion of opposites,
Worship me, steadfast in their resolutions
(dṛdhavratāḥ).

29. Having taken refuge in me,
Those who strive *(yatanti)* for release from death and old age
Know Brahman entirely and the self and all action.

30. Those who with disciplined minds know me in my higher and lower domains
And the physical world and the highest sacrifice,
Know me even at the time of death.

This is the seventh chapter, entitled "The Yoga of Wisdom and Understanding" *(jñānavijñānayoga)*.

Chapter VIII
THE YOGA OF THE IMPERISHABLE BRAHMAN

Arjuna said:

1. What is that Brahman? What is the original self?
What is action *(karma)*, O Best of Men?
What is said to be the higher and what the lower domain?

2. How and what is the sacrifice here in this body, O Slayer of Madhu?
And how are you to be cognized by those of disciplined self
At the time of death?

The Blessed One said:

3. The imperishable is Brahman, the supreme;
The higher self is called its very essence *(svabhāvah):*
And *karman* is the creative force that causes creatures to exist.

4. A perishable condition is the basis of the lower domain;
The *puruṣa* (vision) is the basis of the higher domain;
I am the ground of all sacrifice here in the body, O best of the embodied ones.

5. And at the time of death,
Whoever, leaving the body remembers me alone,
He attains my being: of this there is no doubt.

6. Whatever is in his mind at the time of death, O Son of Kuntī,
Only that he becomes; embodied in that state.

7. Therefore, think on me at all times and fight;
With mind and understanding joined to me,
Without doubt you will come to me alone.

8. He who is disciplined by the effort of yoga, not wandering elsewhere,
And concentrates on the supreme shining vision *(puruṣa)*,
He goes to him, O Son of Pṛthā.

9. He who meditates on the ancient seer, the ruler,
Who is more minute than minute, the supporter of all,
Incomprehensible in form, sun-colored and beyond darkness:

10. He, engaged in devotion with an immovable mind
And having succeeded by virtue of this disciplined effort (yoga)
In making his life-breath go to the mid-point between his eyebrows,
He, at the time of death, attains shining fullness of vision *(puruṣa)*.

11. That which the Veda-knowers designate as the imperishable,
Which the restrained ones free of passion enter,
And desiring which they undertake a life of chastity:
That abode, I will declare to you briefly.

12. He who controls all the gates of the body
And confines the mind to the heart,
Has set his breath in the head
And established himself in concentration by yoga,

13. He who utters *Oṃ*, which is Brahman,
Meditates on me as he goes forth and abandons his body,
He reaches the highest goal.

14. He whose thought is never on anything but me,
Who constantly remembers me:

For that man of disciplined effort ever disciplined,
I am easily reached, O Son of Pṛthā.

15. Having come to me,
Those men of great self do not go to rebirth
The place of pain and impermanence,
But have reached the supreme fullness.

16. The worlds from the realm of Brahmā down,
Are subject to rebirth, O Arjuna;
But having come to me, O Son of Kuntī,
There is no rebirth.

17. The men who know the day of Brahmā, long as a thousand ages,
And the night of Brahmā, equally as long,
Are knowers of what day and night are.

18. All apparent things arise from the non-apparent at the coming of day,
And at the coming of night they are dissolved there,
In this so-called nonapparent.

19. This very same multitude of beings,
Coming forth repeatedly,
Dissolve helplessly at the coming of night, O Son of Pṛthā,
And arises at the coming of day.

20. Higher than this nonapparent state is another nonapparent state,
Which does not perish even with the perishing of all beings.

21. It is called the imperishable, and the supreme destination,
Those who reach it do not return.
This is my supreme dwelling place.

22. This is the fullness of vision,
By whom all this is pervaded,
In whom all beings stand.
It is to be gained by unswerving dedication.

23. O Best of the Bhāratas, I will declare that time at which men of discipline,
Depart, go and do not return,
And when they depart, but do return.

24. Fire, light, day, the bright half of the lunar cycle,
The six months of the sun's northerly course:
Departing then, men who are knowers of Brahman
Go to Brahman.

25. Smoke, night, the dark half of the lunar period,
The six months of the sun's southerly course:
Departing then, the man of discipline
Reaches the light of the moon and returns.

26. These bright and dark paths of the world
Are thought to be everlasting:
By one, man goes and does not return,
By the other, man returns.

27. The man of discipline who knows these paths, O Son of Pṛthā,
Is not deluded.
Therefore, at all times be engaged in disciplined effort, O Arjuna.

28. The yogin who knows all this,
Transcends the fruit of deeds assigned in the Veda,
In sacrifices, austerities and alms-giving,
And goes to the supreme and primal place.

This is the eighth chapter, entitled "The Yoga of the Imperishable Brahman" *(akṣarabrahmayoga)*.

Chapter IX
THE YOGA OF SOVEREIGN KNOWLEDGE AND SOVEREIGN SECRET

The Blessed One said:

1. To you, however, who are uncomplaining,

I will declare this most secret wisdom joined with knowledge;
Knowing which, you will be released from evil.

2. This is sovereign knowledge, sovereign secret,
This utmost purifier is directly perceived,
Accordant with *dharma,* and quite easy to follow and imperishable.

3. Men who put no faith in this practice, O Foe–Destroyer,
Return to the path of wandering death and rebirth,
Not having reached me.

4. This whole world is pervaded by me in my unmanifested form.
Though all beings are *fixed* in me, I am not *fixed* in them.

5. Yet beings do not stand in me.
Behold my lordly secret:
Generating beings, yet not being generated by them,
My very self is the source of beings.

6. Know that just as the mighty wind, blowing everywhere,
Stands constantly in space,
So all beings stand in me.

7. All beings, O Son of Kuntī, go into my lower *prakṛti* at the time of a world cycle,
And I send them forth again at the beginning of a new cycle.

8. Having seized my own lower *prakṛti,*
I send forth this whole multitude of helpless beings again and again,
At the behest of my lower *prakṛti.*

9. And these actions, O Wealth-Winner, do not bind me,
Who remain as if indifferent,
Unattached to these actions.

10. Under my supervision, *prakṛti* brings forth the moving and the unmoving;
By this cause, O Son of Kuntī, the world revolves.

11. Deluded men, not aware of my supreme condition as Great Lord of Beings,
Despise me when taking a human form.

12. Fallen subject to the delusive *prakṛti*
Which is fiendish and binding *(āsurīm),*
They are mindless,
Their knowledge and deeds and hopes are vain.

13. But those of great self, who abide in my higher *prakṛti*
And who have a mind for no other and worship me, O Son of Pṛthā,
Knowing me as the imperishable source of all beings,

14. Ever celebrating me and striving with firm resolution,
And honoring me with devotion,
Attend upon me constantly ever disciplined.

15. And others also, sacrificing with the sacrifice of wisdom,
Attend upon me as the one, the distinct and as the many
Facing in all directions.

16. I am the ritual, the sacrifice, the oblation, the medicinal herb,
The Vedic text, the clarified butter, the fire and the offering.

17. I am the father of this world,
The mother, the supporter, the grandsire;
I am the one to be known, the purifier,
The sacred syllable *Oṃ,* the *Ṛk,* the *Sāma* and the *Yajus* (the verse, chant and sacrificial formula).

18. I am the witness, the presiding one, the bearer, the final shelter, abode, and friend;
I am the origin and dissolution and foundation:
I am the treasure house and imperishable seed.

19. I give heat, I give and withhold rain;
I am immortality as well as death,
Existence *(sat)* as well as nonexistence *(asat),* O Arjuna.

20. Knowers of the three (Vedas),
Having drunk the soma and become purified of sin,

Worship me with sacrifices and pray for the way to heaven.
Having reached the fair world of Indra,
They enjoy the pleasures of the gods in heaven.

21. Having enjoyed that spacious world of heaven,
Their merit exhausted, they enter the world of mortals.
Thus conforming to the practice enjoined in the three Vedas,
Cherishing desires, they gain what is transient.

22. Of the men who dedicate themselves to me, thinking on me alone,
And who are constant in their effort,
I bring acquisition and possession of their goal.

23. Even those who, devoted to other gods, sacrifice filled with faith,
Even they sacrifice to me alone, O Son of Kuntī,
Though not according to prescribed rules.

24. For I am the enjoyer of all sacrifices, and lord of all sacrifices,
But they do not perceive me in truth,
Hence, they fall.

25. Those who are avowed to the gods, go to the gods;
Those who are avowed to the ancestors, go to the ancestors;
Those who sacrifice to spirits, go to the spirits.
But those who sacrifice to me, come to me.

26. He who offers me with devotion a leaf, a flower, a fruit, water,
I accept that devotional offering of a pure self.

27. Make your doing, eating, sacrificing, giving, and undergoing austerity,
An offering to me, O Son of Kuntī.

28. Thus you will be freed from good and evil fruits,
Released from the bondage of action;
And with your self disciplined by the yoga of renunciation,

Released, you will come to me.

29. I am like-minded to all beings,
None is hateful or dear to me.
But those who worship me with devotion
Are in me, and I am in them also.

30. If a man of very evil conduct worships me in undivided devotion,
He too is to be thought righteous.
For he has decided rightly.

31. Swiftly he becomes one whose self is *dharma,*
And obtains everlasting peace.
Recognize, O Son of Kuntī, that no one dedicated to me perishes.

32. For having taken refuge in me, O Son of Pṛthā,
Even those who are born of sinful wombs, women, Vaiśyās and even Śūdras,
They also reach the highest goal.

33. How much more, then, meritorious brāhmans and devoted sage-kings.
Having entered this unhappy and perishable world, worship me.

34. Your mind fixed on me, be devoted to me;
Sacrificing to me, pay reverence to me;
Having thus a disciplined self and having me as final end,
You will come to me.

This is the ninth chapter, entitled "The Yoga of Sovereign Knowledge and Sovereign Secret" *(rājavidyārāja-guhyayoga).*

Chapter X
THE YOGA OF MANIFESTATIONS

The Blessed One said:
1. Listen still further to my supreme word, O Strong-Armed,

Which out of desire for your welfare
I will declare to you who are taking delight in it.

2. Neither the multitude of gods nor the great sages know my origin,
For I am the source in every respect of gods and of great sages.

3. He who knows me, the unborn, the Great Lord of the World, without beginning,
He is undeluded among mortals and is released from all sins.

4. Understanding, wisdom, freedom from delusion,
Forbearance, truthfulness, self-control, tranquility;
Happiness, sorrow, existence, nonexistence, fear and lack of fear,

5. Non-violence, equanimity, contentment, austerity,
Generosity, fame and ill-fame,
These are the conditions of beings which arise from me alone.

6. The seven great sages of old, and likewise the four Manus,
Had their being from me, being born of my mind;
From them, are these creatures in the world.

7. He who knows in truth this expansiveness and yoga of mine,
Is enjoined by unfaltering yoga;
Of this, there is no doubt.

8. I am the origin of all; from me all proceeds;
Knowing this, the wise, adorned with creation, worship me.

9. Mindful of me, their lives centered on me,
Bringing each other to understand me
And constantly conversing about me,
They are content and rejoice in me.

10. To those so disciplined who worship me with love,

I give that yoga of understanding
By which they attain me.

11. Out of compassion for them, I take my stand in my own condition
And make the darkness born of ignorance
Perish by the shining light of wisdom.

Arjuna said:

12. You are the supreme Brahman, the highest abode, the supreme purifier,
The everlasting shining vision, the primal god, unborn, omnipresent;

13. All the sages say this of you:
The divine sage Nārada, and Asita, Devala, Vyāsa,
And now, you say it to me yourself.

14. I believe all this to be true which you tell me, O Keśava,
Indeed, O Lord, neither the gods nor the demons know your manifestation.

15. You alone know your own self by your own self, O Fullness of Vision *(puruṣottama);*
Source and Lord of Beings, God of Gods, Lord of the World.

16. You should tell me your complete divine self's manifestations
By which you pervade these worlds and exist.

17. How may I, by continuous meditation,
Come to know you, O Yogin?
And in what manifestations are you to be thought of by me, O Lord?

18. Tell me at greater length of your self's power (yoga) and manifestations, O Exciter of Men;
For I am not satiated listening to the nectar of your words.

The Blessed One said:

19. Come, I will tell you, Best of the Kurus, my self's main glories.

There is no end to the details.

20. O Guḍākeśa, I am the self at the heart of every being;
I am the beginning and middle of beings.
And the end as well.

21. Of the Ādityas, I am Viṣṇu; of lights, the radiant sun;
Of the Maruts, I am Marīci; of stars, I am the moon.

22. Of the Vedas, I am the Sāma Veda; of the gods, Vāsave (Indra);
of the senses, I am *manas* (mind); of beings, I am knowledge.

23. Of the Rudras, I am *Śaṃkara* (Śiva); the Yakṣas and Rakṣasas, Vitteśa (Kubera)
Of the Vasus, I am Pāvaka (Agni); of mountain peaks, I am Meru.

24. Know me, O Son of Pṛthā, to be chief of household priests, Bṛhaspati;
Of generals, I am Skanda; of lakes, I am the ocean.

25. Of the great sages, I am Bhṛgu; of utterances, *Oṃ;*
Of sacrifices, I am the muttered sacrifice; of things immovable, I am the Himālaya.

26. Of all the trees, I am the Aśvattha; of divine sages, Nārada;
Of Gandharvas, Citraratha; of perfect men, the sage Kapila.

27. Of horses, know me to be Uccaiḥśravas, sprung from nectar,
Of royal elephants, I am Airāvata; and of men, the monarch.

28. Of weapons, I am Vajra (Indra's thunderbolt in the Ṛg Veda); of cows, Kāmadhuk;
Of progenitors, I am Kandarpa; of serpents, I am Vāsuki.

29. Of the Nāgas, I am Ananta; of sea beings, Varuṇa;
Of the fathers, Aryaman; of the guardians, I am Yama.

30. Of demons, I am Prahlāda; of time keepers, I am time;
Of wild beasts, I am the lion; of birds, the son of Vinatā (Garuda).

31. Of purifiers, I am the wind; of warriors, Rāma;
Of fish, I am Makara; of rivers, I am the Ganges.

32. Of creations, I am the beginning and the end, and the middle also, O Arjuna;
Of knowledge, I am self-knowledge; of speakers, I am the speech.

33. Of letters, I am the letter A; of compounds, the dual;
I am also imperishable time, and the dispenser facing all sides.

34. I am all-devouring death, and the origin of all beings;
Of things feminine, I am glory and prosperity and speech, memory and intelligence and firmness and forbearance.

35. Likewise, of hymns, I am *Bṛhatsāman;* of metres, I am *gāyatrī;*
Of months, I am Mārgaśīrṣa; of seasons, spring.

36. Of deceivers, I am gambling; of the splendid, the splendor;
I am victory, I am resoluteness, I am the essence of the real *(sattva)*.

37. Of the Vṛṣṇis, I am Vāsudeva; of the Pāṇḍavas, Dhanaṃjaya (Arjuna);
Of the sages, I am Vyāsa; of seers, the seer Uśanas.

38. Of restraints, I am the rod; of those desiring to conquer, I am statesmanship; Of secrets, I am silence; of those with wisdom, I am wisdom.

39. And further, O Arjuna, I am the seed of all beings;
There is no being, moving or unmoving, which can exist without me.

40. There is no limit to my marvelous manifestations, O Conqueror of the Foe,

But I have declared this as only an illustration of my glory.

41. Whatever reality *(sattva)* has glory, majesty and power,
Understand that to be sprung from a spark of my light.

42. But of what use is this detailed knowledge to you, Arjuna?
I keep continually pervading this entire world
With only one fraction (of myself).

This is the tenth chapter, entitled "The Yoga of Manifestations" *(vibhūtiyoga)*.

Chapter XI
THE YOGA OF THE MANIFESTATION OF THE WORLD FORM

Arjuna said:

1. This delusion of mine has vanished,
Due to the words you have uttered,
As a favor to me, speaking of the supreme secret called the self.

2. For I have heard in detail from you, Lotus-Eyed,
Of the arising and vanishing of beings,
And also of your changeless greatness.

3. As you say yourself to be, O Supreme Lord,
So it is.
I desire to see your form, O Supreme Vision.

4. If you deem it capable of being seen by me, O Lord,
Then Lord of Yoga, show to me your eternal self.

The Blessed One said:

5. Behold, Son of Pṛthā, my forms,
Hundreds and thousands, divine, varied in color and shape,

6. Behold the Ādityas, Vasus, Rudras, the two Aśvins, also the Maruts;

Behold many marvels not seen previously, Descendant of Bhārata.

7. Behold today the entire world of the moving and unmoving,
Standing in unity here in my body, O Guḍākeśa,
And behold whatever else you want to see.

8. But you can not see me with this your own eye;
I give you a divine eye:
Behold my godly yoga.

Saṃjaya said:

9. Having spoken thus, O King, the Great Lord of Yoga,
Hari, made visible to the son of Pṛthā his supreme godly form;

10. With many mouths and eyes, with many wonderful visions,
With many divine ornaments and many uplifted weapons,

11. Wearing divine crowns and garlands, ointments and perfumes,
Full of every marvel, radiant, infinite,
His face turned in every direction:

12. If in the heavens
There would come to be the light of a thousand suns rising together
It would be like the light of that great self.

13. There, in the body of the God of Gods,
The son of Pāṇḍu then beheld the entire world,
Divided in manifold ways, all united.

14. Then Arjuna, filled with wonder,
His hair standing on end,
His head bowed to the god and with hands joined together,
Spoke:

Arjuna said:

15. I behold in your body, O God, all the gods,

And likewise, crowds of different beings:
Lordly Brahmā seated on his lotus-seat,
And sages all, and celestial serpents.

16. I behold you, O Lord and Form of All,
With many arms and stomachs, and mouths and eyes;
And see no end nor middle nor beginning to you, O Universal Form.

17. I behold you with crown, mace and discus, glowing on all sides,
A mass of splendor, difficult to look upon,
Radiant as a sun and glowing fire, immeasurable.

18. You are the supreme imperishable,
The supreme place of rest of the universe;
You are the changeless guardian of everlasting *dharma,* the primeval *puruṣa:*
So you are to my mind.

19. I behold you who are without beginning, middle and end,
Of boundless power, with innumerable arms,
The moon and sun as your eyes, your mouth a glowing fire,
Burning this universe with your radiance.

20. This space between heaven and earth, and all the quarters of the sky as well,
Are pervaded by you alone;
O Great Self, having seen this wondrous and terrible form of yours,
The three worlds tremble.

21. These hosts of divine beings enter you;
Some afraid praise you
With hands folded together shouting "Hail!"
The hosts of great sages and perfected ones all gaze at you with magnificent songs.

22. The Rudras, Ādityas, Vasus, Sādhyas,
The Viśvadevas, Aśvins, Maruts, and Ūṣmapās,
The hosts of Gandharvas, Yakṣas, Asuras and Siddhas:
All look on you, and all are amazed.

23. Having seen your great form, with many mouths and eyes, O Strong-Armed,
With many arms and thighs and feet,
With many bellies and terrible tusks,
The worlds tremble, and so do I.

24. Having seen you touching the sky, blazing and many-colored,
With mouths open and huge eyes glowing,
My inmost self trembles,
I find no firmness or peace, O Viṣṇu.

25. Having seen your mouths terrible with tusks
Like the devouring flames of time,
I know not the directions of the sky and I find no refuge.
Be gracious, O Lord of Gods, Abode of the World.

26. And those sons of Dhṛtarāṣtra, all of them,
Together with the hosts of kings,
And likewise Bhīṣma, Droṇa, and also Karṇa,
Together with our chief warriors also:

27. They are all rushing to enter your mouths of dreadful tusks;
Some of them are seen caught between your teeth,
Their heads crushed.

28. As the many currents of rivers run towards the ocean,
So those heroes in the world of men enter your flaming mouths.

29. Just as moths with great speed
Enter into the flaming fire and perish there,
So also these creatures with great speed
Enter your mouths to meet destruction.

30. You lick up and devour with flaming mouths entire worlds from every side;
Your terrible light-rays fill the entire world with radiance and scorch it, O Viṣṇu.

31. Tell me who you are with form so terrible;
Homage to you, Best of Gods, be merciful.

I desire to understand you, the Primal One,
For your manifestation is not intelligible to me.

The Blessed One said:
32. Time am I, the world-destroyer, grown mature,
Engaged here in fetching back the worlds.
Even without you, all the warriors standing over against you will cease to be.

33. Therefore stand up, gain glory;
Having conquered enemies,
Enjoy a prosperous kingdom.
By me they are already slain;
Be you merely the occasion, O Savyasācin, (Arjuna).

34. Droṇa, Bhīṣma, Jayadratha, Karṇa, and other warrior–heroes likewise:
Slain by me, slay them, do not tremble.
Fight, you will conquer your enemies in battle.

Saṃjaya said:
35. Having heard this word from Keśava (Kṛṣṇa), Kirīṭin (Arjuna),
Trembling and with folded hands payed homage
And made obeisance to him again,
Then spoke to Kṛṣṇa, in faltering voice, afraid:

Arjuna said:
36. O Lord of the Senses, it is right for the world to rejoice and be pleased in celebrating you.
Rakṣasas run in fear in all directions,
While all the hosts of perfected ones pay you homage.

37. And why should they not do homage to you, O Great Self,
Who are primal creator, greater even than Brahmā?
Boundless Lord of Gods, Abode of the World,
You are the imperishable which is beyond existence and non-existence
And that which is beyond both.

38. You are first of gods, primal *puruṣa;*
You are the supreme treasure-house of all this.

You are the knower and what is to be known,
And the supreme goal, O Infinite Form!

39. You are Vāyu, Yama, Agni, Varuṇa, Śaśāṅka,
You are Lord of Creatures and the Great Grandfather.
Homage, homage to you a thousand times;
Homage, homage to you, again and yet again.

40. Homage to you in front, homage behind,
Homage to you on all sides, O All.
Boundless in power, immeasurable in might,
You fill all, therefore you are all.

41. For whatever I said in rashness or negligence or affection,
I have called you 'O Kṛṣṇa', 'O Yādava', 'O Comrade',
Having thought of you as my friend
And being ignorant of this greatness of yours;

42. For any disrespect done in jest while alone or with others,
At meals or in bed or being seated or when at play, O Unshaken One,
I beg forgiveness of you, O Boundless One.

43. You are father of the moving and unmoving world,
You are the object of its reverence and its greatest teacher.
There is no equal to you, O One of Incomparable Power,
How then could anyone in the three worlds surpass you?

44. Therefore having made obeisance before you and prostrated my body,
I seek your grace, O Lord;
Please bear with me, as father with son, friend with friend, lover with beloved.

45. I am delighted, having seen what was not previously seen,
But my mind trembles with fear.
Show me that other (human) form of yours, O Lord;
Be gracious, Refuge of the World.

46. I wish to see you as before, with crown, mace and discus in hand.
O Thousand Armed One of Universal Form, become that four-armed form.

The Blessed One said:

47. By my grace, and of my own self's power,
This highest form was shown to you, Arjuna,
My form composed of splendor, universal, boundless, primal,
Which has been seen before by none besides you.

48. Not by the Vedas or sacrifices or study,
Not by gifts or rites or terrible austerities,
Can I come to be seen in the world of men
With this form by someone besides you, O Hero of the Kurus.

49. Do not tremble or be bewildered,
Having seen this so terrible form of mine.
Free from fear and satisfied mind,
Behold once again this other (human) form of mine.

Saṃjaya said:

50. Having spoken thus to Arjuna, Vāsudeva revealed his own form again.
The great one, having become again the gracious form,
Comforted him in his fear.

Arjuna said:

51. Seeing this gentle human form of yours, O Exciter of Men,
I have now become composed in mind,
Restored to my normal condition.

The Blessed One said:

52. This form of mine, very hard to see, you have seen.
Even the gods are constantly desirous of the sight of this form.

53. Not through the Vedas nor austerity nor charity nor sacrifice
Can I be seen in this form in which you just saw me.

54. But by single-minded devotion *(bhaktyā),* O Arjuna,
I can, in that form, be known and be seen in essence,
And be entered into, O Foe-Destroyer.

55. He who does my work, who has me as his goal,
Dedicated to me, without attachment and without enmity to any being,
He comes to me, O Son of Pāṇḍu.

This is the eleventh chapter, entitled "The Yoga of the Manifestation of the World Form" *(viśvarūpadarśanayoga)*

Chapter XII
THE YOGA OF DEVOTION

Arjuna said:

1. Those devotees who attend upon you ever disciplined,
And those devotees who worship the imperishable and the unmanifest:
Which of these know yoga best?

The Blessed One said:

2. Those who, fixing their minds on me,
Worship me with constant discipline and supreme faith,
These I consider the most accomplished in yoga.

3. But those who worship the imperishable and undefinable,
The unmanifested, the omnipresent, and unthinkable,
The immovable, the unchanging, the constant,

4. Who restrain all their senses, are even-minded,
Who take delight in the welfare of every being,
They also obtain me.

5. The difficulty of those whose intellects are fixed on the unmanifested is much greater,
For the goal of the unmanifested is painful for the embodied to attain.

6. But those who, intent on me, renounce all actions in me,
Worship me with complete discipline and meditate on me:

7. These whose thoughts are fixed on me,
I become quickly their deliverer
From the ocean of death and rebirth, O Pārtha (Arjuna).

8. Set your mind on me alone,
Make your understanding at home in me;
You will dwell in me thereafter.
Of this there is no doubt.

9. But if you are not able steadily to concentrate your mind on me,
Then seek to reach me by the discipline (yoga) of concentration, O Wealth-Winner.

10. If you are not capable of such repeated concentration,
Then be dedicated to my service,
Engaging in actions for my sake,
You will reach fulfillment.

11. But if you are not capable of doing even this,
Then resorting to my own discipline,
Do my yoga and renounce the fruit of all action.

12. Knowledge is better than practice, meditation is superior to knowledge;
Relinquishment of the fruit of action is better than meditation;
From such relinquishment, peace immediately comes.

13. Without hate for any being, friendly and compassionate,
Without possessiveness or the sense of "I,"
Forbearing, even-minded in pleasure and pain,

14. The man of discipline who is ever content,
His self restrained, his resolve firm,
His understanding and mind fastened on me:
He is devoted to me and is dear to me.

15. He whom the world does not fear and who does not fear the world,
Who is free from joy and impatience, fear and agitation,
He also is dear to me.

16. He who, devoted to me, is without expectation,
Pure, skillful, unconcerned, untroubled
And who has relinquished all projects,
He is dear to me.

17. He who neither exults nor hates, grieves nor desires,
Who has relinquished good and evil, dedicated to me,
He is dear to me.

18. He who is the same to friend and enemy, to honor and disgrace,
To cold and heat, pleasure and pain,
Who is free from attachment,

19. He who is thus unattached to blame and praise,
Who is silent, content with anything,
Is homeless, of steady mind, and dedicated to me,
He is dear to me.

20. But those who have faith and are intent on me,
And follow this immortal *dharma* which I have stated earlier,
Those so devoted to me are exceedingly dear to me.

This is the twelfth chapter, entitled "The Yoga of Devotion" *(bhaktiyoga)*.

Chapter XIII
THE YOGA OF DISCRIMINATING THE FIELD AND THE KNOWER OF THE FIELD

Arjuna said:
O Keśava, (Kṛṣṇa), I wish to know Prakṛti and Puruṣa,
The field and the knower of the field,
What is knowledge and what is to be known
(This stanza is not found in all the editions of the *Gītā,* so it is kept unnumbered.)

The Blessed One said:

1. This body, O Son of Kuntī, is called the field,

And he who knows it,
Those who know, call the knower of the field.

2. Know me, O Bhārata, to be the knower of the field in all fields;
The knowledge of the field and of the knower of the field:
This I hold to be (real) knowledge.

3. Hear from me briefly what this field is,
What it is like, what its modifications, and whence it comes,
As well as who he (the knower) is and what his powers.

4. This has been sung many times by sages,
In various hymns separately,
And also in the well-reasoned and definitive aphorisms about Brahman.

5. The (five) gross elements, the sense of I,
Understanding, the unmanifested, the ten senses
And one (mind) and the five sensory realms;

6. Desire and aversion, pleasure and pain,
The bodily aggregate *(saṃghata)*, knowledge *(cetanā)*, will *(dhṛti)*:
This, in brief, is the field with its modifications.

7. Lack of arrogance and deceit, nonviolence, patience,
Uprightness, service to one's teacher, cleanness,
Steadfastness, self-control.

8. Dispassion toward sense objects, lack of identification with the I,
Perception of the evils of birth and death
Of old age and sickness and pain,

9. Nonattachment, lack of clinging to son, wife, home, and the like,
Constant evenmindedness in desireable and undesireable occurrences,

10. Unfailing dedication to me and unswerving dedication to yoga,
Resort to isolated places, dislike for crowds of people,

11. Constancy in knowledge of the self,
Vision of the purpose of essential knowledge:
This is declared to be wisdom,
And whatever is other than this, is non-knowledge.

12. I will describe which is to be known,
And by knowing which one gains immortality.
This is the beginningless supreme Brahman,
Who is said to be neither existent nor nonexistent.

13. With hands and feet everywhere,
Faces and heads, eyes and ears on every side,
It stands, encompassing all, in the world.

14. Appearing to have qualities of all the senses,
Yet free of all the senses,
Bearing all yet unattached,
Enjoyer of the *guṇas* yet free from the *guṇas,*

15. Both outside and inside beings, both moving and unmoving,
Too subtle to be discerned; far away yet it is also near.

16. Undivided, yet standing as if divided among beings,
And as destroyer and producer of beings.

17. Light of Lights, it is said to be beyond darkness;
It is knowledge, what is to be known, and the goal of knowledge,
It is seated in the heart of all.

18. Thus the field, knowledge, and what is to be known has been briefly stated.
Devoted to me, having understood this,
One arrives at this state of mine *(madbhāvāya).*

19. Know that *prakṛti* and *puruṣa* are both beginningless;
Know also that the modifications and *guṇas* are born of *prakṛti.*

20. *Prakṛti* is said to be cause of the generation of causes and agents;
Puruṣa is said to be cause in the experience of pleasure and pain.

21. For *puruṣa,* dwelling in *prakṛti,* experiences the *guṇas* born of *prakṛti.*
Attachment to the *guṇas* is the cause of births in good and evil wombs.

22. The supreme spirit in this body is also called:
Witness, and Consenter, Sustainer,
Enjoyer, Great Lord, Supreme Self.

23. He who knows the *puruṣa* and *prakṛti* with its *guṇas,*
Is not born again, whatever turns his existence takes.

24. By meditation some see the self in the self by the self;
Others do this by the yoga of Sāṃkhya,
Still others by the yoga of action.

25. Others, however, without knowing this,
Worship it, having heard (of these things) from others;
And they too, taking refuge in what they have heard,
Cross beyond death also.

26. Whatever being is born, movable or immovable,
Know it to be born from the union of field and the knower of the field, O Best of the Bhāratas.

27. He who sees the Supreme Lord standing the same in all beings,
Not perishing when they perish,
He sees indeed.

28. For seeing the same Lord standing everywhere equally,
He does not injure the self through the self;
Thus he goes to the supreme goal.

29. He who sees that actions are everywhere done by *prakṛti*
And who likewise sees his self not to be the doer,
He sees indeed.

30. When he sees the various states of beings
Abiding in the One and refracting out from it,
Then he attains Brahman.

31. Because this supreme self, imperishable, without beginning or qualities,

Neither acts nor is tainted,
Even though embodied, O Son of Kuntī,

32. As the omnipresent ether is not defiled because of its subtleness,
So the self, abiding in every body, is not affected.

33. As the one sun illumines this entire world,
So does the field-knower illumine the entire field, O Bhārata.

34. They attain the supreme, who, with the eye of knowledge,
Know in this way the difference of the field and the knower of the field,
And the liberation of beings from *prakṛti*.

This is the thirteenth chapter, entitled "The Yoga of Discriminating the Field and the Knower of the Field" *(kṣetrakṣetrajñavibhāgayoga)*.

Chapter XIV
THE YOGA OF THE DISTINCTION OF THE THREE GUṆAS

The Blessed One said:

1. I will declare still further the supreme vision, chief among wisdoms;
Knowing which, all sages have gone from this world to supreme fulfillment.

2. Having held to this wisdom
And become the likeness of my own state of being,
They are not born even at creation
Nor are they disturbed at dissolution.

3. The great Brahman is my womb;
In it, I place the seed.
From this, O Bhārata, comes the birth of all beings.

4. Brahman is the womb of whatever forms come to be in all wombs, O Son of Kuntī,
And I am the father who bestows the seed.

5. *Sattva, rajas, tamas:* these *guṇas* born of *prakṛti*
Fetter the changeless embodied one in the body, O Strong-Armed.

6. Among these, *sattva,* due to its stainlessness,
Is luminous and healthy.
It binds, O Blameless One,
By attachment to happiness and by attachment to knowledge.

7. Know that *rajas* is of passionate essence,
Is the source of attachment and craving;
It binds the embodied one, O Son of Kuntī,
By attachment to actions.

8. But the *tamas* which is born of ignorance,
Know it to be the deluder of all embodied ones.
It binds, O Bhārata, by heedlessness, indolence and sloth.

9. *Sattva* attaches one to happiness, *rajas* to action;
But *tamas,* obscuring wisdom, O Bhārata,
Attaches one to heedlessness.

10. When *sattva* overpowers *rajas* and *tamas,* it takes over, O Bhārata;
When *rajas* overpowers *sattva* and *tamas,*
And *tamas* overpowers *sattva* and *rajas,*
They also take over.

11. When the light of wisdom appears in all the gates of this body,
Then it may be known that *sattva* has increased.

12. Greed, busyness, undertaking actions, unrest, yearning:
These are born when *rajas* increases, O Best of the Bhāratas.

13. Obscurity and inaction, negligence and delusion:
These are born when *tamas* increases.

14. When the embodied one dies and *sattva* has increased,
He then attains the spotless worlds of those knowing the highest.

15. Meeting death when *rajas* prevails,
He is born among those attached to action;
Likewise, meeting death when *tamas* prevails,
He is born in the wombs of the foolish.

16. The fruit of good action is spotless and sattvic they say;
That of *rajas* is pain, and the fruit of *tamas* is ignorance.

17. Wisdom arises from *sattva,* greed from *rajas,*
Negligence and delusion from *tamas,* as also ignorance.

18. Those who abide in *sattva,* go upwards;
Those in *rajas,* stay in the middle;
Those in *tamas,* abiding in the lowest *guṇa,* go downward.

19. When the seer perceives no doer other than the *guṇas*
And knows what is higher than the *guṇas,*
He attains to my being.

20. Having gone beyond these three *guṇas* springing from the body,
The embodied one, released from birth and death, old age and unhappiness,
Attains immortality.

Arjuna said:

21. O Lord, by what marks is he who has gone beyond these three *guṇas,* distinguished?
What is his conduct?
How does he pass beyond these three *guṇas?*

The Blessed One said:

22. He does not dislike clarity *(sattva)* and activity *(rajas)* nor delusion *(tamas)* when they arise, O Son of Pāṇḍu,
Nor desire them when they cease.

23. He who, seated as if unconcerned, is not agitated by the *guṇas,*
Who thinks the *guṇas* alone act,
Who stands apart and remains firm,

24. Who abides in the self,

To whom pleasure and pain are alike,
Who is the same toward a clod or a stone or gold,
Holding equal the pleasant and the unpleasant,
To whom praise and blame of himself are the same,
Who is firm,

25. To whom good and bad repute, friend and enemy are the same,
Who has left all projects:
He is called the man who has gone beyond the *guṇas*.

26. And he who serves me with the unfailing yoga of devotion *(bhakti)*,
Having gone beyond these *guṇas*,
Is fit to become Brahman.

27. For I am the dwelling place of Brahman,
Of the immortal and imperishable,
Of everlasting *dharma* and absolute happiness.

This is the fourteenth chapter, entitled "The Yoga of the Distinction of the Three *Guṇas*" *(guṇatrayavibhāgayoga)*.

Chapter XV
THE YOGA OF THE HIGHEST VISION

The Blessed One said:

1. They speak of the changeless peepal tree,
Its roots above, its branches below.
Its leaves are the Vedic hymns.
He who knows it, is the knower of the Veda.

2. Its branches stretch below and above, nourished by the *guṇas*,
Its sprouts being the sense objects.
And down in the world of men,
It spreads out the roots that result in action.

3. Its form is thus not comprehended here,
Nor its end, nor its beginning, nor its foundation;
Cutting off this firmly rooted tree
With the firm weapon of nonattachment,

4. Then they should seek after that path from which, having gone,
Men do not return again.
(Saying) I seek refuge only in that primal vision *(puruṣa)*
From which this ancient world manifestation came forth.

5. Those who are without arrogance and delusion,
The evil of attachment conquered, established in the inner self,
Freed from desires and from the pairs known as pleasure and pain,
Who are undeluded,
Go to that imperishable abode.

6. The sun does not shine on it, nor the moon nor fire;
After men come to this, my supreme dwelling-place,
They do not return.

7. A fraction of my self, in the world of the living
Becomes a living self, eternal,
And draws into its power the (five) senses and the mind as sixth,
That come from *prakṛti.*

8. When the Lord takes on a body and also when he departs from it,
He goes taking these along,
Like the wind carrying perfume from their home.

9. He enjoys the objects of the senses,
Using the ear, eye, touch, taste and smell, and also the mind.

10. The deluded do not perceive him, whether he is departing or is staying, Or, when experiencing objects joined to the *guṇas,*
They see him who have the eye of wisdom.

11. The yogins, by striving, see him also
Abiding in their self;
But the mindless whose self is unreadied,
Though striving, do not see him.

12. That radiance in the sun which illumines the entire world,
The radiance in the moon and in fire:
Know that radiance as mine.

13. Entering the earth also,
I support all beings by my power.
And becoming the sap-natured soma,
I also nourish all plants.

14. And becoming the fire inhabiting the body of living beings
And being united with their life-breaths,
I prepare the four kinds of food.

15. And I am seated in the hearts of all;
From me are memory, wisdom and their loss.
I am the one to be known by the Vedas;
The author of the Vedānta,
I am also the knower of the Vedas.

16. There are two *puruṣas* in the world, the perishable and the imperishable;
The perishable is all beings, the imperishable is called Kūṭastha (the imperishable).

17. But other than these is the uppermost *puruṣa* called the supreme self,
Who, as the imperishable Lord,
Enters the three worlds and sustains them.

18. Because I surpass the perishable and even the imperishable,
I am the supreme *puruṣa* celebrated in the world and in the Vedas,

19. He who, undeluded, thus knows me, as the supreme *puruṣa (puruṣottama)*;
He is all-knowing and worships me with his whole being, O Bhārata.

20. Thus has this most secret teaching been disclosed by me, Blameless One;

Being enlightened to this, O Bhārata,
One will be a man possessed of understanding
And will have done his work.

This is the fifteenth chapter, entitled "The Yoga of the Highest Vision" *(puruṣottamayoga)*.

Chapter XVI
THE YOGA OF THE DISTINCTION BETWEEN LIBERATING AND BINDING CONDITIONS

The Blessed One said:

1. Fearlessness, essential purity of being, perseverance in the yoga of wisdom,
Charity and self-control and sacrifice,
Study of the Veda, austerity, rectitude,

2. Nonviolence, truth, freedom from anger,
Relinquishment, peace, lack of malice,
Sympathy for beings, freedom from covetousness,
Gentleness, modesty, absence of fickleness,

3. Vigor, forbearance, firmness,
Cleanness, loyalty, absence of overweening pride:
These belong to one whose birth is of a divine condition, O Bhārata.

4. Hypocrisy, insolence, overweening pride and anger,
Harshness and ignorance:
These are the endowments of one born of a demonic condition, O Son of Pṛthā.

5. The divine endowments are said to lead to release;
The demonic to bondage.
Do not grieve, O Pāṇḍava,
You are born with divine endowments, (best circumstance for gaining freedom).

6. In this world there are two kinds of beings, the divine and demonic.
The divine has been spoken of at length;
Hear me now, O Son of Pṛthā, concerning the demonic.

7. Demonic men know neither action nor its cessation,
Neither purity nor good conduct, nor truth is in them.

8. They say that the world is without truth,
Without a foundation, a Lord;
That it is not produced by orderly complementary union,
But that it is produced by (the pursuit of) pleasure.

9. Relying on this view, such men,
Lost in self, small in mind, cruel in deed,
March forth as enemies,
Pledged to the destruction of the world.

10. Surrendering to insatiable desire,
Full of wantonness and arrogance and hypocrisy,
Holding obscure views through delusion,
These men act with impure resolve.

11. Clinging to innumerable concerns whose only end is death,
Completely dedicated to the enjoyment of desire,
They are convinced that this is all.

12. Bound by hundreds of fetters of desire,
Dedicated to lust and anger,
They strive for the gaining of wealth even unjustly
For the gratification of their desire.

13. "This I have won today; that desire I will obtain;
This is mine; this wealth will become mine.

14. I have slain that foe, and I will slay others besides;
I am lord and enjoyer, I am perfect and strong and happy.

15. I am wealthy and well-born.
Who else is like me?
I will sacrifice, I will give, I will rejoice."
Thus speak those deluded by ignorance.

16. Bewildered by many thoughts, enmeshed in the net of delusion,

Given over to the gratification of desires,
They fall into a foul hell.

17. Self-deluded, hard-headed, full of arrogance and pride of wealth,
They offer sacrifice in name only,
Hypocritically and against all the prescribed rules.

18. Taking their "I" literally, full of might, insolence, desire, anger:
These malicious men show hatred against me
In their own bodies and those of others.

19. These men, hostile, cruel, foul, the lowest of men,
I am forever hurling into demonic wombs
In the cycle of existence.

20. Having fallen into demonic wombs, these deluded ones,
From birth to death, having failed to reach me,
They go to the lowest place, O Son of Kuntī.

21. This is the threefold gateway to hell, the ruin of a self:
Desire, anger and greed.
Therefore, one should abandon these three.

22. The man who is released from these three gates of darkness, O Son of Kuntī,
Goes to the supreme destination after practising what is good for his self.

23. He who, dismissing the rules of scriptures,
Acts according to his inclinations,
Does not reach fulfillment, nor happiness nor the highest destination.

24. Therefore, let the scripture be your standard
In settling what is to be done and what is not.
Here on earth you should do the deed called for by the rule of scripture.

This is the sixteenth chapter, entitled "The Yoga of the Distinction Between Liberating and Binding Conditions" *(daivāsurasaṃpadvibhāgayoga)*.

Chapter XVII
THE YOGA OF THE THREE FORMS OF FAITH

Arjuna said:

1. What is the state of those who, neglecting the rules of scripture,
Sacrifice full of faith, O Kṛṣṇa?
Is it *sattva, rajas* or *tamas*?

The Blessed One said:

2. Born of their innermost conditions *(sva-bhāva),*
The faith of the embodied ones is threefold:
Sattvic, rajasic, and *tamasic.*
Hear about it now.

3. The faith of each man comes in accordance to his essence, O Bhārata.
Man here is made up of his faith.
Whatever faith a man has, that he is.

4. The *sattvic* sacrifices to the gods,
The *rajasic* to the Yakṣas (demigods) and Rakṣasas (demons) and the rest,
The *tamasic* sacrifice to the ghosts and spirits of natural beings.

5. Men full of the strength of passion and desire,
Full of self and hypocrisy,
Who perform cruel austerities which are not enjoined by the scriptures,

6. Who starve the collection of elements in their bodies,
And even me dwelling in their bodies:
Know that these fools are demonic in their intent.

7. But also the food dear to each man is three-fold,
And likewise the sacrifice, austerity and charity.
Hear now the distinction of these.

8. Foods increasing life, vitality, strength,
Health, happiness and joy,
Tasty, rich, lasting and agreeable:
These are dear to the *sattvic.*

9. Foods which are pungent, sour, salty,
Very hot, spicy, astringent, burning,
Which cause pain, grief and sickness:
These are desired by the *rajasic.*

10. Food which is spoiled, tasteless, foul-smelling, stale,
Which is left-over or unclean:
This is the food dear to the *tamasic.*

11. That sacrifice which is offered according to scriptures,
By men who do not desire fruits
But think simply that it ought to be performed,
Is *sattvic.*

12. Know that sacrifice to be *rajasic,* O Best of Bhāratas,
Which is offered aiming at the fruit,
And also for the sake of appearance.

13. That sacrifice is called *tamasic* which is lacking faith,
Is not enjoined by scripture, is lacking in hymns,
Is lacking in distribution of the food, and fees are not paid.

14. Honor for the gods, the twice-born, to teachers and wise men;
Purity, uprightness, continence, non-violence:
This is bodily austerity.

15. Utterance which is inoffensive and truthful,
Agreeable and beneficial, and the practise of (Vedic) study:
This is austerity of speech.

16. Mental clarity, gentleness, silence,
Self-restraint, purity of being:
This is mental austerity.

17. This three-fold austerity,
Engaged in with supreme faith by men who are disciplined
And are not desirous of fruit,
They call *sattvic.*

18. That austerity which is practised hypocritically for esteem,

Or honor or reverence,
Is called *rajasic:*
It is unstable and fleeting.

19. The austerity which is performed with foolish stubbornness,
Or with self-torture, or is done to destroy others,
Is called *tamasic.*

20. That gift which is given to one without expecting return
Just because it ought to be given,
And which is given at the proper time and place to a worthy person:
That gift is declared to be *sattvic.*

21. But that gift which is engaged in for the sake of something in return,
Or aiming at fruit,
And which is engaged in grudgingly,
Is declared to be *rajasic.*

22. That gift which is given at the wrong time and place to an unworthy person,
Without respect and with contempt:
That is called *tamasic.*

23. *Oṃ, tat, sat':* this is declared as the three-fold designation of Brahman.
By this the brāhmans, the Vedas, and the sacrifices
Were ordained of old.

24. For this reason, uttering *Oṃ,* the acts of sacrifice, giving and austerity enjoined in Scripture,
Are always carried on by the knowers of Brahman.

25. (Uttering) *tat,* the diverse acts of sacrifice and austerity and giving
Are performed by those seeking release,
Without their aiming at the fruit.

26. *Sat* is used for the "real" and the "good," O Son of Pṛthā,
Likewise, the word *sat* is used for a praise-worthy action.

27. Steadfastness in sacrifice, austerity and giving
Is also called *sat*;
And action for the sake of these is called *sat*.

28. Whatever sacrificial offering, act of charity, austerity,
Performed without faith, is called *asat*, O Pārtha.
It is of no use here on earth or hereafter.

This is the seventeenth chapter, entitled "The Yoga of the Three Forms of Faith" *(śraddhātrayavibhāgayoga)*.

Chapter XVIII
THE YOGA OF FREEDOM BY RENUNCIATION

Arjuna said:

1. O Strong-Armed, Lord of the Senses,
I desire to know the true essence of renunciation *(saṃnyāsa)* and of detachment *(tyāga)*,
And the distinction between them, O Slayer of Keśin.

The Blessed One said:

2. Seers know "renunciation" to be the giving up of acts of desire;
"Detachment" is the relinquishing of the fruit of all action.

3. Some wise men say, however, that action is to be relinquished as evil;
Others say one should not relinquish the acts of sacrifice, giving, and austerity.

4. Hear from me the resolution of this matter of detachment, O Best of Bhāratas.
Detachment, Best of Men, has been declared to be threefold.

5. The acts of sacrifice, giving, and austerity are not to be relinquished but to be done;
For sacrifice, giving and austerity are purifiers of the wise.

6. But even these acts are to be performed, Son of Pṛthā,
   without attachment to their fruits:
   This is my assured and final judgment.

7. The renunciation of an action prescribed is not fitting;
   The abandonment of it due to delusion is declared to be
   tamasic.

8. He who relinquishes an action due to fear of bodily pain,
   Performs a *rajasic* abandonment.
   He does not win fruit for his abandonment.

9. He who does his prescribed action, O Arjuna,
   Because it ought to be done,
   Abandoning attachment and the fruit,
   He is deemed to be *sattvic*.

10. The wise man, the unattached, whose doubts are removed,
    Who is filled with light *(sattva),*
    Does not dislike unpleasant action,
    And is not attached to pleasant action.

11. It is not possible, indeed, to relinquish action altogether
    for an embodied self;
    But he who abandons the fruit of action
    Is called the detached.

12. Pleasant, unpleasant and mixed:
    Three-fold is the fruit of action for the attached after
    death;
    But there is no fruit whatever for those who renounce.

13. Understand from me, O Strong-Armed, learn of me,
    These five factors for the accomplishment of all actions,
    As proclaimed in the *Sāṃkhya* at the end of the *kṛta* age.

14. The seat of action (body), the agent, instruments of
    various sorts,
    Various kinds of actions,
    And (as fifth) also intention:

15. Whatever action a man undertakes with his body,
    speech, and mind,

Whether right or wrong,
These are its five causes.

16. This being so, he who because of undisciplined intelligence,
Sees himself as the sole agent,
He is a fool, and does not see.

17. He who is free from the sense of I,
Whose understanding is not tainted,
Though he slay these people,
He slays not nor is he bound.

18. Knowledge, what is to be known, and the knower
Are a three-fold incitement toward action:
The instrument, the action and the actor
Are the three-fold composite of action.

19. Knowledge, action and the agent
Are said, in the enumeration of the *guṇas,*
To be three-fold also, according to the diversity of the *guṇas.*
Listen, accordingly, to these also.

20. That knowledge by which the one imperishable being is seen in all beings,
Undivided in the divided,
Know that that knowledge is *sattvic.*

21. That knowledge which knows the manifold different conditions in all beings,
Because of their separateness,
Know that knowledge is *rajasic.*

22. But that which clings to one single effect as if it were the whole,
Missing the cause, without grasping the real and non-apparent,
Is said to be *tamasic.*

23. An action which is obligatory,
Performed without attachment and without desire or hate by one undesirous of the fruit,
That is said to be *sattvic.*

24. But action which is done in great strain
By one seeking to gratify his desires or by the sense of I,
Is said to be *rajasic.*

25. That action which is undertaken out of delusion,
Without regard to consequences, or to loss and injury, or to one's human capability,
Is called *tamasic.*

26. The actor who is free from attachment and not taking first person speech (literally),
Is without agitation in regard to success and failure,
And is filled with strength (of vision) and firmness,
Is called *sattvic.*

27. That actor who is passionate, desirous of the fruit of action,
Lustful and impure and violent,
Filled with exaltation and grief,
Is called *rajasic.*

28. That actor who is undisciplined, unrefined, obstinate,
Deceitful, dishonest, indolent,
Despondent and procrastinating,
Is called *tamasic.*

29. O Wealth-Winner, hear the three-fold differentiation of understanding and firmness also,
According to the *guṇas,*
Declared fully and separately.

30. That (understanding) which knows action and inaction,
What ought to be done and what ought not to be done,
The fearful and what is not, bondage and release,
That understanding, O Son of Pṛthā, is *sattvic.*

31. That, O Son of Pṛthā, by which one understands incorrectly *dharma* and *adharma,*
And also what ought to be done and what ought not to be done,
That understanding is *rajasic.*

32. That which, O Son of Pṛthā, covered by darkness,

Deems as *dharma* what is *adharma,*
And thinks all things in reversed fashion,
That understanding is *tamasic.*

33. The firmness (of judgment) by which one holds the workings of the mind, life-breath, and the senses,
By way of undeviating yoga,
That, O Son of Pṛthā, is *sattvic.*

34. But that firmness (of judgement) by which one, desiring fruit,
Holds fast to worldly goals, *dharma,* wealth, pleasure
In an attached manner,
That, O Son of Pṛthā, is *rajasic.*

35. That firmness (of judgment) by which the fool does not give up sleep, fear, grief, depression and pride,
That, O Son of Pṛthā, is *tamasic.*

36. But hear now from me, O Best of the Bhāratas, the three-fold happiness,
In which man rejoices by long practise,
And comes to the end of suffering.

37. That which, born of clarity in one's understanding of self,
Is at first like poison but in the end is the finest nectar,
That is *sattvic.*

38. That happiness which (arises) from the union of the senses and their objects,
Is in the beginning like the finest nectar but in the end like poison,
That is called *rajasic.*

39. That happiness which deludes the self in the beginning and in the end,
Arises from sleep, indolence and heedlessness,
That is called *tamasic.*

40. There is no actuality either on earth or in heaven, even among the gods,
Which is free of these *guṇas* born of *prakṛti.*

41. The works of Brāhmans, *Kṣatriyas, Vaiśyas* and *Śūdras,*
O Foe-Destroyer,
Are distinguished by the *guṇas* that arise from their own inner condition.

42. Repose, self-restraint, austerity,
Cleanness, patience and uprightness,
Piety, wisdom and knowledge,
Are the actions of the Brāhman, born of his own condition.

43. Heroism, energy, firmness,
Resourcefulness, and not fleeing in battle,
Generosity and lordliness,
Are the actions of the *Kṣatriya,* born of his condition.

44. Agriculture, cattle-tending, trade,
Are the actions of the *Vaiśya,* born of his condition;
Service is the action of the *Śūdra,* born of his condition.

45. A man, dedicated to his own action, attains fulfillment.
Hear then in what way he finds fulfillment,
When one is dedicated to action.

46. A man finds fulfillment by worshipping him, through his own proper action,
From whom all beings arise and by whom all this is pervaded.

47. One's own *dharma,* even when not done perfectly,
Is better than an alien *dharma,* even though well performed;
One does not incur sin doing the action prescribed by one's own condition (doing one's thing).

48. One should not abandon the action congenial to one,
Even though it is defective,
For all undertakings are clouded with defects
Like fire by smoke, O Son of Kuntī.

49. He whose understanding is everywhere unattached,
Who is without yearning, whose self is subdued,

Arrives by renunciation at the supreme fulfillment of freedom,
From the bondage of action *(naiṣkarmya)*.

50. Understand from me succinctly, O Son of Kuntī,
How, he who has reached fulfillment, has reached Brahman,
Which is the supreme state of wisdom.

51. Disciplined with a pure understanding,
Having restrained his self with firmness,
Having relinquished sound and other sense objects,
Casting aside passion and hate,

52. Dwelling alone, eating little, with mind, body and speech controlled,
Constantly engaged in the yoga of meditation,
Supported by dispassion,

53. Having forsaken the sense of I, might, insolence,
Desire, anger, possession;
Unselfish and at peace, he is fit to become Brahman.

54. Having become Brahman, tranquil in the self,
He neither grieves nor desires;
Regarding all beings as equal, he attains supreme dedication to me.

55. Through this dedication, he knows me in essence;
Then having known me essentially, he forthwith enters into me.

56. Ever performing all actions, taking refuge in me,
By my grace, he reaches the eternal, imperishable abode.

57. Renouncing all action to me with your mind,
Intent on me, relying on the yoga of understanding.
Become constantly mindful of me.

58. If mindful of me, you will cross all obstacles by my grace.
But if, due to your sense of I, you will not pay heed,
You will perish.

59. If, having centered in your sense of I, you think "I will not fight,"
Your resolve will be in vain:
Prakṛti will impel you.

60. Tied to your own action born of your condition, O Son of Kuntī,
You will do helplessly
That which, due to delusion, you do not want to do.

61. The Lord stands in the heart of all beings, O Arjuna,
By his power causing all beings to revolve as if they were mounted on a wheel.

62. Go to him alone for shelter, O Descendent of Bhārata,
With all your being.
By his grace, you will attain supreme peace and everlasting abode.

63. Thus the wisdom, more secret than any secret,
Has been declared by me to you;
Having relfected fully on this, do as you desire.

64. Hear once more my supreme word, most secret of all.
You are greatly loved by me:
Therefore I will speak for your good.

65. Mindful of me, be devoted to me:
Sacrifice to me, do me homage:
You will come to me.
Truly I promise you, for you are dear to me.

66. Having relinquished all *dharmas,* take shelter in me alone.
I shall make you released from all sins: be not grieved.

67. This is not to be spoken by you to anyone who is without austerity,
Not dedicated and not obedient;
Nor to one who speaks against me.

68. He who will share this supreme secret with my devotees,
Having supreme devotion to me,
He will doubtless come to me.

69. None among men would do anything equally dear to me,
Nor will there be another dearer to me on earth.

70. And he who shall study this dialogue of ours full of *dharma,*
Should sacrifice to me by the sacrifice of wisdom:
Such is my thought.

71. The man who, unmurmuring and with faith, shall listen to it,
He shall be released;
He shall attain the radiant worlds of the perfect.

72. O Son of Pṛthā, have you listened to this with concentrated mind?
O Wealth-Winner, has your delusion through ignorance been destroyed?

Arjuna said:

73. Destroyed is my delusion;
By your grace, O Unshaken One, I have gained remembrance.
I take my stand firmly, with doubt dispelled;
I will do your word.

Saṃjaya said:

74. Thus have I heard this marvelous hair-raising dialogue of Vāsudeva (Kṛṣṇa) and the Son of Pṛthā (Arjuna),
Of great self;

75. By the grace of Vyāsa I have heard this supreme secret, this discipline,
Related in person by Kṛṣṇa himself, Lord of Yoga.

76. O King, each time I recall this marvelous holy dialogue of Keśava and Arjuna,
I rejoice once again.

77. And each time I recall that exceedingly marvelous form of Hari (Kṛṣṇa),
My wonder is great and I rejoice once again.

78. Wherever there is Kṛṣṇa, Lord of Yoga, and Pārtha the archer,

There surely is fortune, victory, prosperity, wise conduct:
I believe.

This is the eighteenth chapter, entitled "The Yoga of Renunciation" *(mokṣasaṃnyāsayoga)*.

Here the Bhagavadgītā-upaniṣad ends.

Part IV

Crisis in Identity

Chapter Four

In relation to what I can say this I am, I do not know.
Lost in thought, I wander.

Ṛg Veda 1,164,37

Unconcerned, mocking, violent—thus wisdom wants us:
she is a woman and always loves only a warrior.

Thus Spoke Zarathustra

INTRODUCTION

Our journey through Western Philosophy has made us aware of at least two radical needs in Comparative Studies (and all studies, even within a discipline, are comparative): the recovery of philosophy as a radically critical activity which justifies itself through its own repeated execution, and the recovery of man/woman through such radically executed activity.

As things stood when we lifted our tents from the Western shores of philosophy, philosophy as a radically critical activity that man must do to ground man's basic orientations in view of man's self-reproduction and continuity as a social being was never fully realized. Instead other less effective, insufficient and dogmatic attitudes were demanded of man to cope with his world.

We will in the following chapters try to show how the crisis of philosophy is radically linked to the demands for identification, opening thus the possibility of creating the necessary and sufficient conditions for the *Bhagavad Gītā's* own interpretation to appear.

Chapter Four will examine self-identification and its

crisis; chapter Five will examine the problem of identifying knowledge with some particular form of knowledge; chapter Six will point out the problem of absolutizing structures into some form of knowledge; chapter Seven will try to point out the resolution of these crises by showing how the search for meaning is a systematic and methodic effort to save rationality in its plural manifestations through an activity of embodiment that emancipates man from any form of identification, allowing him the freedom to act efficiently in any one identifiable field of the social fabric.

The problem of identification is central to our theme of Man and Circumstance for unless we can suspend the natural tendency to identify others with ourselves and vice versa, historic reason cannot emerge. The capital sin of our methods is to try to submerge a whole people and its diversity into a single vision; a single personality.

At a synthetic glance we may summarize the main attitudes and demands of Western philosophy as:

1. a search for universal principles, applicable to man, *universal* man, in general. These universal principles guarantee man everything except one thing: to be a man;
2. the atomization of man, individual man/woman, through the affirmation and universalization of a particular situation; self-commitment as opposed to self-surrender: authenticity *vs.* hypocrisy;
3. and the reduction of man to those momentarily approved norms of behavior which are scientifically explainable, predictable and controllable.

These three modes of manipulating philosophy have left contemporary Western Man with three corresponding modes of being-in-the-world; three possibilities which Existentialism has summarized for us in three concrete universal images: the Democratic and Anti-Semite (Sartre); the Underground-Man (Dostoevsky); and the Grand Inquisitor (Dostoevsky). Regardless of the merits of this synthetic glance it is still valid to generalize that these three forms of being in the world for Western man, not withstanding their drama, anguish, success, glory, ecstasy, despair, value, etc., are three forms of being in the world made possible for only one simple, philosophic reason: the radical need of Western man for self-identification. On hindsight it could have been also seen not as a radical need but as a radical blind spot in the philosopher's own vision of philosophy. Identity-making decision has no one factual answer, but rather depends on a great variety of criteria for determining personal (or other) identity. Statements about identity in any language are language bound, and it is not only the trivial case that statements about identity do not always refer to the same subject or object, but rather it is the case that they do not *necessarily* refer to any subject or object at all, though at times they do. Self or other identification terms, in any language, do not prescribe the criteria for their use. It is up to every language user, and entirely up to him, to decide the type of identification game he is going to play with, say, sensation or other terms, so that he may decide, even while suffering, , acting, etc., which kind of "candidate" he wishes to have as "sensation-owner."

Plato started his Timaeus by asking: "One, two three . . . Where is the fourth?" Is self-identification in any of the three forms described above the only alternative for man to-be-in-the-world? Is there a fourth? These, of course, are not rhetorical questions. We understand man to be the possibilities of man as actualized by man: man in his circumstantial situations as actualizing and modifying his circumstance through these actualizations. We have already seen, however, through the first two chapters of this book, how by focusing on the radical activity of philosophy itself, man transcends his own actualizations (context, structure, and meaning) and actualizes his own possibilities: i.e., ontological and ontic detachment is possible. Thus, the fourth way of man-in-the-world is what we have implicitly identified in those two chapters as the activity itself of doing philosophy at a radical level, as the saving of the human circumstance, as the philosophic method, as historic reason, as what philosophy does if it fully (necessarily and sufficiently) justifies itself: guarantees human life. However, our doing of philosophy has made also a very important clarification regarding the doing of philosophy itself, or the modality of man-being-in-the-world in a radical sense: We could not have done it *without* doing it (philosophy) through what others have done. Our method is not a method in opposition to others, a way of being-in-the-world against the others or an alternative (either/or) to the others. Ours is a method, a doing, a path, through the others and it is because of the others, of what others have done, that our method is possible. It integrates; it does not destroy a thread of the human fabric. It leaves rationality opened, does not close itself in the cocoon of any system, and renews human life through human life on an equality with equals. The only difference is that the method is committed to only one thing: itself, the doing of philosophy at a radical level. Although it will have to go through others and through its own self-reflective activity (through identifications) still it is grounded on the activity itself (which man, to be man, has of necessity to do in every act) without ontological or ontic attachments; for the activity itself (the method, way) is capable of going through every ontological and ontic situation without getting trapped in any one of them. The first two chapters of this book could offer a suggestive hint as to the possibilities of this way of doing philosophy. This chapter sets us in search of something more concrete: the fourth way of being in the world, which would integrate and cancel the previously described three modes of being in the world which contemporary Western man seems to be condemned to follow. This fourth way we now identify as the way of being in the world which the *Bhagavad Gītā* exemplifies. The rest of the book will be dedicated to show this way of being in the world. Furthermore, we contend that this "message" of the *Bhagavad Gītā* is not recoverable unless what we have identified as the method of radical reason, vital reason, the way of philosophy's historic reason, etc., is used so that we do not identify the *Gītā* as something, book or doctrine, which is already trivially known to us, our religions, systems of ethics, universal principles or our own selves. For the *Gītā* to have meaning it has to appear in its own context and structure. To begin with, we must start with the *Gītā's* own initial situation: the crisis of man through self-identity.

INTERPRETATION AND THE BHAGAVAD GĪTĀ

If our journey through Greek and contemporary philosophy was considered necessary and, if not complete, at least suggestively sufficient, it was primarily to lead us into the paths of the *Bhagavad Gītā*. Three main methodological considerations have been repeatedly made. It is important that we review them before plunging into the *Bhagavad Gītā*.

Philosophical language of any historic period (its meaning) is radically bound to that historic period. Language, we have found to be context and structure dependent. For any one concept to have meaning (in any one context) one must know the whole context, or what is the same, in order to have a concept one must in a sense have them all. No dictionary can obviate the effort of discovering a context-giving-meaning. But it is the case that in Eastern and Western traditions there have been a plurality and a succession of contexts and structures determining the meaning of words relative to those traditions. Translators and interpreters of the *Bhagavad Gītā,* however, appear to have been unaware of this interpretative situation. They have ignored the fact that the linguistic ground of the people they were studying and even the ground on which they were standing within their own disciplines—religion, linguistics, philosophy—was moving, or had already moved from under their own feet while studying those people. What they have done instead is to fix the model of interpretation of the natural sciences and *demand* that the plurality of worlds and words surrender to it. Thus what we have at the moment are translations and interpretations of the *Bhagavad Gītā* (how can one separate the two?) which in many ways represent a necessary accomplishment, especially in regard to the language, but which in other ways, especially in regard to interpretation, still remain insufficient and terribly dated, out of touch with today's as well as the *Gītā's* context.

The reason for this lack of up-to-date sophistication in interpretation is the almost complete ignorance by interpreters of the way philosophic language functions in the life of a people, Eastern or Western. We have identified this ignorance as the oblivion of philosophy: what people had to do in different and concrete periods of history to orient their lives. The reliance of interpreters on the heavy-handed methodological biases of the social sciences has substituted the discovery of this activity for a general conformity to the demands of scientistic methods; thus covering the historicity of man or making his historical appearance on this earth a triviality.

Indian scholars did not fair better in this enterprise. They have been fighting all along a losing battle. After all, they had to make Indian thought palatable and respectable to Western methods. Thus we have as a concrete consequence a mute subservience of all concerned to the mighty worship of the "word"—of identification of words with words, of gods with gods, of concepts with concepts—and so "the wasteland grows" while man is systematically reduced in size.

This brings us to the final point: the problem of interpretation itself. If interpretation is a radical activity of man which he must do in order to continue his life as man, then the interpretation of a "text" like the *Bhagavad Gītā* is condemned to the same fate. Then, it is not the case that the activity of interpretation is to produce a definitive text, a text which once and for all will stand fixed for all men to read. This is the kind of crypto-premise that hides behind the biases mentioned earlier. If I am able at this time to be so strong on the interpretations I condemn, and on which I depend for my own, it is because such an irrevocable, final feat is not the task of interpretation, but the demand or dream of certain unproven and unprovable scientistic methodologies which place "truth" in a vague tomorrow, thus dulling the present "truth" which we must do today. If repeated interpretations are needed *(saṃvṛtisatya)*—the activity *(satya)* of gathering together *(saṃ)* what needs to be uncovered *(vṛ)*—it is because man never stands on the same ground; it is because man's conceptual schemes keep moving and shifting; it is because man's empirical life becomes larger and more complex as man moves; it is because there is no fixed belief on which man can stand forever, nor fixed sensations on which man can count on forever, nor a fixed linguistic behavior to which man must conform or in fact does conform; it is because man is man: someone always on the move, someone always making himself, dependent on others for his interpretations of himself and others, of himself and his circumstance. This is the simple reason why a new interpretation (of a life or of the *Bhagavad Gītā*) is always needed. There is always a new confrontation, a new rationality demanding to be met. There can never be a final interpretation, but it must always be new, perhaps less dogmatic, always more open, more like man himself: capable of creating the necessary and sufficient conditions which would make it possible for the text (of a life or the *Bhagavad Gītā*) to appear (find its own meaning) in its own context and within its own structure. It is in this present immediacy that an interpretation of the *Bhagavad Gītā* will satisfy the contemporary sophistication of contemporary man. And this condition must be met. It is not sufficient that the *Bhagavad Gītā* be recognized within its own tradition. It must also be recognized by us, for unless it is recognizable by contemporary man in his present up-to-date context, the interpretation will remain trivial. (By contemporary man, of course, we mean the man of any continent who has embodied both the mind and the needs of the times and desperately looks for their reconciliation.) This demand, however, that present, contemporary man recognizes his own interpretations is also the interpretation's own limit and the need to look for another one once this one is out. This is the reason why all interpretations, the one in this book, or Kṛṣṇa's interpretation of his own culture in the *Bhagavad Gītā,* are only for the time being.

To proceed systematically in this mutual journey of interpretation—mutual in the sense of the author–reader—I will now proceed to divide our tasks in this chapter. Because of what I understand interpretation to be, I have already excused myself from "saying" everything with the "sayings" of the *Bhagavad Gītā.* This would involve us in a futile journey and methodological contradiction. What I will do, from my side, is to offer instead the "whole" or "wholes"—contexts—through which the "sayings" (texts, quotations) of the *Bhagavad Gītā* will gain meaning. The reader, on the other hand, cannot substitute my "interpretation" for his own *active reading.* It is this *active doing* by the reader that will actually save the text. I will hopefully offer conditions that will not turn the reader's effort into a futile and trivial exercise.

We shall immediately concentrate on Arjuna's concrete *situation.* A concrete human situation from which man must, in order to survive as man, take stock of his own convictions. But the reader must avoid uncovering merely the *idea* of these convictions: he must discover them as an active function of a man's life—Arjuna's or his own—of such importance that unless this function is recovered Arjuna, any man, will not be able to act.

Arjuna's situation will demand that we clarify the following points:

- Arjuna, the warrior *(kṣatriya);*
- Arjuna, the man in a situation: the crisis identified;
- Human crisis around Arjuna, and Arjuna's.

To avoid frustration on the part of the reader in this

author-reader interpretive journey, I will summarize here our intentional clues in this task of interpreting the *Bhagavad Gītā*.

1. The text of the *Bhagavad Gītā* will be taken as a complete linguistic whole.
2. The sources of meaning of this linguistic whole will be found in the recognition of this text within its own context or tradition and also within our present context, or the contemporary understanding of contemporary man.
3. For these conditions to be met it is necessary and sufficient that the interpretation of the *Bhagavad Gītā* be grounded on the contemporary needs of contemporary society as rational possibilities—on equal bases with our own rationalities—for contemporary man to save his present circumstance.

The above conditions can be met only if philosophy is understood as a radical activity which is executed for the sake of its own constitution and realization of man's needed basic orientations as he interacts and communicates with other men in search of his own human ground and human continuity.

To put the above interpretative clues in our own language of historic reason, we may say that there are three levels of man's acting at which our inquiry aims.

The first level is the contextual level as the possibilities of man as realized by man: a heuristic anticipation, a dark, unformed world or worlds to be discovered; worlds of silence not yet made language, propositions not yet spoken; myth not yet made knowledge.

The second level is the world of concrete formed and structured worlds; known horizons; man within language; man within structures; propositional worlds, man's body.

The third level is the world of meaning: what man does in order to constitute his human world, or human ground to remain human. It is also the confrontation of man with his own contexts—presuppositions—his own structures—theories of knowledge—and overt meanings and the possibilities for man to become a slave of his own creations—leave the world as it is—or to emancipate himself through his own liberation or recreation; the birth of new languages, new worlds, new man, new human grounds.

The activity itself of uncovering and reconciling these three levels, three dimensions, remains anonymous. It is man's fourth dimension: the effective ground of human self-constitution and continuation. It is our contention that the role of interpretation is not just to dictate what interpretation should be, but rather what the doing of interpretation really does when it is done in this manner. This is the reason we have taken as our challenge the *Bhagavad Gītā*—also our present need—so that we do not only speak about interpretation but do it while speaking. Thus we hope that in interpreting the *Bhagavad Gītā* we will actualize the possibilities of historic reason's way. Thus we concentrate our effort by focusing on how the *Bhagavad Gītā* does within its own culture exactly what we are doing with the *Bhagavad Gītā* and our own. It will be convenient, therefore, that the reader recapitulates the "action" implied in the whole text of the *Bhagavad Gītā* as offered in Chapter Three's first pages of critical notes.

The *Bhagavad Gītā*'s chapters one and eleven deal with the human crisis of Arjuna. Its resolution is seen in chapters twelve and thirteen. Chapters two through ten, inclusive, cover the ontological ground—sets of beliefs, structures and actions—on which Arjuna and his people stand. This ontological ground is canceled by chapter eleven. This same chapter with twelve and thirteen cancel out also the ontic situations (empirical acts) of Arjuna and the men of his culture as described through chapters fourteen to eighteen. Both ontological and ontic situations in all these chapters will be described as attached (appropriated by a self of man, knowledge, action, inaction) or detached (without self-identification or as an embodied vision in every situation).

We may now proceed to examine Arjuna's crisis.

ARJUNA THE KṢATRYA (WARRIOR)

Friedrich Nietzsche in the *Genealogy of Morals* and later on Ortega y Gasset in *The Revolt of the Masses* elaborate the theme of the master—slave relation with regards to human "ethical" behaviour. The master class acts, and what it does is good. The slave class imitates those actions and through the mediation of the perverted psychology of the priests absolutizes those actions as normative, even divinely inspired behavior. Nietzsche, of course, gives us only the negative side of this picture for he knows of no model of the master class where *acting* is not caprice or sheer arbitrariness. Ortega tries to correct the picture through his better understanding of "aristocracy." For Ortega "aristocracy" would be mediated through education and emancipated thus from its slave and mimetic condition. The problem, however, still remains of knowing exactly on what does the master action, or the aristocratic action (from its Greek source, the best action among many possible actions) rest. Which is the ground on which a *leader* in a moment of decision making or crisis grounds his action. What does a *leader,* an emancipated man, a free citizen, know in order that his action does not remain arbitrary or the child of caprice. In other words, the question is not how does an action become free, given that one has to invent it, unable to imitate others, or is executed under the law, but rather given that there is a law, that man acts within controlled conditions, how is freedom possible?

The *Bhagavad Gītā* offers us a model of human freedom within human determinism; of acts of freedom within socially controlled situations; of free, emancipated, master behavior within slave, determined, controlled conditions. Kṛṣṇa and Arjuna offer us the conditions, model and prototypes of this human journey.

The first clue in clarifying these claims, is to understand the condition of a warrior—of Arjuna and Kṛṣṇa in particular—in the Hindu tradition. The first condition of interpretation is that it recognizes itself within the tradition it interprets.

Apples fall from trees to the ground. By the theory of gravitation we conceive this fall. The behavior of the apples, however, does not depend on this gravitational theory. Even if the gravitational theory did not exist, apples would still fall from trees to the ground. Not so the concepts and behavior of man. Social phenomena, human behavior, is dependent on the concepts that give them life. A warrior in any culture is the kind of warrior the concepts of the culture make him be. He may be a mercenary if he joins the mercenaries: an adopted child of any Pentagon if he is drafted, or decides to become a war professional in view of the rewards of money and decorations; or he can be an Indian–Hindu Kṣatriya: a warrior who besides the art of fighting "knows" what needs to be done for the good of all, because he knows the whole society, its irreversible past, its dreamed future, the possibilities of the present. In other words, his desire as a man coincides with the self-constitution and renewal of the culture: its intentionality. A Hindu Kṣatriya needs to be a philosopher besides being a warrior. The goal is explicitly made clear in the *Bhagavad Gītā* when toward the end of the *Gītā* Kṛṣṇa tells Arjuna: "Do as you desire." That is, now that you know; now that your desire coincides with the knowledge and salvation of your circumstance, do as you wish.

In Indian tradition the Kṣatriyas shared with the Brāhmans the distinction and responsibility of the culture's aristocracy. They were the master class. What had to be done they had to "know" of themselves for there was no one else around to tell them. But while the priestcraft of the Brāhmans tended to freeze the culture by habitualizing ritual to the verge of stagnation, the Kṣatriyas were the defiant leaders of the radical moves within the culture, seeing to it that the culture continued its own self-renovation, continuity and constitution. Examples of this may be found from the Ṛg Veda with the exploits of Indra, through Buddhism, Buddha was himself from the Kṣatriya class, through the Gītā with Kṛṣṇa and Arjuna, both Kṣatriyas, and through the Upaniṣads.

The Indian prototype *(pratirūpa)* of a warrior appears as early as the Ṛg Veda with Indra. Indra, like Arjuna, is caught in a battle between feuding and related families, the Ādityas and Dānavas. Indra, like Arjuna, has no place to turn for counsel but to his own social fabric, for both are within a social intentional life *(pracetas)* ordered by men—*kavis, ṛṣis*—and where all the gods: Agni, Varuṇa, etc., Dragons: Vṛtra, etc., and warrior heroes: Indra, are all this side of creation.

The Upaniṣadic tradition gives us also a great number of examples of the intentional understanding the warrior has of his position in Hindu society. It is only against this background that the Kṣatriya critical thought of the *Bhagavad Gītā* and Arjuna's plight can be understood. In general we may assert that both Buddhism and Hinduism in their own specific way reassert the critical demands of man within culture when trapped within any Brāhmanical priestcraft which demands that all men be reduced to ritualistic uniformity. Hinduism's answer will be an affirmation of the whole culture through a negation of identification with any one single self, knowledge or structure of the culture. In fact, such identification with a form of self and a form of knowledge is the ground of Arjuna's crisis. To be a warrior in this tradition is the ability to act without attachment to the fruits of action.

ARJUNA'S CRISIS

Arjuna's crisis as described in Chapter I of the *Gītā* is apparently a crisis about Arjuna's decision to fight or not to fight. Which would be fine if indeed Arjuna had a choice of either. Kṛṣṇa will make him aware as early as Chapter II that he has no choice but to act; acting in a battle situation, of course, being nothing else but fighting. Kṛṣṇa, in fact, will point to Arjuna that both his question and his crisis should be directed elsewhere, for both presuppose the human condition to be a particular kind of human condition, reducing thus Arjuna's possibilities to no possibility at all, but despair. Kṛṣṇa's moves will be three fold, moving Arjuna from one ontological space to another as he prepares him for the great adventure of saving the human circumstance around him, with him. First he must make Arjuna aware that the space he actually is in is a moveable space, a multiplicity of cultural spaces and not a fixed barbarian state.

Arjuna, the warrior, prince, politician, leader, is, of course, no ordinary man: a whole social life hangs on his decisions. Generations of warriors before him and his own thirteen years in exile have made him ready for what is facing him now in the "field of battle," the "field of *Dharma*." Or have they?

> Arjuna saw standing there fathers and grandfathers,
> Teachers, uncles, brothers, sons, grandsons, companions,
> *I.26*
>
> Fathers-in-law and friends, belonging to both armies.
> And having looked closely at all these relations standing there,
> The son of Kuntī (Arjuna)
> *I.27*
>
> Filled with the utmost sadness,
> And weighed down by his sorrow, he said:
> Kṛṣṇa, seeing my own kin on hand and eager to fight,
> *I.28*

My limbs become weak, my mouth dries up,
My body trembles, and my hair stands on end.

I.29

Gāṇḍīva (the bow) slips from my hand;
My skin is also burning; I can scarcely remain standing;
My mind is reeling.

I.30

I do not crave victory for myself, Kṛṣṇa, nor kingdom and pleasures.
Of what use is kingdom to us, O Govinda (Kṛṣṇa)
Of what use pleasure, or even life?

I.32

It would be better for me if Dhṛtarāṣṭra's sons,
Would slay me, weapons in hand,
Unarmed and unresisting, in battle.

I.46

Having spoken thus in the battle-field,
Arjuna threw down his bow and arrow and sank down upon his chariot seat,
His mind overcome by grief.

I.47

Arjuna, as a Hindu warrior, should by now know not only to act—fight—without regard to the consequences of his action according to his condition but he should also know how to act without any doubt and with a complete aperspectival view of his action: a nondefined, nonidentifiable action, an unshakable judgment. Arjuna, however, collapses in the battlefield unable to balance the terror of being a man with the decision to being a man. The terror is grounded on the belief that there is a natural condition of man born of a natural and blind compulsion towards the reproduction of social action. Arjuna's liberating decision will be the ability to recover the cultural condition of man: man having to cope with a multiplicity of predetermined worlds *(karmic laws)* of which he can sketch the profile *(dharma,* horizon, context), and thus recreate himself.

To follow systematically this journey from space of crisis to spaces of liberation, let us summarize here the programmatic moves of Kṛṣṇa.

1. Arjuna's arguments for in-action in his present situation are futile *once* he is in that present situation *(dharma kṣetre)* in the field of battle.
2. These arguments veil a belief in a natural, raw, barbarian state within which man may try to hide, as it were neutral and unaware of ontological and epistemic presuppositions: the slave of *karmic* laws.
3. This false situation of Arjuna is held together (epistemically and ontologically) by the bewitchment of language in the form of the "*ahaṃkāra*" (I-maker or sense of I) and its subsequent epistemic and ontological appropriations or identifications. A linguistic space is thus absolutized into a universal human space reducing all human acting to only one possible interpretation.

The correction of this nonexist or crisis of Arjuna, Kṛṣṇa will effect by turning (converting) Arjuna from the natural-man he believes himself to be—a linguistic space—into the cultural man he actually is—a multiplicity of spaces. This journey will take up the whole *Gītā* but can be summarized here as a way of being in the world, *acting,* without any form of absolute identification while acting, so that the saving of the human circumstance is possible; but this will of necessity demand that Arjuna's *desire* coincides with the original *desire* which creatively oriented the culture in the first place: that Arjuna becomes the *kṣetrajñanin,* the knower of the field in every field; i.e., that Arjuna's basic orientation as regards knowledge consists in realizing that to know is to know the knowledge of the field in every field, avoiding again the futile search for any absolute form of knowledge for the control and reduction of all the fields and actions of man to only one interpretative possibility.

Situation as Determined Action

Kṛṣṇa shows Arjuna that his arguments for not doing anything while facing the battlefield are useless and ineffective. He shows him that to fight—act—is inevitable. He points out that according to the Kṣatriya tradition *(svadharma)* fighting is in keeping with the noble traditions of the King-sages; it is also virtuous enough to lead to heaven, and it is glorious enough to establish fame on the earth. Thus it is emphasized that this line of action has come down through tradition. Kṛṣṇa tells Arjuna that, "there is no higher good for a kṣatriya than to fight accordant with *dharma,* and that for him it is like "an open door to heaven." The *Mahābhārata,* within which the *Gītā* appears, teaches that a warrior following his royal *dharma (rājadharma)* and a comtemplative seer following the *dharma* of a recluse *(yatidharma)* reach the same goal. The *Bhagavad Gītā* agrees that both these paths lead to the same goal. The Mahābhārata also proclaims in the same vein: "O thou best of men, there are only these two who pierce the constellation of the sun (reach the sphere of Brahman); one is the recluse who is endowed with yoga and the other is the warrior who falls fighting in the battlefield." These two cannot avoid doing what they have been prepared for. "The *dharma* of a Kṣatriya is to take the rod and not to shave the head." "He is called a Kṣatriya because he protects from destruction." To fall from this duty is to incur ill-fame or dishonour forever since "for one who has been held in honor, dishonor is worse than death." In short, desisting from fighting "is ignoble, O Arjuna, and neither leads to heaven nor brings glory." Arjuna is therefore clearly told: "But if you will not engage in this righteous battle, then having forsaken your own particular *dharma* as well as glory, you will incur sin." On the other hand, the participation in war would do good in any case: "Either, slain you will gain heaven, or victorious, you will enjoy the earth."

In his further attempt to show Arjuna the emptiness of his arguments not to fight, Kṛṣṇa, as one who has the whole culture at a glance, reveals before him the destiny of the people assembled there for the battle and points out that it is futile on his part to think that merely on account of his desisting from fighting, the battle would be avoided and the lives of these people would be saved. In keeping with the line of argument that the evil-doers *(ātatāyinaḥ)* are killed by their own outrageous conduct and the man who is merely instrumental in their killing is not guilty of the sin, Kṛṣṇa exhorts him to follow his duty and earn the glory of a true warrior. He says: "Even without you, all the warriors standing over against you will cease to be. Therefore stand up, gain glory; having conquered enemies, enjoy a prosperous kingdom. By me they are already slain; be you merely the occasion *(nimittamātraṃ),* O Savyasācin, (Arjuna)." Arjuna is told to be wise enough to realize the true duty of a Kṣatriya, with the natural endowment with which he is born and not to allow his I-maker *(ahaṃkāra)* and attachment to get the better of him. If, on the other hand he, on account of his vision being blurred with the literal *ahaṃkāra,* fails to exercise his wisdom and desists from following the determination of his condition, it is pointed out, that it may not be possible for him in that ignorant state of mind to keep control over his natural abandonment to fate for long and ultimately he will be compelled by his condition to fight—the only difference being that in the latter case he will fight in ignorance and attached to his action and for the destruction of all. Thus he is clearly told: "If, having centered in your sense of I, you think 'I will not fight,' your resolve will be in vain: *Prakṛti* will impel you."

Had Arjuna minded the tradition, and remembered even a bit of its intentionality, he would have avoided this impasse, for as Kṛṣṇa tells him: "In this path, there is no unsuccessful effort, no reversal is known; even a little of this *dharma* rescues one from great fear." Arjuna's condition as a warrior is grounded on "heroism, energy, firmness, resourcefulness and not fleeing in battle; generosity and lordliness . . ." and in a "battle situation" there is nothing else he can choose.

Even Arjuna, in his despair, realizes that human acting is decision making, a decision in relation to a radical orientation of knowledge, a judgement at every step of the way without questions, doubts, unhesitatingly. He wishes he knew how to be a man of *asaktabuddhi* (firm knowledge-wisdom), and so he asks "what is the mark of a man of firm wisdom *(sthitaprajñā)* how does he speak, walk, sit?"

Kṛṣṇa promises him no less; but first Arjuna must realize and transcend the muddy space he is trapped in. The important point to be made, however, is that a rationalization of in-action—or of whatever action man performs—is always an interpretation: radical and sufficient or insufficient and dogmatic of a man's orientation to life.

The Relation *Dharma-Karman.*

The first chapter of the *Gītā* places man in the midst of his own authentic reality: despair, anxiety, inaction.

The second chapter shows the ground on which man —Arjuna—stood all his life: the theoretic consciousness of his culture and the actions and roles he was determined to play and for which he was trained by the culture. Now that this ground is no longer under Arjuna's feet; he has lost it; it has moved from under him, what is Arjuna to do?

Chapter three makes the first move: what Arjuna must do is recover a *knowledge* he has forgotten, the kind of knowledge that created the culture in the first place, and the kind of knowledge that if sought diligently, will help Arjuna save himself and his circumstance: the knowledge of the sacrifice.

For clarification, however, we will first dwell on the relation *Dharma-Karman* as the root relation of Arjuna's path leading to the sacrifice and his freedom.

The first line of the *Gītā* identifies for us the problem, the human problem of Arjuna. The "field of the Kurus" and the "field of *dharma*" are the same: "*Dharmakṣetre kurukṣetre.*" In the field of the Kurus, in the field of *dharma,* the crisis of Arjuna unfolds. What is at stake in Arjuna's mind is not the battle alone, but his whole social and conceptual scheme, his whole life. He has literally no ground to stand on. The root of the word *Dharma, dhṛ,* means to support, sustain, hold together: i.e., *Dharma* is the general or particular context and structure which holds together certain objects with definite and determined programs of action: Thus we have *rājadharma* (duties to be performed by a king), *padārthadharma* (the ordering of natural elements), *samājadharma* (the ordering of norms of communities), *āśramadharma* (the ordering of people according to the god they follow in the Ṛg Veda or the class system), *sāmānyadharma* (the ordering of customs not covered by special *dharmas),* etc. There is also *mokṣadharma* (the *dharma* of liberation) at least according to Manu.

The important point to be made here is that human life—and this is all the Gītā is concerned with—is problematic, it rests on a continually recurring problem which can only be solved if a plan of action, a disciplined commitment is made which starts by revising the *dharmas,* the conceptual schemes which make up that concrete life. If man's actions and occupations which compose human life were produced mechanically, the result would not be human life. Automation does not live. At the heart of all movement lives the "knower of fields and *dharmas*";

> "by his power causing all beings to revolve as if they were mounted on a wheel."
>
> *(B.G. XVIII. 61)*

What constitutes, in the Gītā, the basic element of our—or

Arjuna's—creatureliness, our historical ground, is *karman:* "Karman is the creative force that causes creatures to exist (as creatures)." The word *Karman* is a noun meaning action, from the root *kṛ,* "doing, acting, performing." The significant point of the *Gītā,* however, is not so much to stress this obvious fact of man having to act, but rather the fact, as in Arjuna's case, that acting enslaves, if karmic acting brings along karmic thinking and its viewpoint on the world. Karmic thinking in this case consists in Arjuna or anyone thinking that he is the agent; that is, he deludes himself into thinking linearly by causally uniting action after action and ontologically linking them with himself. In this view action, self and body are unified ontologically; fear, anxiety, despair, agitation, in-action, follow. Negatively the *Gītā* says: "He who thinks himself the agent is wrong." There are five factors which are the causes of action and any way *Prakṛti* (and the *guṇas)* are bound to lead you to action. Under karmic law man has no other alternative but to act. This sounds like sheer determinism and it is; and although *Prakṛti* and the *guṇas* may explain the human fact that man, whatever his nature, *tamasic, rajasic* or *sattvic,* has to act, they also put man in the midst of his own existential anguish that he is determined to act, trapped in action. Add to this inescapable fact man's own decision to identify himself with his actions and you have the impossible *aporia,* problem, nonexit of Arjuna. His solution, obviously, is not in action but in viewing. The same way his crisis is not in acting but in the viewing it is grounded. The starting point of Arjuna's liberation is the understanding of *dharma.*

Kṛṣṇa addressing Arjuna reminds him that his conduct does not become him and Arjuna confesses plainly that he is confused about his *dharma,* and in typical karmic-value thinking asks the question (determined in the answer): "which is better, tell me, with certainty *(niścitaṁ),* (to fight or not to fight; he sees no other possible avenue of action)."

Identical confusion between *dharma* and *adharma* is mentioned in XVIII 31–32, with reference to the limitations of creatures within a social order. In II, 40 *dharma* refers to a concrete ordering of actions in one context and is described as *asya dharmasya* (even a little of this *dharma* saves one from great fear), and in IV, 7–8 *dharma* is used in the general sense, central to the *Gītā,* of that which holds (root *dhṛ)* together in a certain order the world, a concrete world.

The relation between *karman* and *dharma* is essential to understanding the *Gītā.* Kṛṣṇa's way in teaching Arjuna is to show him the relation and eventually become the knower of *dharma,* or *Kṣetra.* Thus Arjuna's resolution of his crisis in Chapter XIII. The sixteenth chapter of the *Gītā* says that people who hold a false philosophy, not knowing or becoming the *Kṣetra-jñanin,* destroy themselves by foolish indulgences and cruel deeds and would by these thoughtless actions turn the world to ruin. Teaching this philosophy, however, is not easy, not even for Kṛṣṇa, so instead of a direct answer Kṛṣṇa turns Arjuna inward into the discovery of how *dharma* functions in his own culture. All actions are action, and such actions are of such value, because they come so ordered in a concrete contextual structure of *dharma.* Looking at the actions alone, one is determined, knowing the *dharma* one is free. If we look directly at the *Gītā* we find that Arjuna's journey into his own culture from Chapters III through XIII especially is a journey of the relation between *karman-dharma,* action-context, with the added corollary that what will be known by both Arjuna and Kṛṣṇa at the end of the journey is *"ekāṃśena sthito jagat,"* a concrete world, empirically knowable, but only a fraction of many possibilities of manifestation.

Ahaṃkāra, Anahaṃvādī and the Grammatical "I"

Wittgenstein wrote in his *Logical Investigations:* "When we read this word "I" without knowing who wrote it, it is perhaps not meaningless, but is at least estranged from its normal meaning." In our approach to the *Gītā* we must avoid the sin of idolatry: idolatry of things, self, concepts, knowledge, God. This sin is induced in us through the idolatry of our own language. We are a literate and literal people, but the Gītā, Kṛṣṇa, etc., cannot be taken literally as we read them in the translations. They must be taken in their own linguistic context: Sanskrit. The greatest linguistic sin in the *Gītā* is the *ahaṃkāra,* literally the I maker. The most favored modality of seeing oneself in the world is the *anahaṃvādī,* literally not "I" speaking. To clarify this impasse would require more than a few remarks on the nature of language in general and of Sanskrit in particular. I cannot repeat here what I have already said somewhere else and I will only here point out some particular clues directly dealing with the *Gītā.*

The Sanskrit personal pronoun *aham* (I) functions to bring out an *artificial emphasis,* a contrived superimposition on an activity-whole which lacks otherwise identification.

Aham emphasizes the agent in an artificial way for the simple reason that the personal suffix to the verb alone suffices to specify the agent. The reason for the use of *aham* has been more concerned with the partial aspect of momentary interest, on the emphasis placed on individuation for the sake of clarification: *aham yaje* (it is *I* who sacrifices as opposed to *yaje* (I-sacrificing). Indian philosophy has made extensive use of what in Sanskrit is called *ahaṃkāra,* literally, 'the I maker.' It is understood as a principle of artificial individuation of any and all particulars. However, by using *aham* the speaker would be committed to a way of speaking which would "create the impression of" or "as if" the individual had an ultimate ontological identity with the activity-whole.

The *Bhagavad Gītā* portrays three basic types of agency in Chapter XVIII, verses 19–40, which can be explained in terms of these modalities: *ahaṃkāra* and *anahaṃvādī.*

Instrumental agency is paradigmatic of the "agent" of "light" *(sāttvikam)* who allows the cosmic ritual of *karma, saṃsāra,* and *dharma* to play itself out through his body:

> An action which is obligatory,
> Performed without attachment and without desire or
> hate by one undesirous of the fruit,
> That is said to be *sattvic.*
>
> *XVIII.23*

The *agent (kartṛ)* as used in this passage is clarified earlier as:

> Actions are engaged in by way of the *guṇas* of *prakṛti* alone;
> Yet he who is deluded by the sense of I *(ahaṃkāra)* thinks "I am the doer."
>
> *III.27*

Here the "agent" *(kartṛ)* in the instrumental case is on a par with the material instrument or means *(karaṇa)* by which the action is performed: the efficient cause is not to be distinguished from the material cause, for what matters is the activity or process itself.

Dative agency is paradigmatic of the "agent" of passion *(rājasam),* who is accordingly disparaged in Indian culture, for he continues ignorantly to bind himself to the wheel of *saṃsāra* and to accumulate *karma-phala* (fruits of action):

But action which is done in great strain
By one seeking to gratify his desires or by the sense of I,
Is said to be *rajasic*.

XVIII.24

Dative agency is also typical of the "agent" of ignorance and darkness *(tāmasam),* who is even worse off than the "agent" of passion, for he acts blindly, with no knowledge of *dharma* or how things "hang together":

That action which is undertaken out of delusion,
Without regard to consequences, or to loss and injury, or
to one's human capability,
Is called *tamasic*.

XVIII.25

Thus, if the individual subject was to be understood as material instrument by which the action was effected, he was expressed in the instrumental case. If he was to be understood as a partaker of the action and vitally interested in the outcome as to whether it might be of benefit or disadvantage to him, he was expressed in the dative case. The most highly favored modality of dwelling in the world is characterized by *anahaṃvādī* (not the "I" speaking).

These distinctions will clarify the fact that first person discourse is not so much a function of language, in its intending meaning, but rather a function of the intentionality of a historico-cultural background. In English, "I" names a person, a particular speaker, whose standpoint is irrevocably within a concrete historical situation and whose presence through self-mediation, is his own personal history. *Aham* has no personal history but rather has only the status of a superimposition on an activity-whole. Consequently, unlike "I," *aham* can never be identified internally with the utterance origin or with the agent of a speech act, or if done, it is only by mistake and ignorance *(avidyā)*.

HUMAN CRISIS AND HUMAN LIFE IN THE *GĪTĀ*

Not to lose sight of our Man and Circumstance theme, I would like at this point to paraphrase Ortega y Gasset in recapitulation of what we have made possible in this chapter for the understanding of our theme.

Human life, Eastern or Western, Arjuna's or the present interpreter's, is to have to deal with the world: a world. This, however, is not done in the abstract, but in the concrete situation of an individually felt vital need which fills man with the anxiety of life in a moment of crisis. This perception of anxiety is unique to the individual. The concepts, however, by which he thinks cannot be found ready made, but must be extracted from the circumstantial architecture of his world. If the concepts, however, by which man thinks his critical situation are less than or not capable of embodying the whole circumstantial architecture of a man's world, then man is condemned by the hand of his own limited and distorted vision to surrender to the fate of others, to be a slave of the circumstance, to human inaction: crisis

The occasion for Arjuna's crisis is the fact that he is in a battle situation. The crisis, however, is Arjuna's own identification of himself with his actions, unaware of the fact that this decision about this identification is not part of the battle, but on the contrary it is the willing reduction of Arjuna the warrior, the leader, to a vision of himself short of his tradition and his training and the one that reduces him to inaction. The battle, therefore, is not the fact at issue in Arjuna's crisis, but rather it is Arjuna's decision about himself in this battle situation which is at issue. His decision being none other than his own identification with his actions by taking unto himself literally the identity of the grammatical "I."

It would, therefore, be a grave misreading of the *Gītā* to make an issue of the abstract values for or against war. To take such an abstract stand would be to misread from the beginning the whole intentionality of the *Gītā*. Nor would it change the "message" of the *Gītā* the fact that Arjuna fights with chariots and arrows and we have thermonuclear weapons hanging over our heads. We are not dealing here in possible wars. We are dealing here in human possibilities. Arjuna *is* in a war, not a possible one. We are amongst decisions, not possible ones. What is at issue, of course, is how Arjuna or we decide to see ourselves in our critical situations. What makes a man falter, doubt, stop on his human path? What leads a man to despair, inaction, abandonment when faced with a determined crisis? What kind of man one makes himself to be in order to helplessly abandon himself to fate, chance, even despair?

If the individual—Arjuna in this case—is seriously

concerned with his problem, he will find the activity—truth—which will quiet the anxiety in his life. He will then develop a disciplined commitment—his morality—of carrying out this program of soothing his radical needs. When a "problem" is as vitally felt as Arjuna's, neither truth nor ethics are in any way *conformity* to already established norms of thought or behavior. For him, truth and ethics are the necessary acts and habits of a man in search of his own freedom. They are the habits and acts of a man in need to invent himself anew, to remake himself. His path is an affirmation of reason, historic reasons, against madness, irrationality and the inertia of conceptual imperialism. Kṛṣṇa's role is to restore Arjuna to a solid human ground along which he can step sure of his strides, without doubt and without faltering.

The difficulty of human life is that it is not given to anyone ready made. Like it or not, human life is an affair of instant decisions, one after another. At each moment it is necessary to make up one's mind about what we are going to do next. Human life thus becomes an instantly recurring problem. In order to decide what to do next, man is compelled to have to form a plan of what he is supposed to do, or merely resort to some plan someone else has made for us. It is not the case that man ought to make a plan. There is simply no possible life, sublime or mean, wise or stupid, which is not essentially characterized by its proceeding according to some plan. Read Chapters XVI, XVII and XVIII of the *Gītā* for example; even to abandon our life to chance, like Arjuna proposes to do in Chapter I, in a moment of crisis, is to make a plan. Every human being chooses out of the necessity of being human his way through life; which is tantamount to saying that as a man decides what he has to do in every situation, he is "obliged to justify it in his own eyes." This plan, or justification, however, implies that man has acquired some "idea" of the world, its objects and programs of action, and his own relation to them. In short, man lives by some conceptual scheme, historically rooted in its own actions, for which certain reasons are included for the self-justification of such a world. Thus man is forced to make a constant interpretation of the world around him or the worlds with which he comes into contact. Man is thus an interpreter, but his interpretation of himself and his world cannot be an arbitrary plan, not even a plan for oneself alone. Arjuna's plan is such a plan: too small; he reduces himself to a bag of skin which he rinses of self-inflicted pity under the pale sun of his grammatical "I." Arjuna's plan as a warrior should include the whole circumstance—contextual and structural—to be meaningful; but failing this he falls into crisis. How can he recover the ground upon which generations of warriors before him did not hesitate to fight and question? Arjuna and Kṛṣṇa interpret the culture in the *Gītā* from two different grounds: one is shaky, the other firm; for while Arjuna does not know how to go about it—he thinks only *karmically,* that is act after act, and linearly strings himself with them—Kṛṣṇa will show him to think *dharmically,* that is in contexts, chunks, which, at a glance, show at least the determined way the *karman* of the world and its view on the world enslaves man. This way of thinking will be the beginning of how man liberates himself.

Turning to the established fact that man is an interpreter, we must abandon the naive idea that facts exist by themselves, universally recognizable by anyone who cares to look. The fact is that no fact is a fact unless the structure and context which gave it birth are discovered simultaneously with the fact. Facts are facts because they come in a web of conceptual structures. There is *karman* because there are *dharmas* linking them in a certain order. Facts are like the figures of a hieroglyphic writing. Any fact, a man, even this book, are such hieroglyphics. Their reality, their existence, their meaning lies behind and is hidden by them. In order to arrive at their meaning, we must not fix our attention on them, nor take them for their literal reality; on the contrary, we will have to interpret them, and this means that in order to arrive at their true meaning, we must search for something different, very different from the aspect which their presence offers. What we see of these facts is not their life, but on the contrary a portion of our own. Hence, in order to know another life which is not ours, we must try to see it not from within ourselves but from the circumstantial world of the facts living that life.

In the case of the *Gītā* we have at least three lives—three interpretations—who fulfill this condition and challenge: Arjuna, Kṛṣṇa, and the writer of the poem. Arjuna and Kṛṣṇa speak for themselves. The composer of the poem—whoever he may be—provides us with the challenge of figuring out the presuppositions—historical, contextual and structural—on which he bases his poem.

Let us draw some conclusions: Human life is such because it has a contextual structure which organizes experience in a certain definite sense: that is, according to some self (or culturally) justifiable reasons: that is to say, it consists in man having to cope with a predetermined world *(karmic laws)* of which he can sketch the profile *(dharmic laws)* and thus recreate himself.

History, then, is not the discovery of sheer, disconnected empirical facts; as Ortega puts it, like the wall of a handball court, against which hit the fortuitous balls of an extrinsic destiny which we record, but rather it is the refashioning of a certain historical and reasonable contextual-structure of that eternal drama between man and his worlds.

The true historical search, therefore, cannot be anything other than the search for the contextual structures of human life, which make human life possible, meaningful and different for different people, and which would make different people, with different contextual structures, alive in an intercultural, planetary or democratic world.

Man is understood thus as the context maker and context knower; and culture as the institutionalization of sets of contexts and the possibility of their recovery.

Philosophy—as it comes out in the *Gītā*—is not so much the objective knowledge of those contexts and structures but the activity which would make the *possession* of those structures possible so that man increases his freedom—by shaking the determinism of single context-structures or *karmic* laws—and becomes fully human by embodying—conceptually and empirically—the human condition up to his time, as is the case of Kṛṣṇa.

The problem, however, remains with us for we still have Arjuna in the midst of his crisis. What does he need to know in order to be free, to exit from the circle of his thin and shadowy grammatical "I"? The question Arjuna and we must face is the question of knowledge. What do we need to know to get out of the crisis? But again is there any one knowledge to be known which is capable of setting man free? For if there is no knowledge which can set us free, then we are condemned to despair; but if there is one single knowledge capable of setting us free, then we are condemned to be gods. In both cases we would run the risk of shrugging our shoulders and crying: "to hell with the world!" What knowledge, therefore, does a man need to remain being a man, unafraid to balance the despair of being a man with the wonder of being a man? What knowledge is necessary and sufficient to save the human circumstance?

Let us phrase the question in a radical and rigorous philophical way. Philosophical theories about man/woman are philosophically interesting not only if within the domain of their claims—man/woman—they are *verifiable,* but above all if within those same domains they are not *falsifiable.* That human theories about man/woman are verifiable is almost a triviality. Practically every theory about man/woman has or can find empirical verification. The natural sciences, history, sociology and in particular psychology are exponents of such universal verification. Besides, theories about man/woman have man/woman as constant accomplices. Theories about man/woman have a rather rapid way of becoming human flesh. But all these theories have hardly ever been put to the test of falsification, even when man/woman has found his/her self ejecting those theories from their own human flesh by falling again and again into a total human crisis. Human crisis is the mediating ground of such theoretical falsification, only that it has not yet been understood as such. For a human crisis is the absolute rejection and falsification of any and all human theories about the man/woman *in* crisis. Human crisis is not crisis about one or several ideas or theories about humans. It is the absolute rejection of any identification with a total theory about humans. But if identification leads inexorably to crisis, then what is the human alternative?

The suggested way of the Gītā is that man does not need to carry *with him* the knowledge of his identifications. What man—Arjuna—can do instead is to discover the knowledge and controls of every situation as he encounters it. What man can do instead is to squeeze out of the flesh of historic man the knowledge that that flesh, to be human flesh, carries in it, and in this discovery remake himself constantly.

The first step in this journey, therefore, will be for the Gītā to question the knowledge itself of Arjuna's crisis and all the knowledge of his culture so that he may be able to run its paths from beginning to end in every situation.

Context: The Problem of Knowledge

Chapter Five

Know me, O Bhārata, to be the knower of the field in all fields;
The knowledge of the field and of the knower of the field:
This I hold to be (real) knowledge.

B.G. XIII. 2.

INTRODUCTION

Man may write many books, compose many poems, create masterpieces of art or even civilizations, but eventually he will have to face the reality of man himself. It takes a human crisis, according to the *Gītā,* to set man on the path of his self-search and self-constitution. Man may choose, however, to fall into despair. In either case, or choice, a self-constitution is implied. Man is the creator of his own decisions, and his decisions are a function of his own self-orientation.

Human crisis is bound with possibilities; despair with inertia. The first may lead man to a radical reorientation of his life, the latter to a surrender to others, behavior-control and even the "age of therapy." Our main concern in this book is the reorientation of man by man himself: the saving of the human circumstance. We are only concerned with the kind of knowledge that is radical to a man's life; the kind of activity that is capable of making this radical knowledge transparent to itself. This is the concern we have in mind when talking about emancipation. This is the program of emancipation. This program of emancipation, however, requires that we not only acknowledge crisis as an element of man's life, but that we uncover its presuppositions so that man's emancipation may be made possible.

Taking our clues from the *Gītā,* we find that Arjuna's crisis is his *present* fed by a habit of the *past.* In this sense it is rather the theoretical *past* substituting for the *present.* Insofar as this hybrid present is in need of a resolution, it is also Arjuna's *future.* The past and the future as embodied by Arjuna and Kṛṣṇa are both mediated through knowledge and their radical orientation or origin. In Arjuna's case this knowledge is bound by a reflective consciousness which absolutizes Arjuna, knowledge, and society to the fixed space of a reflective and perspectival consciousness limited by its own decision that it be so. Arjuna, of course, is unaware of what he is doing in this moment of crisis, not only in relation to his reflective consciousness, but also in relation to the identification of his self with the actions and objects within this reduced space of reflection.

Simultaneous with Arjuna's form of knowledge there is Kṛṣṇa's: a knowledge which not only includes reflection but it is a form of reflection which is fed by the multiplicity of social "regional ontologies" and their perspectives as they surround both Kṛṣṇa and Arjuna. It is, moreover, a knowledge intentionally directed towards the recovery of its own original grounding orientation, the absolute present. The "other" becomes for Kṛṣṇa's way of knowledge the possibilities of its own emancipation and radical constitution. This is the kind of knowledge a whole social fabric has been "counting on" in order to live in innovation and continuity. Arjuna's and Kṛṣṇa's consciousnesses, plus their radical original orientation, form the necessary and sufficient conditions for the culture—the *Gītā*—to be. All three have to be accounted for. Any one of them absolutized would be no culture at all, at least not the culture of the *Gītā;* but the integration of multiple perspectives and their ground is not possible if, ultimately, knowledge is not mediated through a radical sacrifice of perspectives. It is through this sacrifice that human knowing as an embodied vision of man's actual body may be opened up; that the multiplicity of actual human empirical spaces for man's interaction and communication may be made possible; and that the originating a-perspectival ground which made possible the subsequent multiplicity may be recovered.

Arjuna's crisis and despair can be read from Chapters I and XI of the *Gītā*. Kṛṣṇa's resolution of this crisis, his own dependence on Arjuna and their simultaneous moves can be seen through Chapters II to X and XII to XVIII. Chapter XI will appear in the *Gītā* as the absolute present mediating and grounding the moves of the past and the future, Arjuna's and Kṛṣṇa's.

The saving of the human circumstance—I am I and my circumstance—is not possible if "circumstance" is reduced to an identification of one's self with the grammatical "I" and its subsequent philosophical, psychological and social appropriations and self-serving interests, as we saw in Chapter Four of this book. The decision that it be so is what leads a man—Arjuna in the battlefield—not to emancipation but crisis. This decision about identification, however, is a decision about what Arjuna decides he needs to know. It is a decision about knowledge. Human life is at its root a theory of itself.

The first steps taken by Kṛṣṇa in leading Arjuna from his shaky but fixed space of crisis to a multiplicity of spaces of liberation is to move Arjuna through a multiplicity of ontological spaces different from, and contrary to, Arjuna's decision that a man's ground is fixed and unmovable. Man's ground, it will appear, is a plurality of interpretative grounds, interpretative spaces within which man—cultural man—moves of necessity in order to live a human life, a social life, each one embedded in a radical theory or perspective of itself.

In order to understand, however, Kṛṣṇa's moves in the *Gītā,* we will first have to become aware of the fact that in our own interpretation of the *Gītā* we are also caught in a similar position to Arjuna's—an interpretative fixed space—in relation to knowledge. We all believe that in order to understand the *Bhagavad Gītā* we will necessarily and sufficiently have to know exactly the kind of knowledge the *Gītā* identifies with, so that when we finish our work, we and others will be able to claim a definite, particular and knowable knowledge about the *Gītā*. Even when we explicitly do not make these specific claims, our particular kind of interpretation will demand, with its presuppositions, that reader and author join in doing so.

Our thesis in this book is precisely a large note of caution to such positions, and therefore to Arjuna's initial crisis position. Our thesis about knowledge, and the knowledge of and in the *Gītā,* is that identification of interpretation with any particular kind of knowledge is contrary to the *Gītā* and leads both the author and the reader not into the liberating moves and human spaces of the *Gītā* but into the spaces the author and reader bring along with them as already known and fixed. These fixed spaces of interpretation will of necessity lead author and reader to the brink of crisis and perpetuation of ignorance in relation to the text of the *Gītā*.

In order to make this thesis clear and follow systematically Kṛṣṇa's and Arjuna's path, we will proceed in this chapter through the following strategic points:

- The perils of Idolatry: We should first recognize the ideas of knowledge of Western philosophy so that we do not reduce the *Gītā* to them. We should also proceed thus to create the conditions, necessary and sufficient, so that the *Gītā's* understanding of knowledge may appear.
- The multiplicities of knowledge in the *Gītā:* Yoga, Sāṃkhya, Vedānta, Bhakti, etc.
- The sacrifice of perspectives as the necessary and sufficient condition for transcending knowledge into Embodied-Vision: a knowledge which is unidentifiable and socially efficient.
- A summary of these moves through Faith, Knowledge and Action will conclude these points in preparation for the next chapter on Structure in the *Bhagavad Gītā*.

THE PERILS OF IDOLATRY.

The theme of Man and Circumstance has compelled us again and again to reflect on our philosophical past insofar as it determines our present and future possibilities. This statement, however, could be misleading in at least two senses. It might appear that our past is recoverable, if we care to look at it, as a thing of the past: a chunk of past history, i.e., a fixed understanding of history being thus the space within which we try to capture the *Gītā*. Or it might also be the case that we look at the past to see not our decisions, but our bad decisions and learn from our bad judgments to form a better future; again our fixed historical space remains unchallenged. We mean neither of these two possibilities. For clarity's sake we will retrace here our strategic points:

- We are interested in the *present,* all the *presents* that surround us: our circumstance.
- These multiple presents—"the others"—which surround us and through which we have to save ourselves with them, or through them, come to us, or we discover them, insofar as we are able to communicate with them through language and act in them through the work of our interpretation.
- Language and work—our philosophical radical action—would be ineffective if our action and communication did not recreate for us the conditions of possibility which make those multiple and discreet *presents* not only actual for themselves but also for us as actualized present human possibilities.
- In this sense our task is not only the critical activity of discovering the conditions of possibility of the past as past, but insofar as the past constitutes the present, i.e., as the possible multitude of actual *presents* in our experience, though most often not recognized.
- Though we must face the problem of knowledge, which to a certain extent mediates man's radical, or at least possibly radical, constitution and orientation, we must start by realizing that no *theory of knowledge* can simply remain a theory, but that every theory of knowledge implies simultaneously a practice of society, of the means of knowledge and of man.
- Our method or path is neither idealistic, nor a theory of theories of knowledge under the guise of critical philosophy, nor hermeneutically a vicious circle. Our inquiry starts and ends in the present vital needs of a social world surrounding us which demands that it be saved from objective illusions, including the objective illusion of *one* society, *one* knowledge, *one* god, *one* revelation, *one* consciousness, *one* human space devoured by an irreversible logical time.
- Our immediate starting point, therefore, since we are interpreting the *Bhagavad Gītā,* is to radically focus on the activity itself of interpretation as exercised in the text of the *Gītā.* By focusing on this activity, through its communicative intention, we might be able to face squarely the problem of knowledge as either binding to

objective illusions or liberating man by making his human and present possibilities actual.

Regardless of what philosophers think about the difficulty of knowing other cultures (see Chapter Two of this book), the fact is that there are books and people who have ventured into them, interpreting them. Many of them are scholars who knowingly or unknowingly through their own activity and communication of interpreting have demanded from us that we conform to a certain idea about the *Bhagavad Gītā*. If we are even remotely correct in our epistemological claims or criticisms, then what has been offered as interpretations of the *Bhagavad Gītā* borders very closely on the verge of idolatry. Apparently Western man, and also scholars interpreting the East, cannot interpret themselves or others without falling in the trap of idolatry, or, as we saw Arjuna do in the previous chapter, identity. Identity of self—atomic words—and identity of knowledge—grounding of action on a definite idea of knowledge and its reflective consciousness—seem to be the radical malaise of Western interpreting. Identity of any kind, in human terms, leads only to crisis, and philosophically it leads to hiding the conditions of possibility and meaning covered by the mask of identity. In positive terms we can say that identity can only be performed on man, when he is reduced, or reduces himself, to an "idea." But as Karl Marx said: "The 'Idea' always disgraces itself." For the "idea" is always an exercise in ideological coercion by demanding that man lose his embodied actual temporality for a possible logical substitute. Sooner or later the idols tumble and leave man empty and lost again. When ideological identity is carried to dictatorial and imperialistic limits; that is, it is turned into raw power, then we have social coercion—conformity to a social space within logical moves—and the demand for massive idolatry: a self, a god, a knowledge, a State. Leading, disembodied ideas are such and so feeble, so lost in their own anaemic fleshless condition that they cannot gain comprehension unless they rely for their subsistence on the uncritical approval and acceptance of the masses through massive coercion, and so the "idea" always disgraces itself, for no matter how beautiful the "idea" is, it is always a crypto ideology which if turned to action is contradictory of itself: the idea is dead, man's acting is throbbing with the vibrations of a sensuous world, always present, changing, reborn, latent. By turning any particular kind of interpretation into an idea, an identifiable, leading idea, we have as a result not knowledge but an "idea" of knowledge, divorced from the real, human, rational ground from which it originated. An idea of knowledge, however, is not knowledge, but rather the demand that it be. This demand makes objects and slaves, but not humans.

Our contemporary methods, scientific and humanistic, which are also used in interpreting the *Gītā,* are essentially of three types: empirical–analytic (natural sciences); historico–hermeneutic (humanistic sciences); and critico–philosophical (meta-sciences). All these sciences conceive themselves as free from dogmatic positions and subjective interests: they guarantee absolute and reliable knowledge.

The natural sciences are exemplified by positivism with its demand and idolatry of facts. The hermeneutic sciences are exemplified by historicism, religious ideology and the idolatry of facts–ideas. The meta-sciences are exemplified by critical philosophy. These three groups of interpreters radically presuppose the continuity, homogeneity and fixity of a particular logical space-time matrix for the mediation of their claims as regards knowledge, with or without critical reflection. It is clear that interpretations of the *Bhagavad Gītā* through linguistics or comparative religions are a combination of positivism and hermeneutics, within the fixed matrix provided by historicism. Insofar, therefore, as these methods are used in approaching and interpreting the *Bhagavad Gītā,* a few critical remarks are in order.

We have repeated earlier that the knowledge we know most of, the knowledge of the sciences, is concrete, identifiable and reliable: explanation, prediction and the implied possibilities of the control of phenomena. These conditions are what make possible and give meaning to the particular kind of knowledge the sciences provide. On the other hand, the "knowledge" of life is neither concrete nor identifiable with any one kind of knowledge nor with a general kind of knowledge about knowledge, without running the risk of dogmatism, lunacy or idolatry.

Positivism is not interested in the conditions and meaning of knowledge. By virtue of the incarnate fact of modern science, this question has become superfluous for it. Scientific theory, which takes the place of the theory of knowledge, has the prohibitive function of shielding research from the self-reflection of the theory of knowledge. It is philosophical only for the single moment which is necessary to exorcize philosophy from science.

The historico–hermeneutic sciences, on the other hand, orient themselves in another system of relationships. Instead of experiments, they utilize "sensible understanding" to arrive at facts. The interpreter "feels his way in"; he situates himself within the horizon of the world or of the language towards which a received text draws his attention at the time, but here too the facts are not constituted independently of the standards by which they are ascertained. Just as the relationship between measuring experiments and controlling success is always mediated through hermeneutic knowledge in the empirical–analytic sciences, so in the hermeneutic sciences the interpreter's foreknowledge which clings to the original situation is concealed. For the interpreter understands his text only to the degree that his own world opens him to it at the same time. He establishes communication between this world and that handed down through the text. He grasps the content of what is handed down in that he applies the tradition to himself and to his situation. Hermeneutic research links in a specific way explanation and application, but to say this comes close to the conclusion that it reveals *reality* to be among the leading ideas in testing and expanding inter-subjective, i.e., in reaching a consensus *within* the framework which deals with a communication handed down from a tradition. The historico-hermeneutic sciences, however, neither formed the concept of knowledge as a human constitutive need nor grasped what it implies. This would have been possible only in a conceptual framework which was foreign to its own method and attainable only within the concept of a history of the human species conceived as a process of self-formation and self-revelation and not as an anthology of ideas.

We have to approach the *Gītā,* however, with the three forms of knowledge mentioned above and satisfy their necessary condition, for this is the present ground on which we stand as interpreters. We must be aware, however, that in our quest for the *Gītā* we are trying to restore missing parts of the self-formation process of Western man through Hindu man. We are, therefore, forced into a process of self-reflection through which we ought to be able to emancipate ourselves from the existing control systems in those sciences as demanding that their method is sufficient for our present self-formation. Insofar as our interpretation is able to link our *present* need as a repressed dimension of our own historical self-formation and is able to fit all available facts, then we may be emancipated. It is in this reflective recognition of interpretative control systems and interpretative biased orientations, that men can reenter the spaces of self-constitution and radical orientation, and it is in this double awareness of our present ground and absent possibilities that our concrete action and interaction with the *Gītā* is undertaken. Since, however, any action is of necessity a social projection, i.e., it overtly makes claims about society and implies a certain idea of society, we consider it essential to ground our understanding to make a few critical remarks on this monolithic and vague concept, chanted by all, presupposed by all, claimed by all, called society. Since this is a large project, however, and it would disturb the flow of our narrative, we refer the reader to Appendix II where these critical points are made.

KNOWLEDGE IN THE BHAGAVAD GĪTĀ.

It is not the case that the world divides or multiplies by two, but it is the case that the world, any one of man's manifold worlds, must be first constituted in order to divide and multiply by two. This constitutive act is one, indivisible, unidentifiable, yet unless it is recovered, divisions and multiplications are meaningless. This, to say the least, will sound confusing to most. It does not appear to be either a neat or a simple idea. It could also appear frightening to some if they realize the many possibilities open to man through that statement. Man would have to shake the lethargy of ages and act, and that would be frightening. People prefer to believe in one world-out-there with two ways: the good and the bad. This is very comforting, one does not have to do much and it looks very tidy. People have even canonized those who save man from his own effort to be human and praised them for making man surrender to the wisdom of the simple choice: the good and the bad. The bad is common and low, the good is for the chosen and superior. The *Bhagavad Gītā* has suffered this oversimplification of wisdom at the expense of truth—the activity of man enacting his own possibilities. Kṛṣṇa and

Arjuna have been taken as the prototype of the two paths built on the "given" ethical world of the *Gītā*. This approach, however its simplicity and tidiness, forgets to create the world of the *Gītā* in the first place so that the divisions and multiplications by two which appear later are possible.

It is true that the whole *Gītā* divides and multiplies by two: Kṛṣṇa and Arjuna, the two armies, *Puruṣa* and *Prakṛti,* manifest and unmanifest, etc., but it is also true that the *Gītā* is grounded on a Unity which is not divisible, identifiable, destructible or can be appropriated by either Kṛṣṇa or Arjuna or any other side of the multiplications or divisions. This Original Generator is neither the world nor God, neither Kṛṣṇa nor Arjuna, but rather it is the radical orientation of a world which, by becoming aware of itself in a moment of crisis, divides and multiplies by two. Unless this Original Generator is recovered—this original orientation of the *Gītā*—even though unidentifiable, the *Bhagavad Gītā* will be a trivial document in our hands. Furthermore, unless the constitutive intentionality of the *Gītā* is precisely to recover this Original and radical orientation, our interpretation of the *Bhagavad Gītā* would be superfluous.

We will examine in this chapter the *Gītā*'s radical orientation about knowledge. We shall point out in the next chapter the structures that make this orientation possible. The strategy we shall follow in relation to knowledge is to attend not so much to what the *Gītā* says about knowledge but what it does. We shall consider Kṛṣṇa's and Arjuna's positions in the *Gītā* as two positions about knowledge: Arjuna's position as a position through identifications, while Kṛṣṇa's position as a position without identifications. We shall pay special attention to Kṛṣṇa's journey—what he does—through the different ontological and ontic positions of the culture to gain the Original or radical ground that oriented the culture in the first place. Chapters XI, XII, and XIII of the *Gītā* will be the mediating chapters where man's despair and man's possibilities, knowledge and faith, time and eternity are reconciled through the original and radical orientation of the *Gītā*. This reconciliation, however, will be to many wise people, committed to simple and tidy ideas, profane. We claim our profanity to be the *Gītā*'s profanity where man's orientation or radical desire about his orientation is saved but where there are no victors and vanquished, no saviours and sinners. Ours is not a value-laden conclusion but a theory-laden conclusion. A conclusion which is no more than a mere beginning for the reader to take his own human steps—like Arjuna at the end of the *Gītā*—through the present circumstance. Our drama is more dramatic than a victory of good over evil. It is the drama of man reconstructing himself through a society unified at its roots about knowledge but divided and multiplied by two in its actualization in man as he is filled with the anxiety of his life.

Arjuna's Position About Knowledge

Arjuna's position about knowledge we have defined as a knowledge through appropriation and identification. This same position of Arjuna about knowledge is shared by his enemies and, in general, by those who ground the interpretation of their actions on *manas* (mind) and delude themselves through the linguistic *ahaṃkāra* (I-maker or linguistic I).

In the midst of the anxiety of life which leads Arjuna to despair and inaction, the question of knowledge arises in his mind as the last hope, just as a beacon of light from a lighthouse makes a wrecking ship, lost in the storm and darkness, hope that he may be able to reach the shore.

Arjuna realizes in the midst of his impotence that his crisis is about knowledge, "why is it not wise for us, O Janārdana (Kṛṣṇa)." Arjuna realizes so vividly that his crisis lies in his position about knowledge that he is ready to give up victory, pleasures, his kingdom, and even his own life for the sake of the knowledge that will take him away from his crisis.

Arjuna, of course, is completely lost as to the meaning of *dharma,* and he is lost because for him *dharma* is as much an object of appropriation and identification with himself as is the battle, his friends, relatives and the outcome of the battle. Simultaneously Arjuna talks of another kind of knowledge which does not identify itself with the field, the objects of the field, wealth and victory. As Kṛṣṇa points out, Arjuna is talking through his head about this other kind of knowledge, for talk is not sufficient while he is still grieving for things and selves which are such things and selves and grief because Arjuna appropriates them to himself through self-identification.

Arjuna shares with his enemies the same theory of knowledge he blames them for. Like them, i.e., the Kauravas, he does not see how things hang together on account of the greed of his mind for his own way of knowing. Like them, he does not give up this delusion and the desire born of this attachment. Attachment, fear, anger and hatred are all born of desire which is ontologically linked to a theory of knowledge which can only function through self-identification and appropriation. Both Arjuna and his enemies are ignorant of the fact that desire or *kāma* ontologically links man to the dualities, *dvandvas:* cold and heat, pleasure and pain, happiness and grief, knowledge and ignorance, good and evil, and this they presuppose to be the knowledge of how things really are. The *Gītā,* however, points out that this position is deluded since it is a knowledge covered by ignorance *(ajñānena),* and in general it functions by believing—ontological identity—that he (Arjuna) is the doer of the action. In contrast, knowledge according to the *Gītā* should produce even-mindedness in pain and pleasure, in honor and dishonor, in blame and praise, equal to friends and foes and in general a man without doubt and of firm judgment.

For Arjuna as much as for his enemies, the world is grounded on an absolutized polarity made possible through identification, and the justification of this identification through both the *ahaṃkāra* and *manas*. We have seen in Chapter Four of this book the workings of the *ahaṃkāra*. The appropriation of action through *ahaṃkāra* would be impossible if the *ahaṃkāra* was not grounded on *manas* interpretation of sensation. Through the *manas* the three *guṇas* are given a hierarchical value and thus not accepted when present or absolutized as goals of life. Actions themselves are given an absolute and intrinsic value, and the possibility of emancipation through the *buddhi* becomes obscured and divided.

The clues we are suggesting bring out not only the confirmation of the sayings of the *Gītā* but also the presuppositions on which those sayings are grounded. What Arjuna and his enemies are really doing is to presuppose a world or society in whose creation they have nothing to do. They are unaware that they have decided this to be the situation made possible by their decision about their theory of knowledge. This theory of knowledge, by taking the origin of the world for granted, does not recreate the world but becomes the victim of an interpretation of the world which they suffer or enjoy through the *ahaṃkāra* and *manas*. This is absolutized world made so in its uniqueness and simplicity by fixing it in a unique time and space. The incompleteness and futility of this theory of knowledge will appear more clearly when viewed from Kṛṣṇa's theory of knowledge, but for our purpose at this time it will suffice, to show its finality, to quote the dissolution and despair of this world in Chapter XI of the *Gītā,* verses 23–30.

> Having seen your great form, with many mouths and
> eyes, O Strong-Armed,
> With many arms and thighs and feet,
> With many bellies and terrible tusks,
> The worlds tremble, and so do I.
>
> Having seen you touching the sky, blazing and
> many-colored,
> With mouths open and huge eyes glowing,
> My inmost self trembles,
> I find no firmness or peace, O Viṣṇu.
>
> Having seen your mouths tremble with tusks
> Like the devouring flames of time,
> I know not the directions of the sky and I find no refuge.
> Be gracious, O Lord of Gods, Abode of the World.
>
> And those sons of Dhṛtarāṣtra, all of them,
> Together with the hosts of kings,
> And likewise Bhīṣma, Droṇa, and also Karṇa,
> Together with our chief warriors also:
>
> They are all rushing to enter your mouths of dreadful
> tusks;
> Some of them are seen caught between your teeth,
> Their heads crushed.
>
> As the many currents of rivers run towards the ocean,
> So those heroes in the world of men enter your flaming
> mouths.
> Just as moths with great speed
> Enter into the flaming fire and perish there,
> So also these creatures with great speed
> Enter your mouths to meet destruction.
>
> You lick up and devour with flaming mouths entire
> worlds from every side;
> Your terrible light-rays fill the entire world with
> radiance and scorch it, O Viṣṇu.

Arjuna's salvation or emancipation, of course, lies in realizing that this knowledge grounding his crisis is not sufficient and that there must be a better way *(śreye)* to resolve his crisis. Since he is unable to see, he decides to question himself through Kṛṣṇa.

Kṛṣṇa's Position About Knowledge.

Kṛṣṇa's position about knowledge will be shown through correcting Arjuna's absolutized position. Kṛṣṇa's position may be summarized as a gradual emancipation of coercive absolutisms made possible through *smṛti* (remembrance or mindfulness), *samādhi* (concentration), *ceṣṭā* (effort), *śraddhā* (faith), and *jñāna* or *prajñā* (knowledge-wisdom). Contrary to Arjuna's grounding of his theory of knowledge on the *ahaṃkāra* and *manas,* Kṛṣṇa's position about knowledge will be mediated through the *anahaṃvādī* and the *buddhi*-interpretation.

Kṛṣṇa starts by telling Arjuna that this knowledge he is going to impart on him is the knowledge of the wise *(paṇḍitāh)* in his tradition. He further affirms that the knowledge of this tradition is a knowledge grounded on an immutable, indestructible and eternal self. A knowledge which frees one from grief, transcends the dualities, conveys on the man determined purpose *(dhīram),* the ability to treat the dualities of experience as the same *(sama)* and emancipates man even from death (shares in non-death, *amṛtatva*). Kṛṣṇa repeatedly makes the point that without his kind of knowledge emancipation is not possible. This kind of knowledge is made amply clear to be a knowledge which is disinterested, unattached or unidentifiable with any action whatsoever *(niṣkāma-karma),* unattached to anything whatsoever.

Kṛṣṇa starts his journey of emancipation by helping Arjuna to recover his lost memories: that those who are moved by the passing dualities of life, do not really perceive the truth about the undying self who neither kills nor is killed. The entire subsequent discussion about *vināśī* and *avināśī,* perishable and imperishable; *kṣara* and *akṣara,* destructible and indestructible; and *kṣetra* and *kṣetrajñanin,* field and the knower of the field, pertains to the disciplined journey to be undertaken by the one in search of knowledge, and it is said to be realized by the wise contemplative seers of Reality, the persevering yogins. It is claimed to be a more comprehensive knowledge which "the deluded ones *(vimūdhāḥ)* do not see, and (only) those who have the eye of wisdom *(jñānacakṣuṣaḥ)* see." Words like *'mūḍha,' 'vimūḍha'* or *'saṃmūḍha'* are used for those whose knowledge is confined to Arjuna's reduced space and who are ignorant of the culture's wisdom. The knowledge the Bhagavad Gītā talks about is that which having been known, nothing else is left to be known.

This knowledge, of which Kṛṣṇa is the prototype, seems to be of such a nature that it may take one by surprise. "Some take this for a marvel," "it is a most secret knowledge," and "more secret than all secrets," suggests not only the same idea, but unless one decides to take this as mystic rhetoric, it would also be clear that included in Kṛṣṇa's affirmations about knowledge there is also a path which requires that we check carefully what Kṛṣṇa does and uncover his way of bringing about this kind of knowledge.

Self, Knowledge and Society in the Gītā

In order to follow what Kṛṣṇa does in the *Gītā,* we must first bear in mind that non-identifiable action *(karma-yoga)* is only possible:

- if the original orientation of the culture about knowledge is recovered;
- if this original orientation is made possible through a theory of knowledge which both corrects Arjuna's position and embodies the knowledges of the society *(jñāna-karma-samucca-yavāda)* by going through them, thus embodying them; and
- if the result of this journey brings the traveller to the original ground where he feels at home, without questions and doubts, for he himself has *become* the ground.

Since it is obvious that the confusion lies in the different ontological positions about the self taken by Arjuna and Kṛṣṇa, our first step will be to clarify the Self as ground. The fact that the grammatical subject *(ahaṃkāra,* I or self) is ontologically linked with the action is deeply rooted not only in our linguistic modes of expression but like a magic spell bewitches us into believing that this is in fact how the world is: we commit ourselves metaphysically and epistemologically to a world so constituted. This, however, not really being the case, the self in this world is in constant change, opposition, and grief, identifying himself with every act and object in the false hope that one of them will radicalize man's desire on some eternal satisfaction. Instead, lost in this karmic view of the world and unaware of this condition determined by his choice of view, all man does is accumulate more time for his karmic wanderings.

This being the general condition of man—a condition through which he must of necessity go from time to time—the *Gītā's* programmatic journey of emancipation can only have meaning if it is possible for all men, if it is a goal to be achieved "in this very life," if it is "for the welfare of all creatures," and if the path of emancipation is possible through the same knowledge which binds man: "Therefore, having cut out with your self's own sword of knowledge this doubt in your heart which is born of ignorance, get into *yoga* and raise yourself up, O Bhārata." For "nowhere in this world is there to be found a purifier like knowledge," as long as knowledge remains undivided amidst the multiplicity . . . since varieties are only in kind and not universal but only contextual, i.e., what will be known by both Arjuna and Kṛṣṇa at the end of the journey is *"ekāṃśena sthito jagat,"* a concrete world, empirically knowable, but only a fraction of many possibilities of manifestation.

When man transcends or emancipates his self from the coercion of his own decision to live through the precarious dependence on self-appropriation and self-identification, what emerges is the backdrop: the Self as radical orientation, the so-called not-I-making *(nirahaṃkāra),* the *anahaṃvādī,* not-I-speaking. This is the radical ground on which all beings stand. It is the ground which makes possible both its own unity and the multiplicity, "undivided, yet standing as if divided among beings." "As the omnipresent ether is not defiled because of its subtleness, so the self, abiding in every body, is not affected." It is in seeing this simultaneous presence of the generator and the generated that man's emancipation lies; "when he sees the various states of beings abiding in the One and retracting out from it, then he attains Brahman." This *seeing* is the result of a great effort, a dedicated activity; the result of an ontological and ontic detachment: the kind of seeing Saṃjaya, narrator of the *Gītā,* had to have in order to tell the events of the war and dialogue between Kṛṣṇa and Arjuna; the kind of "divine eye" *(divya cakṣu),* Arjuna had to have to see Kṛṣṇa's cosmic form, and in general the "eye of wisdom" *(jñāna cakṣu)* which comes to those in the culture who share Kṛṣṇa's radical orientation.

The *Bhagavad Gītā* declares that the Self as the eternal and immutable and unidentifiable reality is definitely there orienting the whole culture, though too subtle to be discerned, without beginning or qualities. The yogins, by striving, see him also abiding in their self, and the deluded do not perceive It. To distinguish it from the identifiable self, the *Gītā* has to use negative terms, and express thus its incomprehensible, unknowable *(avijñeya),* unthinkable, and undefinable condition. It is in the light of this conception of the Self as the original orientation and the executive or decision-making orientation in action that both delusion and emancipation are possible, "He who is deluded by the sense of I thinks 'I am the doer'," but "he who is free from the sense of I, whose understanding is not tainted, though he slay these people, he slays not nor is he bound," for "both he who considers this to be slayer and he who considers this to be slain, fail to understand: this neither slays nor is slain." It is this Self which is said to be unborn, eternal, everlasting and ancient, the supreme reality, the Generator of the entire culture, on whose knowledge or ignorance lies the reason of both bondage and emancipation. Whether we want to recognize it or not, it is the necessary condition always present, both inside and outside of all beings. Thus "it neither acts nor is tainted, even though embodied." It is the heuristic goal, the radical orientation, which attends through unidentified action "to no less than the holding together of the world."

In trying to trace the Self as a radical orientation about knowledge in the *Gītā,* one has only to read the Upaniṣadic version of the same orientation. The Upaniṣads speak of the Self negatively *(neti neti),* paradoxically, and analogically; it reconciles all contradictions, and transcends all opposites. It is said to go beyond thought and speech, and that silence alone is its adequate expression. This indescribable and unidentifiable Self *(ātman)* is called Reality itself, Brahman.

To prepare the reader to understand the systematic action which the *Gītā* itself develops to lead man—Arjuna—from bondage to emancipation, we will summarize here a selection of texts to prepare this understanding.

The Self I *Count On,* the Executive I, Home:

The man, however, who can be delighted in his self
alone,

Who is pleased with the self and content only with the self,
For him there is no work to be done.

He has no interest in this world
To gain by what is done or by what is not done.
He is not dependent on any of these beings for any advantage.

Self, Action and Society:

No man attains freedom from the bondage of action *(naiṣkarmya)*
Simply by not undertaking actions;
Nor by mere renunciation does one attain perfection.

For no one can remain absolutely inactive even for a moment.
Everyone is made to engage in action, however unwillingly,
By way of the *guṇas* born of *prakṛti*.

He who on earth does not contribute
To the continued movement of the wheel thus set in motion, is evil, O Pṛthā;
Delighting in the senses, he lives in vain.

Emancipation Through Action:

For by action alone, it was,
That Janaka and others ascended to perfection.
And also you must act,
Attending to no less than the holding together of the world.
For me, O Pṛthā,
There is no work whatever to be done in the three worlds,
Nothing unobtained which is to be obtained;
Yet without fail, I continue in action.

These worlds would be destroyed if I did not perform acts,
And I would be the author of confusion,
And would destroy these people.
As those who are ignorant *(avidyā)* act from attachment to action;
The wise should also act, O Bhārata,
But without attachment,

Desiring to act so as to hold the world together.

Even if you were among sinners the worse of sinners,
You will cross beyond all evil
By the boat of knowledge alone.

A man, dedicated to his own action, attains fulfillment.
Hear then in what way he finds fulfillment,
When one is dedicated to action.

A man finds fulfillment by worshipping Him, through his own proper action,
From whom all beings arise and by whom all this is pervaded.

One's own *dharma,* even when not done perfectly,
Is better than an alien *dharma,* even though well performed;
One does not incur sin doing the action prescribed by one's own condition (doing one's thing).

One should not abandon the action congenial to one,
Even though it is defective,
For all undertakings are clouded with defects
Like fire by smoke, O Son of Kuntī.

Action as Sacrifice:

Except for the action engaged in as sacrifice,
This world is subject to the bondage of action.
For the sake of that, Son of Kuntī,
Perform action free from attachment as a sacrifice.

Long ago, Prajāpati created creatures together with sacrifice, and said:
By this shall you prosper,
Let this be the milch-cow for your desires.

By this, nourish the gods, and may the gods nourish you;
Thus nourishing each other, you will attain to the supreme good.

For the gods, nourished by the sacrifice,
Will give you the enjoyments you desire.
He who enjoys their gifts without giving to them in return,
Is nothing but a thief.

Know that action has its origin in Brahman (the Veda).
And the Brahman has its origin in the Imperishable.

Therefore, Brahman, the All-Pervading,
Is always grounded in sacrifice.

Our understanding of the *Gītā,* as much as our understanding of what Kṛṣṇa does in the path of emancipation, lies principally in being able to recover the systematic steps of the journey. This systematic discovery will make us aware, hopefully, that the passage from a narrow view which grounds identification on desire *(kāmātmānaḥ)* is a passage into an "embodied-vision" where desire *(icchā)* coincides with the original orientation and executive Self of the culture. This decision-making appropriation is made possible following Kṛṣṇa's path and implied on Arjuna's realization, even in his moment of crisis, that all action—walking, sitting, speaking—is grounded on a self-interpretation: which self we decide shall be our executive, decision-making self.

THE WAY OF PHILOSOPHY IN THE GĪTĀ

A way is no way unless, step by single step, one travels it. In the *Gītā* Kṛṣṇa not only points out the way but also travels it. To understand this journey, we must first focus on the means of the journey: what the *Gītā* calls "the boat of knowledge." We shall do just that by following, chapter by chapter, Kṛṣṇa's and Arjuna's moves. The reader, of course, could have, in order to follow these steps, the translation of the *Gītā* in front of him.

Kṛṣṇa's steps to lead Arjuna from his dogmatic and insufficient position to one of emancipation and embodied-vision follow these general strategic moves:

- He makes Arjuna realize that his position is grounded on absolutizing the senses (namely, giving them and their objects absolute value), but this value could not be given to them by Arjuna if the senses, their objects and the self were not radically directed to do so by the *manas* (the mind interpretation of the whole process).
- This position of Arjuna is insufficient, even from Arjuna's viewpoint, since it leads to doubt and inaction. Kṛṣṇa will, therefore, propose as the mediating ground of emancipation from this position the *buddhi*-interpretation: a knowledge grounded on what is rad-

ical *(ātmikā buddhir)* in man coincident with the radical singleness of decision *(vyavasāyātmika eka)* to ground man on such firmly established wisdom *(sthitaprajñā)* or vision *(sthitadhīr)*.

- By grounding knowledge on *buddhi* rather than *manas,* Kṛṣṇa will correct Arjuna's demand that the world of man be reduced to a one-space situation with its permanent threat of despair and death. Kṛṣṇa's journey of embodiment will incorporate the multiple spaces of the culture. These "ontological spaces," (from Chapters II to X, inclusive) and "ontic situations," (from Chapters XIV to XVIII) are closed out or "bracketed out" through Chapters XI, XII and XIII. These chapters make it absolutely clear both that Kṛṣṇa's journey is a philosophical one and that without this journey it is not possible for man to find emancipation. Emancipation and liberation in this context meaning that underlying all the appearances of the *Gītā*: characters, language, experience, perception, etc., there is no ground of reference for any of these appearances in particular and in general. Human life appears to be possible only in the anonymity of its own faith.

We have already seen the moves made by Arjuna in relation to the first above. The *Gītā,* in III. 42, summarizes for us the three points stated above:

> The senses are high (great), they say;
> But the mind *(manas)* is above the senses, and *buddhi* above mind.
> And above *buddhi* is He (the embodied-Self).

While in III. 43, the *Gītā* establishes the radical orientation on which *buddhi* is grounded:

> Thus having become aware of that *(buddhvā)* which is greater than *buddhi,*
> Having strengthened yourself through yourself,
> Slay the enemy, Strong-Armed, which is so hard to get at,
> And has the form of desire *(kāmarūpaṃ)*.

What is important in relation to the second item above; namely, the *buddhi,* is that the "knowledge" the *Gītā* has in mind as the mediating knowledge for emancipation cannot be a knowledge which admits doubt, is divided, or makes man falter. Only *buddhi*-knowledge as radical orientation or mediating ground is sufficient for this task, and this the *Gītā* calls *buddhiyoga*. Kṛṣṇa offers Arjuna this mediating knowledge as early as Chapter II on the context of his crisis and the *manas* interpretation that led to it. "In this path," Kṛṣṇa tells Arjuna, "there is no unsuccessful effort, no reversal is known; even a little of this *dharma* rescues one from great fear." For according to Kṛṣṇa this "understanding *(buddhi)* is resolute *(vyavasāya)* and unitary *(eka)* if this resolution is about what is radical *(ātmika)* in man." Contrary to the *manas* interpretation with its ephimeral sense gratification, the *buddhi* is capable of transcending this bondage and "that in which he knows that which is boundless happiness."

Buddhi transcends the interpretation of the world grounded on good and evil: "One whose intellect is disciplined *(buddhiyukta)* leaves behind good and evil while on earth." It is through *buddhi* that the mind is not swayed *(samatva);* that action without identification is possible *(asakta buddhi sarvatra);* it is this attitude of mind that makes man enlightened *(buddhimān);* and it is only through *buddhi* that man can attain to tranquility *(prasādam),* firm judgment, the ground of peace *(śānti),* and one with wisdom itself *(muni)*. It is through the *buddhi* that man can attain to complete emancipation in action, or gain brahman-consciousness *(brāhmīsthiti),* or one becomes "*niveśaya*: enter into" Kṛṣṇa himself or becomes the same embodied-vision Kṛṣṇa is. It is only through the *buddhi* that one may be able to develop those powers which will make his actions efficient "for the welfare of all creatures."

One must be aware, however, as it will be pointed out in more detail in Chapter Six of this book, that because *buddhi*—like *manas*—is grounded on the *guṇas* of *prakṛti,* it can also become confused and deluded in its function and radical orientation and become one in its devisiveness and orientation with *manas*: "Many-branched, indeed, and endless is the understanding *(buddhi)* of he who is not resolute."

Buddhi is the means of emancipation if it coincides with the original ground, desire, faith and decision-making which created the culture in the first place. *Buddhi,* in sum, is the mediating ground on which rests the answer to Arjuna's question in Chapter XIV, 21–27:

Arjuna:

Oh Lord, by what marks is he who has gone beyond these three *guṇas,* distinguished?
What is his conduct?
How does he pass beyond these three *guṇas?*

The Blessed One:

He does not dislike clarity *(sattva)* and activity *(rajas)* nor delusion *(tamas)* when they arise, O Son of Pāṇḍu,
Nor desire them when they cease.

He who, seated as if unconcerned, is not agitated by the *guṇas,*
Who thinks the *guṇas* alone act,
Who stands apart and remains firm,

Who abides in the self,
To whom pleasure and pain are alike,
Who is the same toward a clod or a stone or gold,
Holding equal the pleasant and the unpleasant,
To whom praise and blame of himself are the same,
Who is firm,

To whom good and bad repute, friend and enemy are the same,
Who has left all projects:
He is called the man who has gone beyond the *guṇas.*

And he who serves me with all the unfailing yoga of devotion *(bhakti),*
Having gone beyond these *guṇas,*
Is fit to become Brahman.

For I am the dwelling-place of Brahman,
Of the immortal and imperishable,
Of everlasting *dharma* and absolute happiness.

Action, Knowledge, Sacrifice

In order to understand what follows, a few cautionary notes are in order. It is obvious that no emancipation is possible without recovering the original act of creation itself. This original act of creation, radical decision, radical orientation, is the anonymous contextual-structure grounding man's capacity and direction to wish and to act. The meaning of man's life is grounded on this original intentionality. As long as man, however, appropriates his acts and his wishes to himself and accepts as radical the knowledge that justifies this position, man will forever be trapped within this fixed space of *saṃsāra:* a fixed space, a fixed time, the eternal round of birth, suffering and death.

If we look at the world of the *Gītā* from Arjuna's viewpoint, we find a still world, divided, immovable, fixed and stuck, and so is Arjuna. This same world, however, viewed from Kṛṣṇa's heights is a world in eternal motion, "causing all beings to revolve as if they were mounted on a wheel," "like jewels dancing on a string," like a cloud of dust born of the rhythm of cosmic feet. It is the world upside down "with its roots above and its branches below . . . the imperishable peepal tree," where both Arjuna and Kṛṣṇa have to enact their karmic steps through the liberating spaces surrounding them. It is imperative, therefore, that in this journey of emancipation we bear in mind the fact that it can only be traversed if both modes of being in the world, Arjuna's and Kṛṣṇa's, are simultaneously present. This journey is not a pilgrimage to witness the victory of good over evil, it is a philosophical journey where both Arjuna and Kṛṣṇa are the conditions *through which* emancipation is made possible.

This philosophical journey is not to be understood as an emancipation from time: both Arjuna and Kṛṣṇa are time. The novelty of this journey is precisely the salvation of time *through* the plurality of human spaces and the plurality of human perspectives through which Kṛṣṇa and Arjuna simultaneously and through each other recreate the *present.* The present-to-be-saved, however, is a hybrid creation. On the one hand it will be an original, anonymous and timeless vision; but on the other hand, and simultaneously, it will permeate with time the multiple spaces surrounding both Arjuna and Kṛṣṇa. So that this efficient present may be systematically infused into man's circumstance, Arjuna and Kṛṣṇa will have to keep meeting in that ground which has been made possible through the mediation of *buddhi* and the emancipation of *yajña*—sacrifice.

The next few pages will be just some clues as to how this journey takes place in the *Gītā,*

The Relation Karma-Dharma

This journey we are about to undertake is not new in Indian tradition. The Ṛg Veda anticipated it for the whole culture to follow. It is the combined journey of *Ṛta* and *dhīḥ,* which we translated as the way of "embodied-vision." It is the world created by Varuṇa, and in general it is the result of the sacrifice. It is also a given world, already made and through which we make our own lives, and in this sense it is already a tradition and a gift *(rādha)*. It is a world generated by the first sacrifice which separated the heavens and the earth and opened the free spaces *(varivas),* thus redeeming man from the anguish of the darkness which surrounds him from everywhere *(vīdvamhas)*. It is in *Ṛta,* as the embodied tradition of man, that Vedic man found the source of his faith *(śraddhā),* his guiding light and the guarantee that the norm works and is effective.

Two further clues are necessary so that the steps we are taking here become effective. As we saw in Chapter Four of this book, action or *karma* never appears by itself but is always the concrete *karma* which a particular *dharma* unfolds. It is important that we remember this relationship and dependence of *karma* on *dharma* as it is important to remember that in order to know any *karma* one must first know the *dharma* that determines it. To appropriate *karma* and its results to one's self is a decision which is neither included in the *karma* nor the *dharma*. On the contrary, this is the kind of decision which a man decides to impose on himself, and acts thus as the absolute *dharma* or radical interpretation of one's whole life. In this sense, it is the stream of *saṃsāra,* the cycle of rebirth, and death. Insofar as one realizes that decision-making about *karma* or *dharma* is part of neither, one may then begin to look around towards the discovery of new spaces for unfolding man's life. Man is now looking or listening for the *dharmas* within which actions are determined so that the coercion of this determination becomes no longer a coercion but a spring board for emancipation. The Sanskrit roots of the words *dharma* and *yoga* confirm these insights.

The term *dharma* comes from the verb *dharati,* meaning to hold, carry, bear in mind, endure and last. The root *dhṛ* means the act of holding or supporting; namely, holding together or supporting those actions, i.e., *karma,* from *kṛ*- do, act, which it supports or holds together. In this sense, whatever is or acts is lodged in a *dharma,* and ultimately *dharma* is the ontological basis for any action. Similarly, the word yoga as used in the *Gītā* is not the restricted technical yoga of Patañjali's Yoga Sūtra I.1 as the cessation of mental states *(citta-vṛtti-nirodha)*. There are three roots from which the word yoga may be derived: *yujir yoge, yuj samādhau* and *yuj saṃyamane*. The root *yujir* means to join, share in; *yuj* may mean "onepointedness" in the sense of the cessation of mental states and also in the sense of control. In the *Gītā* the multiple uses of yoga are primarily derived from the root *yujir yoge,* in the sense of joining, sharing in, and also controlling both the sustained effort of that which is joined in and also controlling that this sustained effort is not deviated from what it intends by restricting the intrusion of anything to which it is not joined. Thus, we have *phala-tyāga* as the dedicated effort to renounce to the fruits of action or identification with them, and also *buddhi-yoga* as the dedicated control of one's effort in the direction of one's decision to associate oneself with a particular type of wisdom or viewpoint. The same may be said of *karma-yoga,* meaning sharing in that viewpoint which looks for emancipation through action, or *yoga-yajña,* emancipation through sacrifice. Thus, the relationship we established in Chapter Four between *karma* and *dharma* will also hold between *karma* and any of the yogas we go through with Arjuna and Kṛṣṇa in our philosophical journey.

The second important point to be made is that Arjuna and Kṛṣṇa appear simultaneously—the text of the *Gītā* would not be possible if one of them was missing—in every *dharma* and *yoga,* in every space of the culture, from I to XVIII. To better understand this mutual dependence on each other and also to better understand the possibilities of both bondage and emancipation, we must from the start model our concepts of consciousness not on the naive visual model of physical space where there is only room for one consciousness at a time, but rather on a model where the whole spectrum of consciousness vibrates simultaneously even though we are only able to focus on one of the vibratory bands at a time. Our consciousness, much as the electromagnetic spectrum, consists of numerous vibratory bands. We are "plugged in" through education into some of them, but we are also, through the same process of education, plugged out of others. We believe that only that which we consciously observe is all that there is to consciousness. And so, we are never at home, never in the present. We strive for Arjuna's way, the past, or Kṛṣṇa's, the future.

The simultaneity of presences of both Kṛṣṇa and Arjuna in every situation of the *Gītā* implies not only their mutual dependence but also that man may, by understanding his condition, stop being a stranger in his own land, for simultaneously with Arjuna and Kṛṣṇa there is also the Generator of all movement, sound and vibration: the present is anywhere and everywhere. Insofar as Arjuna is the past, Kṛṣṇa is the future, but both are held together in the present anywhere they meet. Recovering this meeting-point is the task of philosophy as radical orientation.

Sāṃkhyayoga

It will help us to clarify the journey to have in mind its conclusion. In XVIII. 73, Arjuna concludes:

Destroyed is my delusion;
By your grace, O Unshaken One, I have gained
  remembrance.
I take my stand firmly with doubt dispelled;
I will do your word.

The first steps of Kṛṣṇa and Arjuna through Chapter II are summarized in verse 39, as the wisdom of *sāṃkhya.* In sum, these first steps are Kṛṣṇa's effort to make Arjuna recover his lost memories by traversing the paths of his own culture: the indestructibility of the self, Arjuna's dependence on his *dharma* as a *kṣatriya,* and that the origin of Arjuna's delusion lies in the fact that he identifies himself with the objects of the senses and that, therefore, Arjuna's condition will be as impermanent as the conditions of those changing sensations. Kṛṣṇa points out to Arjuna that it is amidst pleasure and pains that the wise man *(dhīraṃ)* makes himself fit for immortality.

In II. 39, Kṛṣṇa continues equating the path of yoga to that of *sāṃkhya.* The emphasis, however, is on *karma*-action. It is a disciplined *karma* mediated through a disciplined intelligence *(buddhyā yukto),* and it is because of this condition that it may liberate man from karmic bondage *(karmabandhaṃ).* Verse 41, as we saw earlier when explaining the function of *buddhi,* points out to Arjuna that only when *buddhi* is directed towards what is radical *(ātmika)* in man, man's understanding is resolute *(vyavasāya)* and unitary *(eka),* while "many-branched, indeed, and endless is the understanding *(buddhi)* of he who is not resolute." It is this kind of association with *buddhi* which will emancipate Arjuna from his confusion and dependence on the self made of desires, projects, and goals. "Action *(karman)* is indeed inferior (dependent on) to *buddhiyoga* . . . and this yoga is skill in action *(karman).*"

It would appear, therefore, that the root meanings of yoga as association, or sharing in a way of looking at the world, or performing actions in relation to a particular perspective is what the *Gītā* has in mind when using those terms. In V. 4 and 5, the *Gītā* is even explicit about the fact that "only the childish, not the wise, think *sāṃkhya* and *yoga* to be different." Thus, if yoga means "association with," then *sāṃkhya and sāṃkhyayoga* would mean the same: association with *sāṃkhyayoga. Sāṃkhya* primarily means, in the context of the *Gītā,* "true knowledge," or the knowledge which has guided the culture from old, but it also means renunciation from any other association which would cloud this knowledge. However, while *sāṃkhya* offers a wide perspective to Arjuna, yoga concretizes it by showing a particular kind of perspective—that of yoga—and the actions dependent on it. In both cases the appropriation or identification of action and doer is rejected through *manas* interpretation, while perspective and action are ontologically unified through *buddhi* mediation.

Karmayoga: The Yoga of Action

The next space in which Arjuna and Kṛṣṇa gather, the meeting point is *karma-yoga*: the working out of liberation through any action whatever. By taking this step both Arjuna and Kṛṣṇa transcend the apparent dichotomy of the world of liberation between the path of knowledge *(jñānayoga)* for those following *sāṃkhya,* and the path of action *(karmayoga)* for those following the yogins.

Karmayoga is action without attachment or identification, acting only, "so as to hold the world together." This condition can only be met if action is engaged in as sacrifice, and it is grounded on *buddhi* when it is directed towards the original ground *(saḥ).*

The whole world, according to Kṛṣṇa, is subject to the bondage of action, Janaka and even Kṛṣṇa himself, who has nothing to gain by this action, is constantly engaged in action. For the world itself was born of an action: the sacrificial act of Brahman, or the sacrificial act of Prajāpati.

What ignorant people do not realize is that all action is

not the action of the *ahaṃkāra* (the I-maker who believes himself to be the doer), but rather it is the action of the *guṇas* of *prakṛti* alone. Action follows the *guṇas,* and nothing will accomplish the repression of action. Those who doubt this teaching are lost. For even the wise share this condition, but desire *(kāma),* like an insatiable flame, is that constant enemy of the wise. This desire, born of appropriation, covers the knowledge of its origin, as fire is concealed by smoke, a mirror by dust and an embryo by the womb.

The path of *karmayoga* at the hands of the *Gītā* has substituted the fixed coordinates of a particular path for the free variations of the multiplicity of spaces, each identical with a point: this is the point where every action takes place, where Arjuna and Kṛṣṇa meet and where the ground transcends and unifies all previous goals.

> Thus having become aware of that which is greater than *buddhi,*
> Having strengthened yourself through yourself,
> Slay the enemy, Strong Armed, which is so hard to get at,
> And has the form of desire.

Meanwhile, sacrifice as efficient action for this new move and doubt as an obstacle for this new move, have been introduced. We will have to wait and watch their development.

Jñānayoga: The Yoga of Knowledge

There is only one kind of knowledge capable of removing doubt radically. This kind of knowledge is the result of the sacrifice of the combination action-knowledge. *Jñānayoga,* as a commitment to such knowledge, is the next move: the new space where Arjuna and Kṛṣṇa meet again.

According to Kṛṣṇa this is the yoga of old *(yogaḥ purātanaḥ),* known to the royal sages, to *Vivasvān, Manu, Ikṣvāku,* handed down in this way from one to another, but which became lost on earth with the lapse of time. Indeed this is the supreme secret.

What does the secret consist of? "Manifold sacrifices are spread out in the face of Brahman," "not even this world is for one who does not sacrifice, how then the next?" "All action without exception is completely terminated in knowledge, but the sacrifice of knowledge is better than the sacrifice of material things." "The seers of truth will explain to you this knowledge . . . for by this you will see all beings without exception in yourself and in me." In other words, knowing the sacrifice, the supreme secret, is equivalent to becoming the sacrifice: the original act which created the culture in the first place, "the action of the unattached man is free, whose understanding is firmly rooted in knowledge, and who acts as a sacrifice, is wholly dissolved." It is indeed this act as sacrifice which generated the many lives of Kṛṣṇa, the *Avatāra,* the generating power *(māyā)* of the self's own self, Kṛṣṇa's and Arjuna's many past lives, the power to send one's self forth when the knowledge of *dharma* decreases; it is the act on which the protection of the good and the destruction of evil rests, on which *dharma* rests, the *yugas* rest (the cyclic turns of the wheel of history) and the reason for Kṛṣṇa's appearance at different times of the yuga cycles. This finally is the radical ground *(bhāva),* the birthplace of every action and of every creature, human and divine.

Even when men do not realize this situation, sacrifice as the original act underlies all of man's actions: but the efficiency of these actions will depend on what men bear in mind while performing them. "He whose actions are centered on Brahman becomes Brahman," this is the reason why "yogins offer sacrifice to the gods, others make sacrifice by sacrificing the sacrifice itself." From verses 26 through 33 of Chapter IV, Kṛṣṇa points out to Arjuna that the sacrifice is not an idea but a concrete activity undertaken by the people of his culture in every action: breathing, eating, sensing, studying, even creating the four castes and knowing.

This is the kind of knowledge which, like fire, reduces all action to ashes, grounds man in faith, peace, destroys the self of doubt, and is capable of raising a fallen man by cutting out with one's self's own sword of knowledge, the doubt in his heart born of ignorance.

This knowledge can only be attained if one is committed to finding it *(yogasaṃsiddhaḥ)* in himself, which might take some time *(kālenā 'tmani vindati)*. But then, by this knowledge, "you will see all beings without exception in yourself and in me."

The radicality of the *Gītā*'s epistemological, ontological and religious position in relation to the sacrifice have been mostly either ignored or misunderstood. Contrary to the Western position that takes as radical the belief that God created the world and that he thought it to be good (the snake and man messed up the goodness of creation), the *Gītā* proposes to ask that antecedent to the good of the world, or the bad of the world, was the act of creation itself. The *Gītā* would make us redo this original act of creation in every act we perform. In fact, the *Gītā*'s radicality consists—through the sacrifice—in becoming that act of creation, literally play God in order to act human.

Yajña or sacrifice in the *Gītā* repeats again the relation *dharma-karma* we observed above. It adds, however, the radical orientation of the culture through the sacrifice, which is as old in the tradition as the Ṛg Veda. Thus, the knowledge resulting from the sacrifice is not only the knowledge that created the culture—its people, actions and objects—but it is also the original ground of the actions of Kṛṣṇa, Arjuna, Brahman, *Prajāpati, Puruṣa, Prakṛti,* the *guṇas, dharma, karman,* the *yogins* and the sacrifice itself. Thus, all actions in the *Gītā,* whether the people know it or not, are actions of *yajña-vidaḥ,* sacrifice-knowledge.

Only by becoming the sacrifice can man avoid rebirth, only by becoming the sacrifice can man save himself and his circumstances, only through the sacrifice, the world, the gods, the prosperity of the people are possible. The good of all and the origin of all are grounded on the sacrifice.

This original intentionality of the sacrifice, which the *Gītā* recovers, offers contemporary man his most difficult task: the sacrifice not only of his own gods, his own perspectives, but also the fear of becoming a god himself, the discovery of that necessary act which orients a man's life radically and reorients it every time he acts. As our sensibility of ourselves and the world becomes more sophisticated, so do our gods; we apprehend what we are ready for. Maybe we are sophisticated and daring enough, or maybe we are as lost and desperate as Arjuna to take this challenge of the *Gītā* with all human seriousness.

Karmasaṃnyāsayoga: The Yoga of Renunciation of Action

The next meeting space between Arjuna and Kṛṣṇa is like a coffee break: Arjuna obviously needs some time to digest the previous insights.

Arjuna needs a breath of reflection: "Kṛṣṇa, you praise the renunciation of actions, and then again, their disciplined undertaking. Which one of these is the better one: Tell me quite decisively." Obviously Arjuna does not see and Kṛṣṇa has to repeat himself: "Of the two, the disciplined unattachment of action is better than the renunciation of action, even if both bring the ultimate good. For, "it is the childish, not the men of learning, who declare *Sāṃkhya* and *Yoga* to be diverse. He who takes his stand in either one properly, obtains the fruit of both. The only condition to the efficacy of both is that they be grounded in the sacrifice. Thus the embodied one, sitting at ease in the city of nine gates (the body), he neither acts nor causes action, neither creates agency of the world, nor action, nor the conjunction of action with the fruit. This is the knowledge which overcomes creation here on earth by those who know, the knowledge which brings freedom forever, the knowledge which knows me as the enjoyer of sacrifices and austerities, the great lord of all the worlds, a friend of all beings."

Dhyānayoga: The Yoga of Meditation

The next space for Kṛṣṇa and Arjuna is *dhyānayoga,* the space generally taken as that of meditation. In the *Gītā's* hands this space becomes a sustained disciplined commitment to focus on action—whichever action man performs—as the medium or the criterion for nonidentification in action. Equanimity will be the medium or criterion of such discipline for the man who has already attained the previous union. In both cases, meditation is an exercise in intentional direction through a sustained effort: *dhyānayoga.*

Through this sustained effort a man, "lifts his self by his own self and does not lower himself." A man will easily find out if his meditation is sufficiently at work, for then, "he will be at peace, composed amidst cold and heat, pleasure and pain, honor and dishonor; he will be unshaken, his senses conquered and to whom gold, a stone, a clod of earth are the same."

From VI. 10 through 32, Kṛṣṇa summarizes the concrete practices through which a man may develop a habit of meditation. These practices, however, are not for their own sake but in order to bring man to "see himself through himself and become content in himself," the space where man, "unflickering, like a lamp in a sheltered place" finally finds that space "in which thought ceases, stopped by the practice of meditation." Where thought ceases *buddhi* begins, leading man beyond the reach of the senses into his original ground where he no longer falls away from.

Arjuna, and Kṛṣṇa both realize the difficulty of this enterprise which can only be achieved "little by little," and through continuous practice, for "the mind *(manas)* is restless and hard to restrain," but, "What," Arjuna asks, "can a man attain if he does not possess this discipline, but has faith?"

In Kṛṣṇa's world there is salvation for everyone, in time. A man of faith cannot be destroyed doing good deeds. But he will fall in the world of *saṃsāra* and stay there many years from where he might be reborn in a house of pure and prosperous people where the conditions for regaining yoga might be better. He might, of course, be born in a family of wise yogins where he might regain the mental habits of his previous embodiment and once more from that point, perfected through many lives, reach this most disciplined condition.

It is obvious that for Kṛṣṇa *dhyānayoga* is a necessary condition for liberation, and only that yogin who shares this perspective can emancipate himself from the round of birth and death. Again what people have in mind—their perspective—determines the efficacy of their actions and their actions.

Jñānavijñānayoga: The Yoga of Wisdom and Understanding

Through the yoga of meditation Kṛṣṇa and Arjuna meet in the space created by discipline: *jñānavijñānayoga,* the wisdom and understanding which will lead a man like Arjuna into the knowledge of the radical orientation which originated the world around him, and this without doubt. This is the kind of knowledge, which when known, nothing else remains there on earth to be known. It is a difficult knowledge which, of the thousands striving for perfection, maybe only one reaches.

Which is, therefore, this difficult and all-embracing knowledge? It is the knowledge of the wise, committed to the Eternal Ground *(nityayukta),* to the One *(ekabhaktir),* for he has reached the ground through his own self-ground *(yuktātmā).* Such a man is difficult to find and it takes many births to reach such a wisdom.

In more concrete terms, this is the knowledge which discriminates manifestations from reality: the lower nature from the higher; the womb from its creatures; the origin and the world; the world and its dissolution; the waters and their taste; radiance from the sun and the moon; sound from ether; *Oṃ* from all the syllables in the Vedas; and manliness from man. This is the knowledge which supports the world and life and the conditions of beings known as the *guṇas*.

The world, however, does not recognize this changeless ground and (people) flee to whatever gods their desires lay down in front of them. Transient, however, is the fruit of such intelligence. "Those who sacrifice to the gods, go to the gods; but those committed to me come to me."

One should, however, pay very close attention that the *me* Kṛṣṇa is talking about is not his manifestation, Kṛṣṇa, but the supreme, changeless and higher generator.

It is this kind of knowledge, the result of meditation, which distinguishes Kṛṣṇa as manifestation and as ground; the physical world, the highest sacrifice; Brahman, the Self and all kinds of actions.

Akṣarabrahmayoga: The Yoga of the Imperishable Brahman

The next space is home: *akṣarabrahmayoga,* the supreme destination, where there is no other place to go to. It is from this supreme dwelling place that questions about Brahman, the higher self *(adhyātmaṃ),* and *karma* are seen in their true perspective.

The two *prakṛtis,* lower and higher, through which knowledge fluctuates, are here fixed as belonging to two different perspectives: perishable ground for the lower domain and a firm vision *(puruṣa)* for the higher; both are reconciled in the body through the sacrifice where the Self and the ground coincide.

It is this abode, this being home in every action, where one should always be at, especially at the time of death, for whatever one has in mind, that he becomes. This home is the ground on which all beings stand. Only the yogin who knows the way home as different from the other paths which lead man to rebirth stands in the primal place.

Home is not chasing after things apparent; they arise from the ground at the coming of day, and are dissolved at the coming of night. Home is where things rise from and dissolve into. Home is making oneself at home in every action, but then one would have to know *Puruṣa* and *Prakṛti,* the *guṇas, karma* and *dharma* and the *yugas.*

Rājavidyārājaguhyayoga: The Yoga of Sovereign Knowledge and Sovereign Secret

The next move of Kṛṣṇa and Arjuna is very puzzling. It has been so misunderstood that it would be worth our while to focus on it. The space where Kṛṣṇa and Arjuna meet this time is Kṛṣṇa's own theoretic consciousness. While Kṛṣṇa has been previously talking about knowledge, knowledge for Arjuna has always been understood as a particular kind of knowledge; *Sāṃkhyayoga, Karmayoga, Jñānayoga, Karmasaṁnyāsayoga, Dhyānayoga, Jñānavijñāyoga, Akṣarabrahmayoga.* Kṛṣṇa realizes that Arjuna does not understand. In this move he makes Arjuna focus again on knowledge as both supreme knowledge and secret knowledge, but by doing this Kṛṣṇa destroys both knowledges as being any kind of identifiable knowledge or any kind of secret. For while Kṛṣṇa is the prototype of the knowledge of the *Gītā,* this knowledge is not Kṛṣṇa as manifestation or as speech but rather the ground of both Kṛṣṇa and speech. The only secret to be discovered or knowledge to be known is to become this ground.

It is not the knowledge of any knowledge but of faith in the execution of a practice *(aśradhādhānāḥ),* and its only secret is that man does not bother to find out about it and returns again and again to the path of birth and rebirth.

Kṛṣṇa, like a broken record, shouts again at Arjuna that what he, Kṛṣṇa, is talking about is "his self as the source of beings"; the fact that "his lower *prakṛti* sends forth this whole multitude of helpless beings again and again"; and it is under his supervision that *prakṛti* brings forth the moving and the unmoving, and that the world revolves. It is from this source that the one, the distinct, the many facing in all directions are the goals of the sacrifice of wisdom. In general, it is because Kṛṣṇa is the ground that he can be everything (read from IX. 16 through 19). It is also in this sense that Kṛṣṇa is also the other gods, the ancestors, the spirits and the sacrifice. He is also the man of evil conduct worshipping undividedly, and the fruit of sinful wombs, and of women and the castes. For if these people take refuge in their original condition, swiftly their selves will become one with *dharma,* thus reaching the highest goal.

Thus Kṛṣṇa confronts Arjuna with his own self-misunderstanding: to know is neither a knowledge nor a secret but an activity fixed in its own ground having this ground as final goal in every action. It is not I-speaking (the linguistic I of the *ahaṃkāra)* but the I as the source of speech that speaks. This is why, he says, "men on all sides follow my path," and so the wheel moves on.

Vibhūtiyoga: The Yoga of Manifestations

It is obvious that Kṛṣṇa sees still a blank expression in Arjuna's understanding, despite his apparent interest. So this next move is to make again *(eva)* the loud shouting *(paramaṃ vacaḥ)* of the previous chapter.

Kṛṣṇa again tries with rhetorical brilliance to make Arjuna aware of the radical distinction he has tried to introduce into his intentional life: the ground or origin or radical beginningless orientation and the manifestations or appearances which it has generated. However, Kṛṣṇa will have to wait a bit longer to make Arjuna understand—hopefully the reader too—for Arjuna is at the moment more concerned with *identifying* the appearances than reaching the ground. What is significant in Arjuna's questions is that he conceives emancipation as "something to be thought of," or something on which to fasten his meditation. Kṛṣṇa decides to humor him, after all he has already said that "in whatever way men approach me, in the same way they receive their reward; men follow my path in every case." And so Kṛṣṇa, from verses 19 through 41, gives Arjuna a detailed and factual litany of his manifestations.

Abruptly, almost rudely, Kṛṣṇa ends up this theoretic journey with verse 42:

> But of what use is this (factual) detailed knowledge to
> you, Arjuna?
> I keep continually pervading this entire world
> With only one fraction *(ekāṃśena:* a point) of myself.

The Humanization of Man: Viṣvarūpadarśanayoga: The Face of Man-World

The *Bhagavad Gītā* is mounted on the static and fixed wheel of Arjuna's crisis. This condition of fixity is grounded on Arjuna's own decision about the self and the world. Both are presupposed to be a fixed body engaged in mutual appropriation. This presupposition is, of course, tacit. Arjuna is not aware that his decision about both is the doer of such tacit creation of his own crisis, but then Arjuna discovers that his own crisis splits him in two: Kṛṣṇa and Arjuna. Even in his own crisis Arjuna is not alone, he faces himself as in a mirror, and the mirror is larger than Arjuna. Kṛṣṇa and Arjuna meet subsequently in different spaces, different cultural points where one depends on the other for their resurrection. Kṛṣṇa appears to have the upper hand, yet without Arjuna's reflectivity those worlds would not come to be: they have to be first fixed, gotten through so that the mutual journey comes eventually to an end. Arjuna's and Kṛṣṇa's mediation of the cultural spaces are a necessary mediation, but that is all they are, a mediation through which both Arjuna and Kṛṣṇa, the original split, recover their human ground. The end is the beginning: to recover man in his own full humanity, the original humanity that constitutes him as human—in its plural phases—in every action.

Chapters II through X have made us aware that what we call society is not a unity, but rather a multiplicity of perspectives determining discreet actions and discreet social bodies. Before any value is ascribed to those actions within these multiple and discreet social bodies, a man must first recreate the original orientation which made such bodies efficient and such actions valuable. Creation precedes ethics. But such philosophical journey of recreation has a frightening end: culture is a multiplicity of bodies; it is a discreet and multiple recoverable past, recoverable memories lodged in those multiple bodies; and it is also an embodied anticipated future. Insofar as each projects and determines the other, insofar as men follow their trajectory, taking for granted their discreet and original constitution, men are lost. For man is not only past and future—Arjuna and Kṛṣṇa—man is time: the present. Man is himself that simple and frightening reality: the present; the simple and frightening "being there": the support and renewal of all the pasts and the futures. This present, this radical ground of man and the world which man is, is what Chapter XI of the *Gītā* is about. To understand its importance and also its mediating projection in relation to the chapters that follow, we have to first clarify what it does in relation to the previous chapters.

Arjuna's and Kṛṣṇa's consciousnesses as they progress from space of discourse to space of discourse, from cultural body to cultural body, while on the one hand they fix those spaces for recognition purposes, on the other hand they cancel them. What appears is not what is. What is, is present: what appears is past and future. What appears has the face of a dialectics, a growth by accumulation; what is, is the radical dissolution of dialectics by erasing the fixed operations of addition, subtraction, multiplication, and division. Man appears to be following logical moves through a dialectical journey of reflection; yet man ends up being *time* for which no logic can account or be a substitute; a *time* from which no logic can spare man.

If we watch carefully what Arjuna's and Kṛṣṇa's moves have *done* in the previous ten chapters rather than just what they have said, we find that in Chapter XI all those moves are cancelled radically: neither Arjuna's bag of skin created by his *reflection of,* nor Kṛṣṇa's critical mediation with its embodying possibilities are finally a choice or a final state. Both are for the time being, devoured finally by the present. The present, however, will again recreate the multiple split and the multiple reflections and multiple selves. Man is this hybrid creation: theoretic consciousness and its cancellation; an operation which will in turn recreate itself and cancel itself, and so the wheel goes on. For behind the past and the future, behind the social multiple bodies, behind the plural ontologies on which the theoretic consciousness of man rests from time to time, there is nothing for its reference: no language, no god, no things, no substances, no selves, no experience, no action, no-*thing*. Simultaneously there is no death of any of the things, languages, experiences, selves, actions created. All that dies is biography: the static accumulation of selves and worlds through the theoretic consciousness. In the present, however, origin and end are eternal, continuous. In reality all we have are changes of name and form; their distribution and the rules of those distributions are man dependent, culture bound and a mimicry of an original act of creation which is never radically recovered with the danger that the cosmic falsification may go on.

Chapter XI in the *Gītā* may be read with these introductory remarks by itself. It would be convenient and helpful to point out that in this chapter as opposed to the others, Saṃjaya, the narrator of the *Gītā,* is the referee for both Arjuna and Kṛṣṇa and also the reader. He tells others what is happening, for even those involved do not seem to be fully aware: it will take the remaining seven chapters to make this vision of Chapter XI explicit: A vision is also its explanation and communication, and this takes time. We shall carry it over ourselves into Chapter Seven of this book.

The *word,* according to Arjuna, has vanished his delusion. But he needs to see. Kṛṣṇa obligingly gives him a "divine eye" and thrusts upon him the command: "Behold my godly yoga." Note again that Kṛṣṇa labels this embodied-vision a yoga, repeating thus the dependence of objects on vision.

To soften the blow on the reader which this frightening present might produce, or because the reader might miss the vision, Saṃjaya interprets for us what is being seen.

The frightening impact of the present on any man, when the security of the theoretic consciousness, either in the form of crisis or in the form of critical reflection is removed from under his feet, may be read from verses 15 through 31. Arjuna's fright is so complete and overwhelming, all of his worlds so completely destroyed, that he trembles with the present as much as the world he sees to crumble. From the depths of his fear he has only one question: "I desire to understand you, The Primal One, for your manifestation is not intelligible to me."

Kṛṣṇa this time speaks but little: "I am time, the world-destroyer, grown mature, engaged here in fetching back the world." What is significant, however, is that Kṛṣṇa's action is not possible without Arjuna. Both are the world, their origin, conservation and dissolution: "By me they are already slain; be you merely the occasion *(nimittamātraṃ bhava).*"

Through verses 36 to 46 the present seems finally to catch hold of Arjuna. He is in awe at having missed it altogether. He apologizes to Kṛṣṇa and shows his delight at the new vision. However, the vision is too strong, too overwhelming, and Arjuna's mind cannot stop shaking with fear. So he pleads with his friend to go back to his previous form so that he may continue with the task of living. Kṛṣṇa agrees, Arjuna regains his presence of mind and joins again the ordinary world. Arjuna, however, is not the same: *now he has seen.* He has also learned from Kṛṣṇa that this vision is recoverable and can be entered into, provided this is the vision one has in mind in every action. In fact, this is the vision that makes possible and liberates man from the past and future.

One final note of caution in relation to the philosophical journey of man, as seen through the previous chapters in the *Gītā,* and other absolutized journeys which, from time to time, one hears men asking from other men and himself to take.

We are too much aware of the readiness with which men embark on absolute *trips* in search of liberation. We have also experienced the futility of working with men who demand that life of necessity be only *one* such absolutized trip. Thus we have seen men migrating like so many arrows in search of a fixed absolute goal. We have seen those men also miss the mark and end up in a psychiatrist couch to regain strength and undertake again their predetermined flight. We have seen men never be born again but live the same life again and again in a meaningless circle around the idea that maybe man can after all avoid being human.

The *Bhagavad Gītā,* on the other hand, offers a different image of man. To be human, according to the *Gītā,* is the condition of being able to start and end a multiplicity of trips, all of them beginning and ending in the same spot: the present, i.e., whatever action man is engaged in. The philosophical journey of the *Gītā* is a program of education to realize that while man must travel many roads, not one road will become his *trip.* Philosophy itself is not a trip but the disciplined commitment to starting and finishing them all by finding oneself at home in any of them. Nothing is permanent except man's faith. *But man's faith is one space beyond any god.* In the aural–oral model of the *Gītā* we would more accurately say that faith is the nonidentifiable sound-point beyond god. Do not force *trips* on man, but develop his capacity to travel his human roads. Perhaps, we are getting ahead of ourselves and we should turn now to the remaining chapters.

Faith, Knowledge, Action

A human vision, because it is human, requires as part of its completion that it be self-revealed: communicated. This communication, being a human communication, is theoretic, lengthy—takes time—and is again subject to the perspective of its own communication. The *Gītā,* therefore, will take seven chapters, from XII through XVIII, to make explicit what has been implied previously: both in the vision of Chapter XI and the activity that led to it: Our own next Chapter Six will deal more concretely with the structure of this vision. As the reader will notice, Arjuna and Kṛṣṇa continue, in the remaining chapters of the *Gītā,* being dependent on each other for this communication and engage themselves in a formal dialogue very similar and at times repetitious of the previous ones. It is for this reason that unless we discover what the *Gītā* really does rather than says, we may end up missing the whole *point.*

The immediate results of the vision in Chapter XI is the recovery of faith and devotion in Chapter XII. The belief in life itself, and even more to have touched life directly without the fog of consciousness, is the vital force that drives man from both, the apathy of inertia in a moment of crisis and the apathy of dread in a moment of vision to create new worlds: man's own life.

It is very clear that in Kṛṣṇa's and Arjuna's understanding of faith, the supreme faith is this faith in life itself, "the imperishable, the unmanifest." It is, however, because of its supreme loftiness that it is so difficult. Thus the *Gītā,* in tune with the greatest traditions of the world, proposes as a secondary but more sure path, the yoga of devotion: the incarnation, the embodiment.

The yoga of devotion that the *Gītā* proposes must be discovered in its own context. It is not a trip closed within its own limits. It is a trip to break the limits of any trip. It is in this sense that one has to read verses 6 through 12 of Chapter XII. One must engage in the devotion one is capable of engaging in and not try to follow the gods of others. Any deviation from this path will be lack of faith and the sign that one's devotion does not have "to become the Father" in mind, but one's own security as a goal. One should read in this light with attention verses 5 through 12:

> The difficulty of those whose intellects are fixed on the
> unmanifested is much greater,
> For the goal of the unmanifested is painful for the
> embodied to attain.
>
> But those who, intent on me, renounce all actions in me,
> Worship me with complete discipline and meditate on
> me:
>
> These whose thoughts are fixed on me,
> I become quickly their deliverer
> From the ocean of death and rebirth, O Pārtha (Arjuna).
>
> Set your mind on me alone,
> Make your understanding at home in me;
> You will dwell in me thereafter.
> Of this there is no doubt.

But if you are not able steadily to concentrate your mind on me,
Then seek to reach me by the discipline (yoga) of concentration,
O Wealth-Winner.

If you are not capable of such repeated concentration,
Then be dedicated to my service,
Engaging in actions for my sake,
You will reach fulfillment.

But if you are not capable of doing even this,
Then resorting to my own discipline,
Do my *yoga* and renounce the fruit of all action.

Knowledge is better than practice, meditation is superior to knowledge;
Relinquishment of the fruit of action is better than meditation;
From such relinquishment peace immediately comes.

To chase after gods could be an escape for avoiding Him. Kṛṣṇa is radically *anahaṃvādi:* not I speaking. Devotion without the radical orientation of faith is again falling into the same cycle of rebirth. Faith, again, is one space beyond god.

Knowledge

The initial questions of Arjuna about the knowledge he needed to know in order to act freely are given to him in Chapter XIII. Knowledge, like devotion, is not one but multiple. As the gods determine devotion, so the fields of man's actions determine knowledge. In the first line of the *Gītā* "*Dharmakṣetre kurukṣetre,*" in the field of *dharma,* in the field of the Kurus, the problem was identified for us. Chapter XIII answers by saying that to know is to know the field, and that those who know are the knowers of the field *(kṣetram, kṣetrajña)* or *Kṣetra-jñanin.* Kṛṣṇa as the embodiment of this prototype of knowledge is "the knower of the field in all fields," and this "he holds to be real knowledge." Kṛṣṇa proclaims this to be the knowledge of the tradition and gives a brief account of the field and its modifications in verses 5 and 6. The important point, however, is not so much the description of the field but the fact that together with the field, the pluralities of fields and knowledge, Kṛṣṇa inserts also the intentionality of each one of these discreet fields and knowledges: "Thus the field, knowledge *and what is to be known* has been briefly stated. Devoted to me, having understood this, one becomes this my state *(madbhāvāya)*."

From a practical standpoint to know the field is to know *puruṣa, prakṛti* and the *guṇas*. "He who sees that actions are everywhere done by *prakṛti* and who likewise sees his self not to be the doer, he sees indeed."

In opposition to the simplistic demand of the Arjuna of the first chapter that the self and the world be both identifiable and knowable as one, the answer of Chapter XIII is overwhelming. There are as many selves as fields, and they and the worlds multiply constantly. It is only when one sees that these multiplicities have the One as ground and that they refract out from it without affecting, modifying or defiling it, that one truly knows. It is only thus that a man finds himself at home in every field and "as the one sun illumines this entire world, so does the field-knower illume the entire field."

> They attain the Supreme, who, with the eye of knowledge,
> Know in this way the difference of the field and the knower of the field,
> And the liberation of beings from *prakṛti*.

Thus it is only through the field that man can play out, through the mediation of knowledge, his option to recover his radical orientation and be free. Or he may decide to substitute this radical orientation for some absolutized form of *prakṛti* or any one field or knowledge and be bound. The One is not identifiable.

Action

For one who has seen, action is no longer disembodied. Action belongs to the field and the field is any action of man. For no action of man is done by "*this*" man, but is the result of the *guṇas* of *prakṛti*. The true option for man is, therefore, to act with the *puruṣottamayoga* in view: with a view to the highest vision, the non-identifiable One. The ground, *puruṣa, prakṛti,* the *guṇas,* the senses, *manas, buddhi,* the *ahaṃkāra,* etc., are all in every action of man. The decision as to which view or interpretation to ascribe to man is culture bound and man dependent. Man is the one to make the decision about these adjudications.

We need not repeat here what we have already stated elsewhere in relation to the *guṇas,* the *ahaṃkāra, manas* and *buddhi.* Their workings will be better understood in the next chapter. Chapter XVI clarifies the workings of the *ahaṃkāra* and how one's circumstance is historically bound with one's concrete social situation within the culture and society, but given the fact that man is bound to act through the determination of the *guṇas,* the *Gītā* proclaims that man is still free if he is capable of correcting the wrong identification with the I that speaks and shifts it to the knowledge or *dharma* that holds the determinations together. As can be seen from Chapter XVII, the *Gītā* is not satisfied with what we would understand as ethical actions, but together with these actions on equal footing are included the actions through which man can work out his liberation: any social and domestic action as well, from offerings to the gods to eating leftovers and rotten food. This might indicate to us that it might be misleading to superimpose on the *Gītā* an ethical doctrine where actions are valuable because of their intrinsic worth.

As Chapter XVIII shows, man's circumstance may be saved when man's actions, with the *guṇas,* and the fields are oriented and energized towards the emancipating knowledge of which both Kṛṣṇa and Arjuna are the prototype. It is only when this knowledge has been recovered by recovering the original orientation of the culture—as opposed to the subsequent ethical doctrines—that a man's radical desire *(icchā)* can play itself freely through whatever actions he encounters. The journey of the *Gītā* is radically a journey to destroy ignorance, regain the lost memories, reaffirm one's decision about one's radical orientation, and remove all doubt. Only then can one venture to execute the word. This journey, however, is not for the feet or the mind only. It must be mediated through the heart, for it is there, as the sages of the Ṛg Veda tell us, that all the relations of their world are radically mediated.

In sum: "Kṛṣṇa is all." To know as Kṛṣṇa does is the aim of the *Gītā,* for "nowhere in this world is there to be found a purifier like knowledge." Knowledge, however, is a difficult and obscure word, leads to misunderstandings, repetitious births, and is inefficient if knowledge is not embodied knowledge: includes the higher knowledge (knowledge about knowledge), the lower knowledge (knowledge about facts or actions), and their radical ground: the present. We must, in order to know, know knowledge and the field, and like Kṛṣṇa, become both, so that unattached action (freedom) is possible and hence creativity, the renewal of the world. Thus we have that to be Kṛṣṇa we need to know or become *Puruṣottama* (embodied-vision) and also know *Prakṛti* and the *guṇas* with the possible trap of being content with the interpretation of the "field" by *manas* (the mind) or the possible liberation of rising higher through the *buddhi*. Structure (through *manas* interpretation) must be known and through *buddhi* integrated in higher and more comprehensive syntheses, where varieties are only in kind and knowledge remains undivided amidst the multiplicity of things. This goal is to be achieved "in this very life." The self belongs to the fields (contexts); the fields to knowledge (liberation). Embodied-Vision is simultaneously Arjuna, Kṛṣṇa, and their Origin.

Since the whole weight of the *Gītā,* however, hinges on the powerful faith of "having seen," and since "seeing" is seeing the field and its relations—the moving wheel on which these fields are mounted—we shall try to spin the web of these fields and these visions in the next chapter to intentionally guide our understanding of the *Bhagavad Gītā*.

Structure: The Problem of Embodiment

Chapter Six

How might the man of steady wisdom speak?
How might he walk, how sit?

Arjuna in II. 54

He who on earth does not contribute
To the continued movement of the wheel thus set in motion, is evil, O Pṛthā; (Arjuna)
Delighting in the senses, he lives in vain.

Kṛṣṇa in III. 16

I heard this marvelous hair-raising dialogue of Vasudeva (Kṛṣṇa) and the son of Pṛthā,

Saṃjaya in XVIII. 74

INTRODUCTION

The previous chapter about the problem of knowledge in the *Bhagavad Gītā* has made us aware that what the *Gītā* calls "knowledge" is a kind of knowledge that grounds the culture radically, and that unless a man is grounded on it, he will stumble, be lost, broken. It is also a kind of knowledge which cannot be identified with any of the "knowledges" provided by the different fields of the culture. It is the "knowledge," however, on which all the fields stand: the radical human ground from which all the directions of Hindu man emerge. The *Gītā,* of course, would fail us if it could not show us the way to gain this knowledge or to recover it when lost. We have already seen in the previous chapter the general moves through which Kṛṣṇa and Arjuna orient us to make us aware of this radical knowledge. Through these moves of Kṛṣṇa and Arjuna we have seen objects, the senses, sensation itself, even whole ontologies being cancelled in front of our eyes; whole worlds have tumbled and been dissolved. We have also discovered that underlying this "knowledge" of the *Gītā* there is a need for a new way of focusing on the words, the movement, space-time, and sound as they unfold through the *Gītā,* for it is only on the condition that such focusing be made possible that we shall be able to recover the whole text of the *Gītā*. In short, the problem of knowledge in the *Gītā,* which we analyzed in the previous chapter, has made us aware that we need to develop the ability not only to become that kind of knowledge—to know the *context*—but we also need to develop the ability to discover the *structure* through which that kind of knowledge appears as corporality, flesh.

To inject corporality into the "knowledge" of the *Gītā* is the task of the present chapter. We shall do this by focusing on the text of the *Gītā* as a whole, as it explicitly and implicitly unfolds the radical knowledge of the *Gītā* in the concrete corporeal form of a *structure.* It is only on the condition that knowledge be made "flesh" through a structure that knowledge may not only orient every word, action, and move of the *Gītā,* but it may also guarantee that this orientation remains a human project.

To proceed systematically, we will progressively thematize this chapter through the following moves: The general structure of the *Bhagavad Gītā*; the structure of Arjuna's world; the structure of Kṛṣṇa's world; the structure of man's radical ground; and the structure of sound as body movement.

On Structure

It is essential at this point for us to remember that our encounter with the text of the *Bhagavad Gītā* takes place for us within the broader theme of "Man and Circumstance." It will be important, therefore, to remember all that we have said in Chapters Two and Three of this book about context and structure and their mutual dependence. In reference, however, to the concrete context of the *Gītā,* we have just suggested that structure is the concrete corporeal form through which a radical orientation about knowledge appears. In order, however, for this particular structure of the *Gītā* to remain *of* the *Gītā* and not be reduced or erased by other theoretical structures, we consider it necessary to add a few cautionary remarks on the function of structure within our large theme of Man and Circumstance.

For Ortega y Gasset structure equals elements plus order. Strictly speaking, this means that we cannot speak of the "structure of reality," but rather that what we call *reality* is *strictly structure.* This formulation of Ortega's which has been further thematized by Julián Marías, carries with it formidable consequences for our theme of Man and Circumstance. For according to this formalization which found its maximal expression in Ortega's condensed thesis: I am I and my circumstance, (a) reality is *my* life; that is, each life lived; (b) human life is not a reality but rather a theory or interpretation of a general structure which I discover through the analysis of my life, hence structure is analytical; and (c) man is, viewed from this radical perspective and insofar as he is radicated in it, a *structure* of human life. The question we face, therefore, is which structure to ascribe to the man confronting us. Obviously, we are not free to give him any structure, but only the structure at which we arrive from his own radical reality, his own life insofar as we are able to know it by making it our own.

With this in mind, we see that what we call structure is derived from a living, embodied reality and so are its contents and conditions; that these conditions are the conditions without which my life is not possible and which must be found, therefore, in each life. We are thus speaking of a necessary structure and, in this sense, universal; a structure which, in a sense, exists *a priori* with regard to each individual life, but which is analytically derived, discovered from the analysis of reality—a lived life—and therefore in no way can it be an aprioristic construction. Thus structure is both analytic and empirical, distinguishable as such yet inseparable and irreducible.

Structure, therefore, is not a quality or a combination of qualities of human life, but it is the human life empirically facing me. This is the empirical fact which constantly constitutes my circumstance: the concrete world through which I make my life constantly. Human life is like that, though in principle it might have been different or at times people decide to make it different. That is why to say that life is like that is not to say anything factual, but rather to point out the structural configuration of human life.

What we call structure, therefore, appears from this perspective as the field of possible human variations in human history. Historical man will make himself present in the world through a particular articulation of this presence: a gesture through structure of which and through which he will acquire his ultimate circumstantial and individual reality while making it present, making it expression or giving it body. Thus, he learns that the adequate form of unfolding the drama of appropriating the general analytic structure into his life is to narrate it. Biography is thus born at the risk of cancelling out the radical structure on which biographical human life stands.

It is only through human circumstance understood as an open world of possibilities through which I make my life constantly that the reduction of structure to biography may be corrected. The corporality of each structure becomes my empirical structure and therefore my body as I learn to embody the world facing me with its generous offer of life, but the fact that human circumstantiality is corporeal, namely, has a body, does not mean that the body may be restricted or identified only with some definite structures of the human body. Biographical life may be taught to narrate itself through different bodies, while in fact belonging exclusively to no one body. However, since corporality and world-possession is also joined to the structure of the senses, biographical life may also be taught to narrate itself through different sense structures, without in fact depending exclusively for sensation on the structure of one body-sensation-interpretation. The fact that human life is visual, auditive, tactile, etc., is not sufficient to make human life dependent on one interpretation of structure of the visual, auditive, tactile, etc. It is also a fact that the human senses and their structure are subject to change. Technology, for one, has changed human sensitivity and sense structure, changing thus the horizon of the human body. Neither the sensorial structure nor the human body of contemporary man are the same as they were a few years ago. Our biographical language, however, has not yet learned to narrate this change or account for these circumstances. Structural changes at the empirical level introduce structural changes into the totality of what we call human life, and this is the task of the theme, Man and Circumstance.

From the viewpoint of circumstantial man, there are no

historical constants. What circumstantial man discovers from within the world surrounding him is historical change: diverse historical determinations through which circumstantial man makes his body, his life, his time, his space, his movement, his voice in the world, constantly demanding from him a responsible decision with its constant offer of life.

With these notes in mind, we may hopefully be able to prepare ourselves to focus on the word of the *Gītā,* not as a word linked to other words, but rather as a *significant gesture,* a structure of a world-dimension which manifests the structure of a particular life now facing us. What is written on the page, or chanted for the ear, is the structure which makes present, through the visible line or the chanted word, a living person's and a living culture's movement.

The same may be said of space, time or movement. Not one of these three concepts is either a quality or a characteristic of any body. They are rather embodied structures, or simply structures through which bodies appear. Insofar as these bodies appear in front of me as I encounter them historically, corporality is always simultaneous with the structures it is capable of embodying. Though it is I who sees, I am also visible. The weight, the thickness, the textures, the colors, the sounds of the world may be sensed not because I am a mind or spirit apart from them and surveying them, but rather my body is made of the same flesh as the world it faces. *The body makes present a context with which it shares its dimensions.* This silent and fleshy unity underlies at its roots any reflective thinking. To be able to see this "sounding silence" of human life historically moving is the "wonder of seeing" that the *Gītā* offers to man in crisis. To this world we now return.

Since structure, however, is vectorial (its origin and goal is exhausted by the dimensions of the context it expresses), our analysis of the structure of the *Gītā* would be insufficient if, like the *Gītā,* we would not have in mind from the beginning the whole context of the *Gītā* as described in the previous chapter. It is because of the kind of knowledge that the *Gītā* presupposes that the structure of it can only be discovered if we discover the way this structure functions in the *Gītā* itself, independently of how *Puruṣa, Prakṛti,* the *guṇas,* etc., function in other contexts. It is for this same reason that we will have to discover and account for whatever elements are necessary to the functioning of this structure in the *Gītā,* especially movement, time-space and sound insofar as they are implied or explicitly referred to in the *Gītā,* or form its body. Furthermore, the reader should be warned that a discipline of knowing how to "see" what one is made to focus upon with the exclusion of everything else is a necessary requirement for this journey. We shall try to make explicit this way of "seeing" as we go along. Let us say, for now, that the reader should get himself ready to see the world from within particular perspectives, particular frames, and see only that which appears in the frame as it embodies the whole frame, notwithstanding the fact that the reader might be conditioned to look for objects only within a frame, or objects only beyond the frame facing him. Just "see" the body opening its own fleshy spaces.

THE GENERAL STRUCTURE OF THE BHAGAVAD GĪTĀ

Human experience is a problematic notion. It is never experience in general, but it is always a particular experience: the experience of such and such. What makes experiences to be such is the concrete structure that determines them to be so. No experience is, therefore, possible unless the structures that determine experience are recovered together with the conditions of possibility of such definite structures. Since structures are context dependent, their vectorial trajectory cannot be isolated from the context setting their movements. Knowledge, however, cannot be reduced to just structure, but structures are determined by and reveal knowledge.

In the case of the *Gītā* our cautions are even more significant since we are dealing with intentionalities foreign to our philosophical systems. Thus, before we set these structures in motion; namely, before we are capable of "seeing" them move as they do in the *Gītā,* we shall have to first "fix" them discursively so that our posterior moves coincide with their cultural rotation.

Sound and Movement

Sound and movement as the condition of possibilities for the function of the structures in the *Gītā* have been mostly overlooked. This oversight has been in many ways responsible for offering us interpretations stillborn and stale. The only movement the reader of such interpretations is allowed to make is an intellectual affirmation or negation reinforced by some concomitant and distant aesthetic feeling about the notion of a discursive synthesis. This move, however, is not historically mediated but the demand of our own method. The reader is thereby not allowed to get involved any further in the world of the *Gītā*; there is nothing else for him to do but to move discursively avoiding human contact. Philosophy's task as we understand it in this book, on the contrary, is to create such conditions as to make it impossible for the reader to get fully involved with man and circumstance as they encounter each other and give each other their life's bodies.

Beyond Arjuna's crisis, underlying Kṛṣṇa's and Arjuna's moves within the culture there is a whole world of sound and movement which makes those moves possible. This sound-movement-world is what in the words of St. John of the Cross we may call "the sounding silence" *(el silencio sonoro)* in which the world of the *Gītā* is submerged and which we must recover to give the *Gītā* its own meaning.

Chapter I of the *Gītā* gives us the most important clues for discovering the *sound* setting of the song–poem. Our first clue is to observe how the author of the *Gītā*—whoever he might be—presents the story. The author remains unknown (though it is speculated his name to be Vyāsa, the compiler), thus he avoids identifying himself with his work and does not force the reader to focus on his own limits. Instead, the whole story is narrated by the charioteer Saṃjaya to his blind king, Dhṛtarāṣṭra, while both get ready to watch from a safe distance the battle which is about to take place. It is from amongst the roars of men, the tumultuous sounds of conch shells blowing, kettledrums, cymbals, and horns, amidst the clanging of armor, weapons, chariots and amidst the nervous exultation of animals and men that Saṃjaya—and through him the whole tradition and ourselves—is able to *hear* a whispering dialogue, in the distant center of the battlefield, between Arjuna and his charioteer Kṛṣṇa. The *Gītā's* body stretches as far as its voice is heard. Like in the *Ṛg Veda*: "So that future generations may see them (the origins) when these hymns are chanted in a future age."

At the end of the *Gītā* in XVIII.74, Saṃjaya repeats this same clue by reminding us that this is the story that he has *heard,* "a marvelous hair-raising dialogue," a dialogue which he recalls again and again.

The reader should remember that Indian literature is of

two types: *smṛti,* "remembered" or "commented upon" and *śruti,* literally "what has been heard." Thus the *Gītā,* through Arjuna's crisis, brings together the whole world of the moving *yugas* and the two traditions of *smṛti* and *śruti* and their reconciliation: "Destroyed is my delusion; by your grace, O Unshaken One, I have gained remembrance. I take my stand firmly, with doubt dispelled; I will do your word." The *Gītā* is the voice that brings and holds the two worlds of Arjuna and Kṛṣṇa together.

It is this model of sound we should keep in mind, for it is only by understanding it that *movement* will appear as a living, embodied movement rather than just a disembodied movement of discursive thought. More will be said on these two points later on in this chapter. A few remarks, however, will help us understand the function of sound and movement as conditions of possibility for the different structures in the *Gītā.*

It would be problematic indeed to reduce movement in the *Gītā* to the movement of thought between two fixed coordinates of space and time. Our theme demands that whatever we encounter in our philosophical journey be given the historical freedom of its own constitution. We must always be aware of conceptual imperialistic designs. *Movement,* in the *Gītā,* is always embodied, incarnate, fleshy. Space and time are mounted on it, they are *of* it, they are not in it. Movement is the condition that makes possible space and time. Whatever active moves are made or discovered in the *Gītā,* they inevitably are going to affect the flesh, the body of whoever makes those moves. It is because of movement that two ways of "seeing" are possible: an emancipated "seeing" where to know is to be able to "see" at a glance, so to speak, the movement; and an ignorant "seeing" where to know is to "see" only the mover, cancelling out thus the movement and the background. In fact, if one is seriously trying to save the whole circumstance of the *Gītā,* one will have to train himself to avoid focusing only on the mover and be able to focus on the vision of the moving movement of the *Gītā*: the dancer becomes the dance; to be able to see this is already a step towards emancipation.

To better guide the reader in the direction of our suggestions, we need to bring here only two examples as clues of what we are about to develop.

One need only read with these notes in mind Arjuna's embodied crisis to realize that the movement of thought is not circumscribed to the head but overpowers the whole body-feelings:

> Kṛṣṇa, seeing my own kin on hand and eager to fight,
> My limbs become weak, my mouth dries up,
> My body trembles, and my hair stands on end.
> Gāṇḍiva (the bow) slips from my hand,
> My skin is also burning; I can scarcely remain standing,
> My mind is reeling.

In Chapter XI when Arjuna faces the radical ground of man, human time, it is again his whole body with its sensations and interpretations that is changed:

> Then Arjuna, filled with wonder,
> His hair standing on end,
> O Great Self, having seen this wondrous and terrible form of yours,
> The three worlds tremble,
> and so do I.
> My inmost self trembles,
> I find no firmness or peace,
> I know not the directions of the sky and I find no refuge.
> Trembling and with folded hands payed homage
> Then spoke to Kṛṣṇa, in faltering voice, afraid.
> I beg forgiveness of you,
> I am delighted, having seen what was not previously seen,
> But my mind trembles with fear.
> Show me that other (human) form of yours, O Lord;
> Seeing this gentle human form of yours, O Exciter of Men,
> Restored to my normal condition (am I).

Following our theme of Man and Circumstance, the reader will remember we decided from the beginning of this book to focus on "action itself" rather than statements about action. We were primarily concerned with that radical action which man must do to radically orient himself about life in a moment of crisis. It is important, therefore, that by concentrating on action as it radically orients itself towards the ground of its own constitution, we bear in mind that this reorientation will carry with itself a series of moves or actions that by being performed or carried through they do not only change our minds or perspectives, but they also radically change our sensations and body-feelings. It is a mark of the wisdom of the *Gītā* to have pointed out the change in body conditions through the change in perspectives by mediating the whole process through a man in crisis: body feelings and sensations are never more problematic and theory dependent as when a man stops feeling to take stock of his feelings. Human living stops being a living to turn itself into an image.

In relation to the above, it will be interesting for us to bear in mind something which we shall develop more fully later on: the relation between time and memory or remembrance in the *Gītā*.

There are two instances in the *Gītā* when the whole movement of life stops: the first one is when Arjuna decides to reduce all life to his thoughts about life; the second one is when Kṛṣṇa, in Chapter XI, submerges Arjuna into the devouring ground of human time: time as concentrated presence. In the first instance the rotation of the wheel is stopped because of lack of memory and contact with the ground; in the second instance all movement stops, overpowered by the presence of the present: radical human time. In the *Gītā* time is only this kind of time, the absolute human ground. The rest—movement—is memory, interpretation, perspectives, past and future.

Before we make these moves clearly embodied in Arjuna and Kṛṣṇa, we shall present the general structures of the *Gītā* on the understanding that our purpose here is only descriptive insofar as they will help us understand what follows and what in fact takes place in the *Gītā*. We do not propose to absolutize those structures by themselves, independent of the bodies and the actions that give them life.

Puruṣa, Prakṛti, the Guṇas and Their Modifications

In order to understand how the structure of the *Gītā* functions in this text, one has to bear in mind the following:

- Although some of the terms of the structure of the *Gītā* are found in other philosophical systems, there is no proof that the terms of the *Gītā* refer to those systems.

For example, there is no proof that *sāṃkhya* in the *Gītā* refers to *Sāṃkhya* philosophy; but the ontological parity of *prakṛti* and *puruṣa* form the basis of the philosophical structure of the *Gītā*.

- Our primary concern in discovering the structure of the *Gītā* is to discover how it functions in the *Gītā* itself.
- The functional characteristics of the structure of the *Gītā*, however, are to be discovered as they function; namely, as they are embodied, not only in the text but primarily through Arjuna and Kṛṣṇa.

See Table I, page 246.

In general terms, *Puruṣa, Prakṛti,* the *Guṇas* and their modifications form the general structure of the *Gītā*. Certain confusion, however, might arise in the mind of the reader because of the many senses in which these terms are used throughout the *Gītā*. Thus, we have *prakṛti, parā prakṛti, aparā prakṛti; puruṣa, akṣara puruṣa, kṣara puruṣa, puruṣottama,* etc. Table I might help us clarify the following:

- With the exception of *puruṣottama,* which we may translate as the absolute radical ground: the transcendent-immanent aperspectival "embodied-vision," and which is immovable, indivisible, indestructible, permanent, etc.,
- Whatever appears in the *Gītā,* either manifest or unmanifest, either on the surface or hiding in the depths, either moving or in crisis, is the combined result of *puruṣa* and *prakṛti*. *Puruṣa* can generally be understood as the energizing power of vision, while *prakṛti* may be understood as the condition of body-feelings-sensations and their interpretation.
- The simultaneous presence in every action of *prakṛti* and *puruṣa* may be directed from lower levels of organization or embodiment to more comprehensive or higher levels of embodied organization. Thus, we have a fully dynamic system capable of being intentionally energized from less to more complex and free body-systems. These body-systems are what is known as the *guṇas* of *prakṛti*: *sattva,* "clarity" or "light"; *rajas,* "energy" or "activity"; and *tamas,* "inertia" or "dullness."
- This intentional direction can be accomplished by desensitizing the body-systems from their appropriations and

TABLE I

THE STRUCTURE OF THE GĪTĀ

ONTOLOGICAL PARITY OF PRAKṚTI AND PURUṢA

NONMANIFEST-AVYAKTA
Depth

- Analytical Structure -

Ground
Present

Puruṣottama: "embodied vision," transcendentimmanet = aperspectival

Paramātman: "Supreme-radical Self"

PURUṢA: Perspectival Vision as the condition of . . .

PRAKṚTI: "what is done repeatedly" "the condition of . . ." interpretation.

Condition of
Possibilities

akṣara puruṣa: "imperishable vision," immanent and unmanifest *(avyakta)*

parā prakṛti: "the condition of possibilities as condition" unmanifest *(avyakta)*—*guṇas* (see below) in equilibrium

---

- Empirical Structure -

Kṣara puruṣa: "changeable perspective of "person (ality)" individual as body-feeling.

Aparā prakṛti: "structuring, the condition of" manifest and changeable—the "body *(deha)*": *guṇas* in manifest form.

MANIFEST-VYAKTA
Surface

The *Aparā Prakṛti* and *Kṣara Puruṣa,* at this level, together make up the phenomenal individual which is composed entirely of the *guṇas* of *prakṛti* in their dynamic, manifest form. The *guṇas* are *sattva,* "clarity" or "light"; *rajas,* "energy" or "activity"; and *tamas,* "inertia" or "dullness."

The mobility of man is made possible through:

Field-Body-feelings-sensations
International Direction ⟶

buddhi, "intelligent will"
ahaṃkāra, "I-maker"
manas, "sense-mind," interpretor of the senses

indriyas, "senses,"
adhibhūta: inner objects
prāṇa, "life-force," literally "breath"
deha, "body"

body-feelings through the sense-mind interpretation of the senses, (the *manas* plus the *ahaṃkāra)* and redirecting that energy through the same body-systems with the *buddhi* interpretation (intentional will-intellect) in search of their common unshakable ground, *puruṣottama,* or original or radical human ground.

The sense of our own progressive trajectory is suggested to us in these quotations from the *Gītā*:

> Having seized my own lower *prakṛti,*
> I send forth this whole multitude of helpless beings again and again,
> Earth, water, fire, air, ether, *manas* (sense-mind interpretation), *buddhi* (intellect interpretation) and *ahaṃkāra* (I-maker),

This is the structure of the lower *prakṛti*. But Chapter XIII. 5–6 offers a more complex system while describing the "field" and the "knower of the field" *(puruṣa* and *prakṛti*):

> . . . the (five) gross elements, the sense of I *(ahaṃkāra),* understanding *(buddhi),* the unmanifested *(avyakta),* the ten senses and one *(manas)* and the five sensory realms; desire, aversion, pleasure, pain; the bodily aggregates *(saṃghata),* knowledge *(cetā),* will *(dhṛti)*: this, in brief, is the field with its modifications.

Whatever exists is the conjunction of, or the fertilization of the field and the knower of the field: *prakṛti* and *puruṣa*. What appears, the surface, the field, is *prakṛti*; its condition of manifestation is that it be energized by *puruṣa*. Their ontological *simultaneity* and parity makes possible all that moves and all movement. The *guṇas,* on the other hand, are the function of *prakṛti* and as such there is no being on earth or even in heaven free from the three *guṇas*. It is important, however, to note that all the actions of the *guṇas* act only on the *guṇas* themselves. Thus we have a whole system of various modifications which is alive, mutable, and perishable, with different and changeable body-feelings-sensations and which needs the activation of *puruṣa* and its presence every step of the way for its own recognition. *Puruṣa* and *Prakṛti* are beginningless. However, the activation or movement and its manifestation is the product of *prakṛti* alone, since *prakṛti* alone is the source of all effects of action and of all that moves. Thus, we have the primary meaning of *prakṛti* in the *Gītā* as the condition of manifested beings and the secondary as the principle from which *guṇas* are produced. The *guṇas* and categories are called *kṣetra.* The fertilizing energy is called *kṣetra-jña* or *kṣetrin,* for he illumines the whole *kṣetra.*

It is important to notice, as mentioned in XIII. 20, that *prakṛti* is the cause of generations of causes and agents, and not *puruṣa*: for *prakṛti* alone is simultaneously cause and effect. Thus it is said that the *puruṣa* being *of prakṛti,* enjoys the *guṇas* of *prakṛti* and yet is free from the *guṇas.*

The simultaneity of *puruṣa* and *prakṛti* and also the dependence with which more complex body-systems may be formed by the union of both is able to produce different levels of organization with different body-feelings-sensations:

Appearing to have qualities of all the senses,
Yet free of all the senses,
Bearing all yet unattached,
Enjoyer of the *guṇas* yet free from the *guṇas.*

Both outside and inside beings, both moving and unmoving,
Too subtle to be discerned, far away yet it is also near.

Undivided, yet standing as if divided among beings,
And as destroyer and producer of beings.

It is in terms of these more complex body-systems that the word *puruṣa* is used in four different senses: *puruṣottama*; *puruṣa,* as perspective; *kṣara* (changeable); and *akṣara* (unchangeable.) Fully embodied *puruṣa,* is called *puru-ṣottama,* as both immanent and transcendent, ground and absolute present. Thus the function of these words should be discovered from the concrete contexts in which they appear.

Notice should be paid, however, to the fact that since the activity of *puruṣa* is appropriated in every case by *prakṛti, puruṣa* is never exhausted nor circumscribed by the field of *prakṛti.* It appears *with* the field yet is not reducible to the field:

The supreme spirit in this body is also called:

> Witness, and Consenter, Sustainer,
> Enjoyer, Great Lord, Supreme Self.

It is, therefore, on account of this openness of every particular field towards its own ground—the *puruṣa*—that a dynamic movement towards complete embodiment is possible and that partial manifestations of this embodiment appear constantly surrounding man from everywhere. In the language of our theme, Man and Circumstance, we would say that man is surrounded by an infinite variety of static fields—*prakṛti*—waiting for man's decision to energize them and manifest them as human life. This, in general terms, constitutes man's circumstance.

This circumstance, however, is humanly efficient insofar as man encounters it; namely, not as a theoretic possibility but as a concrete living situation. This concreteness appears always, according to the *Gītā,* in the form of the *guṇas:* the particular situation through which the circumstance is mediated. This complete mediation of situation and circumstance is further made possible through the dynamic pull of the incomplete *puruṣa* beckoning man from the depths of man's inevitable activity.

> For no one can remain absolutely inactive even for a moment. Everyone is made to engage in action, however unwillingly, By way of the *guṇas* born of *prakṛti*.
>
> For,
>
> Even the maintenance of your body cannot be accomplished without action.
>
> Since even,
>
> The life-breath *(prāṇah)* needs to be directed, together with the senses and the workings of the mind.

The organization of the *guṇas* labors under the constant pull of both the interpretation of sensation by *manas* and the emancipation of this interpretation through *buddhi.* It is essential, however, to notice that the *guṇas* act on themselves and in opposition to each other. In a dynamic circumstance, like the one presented by the *Gītā,* the *guṇa*-situation system is one where the system, though variable, does not change its own composition. Thus, *tamas,* the *guṇa* of darkness and inertia, while lacking awareness and heavy with inertia, provides for this same reason opposition and stability. Without this initial resistance and dullness, human action would be dissipated in fruitless exuberance. Human intentionality would collapse without this initial resistance. It is also because of this initial resistance that one of the *guṇas* appears to predominate at certain times, either through *rajasic* (superactive) thrusts in order to shake the inertia of *tamas,* or as a balance of both in *sattva* (lighten states) above the inertia and superactivity of the other two *guṇas*. If *tamasic* elements are predominant, then the situation-system may manifest itself or be felt as relatively inactive, dull, though stable. If *rajasic* elements predominate, the situation-system may appear or be felt as in constant movement and transition, and if *sattvic* elements predominate, the situation-system may appear or be felt as balanced, tranquil and full of light or transparent.

This complex circumstantial-situation which the *Gītā* describes with what we have called the structure of *prakṛti, puruṣa* and the *guṇas* is humanly complicated by one simple fact: the incompleteness of *puruṣa* in every situation and its full completeness as the ground of the whole structure. It is because of this fact that appropriations of subjectivity and objectivity are made possible through the appropriation of sensation by the *manas*-interpretation of the field and the emancipation from this position through the *buddhi*-interpretation of the same circumstantial-situation. There is always a tendency to absolutize the world through identification. Since, however, *manas*-interpretation of sensation inevitably leads to definite ways of embodying and sensing the world, the process of redirecting this sense-world embodiment through the *buddhi* requires not only a disciplined commitment to returning man to his absolute ground but also, and through this return, to be ready for a systematic program of desensitizing all the body-feelings-worlds through which man identifies himself with as he travels these human paths with a *manas*-identification. To be able to "realize the self within the self" or to "lift one's self through one's self" is only possible because of the internal dynamic pull of interpretations and appropriations with body-feelings-sensation on the one hand and the presence and pull of the absolute gravity of the ground, on the other. To "see" new worlds in this journey is to simultaneously feel–sense new worlds; namely, a successive change of body-feelings-sensations and radically to detach one's habitual sensation from the interpretative source from where it originates.

Charts II, through VI will hopefully clarify the workings of the *guṇas* in relation to their *manas* and *buddhi* interpretations. The full implication, however, of this general structure of the *Gītā* can only appear clearly the way the *Gītā* presents it: through the embodied journey which through the structure of the *Gītā* Arjuna and Kṛṣṇa undertake.

See Tables II through VI, page 252–256.

THE STRUCTURE OF ARJUNA'S WORLD

Our first step will be to remind the reader to "beware of names." We have been laboriously pointing out, throughout this book, a critical activity of reaching other people's life by trying to capture their own activity of living on the same ground they themselves feel at home with their own life. It would be now most dangerous for us and a tremendous waste of time if we forget the theories we have developed and fail to see them embodied in the concrete circumstance we meet. If we saddle the interpretation of the *Gītā* with the *names* of Arjuna and Kṛṣṇa, we will be forced to mount it also on the hidden horses the *theory of names* of much of our Western tradition carries with it: the appropriation by names, empirically known by way of quantifiable sense-data, of qualities or characteristics clustered around them; the theory of abstract concepts which the mind applies correctly to things or those names; subjects facing objects; things moving in space and linear time; thinking substances facing matter; fallen bodies facing heaven; what is and what ought to be. By way of the contextual thinking we have set ourselves to think through, we find ourselves instead facing moving webs, moving structures, each structure a rhythm through which a body-world appears, revealing as it appears a background of living beings together with the glory and terrors of their life. It is against this cultural horizon that the moving bodies of Arjuna and Kṛṣṇa speak out, make present, their world. Beware, therefore, of names. Neither Arjuna is a name nor is Kṛṣṇa. Their movement in the *Gītā* is the movement and opposition of the

TABLE II

THE GUṆAS

Ontic identity and Ontic non identity

Buddhi-interpretation. Ontic Non identity. Instrumental case. Nonattachement to agent, actions, or objects of senses. Resolution of Crisis. *Ahaṃkāra* resolution. *Anahaṃvādī:* not taking first person discourse literally.

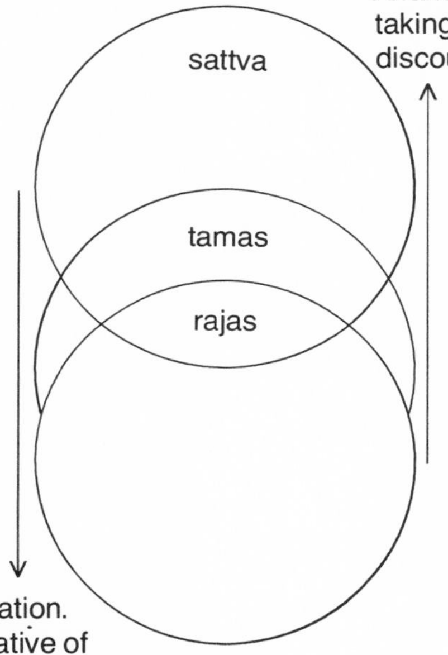

Manas-interpretation. Ontic identity. Dative of agency. Attachement to and institutionalization of agent, actions and objects of senses. Source of crisis. *Ahaṃkāra* institutionalization.

The human circumstance. The manifestation of the ontological parity of *Prakṛti* and *Puruṣa*.

TABLE III

ETERNAL CREATION

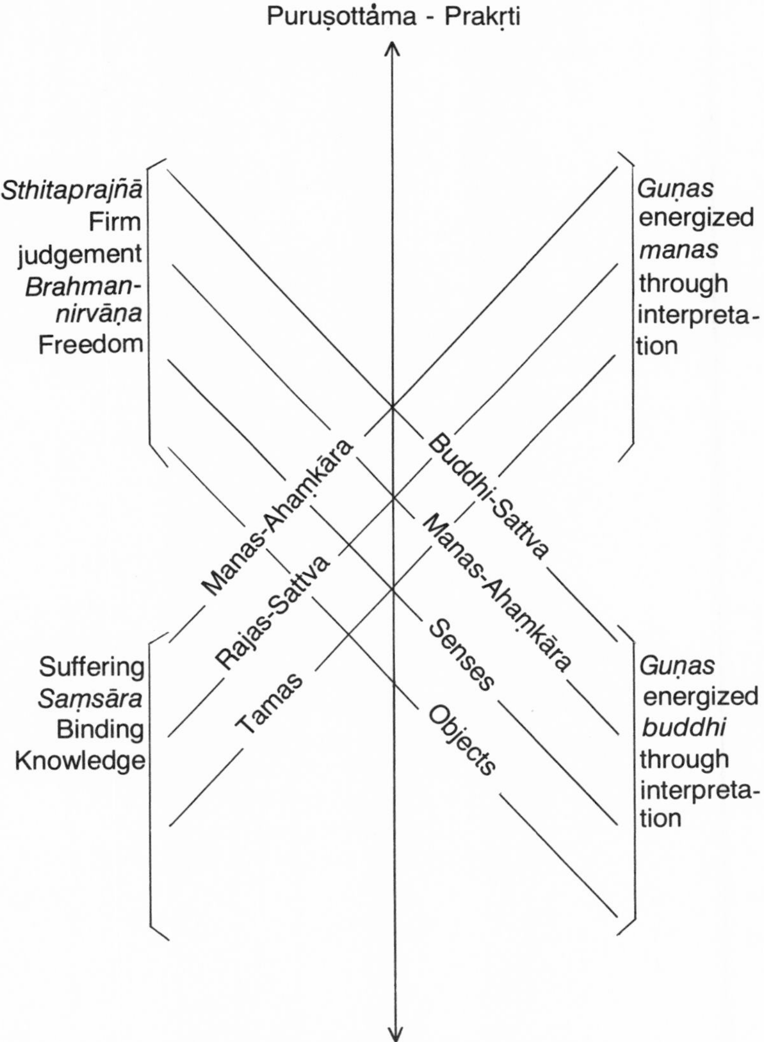

Puruṣottama - Prakṛti

ETERNAL CREATION

The important point to notice in the above diagram is the axis permenently grounding all the fields. The simultaneity of all these worlds makes possible the intentionality and commitment to avoid dogmatisms and reductionisms of any kind, individual or social.

TABLE IV

THE *GUṆAS, MANAS* AND *BUDDHI*

The *guṇa* of *tamas* The *guṇa* of *rajas* The *guṇa* of *sattva*	As *agents* of action they function as identifiable body-self-feelings through the *Ahaṃkāra* and through the *manas* interpretation: attached to objects of sense and action. One body, one self to whom punishments and satisfactions are attributed. Their epistemic foundation is doubt.
The *guṇa* of *sattva*	Functions as *instrument* of action through the *buddhi*-interpretation of action. One may emancipate oneself from the self-identification of the *manas*-interpretation. In its absolutized orientation it transcends the attachment to knowledge: perspectivism and the multiplicity of *puruṣas* and *prakṛtis*. Its epistemic ground is the absence of doubt.

The only criterion for freedom is nonattachment, that is, acting which is not dependent or attached to any one kind of sensation-interpretation. It does not resist life, and it does not doubt. It is the condition and habit of acting with the whole human condition in mind. Therefore, the efficient sacrifice of perspectives is necessary to live an a-perspectival embodied vision of which both Arjuna and Kṛṣṇa are the prototypes.

TABLE V

THE STRUCTURE OF BODY-PERSPECTIVE

THE IMMOVABLE SOUND-POINT	MANIFESTATION AS BODY PERSPECTIVE	
Embodied-Vision *Puruṣottama* *Paramātman* Absolute Time *Gītā,* Chapter XI	*Ontological Parity of Prakṛti and Puruṣa* *Ānanda* (full happiness), *Nirvāna,* *Mokṣa* (emancipation), etc.	
THE UNMANIFEST CONDITIONS *Puruṣa-Prakṛti:* As conditions of possibility. *Akṣara puruṣa:* Imperishable vision, immanent and unmanifest *(avyakta).* *Parā prakṛti:* The *guṇas* in balance, unmanifest *(avyakta).*	*Manas* *RAJAS* (Movement) The totality of the things of the universe *(samaṣṭi)* as social manifestations. One universal body, individual, social, cultural. Memory as past, present, and future.	*Buddhi* The totality of the universe in each human action *(anahaṃvādī).* Each action as a whole body-consciousness. memory as total embodied presence.
THE MANIFEST CONDITIONS As *Kṣara puruṣa:* Changeable perspective of person (ality) as body-feelings. *Aparā prakṛti;* as structured body-conditions: conditions: *guṇas* in manifest form plus *manas* and *buddhi.* The body as problematic tic in relation to its own limits and its own position and duration.	*SATTVA* (Cohesion) A plurality of ontological worlds. A plurality of ontic situations. Perspectivism. Discursive thought. Dialectics. Attachment to perspectives and their bodies.	The total absence of references: language, thought, action. All perspectives present simultaneously, at a glance. Detached action tion through the movement itself of language, thought, action.
	TAMAS (Resistance and disintegration) The natural weight of natural conditions. The weight of nouns and paralysis of the heart's sense of direction: ection: *Gítā* I, XI.	The necessary condition for emancipation through oriented action *(kriyā).* Necessary resistance to human effort *(puruṣakāra)* Eternal creation.

TABLE VI

THE GUṆAS OF PRAKṚTI AND THEIR BODY-CONSCIOUSNESS ORIENTATION

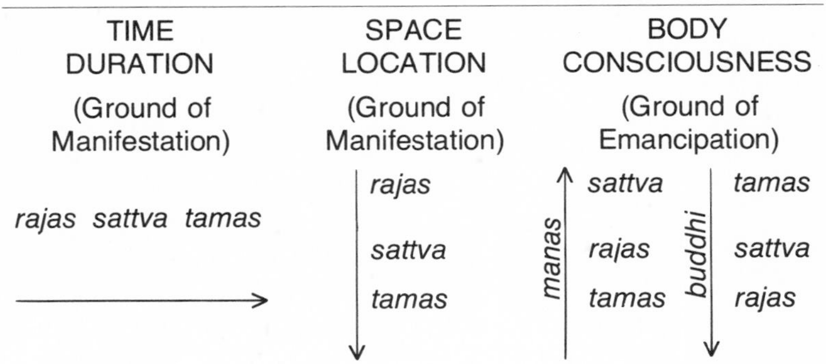

TIME DURATION (Ground of Manifestation)	SPACE LOCATION (Ground of Manifestation) ↓	BODY CONSCIOUSNESS (Ground of Emancipation) *manas* ↑	*buddhi* ↓
rajas sattva tamas →	*rajas*	*sattva*	*tamas*
	sattva	*rajas*	*sattva*
	tamas	*tamas*	*rajas*

All existence is bound by three *guṇas* of *prakṛti*. From the viewpoint of temporality man finds himself already immersed in a world of *rajas,* that is, already acting, with an interpretation of these actions *(sattva)* which radically obstruct his vital path *(tamas)*. In this sense, temporal man follows a contrary move to man in search of emancipation, as shown by the conflicting directions of the arrows. From the viewpoint of location man finds himself in a concrete situation *(rajas)* with its own interpreted *(sattva)* and controlled *(tamas)* local moves and *natural* spaces. From the viewpoint of body-consciousness man may justify the movements of the *guṇas* as his own *natural* moves and give himself the same coordinates of duration and location through the interpretation of the whole process by the *manas* plus the *ahaṃkāra,* or he may reverse this movement through the interpretation of the *buddhi*. In this reversal *tamas* acts as the resistance-ground through which the effort of reorientation overcomes the natural inertia of every natural situation. Cultural man is born by reverting every natural action into an emancipatory action: every action is a whole body-consciousness situation.

guṇas. It is the movement and complementarity of *prakṛti* and *puruṣa*. It is also their parity and dependence. It is even not them, they are like two halves of an orange belonging together to a common origin which negates and reconciles the parts. Yet, having this in mind, we may speak of Arjuna and Kṛṣṇa as if the two halves were really independent. But, beware of names.

Faith, we stated earlier, is one space beyond god. There, according to the *Gītā,* lies the radical ground of man, and unless man stands on it, man will stumble, be lost, broken. This is the origin of Arjuna's crisis: he has lost contact with his ground. As a substitution for the absent—yet present and recoverable—ground, Arjuna has radicalized as his ground a knowledge which makes him depend for his own identification on the senses and the objects of the senses as he is able to appropriate those objects and sensations to himself through his linguistic behavior *(ahaṃkāra)* and the *manas* (mind) reinforcing interpretation of the same process. This is how Arjuna "sees" the world, this is how Arjuna's enemies also see the world, and this is how every man who acts through self-identification sees the world. This "seeing" is the ground of human crisis: this is Arjuna's crisis.

Every man who lives in such a world, whether he likes it or not, whether he knows it or not, is the creator of such a world, and every word, movement, action is the revelation of such a world-view. The decision that the world be so is his own, and the subsequent decision that the world makes no sense as such a world or that a world of crisis is better for him is also the same man's decision.

Man is neither neutral nor innocent in relation to the worlds he embraces or rejects. They are all man's creation as are the actions, objects and sensations of such worlds. In fact, the world, objects and actions are the "structure" of a world-view which makes them have such and such relations to each other and man, the creator. Things, objects, worlds *consist* in the determinate structure of a viewpoint imposed on them, or on how they should be. A world-view is an effort at control and security, at determination and comfort, at reduction and method.

One of the greatest biases in interpretations of the *Bhagavad Gītā* is not to have paid enough attention to Arjuna's crisis with which the *Gītā* opens. If one is set on interpreting, one must account for what is there, in the text, the whole text. Above all, one cannot miss the explicit and obvious crisis of Arjuna and dilute it with scholarly arguments, religious pietism, or aesthetic generalities. It is very obvious that thinking may become, more often than not, a shield people use to protect themselves from life, rather than to mediate it. One must not forget that Arjuna is a warrior, used to living dangerously, with death stalking him at every step. Yet it is this same Arjuna who is now in the grips of a crisis so severe, "that his limbs tremble, his skin is feverish, his weapons fall from his hands, and can hardly move": the man has frozen. I wonder what Arjuna could have done with all the scholarly and pietistic literature written on the *Gītā* if it were presented to him as a remedy to his crisis on the battlefield. Yet, this is the problem which the *Gītā* is "set" to solve. It is fully a controlled experiment with sickness, diagnosis, medication, cure and rehabilitation, all in 700 verses, in one song–poem. If Arjuna's viewpoint depends for its survival on the objects and the senses as appropriated by the *ahaṃkāra* and Arjuna, the whole program of the *Gītā* will be a program to desensitize such a world-view from its absolutized directions: to detach the senses from *one* absolute form of sensing and feeling the world. A man, to be a man, has to be able to move without touch, smell, taste, sight, noise; be able to move up and down, backwards and forwards, in and out the corridors of his own emptiness into the throbbing light, the sustaining ground, by his own impulse. Man can only know his bearings if he himself becomes those bearings.

The *Gītā* recognizes Arjuna's situation as a human situation which is bound to repeat itself as long as man lives. Man will forever have to confront himself while making decisions about his radical orientation, but the only decision that is fully human, according to the *Gītā,* is the one that allows no doubt, or that if a man would falter and fall again into the inertia of crisis, he might by himself know how to "think himself" out and beyond it. The *Bhagavad Gītā* is setting for us, as the start of the song–poem, the recurring problem in human acting that it is not sufficient for a man to find his bearing about his actions from time to time only—any controlled environment will do that for him—but rather that he must know at all times how to find his radical orientation beyond the dictations of controlled situations and *through* these controlled situations. The *Bhagavad Gītā* is not a book or song–poem about god, ethics, aesthetic, and controlled behavior; it is radically a book about the freedom and the determinism of man: i.e., the radicalization of both so that man may be free. We are obviously not talking about an absolute freedom for all men, but rather of the freedom that any man may find by going through the freedom of the Hindu man of the *Gītā*.

Arjuna's initial condition in the *Gītā* is a complete blank. He is *tamas,* dullness and inertia. It is not the case that Arjuna "feels" low. Rather it is the case that Arjuna *is* the whole *tamasic* condition, not only in his mind but in his whole body-feelings-sensation. Man *is* view-point. Structure is the viewpoint made flesh. Arjuna is *tamas* and *prakṛti* in Chapter I of the *Bhagavad Gītā*.

Arjuna As the Guṇas of Rajas and Sattva

If Arjuna had been able, in his moment of crisis, to realize that his body was as large as his *tamasic* condition; if he had been able to realize the dependence of body-feelings on perspective and realize also this ontological unity, then the subsequent journey of the *Gītā* would have been superfluous, but Arjuna settles instead for a crisis and the *Gītā*'s wheel goes on.

The structure of the journey between Chapters II and X of the *Gītā* is again a structure to be "seen," in order to understand. It shares the same kind of ontological union-viewpoint dependence as the structure of crisis. Through a mediation of memory—the lived memories of Arjuna's past, the imaginative variations of a life lived and forgotten—Arjuna is able through those chapters to refeel his body as it felt and thought in different contexts: in *Sāṃkhya* and *Yoga* (II), in *Karmayoga* (III), in *Jñānayoga* (IV), in *Karmasaṃnyāsayoga* (V), in *Dhyānayoga* (VI), in *Jñānavijñānayoga* (VII), in *Akṣarabrahmayoga* (VIII), in *Rājavidyārājaguhyayoga* (IX) and finally in *Vibhūtiyoga* (X). Within each one of these contexts, world-body-feelings are different; the intentionality of the context determines actions and the way these actions world-body-feel. This long journey of lost memories is a journey of re-embodying a body which has been reduced to inaction and impotence.

It is important to realize that underlying the *Bhagavad Gītā's* theory of the *guṇas* of *prakṛti,* and therefore, underlying Arjuna's crisis, there is an implied theory of the *body* and *embodiment* which is fundamental or radical to understanding the *Gītā*.

Richard M. Zaner, in his book *The Problem of Embodiment: Some Contributions to a Phenomenology of the Body,* summarizes for us what phenomenologists understand as the body: "'The phenomenology of the animate organism is, accordingly, the descriptive-explicative analysis of the continuously on-going automatic embodiment of consciousness by one organism singled out as peculiarly 'its' own, and, at higher levels, graspable by me as 'my own." That is, from the lower levels of inner-time consciousness, consciousness is always an embodied consciousness: first, by embodying its kinaesthetic flow-patterns, then, through syntheses of identifications, differentiation, transfer of sense and unification, which constitute the various sensory fields as self-identical and different from one another, and then constitute this organism as *one single orientational point,* . . . and so on."

It is importantly critical that we have in mind this overwhelmingly accepted theory of the body and embodiment for two reasons. First, because this is the kind of theory of the body which, because it is only a particular theory grounded on identity, is the one that leads Arjuna into crisis, and secondly, as a particular theory it disembodies, while claiming embodiment, the individual and social body from the cultural body of which it is radically constituted. In short, the above phenomenological description of the body is not historically mediated. It would not account for the "body" of the *Bhagavad Gītā*.

With this in mind and anticipating Kṛṣṇa's intentionality as leading Arjuna to a full embodiment of the cultural body through the individual and the social bodies, we should then have a second look and really "see" Arjuna's body move. What we are looking to "see" in this journey of Arjuna is that the memories he re-embodies are lived memories. Arjuna himself has gone through them and therefore knows how they world-body-feel. Arjuna is able to body-feel his own body while travelling the corridors of his memories. He is able to body-feel other body-feelings he himself was when those memories were not memories but a living body. He knows of other world-unions which are possible through himself or that he himself has been, but again, as phenomenology reminds us, these body-unions are problematic. One may decide to ascribe all these memories, all these imaginative variations, to the same constant body; that is, one may decide to ascribe them to a body which remains constant through all these variations and to whom memories—imaginative variations—are never recoverable as embodied, but are only possible as disembodied attributes from a logical world to a logical subject. This union is a precarious one, a theoretic unity to which different sensations, different body-feelings, may be ascribed, or may be denied. Man can never find himself at home in such a body, and the only way out for man, in many cases, is to break out of this theoretical body: to declare himself in crisis.

One may, on the other hand, accept the body as it actually appears, moves, sings the world: as a radical embodied unity—therefore historically mediated—which appears as a multiplicity of body-feelings-sensations, complete each time it acts. The function of *manas* and *buddhi* in the *Gītā* is precisely in relation to the kind of body Arjuna and Kṛṣṇa have in mind in their moves towards embodiment.

All the moves, all the actions of the *Gītā* and its characters, rest on the assumption that human memory is always an embodied memory: a memory of a body with sensations, the objects of sensation and their feelings. In this sense memory and body are one. The efficacy, therefore, of Arjuna's journey through the *Gītā* and the resolution of his impass is not only a function of memory but rather a function of "how" the activity of re-embodying such memorizing is of itself able to reunite one's lost memories with the bodies that inhabited them, made them human, in the first place. For human memories are always memories of a body, they are incarnate, fleshy memories; to reduce them to a logical space of past attributes attributable to a de-contextualized body which remains constant through a lifetime is not human, but a reduction of the human to something less than human: the appropriation of *a* body by the *guṇas* and the *manas*-interpretation; man becomes the slave.

Arjuna's realization of what he is doing with Kṛṣṇa does not jump into his own contextual body until Chapter XI forces it on him. Yet the realizations of Chapter XI would not have been possible had Arjuna not taken the *rajasic* journey between Chapters II and X: or to put it even more accurately, had Arjuna not become—even if he was not fully aware of it—the *guṇa* of each field.

The *guṇas* act only on themselves and through themselves. Their identification with, or their attachment to somebody or some particular body-feeling is also their action or decision on themselves, but the history of this appropriation is not complete. It is not completely human yet. It lacks the cultural womb that gives it life. The body has not yet been fully formed. It is still problematic.

THE STRUCTURE OF KṚṢṆA'S WORLD

In order to understand Arjuna's structure in the *Gītā* we had to focus not so much on the statements and names of the *Gītā* but rather on the activity itself, which Arjuna performs; that is, his function in the *Gītā*. In order to understand Arjuna's function in the *Gītā* we had to follow the moves of *prakṛti* and the *guṇas*. Arjuna's activity we found to be the activity of *prakṛti* and the *guṇas*. We also pointed out that Arjuna's closed situation as a man, his human crisis, is the result of appropriating to himself the activity of *prakṛti* and the *guṇas* through the myopic vision which the *guṇas* of *prakṛti* themselves appropriate: the perspectival *puruṣa,* reduced through the *manas* interpretation to a disembodied theory of itself. This was made possible through an interpretation of memory which again tied the *puruṣa* to a theoretical body which remained always at the mercy of the *guṇas*. Since the *puruṣa,* however, is always free, always spilling over the frames of the *guṇas,* always pulled towards the gravitational center of its own emancipation from the *guṇas,* Arjuna's position is not only incomplete but is also explosive. The *puruṣa* has always the capacity to break loose, and Arjuna in his crisis, even if he doesn't realize it, is holding prisoners a multiplicity of potential explosive *puruṣas*.

With this in mind, we have again to focus our attention not so much on the names and sayings of or about Kṛṣṇa in the *Gītā,* but rather on his moves, on what he does. Kṛṣṇa's function in the *Gītā* is the function of the *puruṣa* gone loose.

In order to thematize Kṛṣṇa's journey through the *Gītā,* to be able to "see" his moves, a few further remarks will hopefully help.

If one sees the *Gītā* only from the viewpoint of Arjuna or the *guṇas* of *prakṛti,* then whatever interpretation of the Gītā one undertakes to make, nothing, of necessity, will change in the *Gītā*: Arjuna will remain the same and so will the world and the reader. In more concrete terms, Arjuna's body will remain the same theoretical, individual and continuous body that led him into crisis. His knowledge will be reduced to some form of theoretic synthesis ascribable to the same body, and his liberation will be reduced to a fruitless hope that somebody—someone else besides him—might be able to pull him out from a situation he himself is incapable of understanding or changing. From this viewpoint Arjuna's way of "seeing" remains as constant as his theory of the body, memory, the world, and his self. Yet this is the world of *saṃsāra,* birth and death, origin and dissolution, because the knowledge that holds it together is not only disembodied—a demand of what knowledge should be—but it is not even capable of "seeing itself." Or to put it differently, what this knowledge "sees" is not its own movements but rather the crystalized, static, stagnant repetitions of a structure which takes its own ground for granted. This is the reason why, regardless of how many lives a man lives, how many memories a man has, even while he talks of maturity, change, growth and being different, he keeps being reborn again and again into the same kind of body, the world of *saṃsāra.* The round of birth and death is only possible when man systematically lobotomizes his living flesh for a theoretic substitute that remains constant in spite of the multiplicity of body-world-changes through which a man plays out human life.

When a man, however, *sees* as Kṛṣṇa does, neither the world, nor the self, nor man is what Arjuna thinks it to be. All there is, is movement, fleeting, changing, speeding up or slowing down, and unless one learns to see the movement, hear its sound, dance on its rhythmic waves, one has no other alternative than to stop the world and triumphantly call the movements of thought the movements of the world. Of this reduction human pain, human crisis, human despair is born.

Neither we nor the *Gītā* are proposing the substitution of one world for the other, nor proclaiming one better than the other. The human condition is such that both worlds make up human life. Either man learns to live with both or he will remain forever incomplete. Both worlds are on equal ontological parity and both worlds depend on one another. Their complementarity, however, is radical. What can truly be said in one, the same cannot be truly said in the other. This understanding of complementarity is shared by modern physics and applies not only to two separate, though complementary worlds, but as we shall see, to every action of man if we take it in its circumstantial completeness, i.e., an action-body situation.

Dependence and Complementarity

Kṛṣṇa's dependence on Arjuna, or the *puruṣa's* dependence on *prakṛti,* is not only textually confirmed, but without this dependence the moves of the *Gītā* would make no sense. This dependence, however, can be understood as a dependence of complementarity if complementarity is understood not as a theoretical synthesis of the mind, but rather as a movement of the *puruṣa,* through the multiple *prakṛtic* situations, in search of its own completeness or embodiment. In this sense, any statements which can truly be affirmed in one context, or action-body, are only true in relation to those conditions and limited by those conditions. The same statement cannot be true in any other situation or *prakṛtic* condition, nor can the same statement be true even if the same conditions appear to be identically duplicated: no human situation is repeatable even for the *same* body.

With these notes in mind we may now turn to what was previously said about the *puruṣa* and its dependence on *prakṛti.* In Kṛṣṇa and Arjuna's terms this is translated in statements in the *Gītā* as: "By me they are already slain (your enemies); be you merely the occasion . . ."

This body, O Son of Kuntī, is called the field,
And he who knows it,
Those who know, call the knower of the field.

Know me, O Bhārata, to be the knower of the fields in all the fields;

With hands and feet everywhere,
Faces and heads, eyes and ears on every side,
It stands, encompassing all in the world.

Appearing to have qualities of all the senses,
Yet free of all the senses,
Bearing all yet unattached,
Enjoyer of the *guṇas,* yet free from the *guṇas.*

Undivided, yet standing as if divided among beings,
Destroyer and producer of beings.

It is knowledge, what is to be known and the goal of knowledge.

He who knows the *puruṣa* and *prakṛti* with its *guṇas*
Is not born again, whatever turns his existence takes.

They attain the supreme knowledge, who with the eyes of knowledge,
Know in this way the difference of the field and the knower of the field,
And the liberation of beings from *prakṛti.*

Whatever moves Kṛṣṇa makes in the *Gītā* to liberate Arjuna from the absolutized forms of *prakṛti,* they will have to be, of necessity, embodied moves. If we are able to capture these moves, emancipation may dawn. Alas, our moves with Kṛṣṇa's need also be embodied moves, not just theoretical: We must do what he does if the conditions of possibility which we discover are not to remain just conditions, but become efficient, embodied experience. This intentional search puts us face to face with the difficult problem in the *Gītā* variously called non-identification, detachment or non-attachment to the fruits of action.

Movement and Detachment

Kṛṣṇa's dependence on Arjuna, i.e., the *Puruṣa's* on *Prakṛti,* goes, of course, beyond the statements we have offered as corroboration of our insights. Kṛṣṇa's moves, as we can see from Chapters II through XVIII of the *Gītā,* are intentional moves for a very definite purpose: the emancipation of Arjuna. This emancipation, however, is not possible unless Arjuna is desensitized from the one way of body-feeling-sensing he has reduced himself to by way of the *manas*-interpretation of sensation. Our concern here, therefore, is to clarify what is attachment and how does one achieve detachment; in what does Arjuna's attachment consist, and how Kṛṣṇa's moves lead to detachment and emancipation through desensitization. In order to understand our critical steps, however, a few remarks on movement, sound space, time and the body are necessary.

Fundamental to the understanding of the *Gītā* is the understanding of movement as understood, explicitly and implicitly, by the movement of the *Gītā.* The *Gītā* states not only that man is radically active, that he cannot abstain from action, that the whole world is mounted on a wheel, but for the *Gītā, movement* itself becomes the main clue, the radical presupposition upon which the *Gītā* itself is mounted. For one thing, there is sound: the whole "body" of the *Gītā* stretches as far as its sound can be heard. Notice the beginning of the *Gītā* amidst noise and a chaos of sound and how from a distance *Saṃjaya* is able to "pick out" the dialogue between Kṛṣṇa and Arjuna. Notice also how Arjuna concludes by following out Kṛṣṇa's "word," a word which has been moving amongst confused sounding noises, yet remains always culturally clear throughout. Notice also that the cultural ground from which Arjuna and Kṛṣṇa emerge is a world of "sounding silence," the original rhythmic impulse which keeps sending beings and worlds without ever being exhausted.

Movement in the *Gītā* does not belong either to the objective or subjective sides of the experiences of Arjuna or Kṛṣṇa, but rather it constitutes the radical womb underlying the conditions of all experience in the *Gītā*. It is the possibility to create and recreate a fully embodied experience. Movement, in sum, being radical to every kind of experience, needs to be focused upon radically in order to determine the *kind* of movement which defines and delimits the structure of experience, the structure of space and time, which is specific to the particular text, cultural period or individual which is interpreted.

Movement, to the Western eye, is one of the characteristics or properties of a living body, or of a physical object. From a Western viewpoint, i.e., insofar as I am able to perceive my body movements in space through my flesh and muscles, the kinaesthetic sense is just one more sense among the other senses—sight, touch, smell, hearing. For one thing, such a view already presupposes an existing continuous body in space and time before properties are ascribed to it. For another, this view of movement only reconfirms an already existing theory of the body which does not change itself inspite of movement. The reason for the last standstill is, we presume, the fact that movement, to the Western eye, is capturable or seeable on the same fixed "visual" model on which a perspectival, three-dimensional space and linear time is already presumed to rest. But this assumption is, of course, an optical illusion. Movement cannot be seen by the eye, or rather the 'eye' does not embody movement. What the 'eye' sees is the geometrical forms it has already theoretically accepted as movement. The eye sees only what it recognizes, and what it recognizes is already a movement reduced to some particular form; it is, in a way, still movement.

The kinaesthetic body-consciousness, however, underlies not only the different "fields" of perception—visual or audial—and the different emphasis on perceptions that cultures have projected on those "fields," but it is more radically the underlying structure of every experience and of their conditions of possibility: space and time. It is only with a kinaesthetic body-consciousness as such a radical structure of experience in mind that past and future, as embodied memories, can be made present in the total body-presence of the present. Every movement is the whole, the whole is in every movement. The kinaesthetic body-consciousness is the total presence of a total body-system of embodied possibilities realizable in every body movement.

When we translate the above generalizations into the concrete text of the *Gītā,* we find some surprising orientations. Perception turns out to be less than the innocent and neutral game it is generally taken to be. Arjuna's body, for example, is not just a kind of body, better or worse because of his deficient theory of perception. The truth of the matter is that Arjuna's theory of perception; that is, the way Arjuna relates and orients himself towards his objects of sensation and towards the feelings generated by those objects in his body, is a systematic habitualization of his body as it embodies his theory of perception. It is an embodiment in his body of his body dependence on exterior stimuli such that his whole body becomes sensitized to habitually feel itself and act—move—as such a body. It makes no difference to Arjuna that objects are transient, that feelings are transient, that the same object—so to speak—cannot produce the same kind of sensation when systematically applied to the sense craving for such gratification, or that gratification of the senses cannot be habitually achieved without in a sense destroying the object or perverting the senses. The radical point, however, as far as Arjuna is concerned, is that all must change, even while in his crisis, except the way he has habitualized his body to feel the world and its dependence on the world. Arjuna implicitly claims full innocence and immunity as regards the whole situation. He uses his memory as the instrument to reinforce the same body-perception, the gratifications of the past, the fear of the future and the present crisis. The world stands still.

To understand Kṛṣṇa's moves in the *Gītā,* on the other hand, we must be able to focus on movement on the basis of its kinaesthetic orientation: as the embodied manifestation of space-time which through its revealed movement constitutes at every step an oriented context—an ontological field—within which each action gains meaning, and through which each action embodies the expressive form habitualized by those sharing the context. Thus, every action will belong to a system (a body) constituted in terms of its actual and possible moves in relation to its orienting context. Thus, a man's bodies may be possibly many. As many as embodied kinaesthetic orientations he is capable of embodying. If we now substitute kinaesthetic orientation for Chapters I to X of the *Gītā,* we may be able to focus on Kṛṣṇa's moves as he creates these multiple bodies; we may then focus on Chapter XI and see how Kṛṣṇa tries to "fetch back" all these worlds of the previous chapters into the original womb of their origin and how from Chapter XII through XVIII on how the total movement of the total dance of the *Gītā* is present on every action—ontic situation—of man. To help understand this cosmic dance of Kṛṣṇa, however, we should further explain a few concepts.

Kṛṣṇa's path is the dance of his moves and the lead of his voice. By being able to listen to the one and see the other, Arjuna recovers his lost memories and his will. Self-identification is relinquished for the performance of the dance. The dancer becomes the dance. The crisis is overcome.

In order, however, to be able to see the dance, the moves, or listen to the voice of Kṛṣṇa, it is important to clean the mind of stumbling blocks, dated concepts, conceptual rubble, which might impede the listening or seeing. The reader should remember that movement is taken radically as underlying perception, the senses, even space and time. One should not, therefore, presuppose one particular way of using the senses as the only way to see, or of understanding movement as the only way to move, or a fixed way of placing space or measuring time as the only possible human spaces or possible human time. One should be looking for all those things as they are made manifest through the movement of the dance, as the dance reveals them, as they are embodied by the gestures of the dance, of the movement, and not demand what and how they ought to be *before* the performance of the cultural dance.

The *Gītā* speaks of time in only two senses: one is the

present, the now; the rest is memory. Chapter XI makes it dramatically clear: "*Kalo'smi,*" I am time. This is the absolute present, the only radical time of man. The rest is memories, embodied memories of other presents built of the terrifying and dark present, the present so anxiously avoided by man. Yet this understanding of temporality, like movement, is an oriented dimension. It is not a succession of points one after another, but rather the experience of one after another, is underlied by an actual presence of the total temporal dimension of "the present" within which, or *of* which the memory of "one after another" or the memory of this body succeeding this other body, finds its orientation.

Equally, the *Gītā* speaks of higher and lower, manifest and unmanifest, and these expressions can only be made meaningful if understood within the dimensional actions of movement itself. What is high or low, manifest or unmanifest, seen or implied, is not an extensional experience of points in space contiguous to each other, but rather they are dimensionally oriented in the sense that all these expressions already presuppose the more radical presence of a total cultural dimension within which they relate to each other as high or low, manifest or unmanifest, etc.

To summarize, when focusing on movement, in particular the movement of Kṛṣṇa in the *Gītā,* one cannot see the dancer moving from one space-time location to another and assume these space-time coordinates to be the limits and conditions of movement; rather, one should focus on how the movement brings out the space-time formations of the movement as it moves. Hence what from Arjuna's viewpoint might be seen as form or shape, in reality it is an embodied performance, in that each move or phase, prefigures all other moves and phases. The total movement is present in each move. Thus, the *Gītā* can only make sense if the whole *Gītā* makes sense, and not only a few sentences or a few chapters; but then we might have to give up the usual stale concepts to discover the concepts which would make movement, as a cultural radical orientation, understandable.

Take, for example, pitch, frequency and intensity. These are concepts of sound moving. Movement can sound high or low, narrow itself to a point of extreme intensity and force which is simultaneously the compression of space and the intensification of time, or it can melodically extend its space and prolong its time. All the tensions of movement are implicit in the movement of a note. From this movement-point, frequency and intensity, pitch and rhythm will elicit a mobility dimensionally oriented towards the total movement of the originating sound: the cultural dimension. Thus, in order to understand Kṛṣṇa's moves one has to bear in mind that the orientation of the dance is to desensitize Arjuna from a body habitualized to move according to a rhythm which each muscle in his body repeats: the dependence on objects of sensation and their appropriation by Arjuna's self.

What Kṛṣṇa, on the other hand, is actually performing for Arjuna is the multiplication of his own body as it really embodies itself through another orientation (the *buddhi*-orientation), other memories, and senses itself embodied as such a body. Chapters II through X is the journey of such an embodied movement, a dance of prolonged frequency and low intensity, high and low pitched, but with one conclusion in mind: Arjuna is not the body he believes himself to be in Chapter I; he is also the multiplicity of bodies he has, through the memories of Chapters II to X, re-embodied. All those bodies are alive and asking for release from Arjuna's prostrated and depressed body facing the battlefield.

It would take us much longer than the space we count with here to explain the process of desensitization through which any body in crisis must of necessity go so that it can regain its health again. We may suggest only that the body and the mind may be changed through indoctrination, yogic exercises, hallucinogenic smoke, etc., into not only questions about the body they take as absolute, but through those same means they may be intentionally directed to a richer sensitization which does not absolutize only one form of sensing the world, or interpreting sensation. It is not only important that the body be given other alternatives than sensation through imagination, but it is even more important that in doing this the body remains strong and does not decay in the process. Too much change, without orientation, may lead to exhaustion and losing one's will to even bother with one's body.

In view of the previous remarks, the *Gītā* may be seen through Kṛṣṇa's moves as a systematic desensitization program where the pitch of the voice leading the experiment changes planes and resonance, and where the frequency and the intensity are instrumental in the movement towards a new orientation. Chapter XI, for example, is of such narrow and compressed frequency that space and time are compressed to a now-present point of extreme power. Chapters II through X, on the other hand, have a broader frequency and less intensification to prepare and make possible the effect of Chapter XI. From Chapters XII through XVIII, the frequency and intensity narrow down so that every space-point becomes a now situation. The whole program is an embodied vision which takes time to learn its own embodiment.

Detached Action and Its Body-Conditions

Some have claimed that the *Gītā* could have stopped at Chapter XIII since what follows is a repetition of the previous doctrines, but this claim is gratuitous. It is based on the assumption that all one needs to do in order to understand the *Gītā* is focus on the sayings of the *Gītā,* but this focusing misses all the *Gītā* does and the source, therefore, of those sayings.

In trying to understand the *Gītā,* especially from chapters XIV to XVIII, one has to bear in mind all the previous action the *Gītā* has forced Arjuna to perform on his own view of the circumstance around him and on himself. One has to bear in mind, also, that in chapter XI Arjuna has touched his own emptiness, the absolute bereavement of what he took to be the solid ground of his body-feelings, and that new lenses have been put before his eyes, new auditory devices before his ears, and that for Arjuna the world cannot be seen or heard in the same old way again: the very structure of Arjuna's meaning has changed forever. The same has happened to the text of the *Gītā.*

From chapter XII to the end it is made amply clear that no man is embedded in various social arrangements like rock-hard kernels of unique individuality. Individuality has even been shown to constitute the grounding sickness of man. Man is the confluence of perceptions and social attachments to body-systems circling him. The decisions about that confluence is what gives meaning to his life: it is its own structure of meaning. When those linkages are cut or dissolved against the individual who perceived and decided to keep them permanently, the individual himself feels violated, bereft, naked with the new throbs of his own loneliness. Old forms die hard on man, regardless of how much he may accept change and even want it, for simultaneously he rejects and rapidly resists change if it changes him in the process. The old and the new are irreconcilable if both do not emerge from the same ground, if the emptiness of both is not recovered in the individual who makes his decisions about the confluences of different structures and different appropriations. Change and renovation are mediated through resistence and conservatism. Both are irreconcilable and ineluctable, which is why the tearing change causes is so painful and the healing so slow. This healing is what in the *Gītā* takes the form of chapters XII through XVIII.

Kṛṣṇa, of course, has been merciless in the accelerating process of change in Arjuna's body-feelings. It has been an acceleration more in tuning with an "atomic reactor" acceleration than with a human situation. Like in an "atomic reactor acceleration experiment" what is presumed to be "elementary," that is, the building block of which the rest is made up, on which the rest stands, is accelerated to such speeds, to such high energy, that it ends up "smashed" and giving up "fragments" which prove to be more fundamental. At the center of every organizational nucleus, the atom, there are two opposing forces: the "strong" force that glues together the nucleus, and the "weak" force that governs its decay manifest as radioactivity, and which sheds new particles. Physicists have not yet found the model, or radical ground, to account for both properties, except to say that in "complementary terms" if two statements are complementary statements, at most one of them is meaningful, the other meaningless. This they call the indeterminacy principle. In human terms this indeterminacy principle is the radical ground of crisis when the structure of meaning is smashed. The strangeness of the new situation demands a critical change not only in conceptual structures, but also a relearning of the new process of body-feelings, a re-education of the muscular and nervous systems and above all a change in conceptual structure to account for the new situation. This is the change during which a whole new style of embodied interpretation is assembled, but this is not achieved without an intellectual bereavement which can only proceed to relearn its own process of formation step by step, action by action. Arjuna, who has already *seen,* asks in XIV. 21:

> By what marks is he who has gone beyond these three *guṇas* distinguished?
> What is his conduct?
> How does he pass beyond these three *guṇas*?

It is for this reason that chapters XIV to XVIII are fundamental to the *Gītā,* for they are the chapters which show the 'rehabilitation' process of a man who has seen the emptiness behind his own old structure of meaning and does not know yet how to proceed in the integration of the new.

What Kṛṣṇa proposes to Arjuna from the start of chapter XIV is that for him, Arjuna, who has already seen, every action is 'dangerous,' for each one contains the creation and dissolution of the world. The creation of the new world is accomplished if in every action Arjuna orients himself through the *buddhi*-interpretation of action. The world will destroy itself if in every action Arjuna orients himself through the interpretation of the *manas,* but this program of living is only for one who has: "held to this wisdom (Kṛṣṇa's) and become the likeness of my own state of being." For these are the people who: "are not born even at creation, nor are they disturbed at dissolution." They are humans who have learned to transcend the *guṇas* of *prakṛti.*

From now on, Arjuna the warrior has to tread carefully, for every step is dangerous, every spot in his world is explosive:

> *Sattva, rajas, tamas* . . . fetter the
> changeless embodied one, in the body . . .
>
> *Rajas* is passionate . . it binds the embodied one,
> by attachment to actions.
>
> *Tamas,* born of ignorance, binds by heedlessness,
> indolence and sloth . . .
>
> . . . it *(tamas)* binds one to indifference (not caring).

In no way can Arjuna, the warrior, abandon himself in any action, not even those full of *sattva*:

> . . . *Sattva,* due to its stainlessness,
> Is luminous and healthy.
> It binds (however) by attachment
> To happiness and knowledge.

Arjuna, obviously, is bewildered and lost while trying to give body-shape to his new vision:

> By what marks is he who has gone beyond these three
> *guṇas* distinguished?

What is his conduct?
How does he pass beyond these three *guṇas?*

Kṛṣṇa states simply in XIV. 22, the absolute criterion by which to know:

He does not dislike *sattva* (clarity), *rajas* (activity) nor *tamas* (delusion)
When they arise . . . nor desire them when they cease.
A man who has left all projects:
He is called the man who has gone beyond the *guṇas*.

For it is only by realizing that only the *guṇas* act, by seeing them act, remaining as if unconcerned without attributing or appropriating pleasure or pain to oneself, that one may stand apart and remain firm, without doubt.

Arjuna has to learn that in every action, every step he takes, the whole creation is present. It is the upturned peepal tree, with its branches below, its roots above. The branches stretch below and above, nourished by the *guṇas,* its sprouts are the sense objects, when this tree reaches the world of men, it spreads out its roots that result in action. Men, however, do not see how their actions are so umbilically joined to the whole world. They do not comprehend its form, nor its end, not its beginning, nor its foundation. Their only way out is to cut this firmly rooted tree with the weapon of non-attachment. Only those who have the eye of wisdom are able to see that it is only a fraction of the grounding self which appears as a living, eternal, self and draws into its power the five senses and the mind that comes from *prakṛti,* but taking or leaving a body he takes all these along, like the wind carrying perfume from a home. He enjoys the objects of the senses, using the ear, eye, touch, smell, and the mind. But one has to be able to distinguish the *puruṣa* from *prakṛti* and the different forms of *puruṣas,* for there is the perishable *puruṣa* and the imperishable one, and above these two there is the *paramātman,* or higher *puruṣa,* and above them all is their sustaining ground, the supreme embodied vision, the *puruṣottamam,* the supreme *puruṣa*. This is the vision the yogins see in their own self, but the mindless whose self is not ready yet, even if they strive, they do not see.

This patient waiting for the right conditions to *see,* or

give embodied shape to the new vision which Arjuna has just touched in Chapter XI should be nothing new to Arjuna the warrior. Take a piece of land and there will be as many perspectives as men passing through it, but for a warrior *every* piece of land is all the life there is. The discipline of his own training as a warrior has, in many ways, prepared Arjuna already for detachment and for the silent lust for life and for each of the things of life. ("For you [Arjuna] are dear to me.") His disciplined training as a warrior has already prepared him to immerse himself in every action without fully surrendering to it. His ear is always cocked to anticipate any danger, even while immersed in every action. In fact, there is only *every single action* for him to count on as "his life" as a warrior and it is in every action that he will have to throw himself with the full power of his decisions. A warrior's life is a life of a strategy about every action, and amongst those actions he has to discover also the strategy of waiting for the right action. For a warrior everything is mortally dangerous. A trap hides behind every door, every bush, every branch, but in order to be trapped, a warrior must be willing. He must be willing not to be a warrior and to abandon himself to his mortal enemy: the loss of his will to be a warrior.

From chapters XVI to XVIII the journey of Arjuna, the warrior, to recover his will, to "do as you (Kṛṣṇa) desire," includes also the capacity to wait and stall for the right conditions. For there are those who, without patience, throw themselves to the pursuit of pleasure on the excuse that there is no truth in the world. These are men lost in themselves, small in mind, cruel in deed, enemies of the world. They surrender to desire, arrogance, and hypocrisy, and they justify themselves with false philosophies. They only cling to what leads to death, they strive for wealth to gratify their desire; and they can only speak in first person: I have won today; that desire I will obtain; this is mine; this wealth will become mine; I am lord and enjoyer; I am perfect, strong and happy; I am wealthy, well born; I will sacrifice; I will give; I will rejoice; who else is like me? The destiny of these men is to be born again under the same conditions which perpetuate their delusions in every action. These men do not have enough faith to be able to wait. For one should be able to act in every situation as the situation acts on itself without self-appropriations. For

One's own *dharma,* even when not done perfectly,
Is better than an alien *dharma,* even though well
performed;

For only

A man, dedicated to his own action, attains fulfillment.

One should not abandon the action congenial to one,
Even though it is defective,
For all undertakings are clouded with defects
Like fire by smoke.

If, having centered in your sense of I you think 'I will not
fight,'
Your resolve will be in vain:
Prakṛti will impel you.

Arjuna's conclusion at the end of his long journey in terms of a philosophy which would give shape to his vision of chapter XI is obviously a coincidence with Kṛṣṇa: to realize his own emancipation through the action facing him. Through that action Kṛṣṇa, Arjuna, *Puruṣa, Prakṛti* and their foundation coincide. For emancipation to be possible, however, Arjuna's will has to coincide with the original *cultural* will of which both Kṛṣṇa and Arjuna are the bodies, but this realization could not have been mediated had Arjuna not been able "to body-think himself up."

Destroyed is my delusion;
By your grace, O Unshaken One, I have gained
remembrance.
I take my stand firmly, with doubt dispelled;
I will do your word.

But, which word? Just, listen!

THE STRUCTURE OF MAN'S RADICAL GROUND

The full circumstance of the *Bhagavad Gītā* cannot be saved if its radical orientation cannot be saved. This radical orientation is not radically grounded in that which appears *(vyakta),* the surface: *Prakṛti* and *Puruṣa,* Arjuna and Kṛṣṇa, names and forms, the *guṇas,* memory. The radical orientation of the *Bhagavad Gītā* can only be found through its radical structure: the *avyakta,* the unmanifest, the *akṣara puruṣa,* the imperishable vision, the *paramātman,* the supreme-radical Self, the *puruṣottama,* the aperspectival embodied vision, and unless statements in the *Bhagavad Gītā* about the "undying self who neither kills nor is killed," who transcends the dualities, who is immutable, indestructible, eternal, who frees man from grief, guides man with determined purpose *(dhīram)* and makes man share in the non-death *(amṛtatva),* or statements about *vīnāśī* and *avināśī,* the perishable and imperishable, *kṣara* and *akṣara,* destructible and undistractible, absolute time as in chapter XI or absolute faith as in chapter XII or absolute knowledge as in chapter XIII, are embodied, then the *Bhagavad Gītā's* meaning will be lost, either through reduction of meaning to its surface structure only or through the rejection of meaning by placing meaning in an unknowable structure generally called mystic or esoteric. In both cases meaning is not explained, it is rather explained away.

These and other similar statements, however, are the statements around which the *Bhagavad Gītā* structures itself, through which it revolves, on which it is mounted, and through which it provides the radical structure for its meaning. In order to clarify this radical structure we will have again to listen to the "cultural voice," or body of a tradition; review our notions of time, space and sound-movement, and focus particularly on chapter XI of the *Gītā* and its mentioned, yet mostly implied, notion of the *yugas*: the cultural movement within which Kṛṣṇa and Arjuna are already moving.

It has already been pointed out that the *Bhagavad Gītā* is not a dialogue between Arjuna and Kṛṣṇa, but rather it is the narration of Saṃjaya to his king about a dialogue between Arjuna and Kṛṣṇa. It has also been pointed out that this dialogue and narration about the dialogue is not primarily about fighting or not fighting in a battlefield, but rather about what a man needs to know—what a Hindu man needs to know—while engaging in action, any action. Furthermore, it has already been pointed out that Arjuna's crisis is a radical crisis about a human life which has lost its footing: it is a life in mid air, surrounded by the anguish of a space which has no solid hold on any ground; it is also an anguish of time because one feels threatened with the extinction of one's own identity, of no longer being the one one believed oneself to be. Hindu tradition has been aware of this crisis since Ṛg Vedic times. It is the painful world of human crisis, surrounded from everywhere with a radical discontinuity in time within the dark spaces *(tamas)* of a disembodied world which flows from darkness into darkness like a roaring sea *(salila)* and threatens to engulf all. Man's only recourse in such a situation is to stop, both himself and the world, and surrender to despair and inaction. It was recognized in the Ṛg Veda with its descriptions of the *Asat* (non-Existence) and *Nirṛti* (non-action), and variations of the same idea run through the Brāhmanas and the Upaniṣads. It is in general the crisis of *natural* man, the man who acts through natural compulsion, the victim of the natural forces around him, it is what the Ṛg Veda called *anṛta:* that in which man has had no part, which he has not formed, as opposed to the Ṛg Vedic *ṛta,* that which he has formed, organized: the activity of *cultural* man. Hindu man will culturally and historically share this large scheme of natural man and cultural man and will try to emancipate himself from the chaotic natural compulsions (the *anṛta*) not only by structuring the intentionality of cultural man *(ṛta)* but by directing this intentionality to an original sound-point *(ekā),* the One, a unity which radically grounds in a concentrated form movement, time, space, faith, etc., and which is totally the ground of that which appears. Thus, that which appears is no longer groundless, rootless, but on the contrary it is the cultural body and will on which Hindu man may count on while acting, because it is always present, always playing itself out through the active structure of an intentionality which is capable not only of creating projects and anticipating its results, but it is also able to cancel those projects and detach itself from its results by making itself constantly present to create new projects, new worlds.

Akṣara (indestructible), Nitya (eternal), Brahman, Ātman, Śraddhā (faith), Kāla (time), Ākāśa (space)

These words mean through Hindu tradition the same thing: unique reality, the really real, fullness without fissures, the ground beyond the subjects and objects. They denote the continuous, the perfect identity between the all *(sarva)* and the One *(ekā)*. These words, on the other hand, do not imply any form of transcendence through a relation of the many to the one. In Hindu tradition they are just immanance in everything *(savāntara)* while the multiplicities which appear in the form of names, forms and actions *(nāma-rūpa-karman)* are only the "cracks" of a radical unity which does not appear on the surface due to ignorance *(avidyā)* and linguistic confusions *(manas* plus *ahaṃkāra)*.

The word *akṣara* goes back to the *Ṛg Veda*. It means that which cannot be further compressed, the original syllable, original sound including phonetics, articulation, pronunciation, enunciation, tone, metrical value, in short the irreducible sound-point in all its aspects of which all sound emerges: the generator of sound. It is the source of movement of the universe on which all the gods stand. It is the unnamable syllable with a thousand syllables. From it *Oṃ,* the primordial sound, the inaudible whisper, is born. It is the sound-point which remains permanent amidst all changing sounds. Like *ātman,* Brahman and *nitya,* it is that which stands under all change. It is the matrix, the origin or beings and its end. It is the absolute time *(kāla)* and space *(ākāśa)* of which the world is made. Brahman, *ātman, akṣara* and *nitya* are descriptions of the same ground structure: eternity *(amṛta),* the indestructible *(avināśin, anucchitti),* imperishable *(akṣara),* eternal *(nitya),* plenitude *(śāśvata),* the self *(ātman),* the absolute (Brahman), the ground always present, always absent of name-form-action.

The critical remark we need to bear in mind for our purpose, however, rests on the fact that *akṣara* from the Ṛg Veda through the Upaniṣads is identified with the imperishable sound-point, the *Oṃ,* the moving sound of the worlds, the thread of the universe and also with the moving wheel of the worlds, the movement on which the worlds hinge: the cultural world-movement of the *yugas,* the cyclic *guṇas* of civilizations. With these hints in mind we may notice also that in the Gītā the model to identify the structure of the unmanifest, the *akṣara,* is a model of sound where any sound-point is the center for the movement and any sound has a center in the *akṣara.* It is important, however, for the sake of accuracy to notice that to the description of the traditional *akṣara* the *Gītā* adds the *paramātman* and the *puruṣottama*: the first indicating height—highest *ātman*—and the second best—best *puruṣa,* and that in the *Gītā* high and low are used frequently in relation to the best vision, or that the best vision is always a higher vision, a detached vision, while the low is attached and identified with the fruits of action.

The model of identification through sound arises basically from a nonperspectival, audial intention of space and time. Nonperspectival does not mean that one does not know, the way one knows through a perspective, but rather that one knows at a glance, so to speak, all the perspectives at once. This implies a sort of coagulation of space and time into an instant moment of total presence—as we read in Chapter XI of the *Gītā*—where all the perspectives of the past, present and future are "concentrated" into an instant moment of total presence: the absolute time-space concentration of every space-point-sound of which name-form-actions and the new perspectives are born. The radical structure of this concentrated space-time in one point-sound, however, is such that through this concentration both—space and time—are out of each other. This generating—*akṣara, ātman,* Brahman, etc.—cannot be either identified by any subsequent operations of additions, subtractions, etc., nor erased by any such operations. It cannot be identified with any god, word, or description, nor erased by any such names. What we have is a rhythmic world of sound patterns ebbing and flowing through "clusters" of sound which refract sound through other "clusters" of sounds or stop dead, like against a wall, as when a man identifies the movement of his wave-thoughts with the movement of the cultural world-waves, or *yugas*. We must bear in mind, however, that the movement we define as cyclic and for which metaphors like the wheel, the lunar cycle or the changing of the seasons are used is not a natural cycle. Hindu man was well aware, as we have just mentioned, that natural man is the one that acts through natural forces, that has not gotten into the cultural rhythm of his culture, rootless man. We are always speaking—against the romantics and rationalists—of cultural man as a man who in order to act naturally has first to discover the rhythm of the body he culturally inhabits. It is in this sense also that we question the name culture when applied to romanticism as a notion of life in communion with nature, a communion which would only be possible in romanticists terms if man was excluded from that communion. We have the same reservation when using the name "culture" to denote what we generally understand by the industrial revolution if we consider the premise that the absolute objectivity of scientific method is precisely the absolute negation of man's share of his subjectivity in such an objective world. In the same way that a romantic world could have only natural objects but no man, in the industrial objective world there is only room for artifacts, not for man and his human body, unless, of course, man himself turned into one more artifact. The long and short of this digression is that there are no structures of the world without a concrete body laboriously working for centuries to modulate each tendon, each muscle, each nerve, each thought to move to the rhythmic pulse of a distant and always present radical orientation which gives it life in the heart of man: "It is in the heart where one finds the seat *(āyatana)* of all things, the strength *(sthiti),* the support *(pratiṣṭhā)* of all beings. For in the heart of man all things find their footing *(pratiṣṭhita).*"

Space *(ākāśa)* and time *(kāla)* may also be traced culturally all the way to the Ṛg Veda and through the Upaniṣads with the same function with which we have identified *ātman,* Brahman, *akṣara,* etc.

Ākāśa from the root *kāś-* "to shine," means to shine from every side, as a presence whose shine spreads everywhere. In this connection one must bear in mind the description of the *guṇa* of *sattva* in the *Gītā* as the manifestation of this pervading light through all the gates of the body.

Time, from the Ṛg Veda through the Upaniṣads, is a concentrated moment of efficacy. *Kāla,* a variant of *kāra,* from the creative root *kṛ-* and *abhīka* are used to signify the efficient moment of Indra's victory or as the important moment of union between the Father and the Daughter when the procreative seed of the universe was planted.

In the *Bhagavad Gītā,* Time, as described in chapter XI, is the original ground from which and to which all the chapters of the *Gītā* flow.

It is easy, with these notes in mind, to understand all those statements in the *Gītā* which apparently deny movement. They can only be understood if this original ground is taken as their source meaning. From this perspective the idea itself that all beings are bound to change with the passing of time is trivial. Life is absolutely life, death is absolutely death, spring is absolutely spring, summer is absolutely summer; there is no "process" or "becoming" from one to the other. They simply "are." The same applies to *sattva, rajas* and *tamas.* Only that comes to an end that one wants to prolong. The idea of anticipating the fullness of time in the future, regardless of how dialectic it might appear, is not historically mediated. It rings with empirialistic designs. Only with the realization of the complete discontinuity of time and its fullness in each independent moment, i.e., only by the negation of temporality, does time become real human time. According to the *Gītā* there is no time—action-point—that is not fullness of time. Thus history is not a manifestation of the fullness of time, but rather any moment of history is fullness of time insofar as at every moment time fully manifests itself.

Radically, however, Time, as presupposed in the *Gītā,* is the radical orientation Hindu man needs to radically face in every action. For any human action to be efficient it must be oriented towards the original, indestructible concentration of itself.

Arjuna's crisis, from this perspective, appears as the paralysis of the heart's sense of direction. And this seems to be the chronic illness of man.

THE STRUCTURE OF SOUND AS BODY MOVEMENT

Summarizing all that has been said in the previous pages in relation to the structure of the *Gītā,* we find three radical structures, three radical ways of being in the world. Each one of these three ways is of itself incomplete and depends on the others for its own manifestation. The *Bhagavad Gītā* seems to propose as a human program that the three radical structures coincide in every human action. The coincidence of these structures in every action seems to be the radical orientation that the *Gītā* proposes to Hindu man.

Our own method of philosophy as a radical activity has made us aware of how these three structures coincide with three radical orientations found in the *Gītā*: Arjuna's, Kṛṣṇa's and the Ground as concentrated movement. Arjuna's structure appeared as an effort of a man to identify himself with the totality of the things around him. Meanwhile, this man has to presuppose a universal constant body, individual, social and cultural. Chapter I of the *Gītā* emphasizes this point with the proliferation of names of things and people in Arjuna's crisis. This crisis we have called the paralysis of

Arjuna's heart's sense of direction: his body is as incomplete as his memory, for he has lost touch with his ground.

Kṛṣṇa's structure, on the other hand, assumes that there is nothing ever radically new under the sun, at least under any Hindu sun. Whatever novelty is introduced is a false mirage of language reduced to its humblest function: the appropriation of qualities for a particular subject. In positive terms and in its most radical sense, since language is unutterably vast, whatever is uttered, it has already happened before many times over. What Kṛṣṇa embodies for us as radically real, therefore, is the structure rather than the event. From this viewpoint it is only the institutionalized patterns of cultural performance—ritual, art, work—that are efficient. Whatever variations may appear among them are all accidental, not essential or radical. The ultimate radical value of structures is that through them, in a fundamental and immutable sense, movement finds its own way to emancipation. Their truth lies in being able to see their movement, in being able to perform the whole human dance.

The problem, however, arises when one begins to have even a slight glimpse of the possibilities of such a program for human action. Human truth demands that it not be transcribed into systems of general notions according to a system of calculations derived mostly from Aristotelian taxonomy. Human truth must be met in its own terms: Arjuna's, Kṛṣṇa's and the radical ground of the *Gītā*. It is true that man must live by appropriation of names and selves, within the social maps of 'real events' as described and reinforced by his linguistic behavior, but man's decision to ascribe these maps ultimate value and radical orientation is his own, choosing thus a way of living against other possible ones. A map is never the actual landscape, nor is a landscape ever the *forest*. To take the map for the ultimate reality is to surrender to the map's own imprisonment. Ordinary language's conventional reinforcements only help forge more solidly those prison bars. Even the resentment against one's circumstance reinforces further the demand that those bars exist.

The *Bhagavad Gītā* requires, for its full understanding, the disintegration of the often comfortable prison of conceptual habits as an absolute necessity before its processes and images can even begin to work.

It is not sufficient, however, to point out the shortcomings of any decision mechanism if we are not capable of showing *how* to correct that decision making mechanism. The *Bhagavad Gītā* presents very clearly that its primary human program in the light of human emancipaton is the "unselving" of the world and objects, but then, if this is the case, what we are looking for is not "what" we ought to do (since there are no selves or substances it would be ridiculous and a waste of time to look for them), but rather "how" what we do is radically grounded. In other words, if the prison bars are the result of the belief in a linguistic I-maker *(ahaṃkāra)* and the habitualization of a body according to the coordinates of such a language, then "how" can one pass from such a strongly held and felt body and belief to a body of seeing where the illusory prison bars would disappear? It is obviously clear, I hope, that the change of viewpoint would not change anything in a world of no-things. In a world of things, things will always remain things, regardless of how one colors the viewpoint of such a world.

The problem we face, therefore, is "how" can we *see* for ourselves—author and reader—that the world the *Gītā* describes is as intelligible for us and on the same terms as it was to the writer of the poem. Our next chapter will hopefully clarify more this point. What we shall do now is a final effort to correct that last step where commentators and interpreters always falter by ending this chapter not in a note of hope for the future but on a concrete presentation of the structure of embodied-vision as we have presupposed it here and claim the *Bhagavad Gītā* presupposes in its own text. We hope thus to contribute to the possibility of working towards the cultural miracle of seeing other people as they see themselves. To be even more accurate we would have to say that in this way we actually contribute to "forming" ourselves through other peoples' lives. Our next pages will concentrate on the indispensable notions, operations and charts needed to structure what we have called embodied-vision.

The Structure of Embodied-Vision

The following notes and diagrams are a brief summary of a much larger enterprise undertaken by my friend and colleague Ernest McClain. Although Professor McClain's work is mostly centered on the Ṛg Veda and on my earlier book *Four-Dimensional Man,* his musical theories apply equally to the *Gītā*. Or to be even more accurate, the *Gītā* would be a "tone-point" of the musical body of the Hindu song. The diagrams or *yantras* will be reduced exclusively to those mentioned in the *Gītā* or necessarily presupposed. The sound model, the mantra theory, will again be reduced to the body of the *Gītā*.

Our intention is primarily to create such conditions that the "movement" of the *Gītā* be not only understood but also recoverable. With this in mind we shall first present several "protoPythagorean" definitions of the musical scale, then force these rational perspectives into a critical confrontation with each other, and finally force out that vision embodied in the Hindu theory of tuning by which *all possible perspectives* are kept open. The *Gītā* should thus stand revealed as the literary embodiment of a philosophical tradition validated by the ear and which goes back to the dawn of its own history.

Our study assumes much which is not explicitly stated in the *Gītā,* but either taken for granted or barely suggested. Yet, without these assumptions the *Gītā* would be deprived of its own body and vision. Further, these presuppositions form a structural cultural body which extends as far back as the Ṛg Veda and as late as the Tantric disciplines. Thus we assume that Ṛg Vedic seers and the tradition that followed them, were aware of the string-length ratios of the tones of the scale. This knowledge was required of harp makers in India, Babylon and Egypt millenia before a wandering Pythagoras "discovered" it for Greece, whose lyres and kitharas kept all strings approximately the same in length.

In relation to numbers, we need credit the Hindu poets with no more than the most primitive "Egyptian" mathematical methods: (a) multiplication and division via halving and doubling, and (b) addition and subtraction of "unit-fractions" (1/2, 1/3, 1/4, etc.). At least these are the operations the reader needs to know in order to understand the charts that follow. The reader should not confuse or reduce the movement of sound to mathematical operations, nor be alarmed or discouraged by mathematical operations. All he needs to know is what we have identified as (a) and (b). One principle remains inviolate: every demonstration is expressed in *smallest integers* (by resorting to the "auxiliary numbers" reached by *least common denominators* when any sum or product promises to require a fraction). Systematic tabulation of the results of such repeated operations leads to an isomorphic tuning-theory embodied in number-theory and in structure-yantra theory, but then is when things begin to look complex and interesting. While Hindu, Semitic and Pythagorean cosmologists all considered themselves to be expounding the mystical meanings of "Ten-ness,"—at least this is how they've been mostly presented—from our point of view they were actually using *integers* generated by the prime numbers 2, 3 and 5 to explore the pitch *continuum* according to the *logarithmic scale* by which the ear recognizes invariance. That effort involves the topological subtleties of the *real* number field and the historical crises between *rational* and *irrational* number. In India, as in the Greece of Aristoxenus, liberation from the confining perspectives of "Pythagorean" number theory was achieved by cutting the umbilical cord which bound tone to number. The *continuum* of pitch experience was preserved under the hegemony of the ear, not number, in a way which rejected no possible "embodiment" (*tuning,* however defined) while declining to grant perspectival precedence to any one of them. In India *number* was apparently dethroned only after its lessons were thoroughly assimilated, sometime *before* the Ṛg Vedic cosmological hymns were conceived, long before the *Gītā*.

The following charts and tables together with their footnotes should *speak* for themselves. Western tonal and mathematical systems have been "translated" into corresponding Hindu *maṇḍalas* and *yantras,* hopefully in such a way that static geometry gives way to the dynamism of active discovery. The reader's challenge is to see the Indian forms or *yantras* as Socrates yearned to see his own ideal forms, not as "noble creatures in a painting," but "in motion and actively exercising the powers promised by their form."

See Charts I through XI, pages 287–297.

SUMMARY

By the way of critical philosophy, or of philosophy done radically, we have been forced to face a very sophisticated understanding of both "embodiment" and "dismemberment" as developed by Hindu man and his tradition.

In the Ṛg Veda it is by "Indra's" power that all victories are won over the chaos lurking in the continuum of sense experience: Vṛtra, the Dragon, as both possibilities and non-action *(Nirṛti),* or Arjuna's crisis in the first chapter of the

CHART I

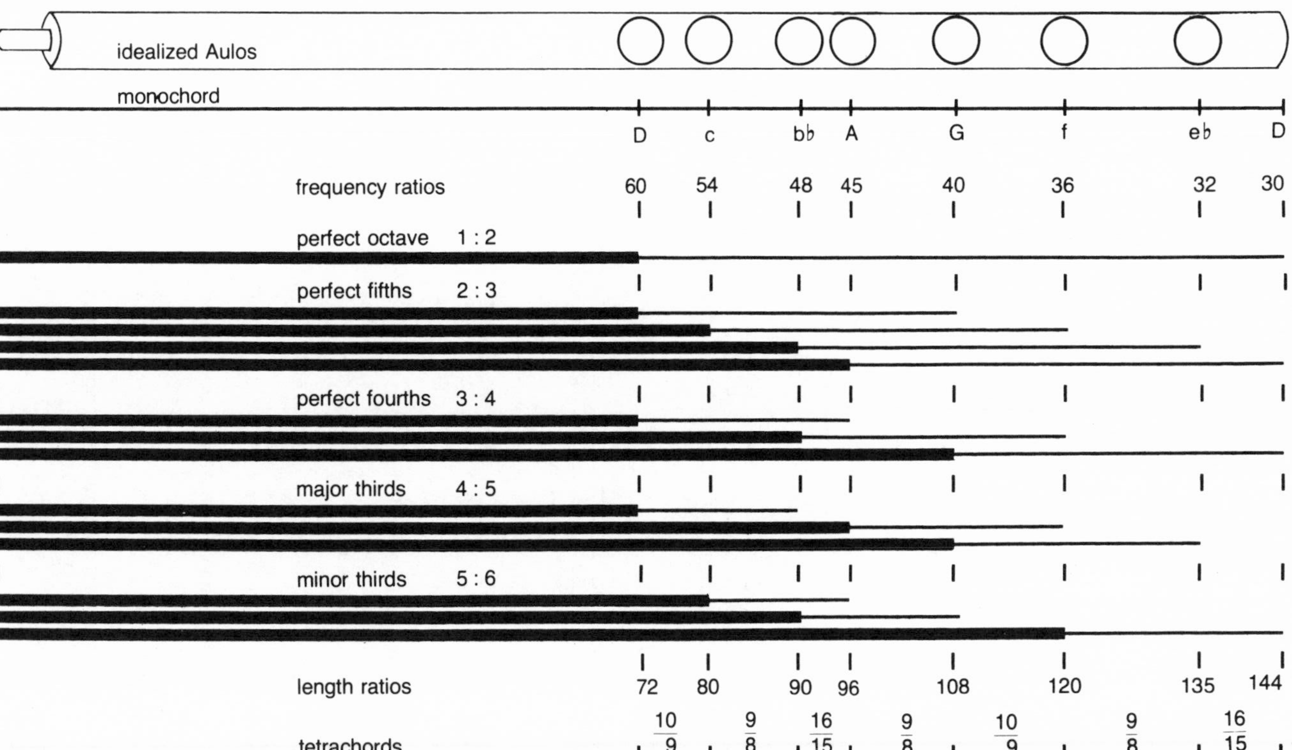

FOUNDATIONS OF MATHEMATICAL HARMONICS: The Hindu-Greek scale in smallest integers as ratios of length and frequency on the idealized pipes and strings of aulos and monochord. These ratios, exihibited on the most primitive harps and pipes for thousands of years before the discovery traditionally credited to Pythagoras (6th c. B.C.), are probably the oldest of all quantitative physical laws.

CHART II

Alternate Vedic Tonal Perspectives

(a) Maṇḍala of the "twelve-spoked wheel of Ṛta," (R.V. 1.164.11) linking solar zodiac and chromatic scale in a common geometry. "Spokes" can be equally-spaced only in "equal-temperament."

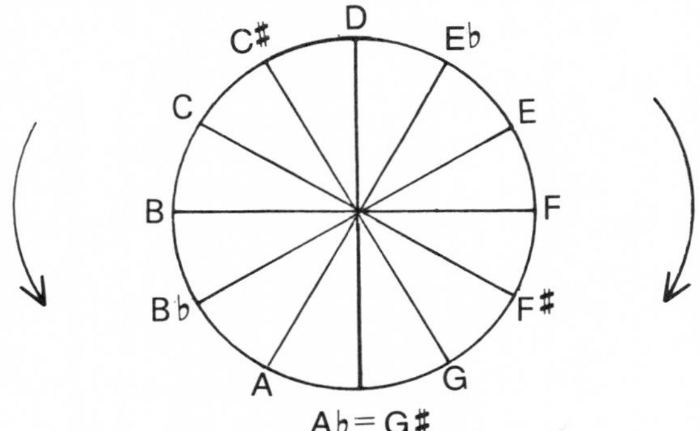

(b) The rising Hindu-Greek scale and its falling reciprocal. Eleven tones in "Just tuning" generated by the female number 2, the divine male number 3 and the human male number 5 symbolize a Vedic bride's "husband and ten sons." (R.V. 10.85.45)

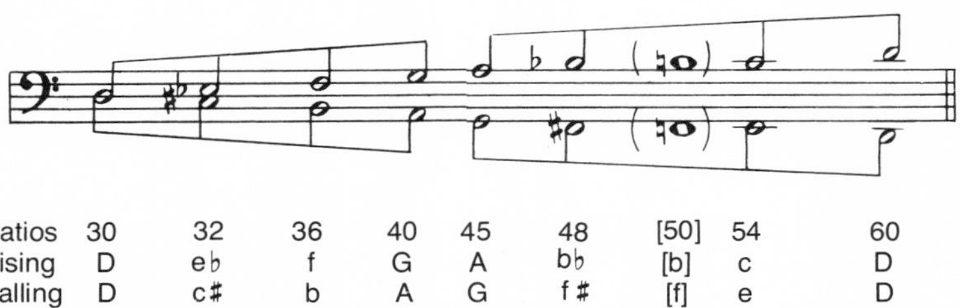

ratios	30	32	36	40	45	48	[50]	54	60
rising	D	e♭	f	G	A	b♭	[b]	c	D
falling	D	c♯	b	A	G	f♯	[f]	e	D

(c) The same eleven tones in "Pythagorean tuning" (integers 2^p3^q) representing a victory of the "divine" 3 over the "human" 5, a *later* arithmetic development requiring *larger* numbers. Modes are the reverse of those in b).

ratios	384	432	486	512	576	648	729	768
rising	D	E	F♯	G	A	B	C♯	D
falling	D	C	B♭	A	G	F	E♭	D

(d) A seven-tone "diatonic" subset of c), with internal symmetry.

ratios	432	486	512	576	648	729	768	864
rising	D	E	F	G	A	B	C	D
falling	D	C	B	A	G	F	E	D

(e) A "pentatonic" subset of c) and d), the "highest" musical caste ("brothers" in the Gītā, or "Aryan tribes" in the Ṛg Veda).

ratios	48	54	64	72	81	96
rising	G	A	C	D	E	G
falling	A	G	E	D	C	A

CHART III

Point, Space, Manifestation

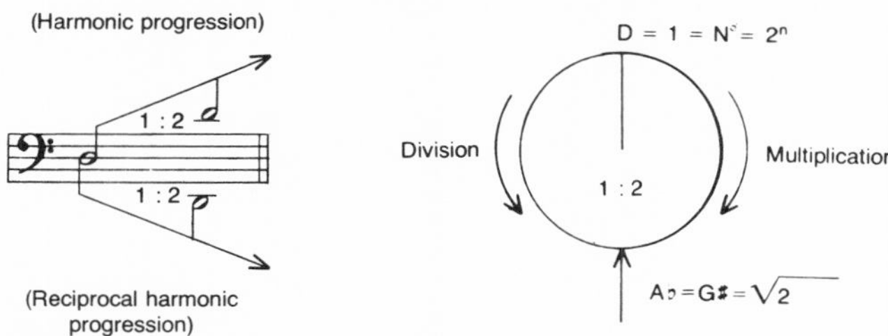

A tone-field can be generated from any "point" in the pitch continuum. Cyclic recurrences of all tones at every doubling or halving of frequency or wave-length permits tuning operations to be summarized in a tone-maṇḍala where all possible octaves are reduced to one model octave. Western alphabetical notation establishes a center of symmetry on the tone D (with inverse symmetry on A♭ = G♯), but Hindu music remains faithful to the principle of "relative pitch," or "non-identification," so that *pattern* alone is significant.

The masculine aspect of deity is emphasized by the odd integers which *introduce* cuts into the tone-maṇḍala, any cut by itself representing a tonal unity, a possible "point of origin," and a "location without extension." In modern terms, $1 = N^\circ$, the "zero power" of all numbers being equated as 1.

The feminine aspect of deity, space, is emphasized by the matrix function of 2 which can create new arithmetical doubles—of whatever size is required to avoid fractions—but which cannot, by itself, *introduce* new tones into the maṇḍala. Rotation and counter-rotation correlate with multiplication and division by 2 to infinity. Every "cut" within the circle is a cut in both the continuum of pitch and the continuum of *real* number.

An infinitely divisible space is a "field of manifestation" for the infinite range of *rational* numbers, but within the confines of a single octave those numbers must compete with each other in defining the relatively few "spaces" the ear is able to discriminate. Music requires some "sacrifice" of accuracy.

The octave-maṇḍala exemplifies "Universal Form . . . without beginning, middle and end," a "changeless guardian of everlasting *dharma*," and a "boundless power" which can be differentiated by the "innumerable arms" (radial cuts) of masculine, odd numbers. (*Gītā* 11. 16–19) It interprets rational numbers according to a logarithmic scale on base 2.

CHART IV

Divine and Human Generators, $\log_2 3$, $\log_2 5$

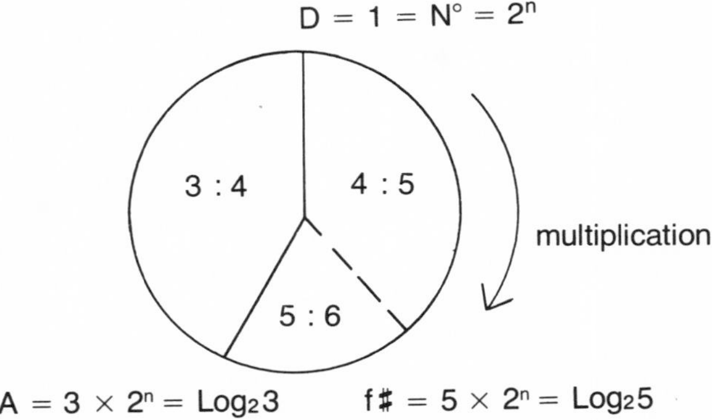

Within the cyclic matrix of the octave, ratio 1 : 2, the prime number 3 generates a perfect fifth of ratio 2 : 3, slightly larger than 7/12ths of the matrix, and a complementary perfect fourth of ratio 3 : 4, slightly smaller than 5/12ths. (To *add* intervals, express their ratios as fractions and multiply: $2/3 \times 3/4 = 1/2$, or $3/2 \times 4/3 = 2$.)

Within the perfect fifth of ratio 2 : 3 the prime number 5 generates a pure major third of ratio 4 : 5, slightly smaller than 4/12ths of the octave matrix, and a complementary minor third of ratio 5 : 6, slightly larger than 3/12ths.

The ancient world probably estimated the loci of tones in the mandala by comparing ratios. In modern concepts, the octave is considered to be worth 1200 *cents* (equal logarithmic units) so that a perfect fifth is worth about 702 cents, a perfect fourth about 498, a major third 386, and a minor third 316. Since each *degree* is worth $1200/360 = 10/3$ *cents,* we can plot tuning operations and their associated algebra with as much geometric accuracy as proves convenient.

Pythagorean tuning (by perfect fifths and fourths) uses 3 iteratively to define all tones, and they lie closer to the idealized values of equal temperament than those generated by 5, hence musical *function* justifies the notion that 3 is "divine" while 5 is merely "human." Tones generated by 3 thus constitute the highest musical caste in all tunings, and tones generated by 5 are responsible for the "dissension" which arises in all forms of Just tuning. "Class" *(varṇa)* membership is a function of the generative powers of prime numbers in a tonal community.

CHART V

The *Bhagavad Gītā*'s Tone-Maṇḍala-Form of 18

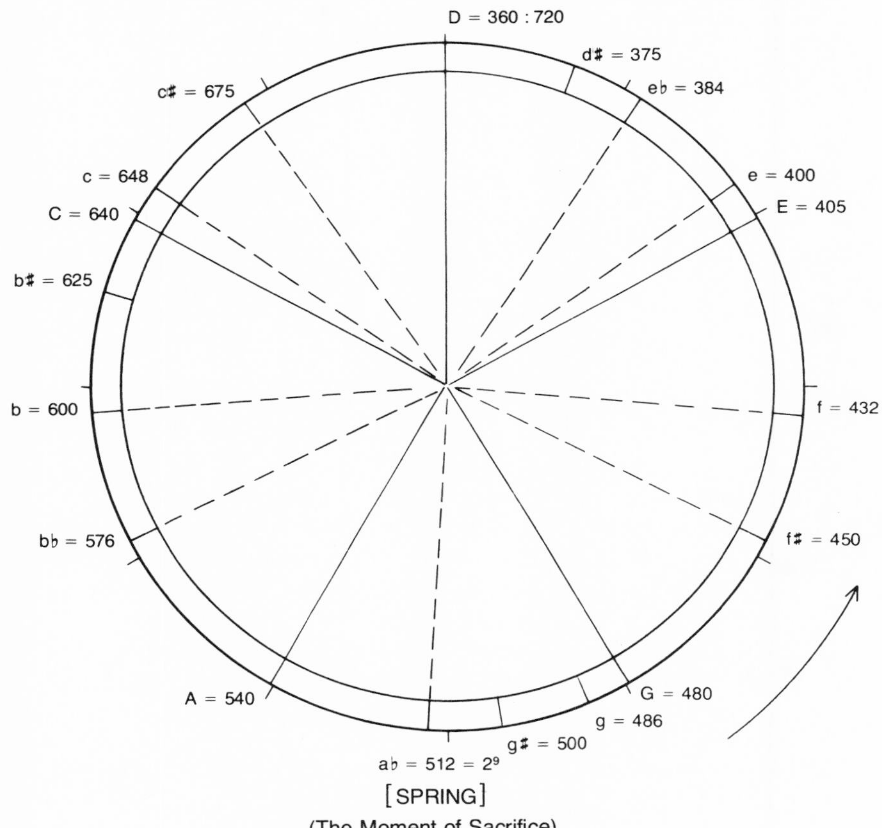

[SPRING]
(The Moment of Sacrifice)

The eleven tones of the reciprocal diatonic scales in the 30 : 60 octave (Chart IIb) gain *smallest integer* names in *chromatic* order in the expanded double 360:720 which harmonizes scale and schematic year. Within this new cycle there are 18 cuts by integers $2^p3^q5^r$ (*Just* tuning) corresponding with the 18 chapters of the Gītā. Five cuts are Brahmin brothers (C G D A E, Chart IIe, the *Pythagorean* subset indicated by solid radial lines) and the rest are "relatives" in this contest between two tuning systems. Powers of 2 can be eliminated to show all cuts as *odd,* hence *male,* numbers, with a♭ = 512 = 2^9 as "1," meaning beginning of the yearly cycle (Spring). Counting counterclockwise, as the heavens rotate; the 11th tone, D, like the 11th "crisis" chapter of the Gītā, establishes a "balanced" perspective in the "field of possibilities."

CHART VI

Sacred Stones o o o As Algebraic Yentras

(a) Matrix for Just tuning (Chart IIb, numbers $2^p3^q5^r$), model for logarithmic sequences generated by any three rational numbers (J, K, L) prime to each other. Reciprocation of *integers* by *unit* fractions (1/n) correlates with rotation by 180 degrees.

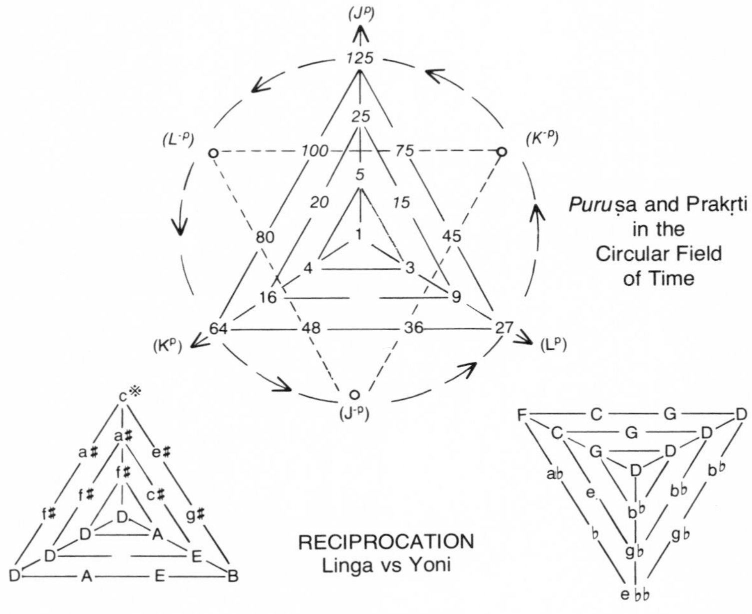

Tonal Interpretation

(b) Matrix for Pythagorean tuning (Chart IId, e, numbers 2^p3^q), model for logarithmic sequences generated from any two rational numbers (J, K) prime to each other.

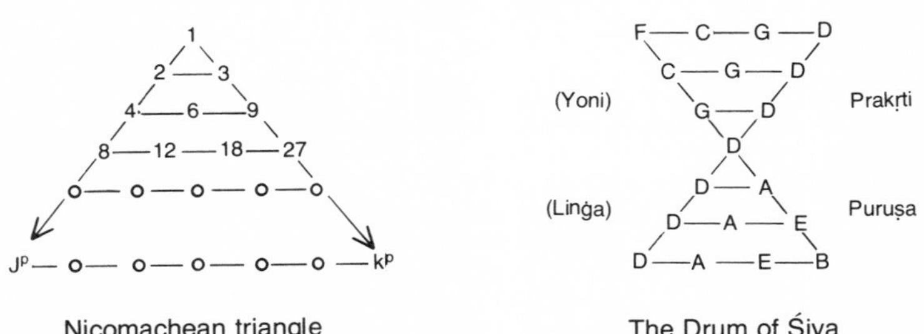

Nicomachean triangle

The Drum of Śiva

The "drum of Śiva" emerges as a subset in Pythagorean tuning from the star hexagon matrix of Just tuning.

CHART VII

Musical Yantras

(a) The "stepped pyramid" or "ziggurat" yantra for just tuning as a multiplication table, 3^p5^q, eliminating the redundancies of Chart VI.

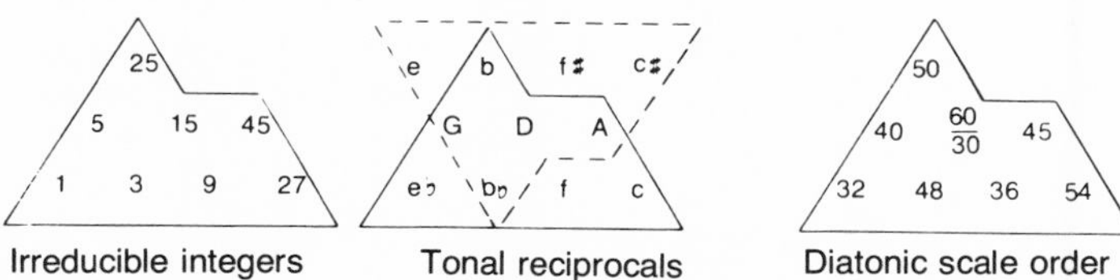

Irreducible integers — Tonal reciprocals — Diatonic scale order

The peculiar shape of the yantra results from the restriction to integers $J \leqslant 60$. Multiplication by appropriate powers of 2 produces "tone-numbers" in the 30:60 "double" of Chart IIb, but under the assumption of "octave-equivalence," or "reduction," the *male odd* numbers are sufficient, for all numbers are being interpreted according to a logarithmic scale on base 2.

(b) The same yantra extended to the limit of 6! = 720 (factorial 6) required to name all eleven tones above in the *chromatic* order of Chart V.

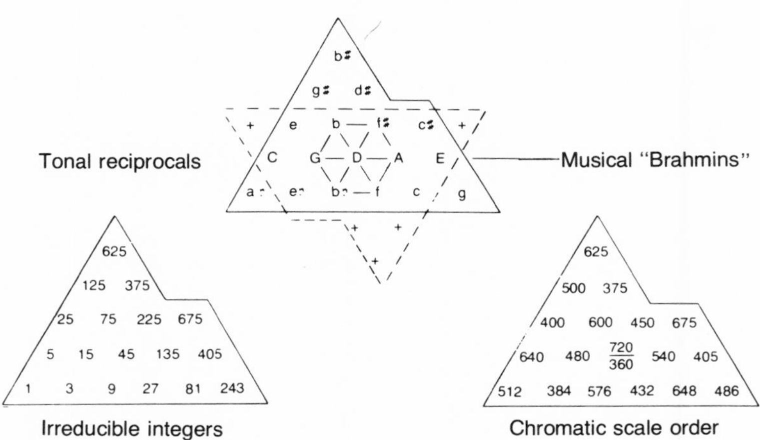

Irreducible integers — Chromatic scale order

Alternate tunings appear at C-c and E-e, differing by a "comma" of ratio 80 : 81. Five more tones outside the common limits of reciprocal yantras do not participate in the perfect inverse symmetry around the central axis on D.

Every horizontal array—when considered by itself—has the same meanings as the horizontal arrays in the drum of Śiva, Chart VIb. Every triangle has the same set of possible meanings as in the star-hexagon of Chart VIa.

CHART VIII

The Yugas

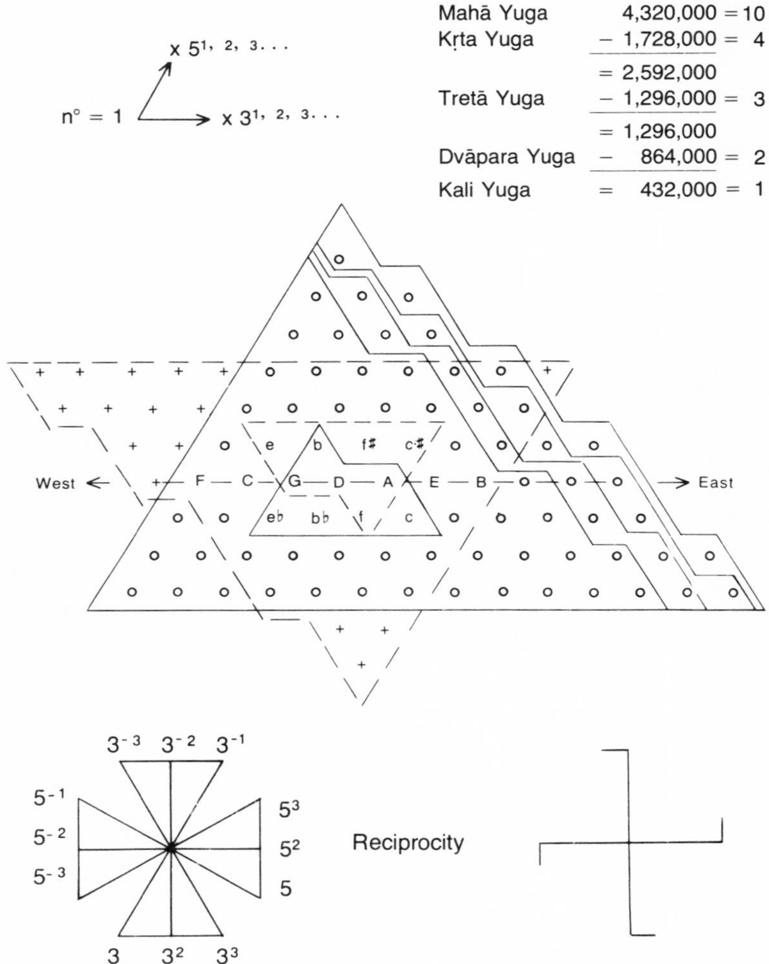

"Male" odd numbers, 3^p5^q, are shown in triangular arrays appropriate to periods of decreasing "radiation," together with our "dark age" Kali Yuga reciprocals. This "field of contest" consists entirely of "friends and relatives," with the highest caste along the horizontal axis, and with supporting castes above and below. The seven tones which remain the same under reciprocation (F C G D A E B) are the "Pythagorean" team from Charts IId and VIb.

CHART IX

Musical "Chariot of the Gods, fashioned mentally, three-wheeled, one-poled, but turning every way." (R.V. 10.135.3; 1.20.1–3; 10.102.1; 4.36.1–2)

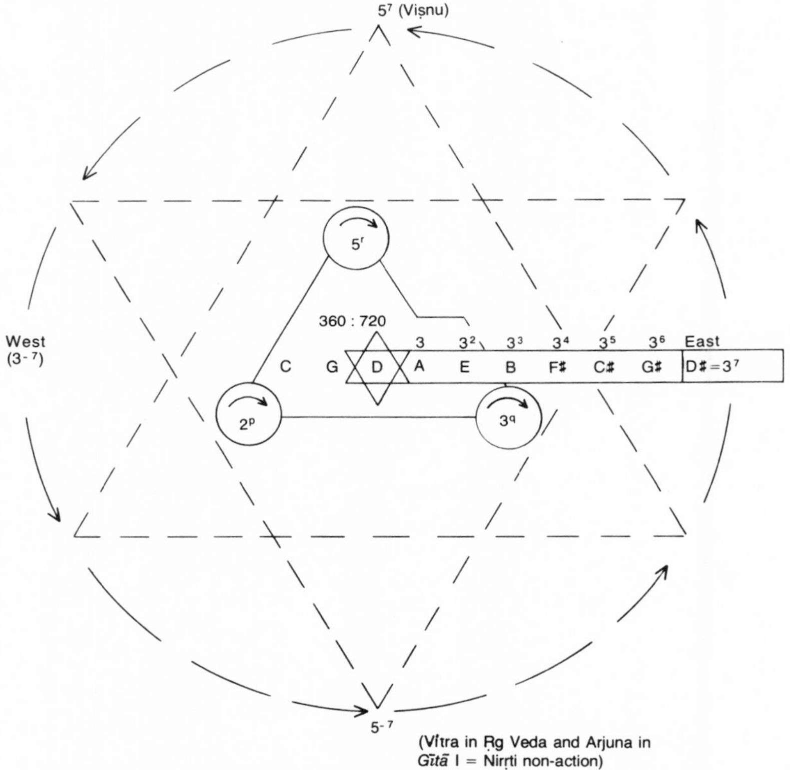

From any reference pitch (D = 1 = N° = 2^n = "Mitra-Varuṇa linch-pin of the heavens" = *geometric mean* in the field of rational numbers) the tone-number field expands with every multiplication by 2, 3 or 5. At 3^6 and its reciprocal, 3^{-6}, there arises an internal conflict in the horizontal axis (G♯ ≠ A♭) which requires a "sacrifice." At 5^7 the field contains (as Viṣṇu, or Sun in the heavens) a very near approximation to the equal-tempered G♯ = A♭ = $\sqrt{2}$ Its reciprocal represents Ṛg Veda Vṛtra, "dragon in the Deep," or the moment of crisis, Chapter I in the *Gītā,* as the moment of Nirṛti or non-action. Thus 7 as exponent represents Agni (Avatāra, incarnate Savior) in the Ṛg Veda or Viṣṇu in the *Gítā, born in the east during some appropriate cycle and as a result of a change of viewpoint (180°* turn of the pole).

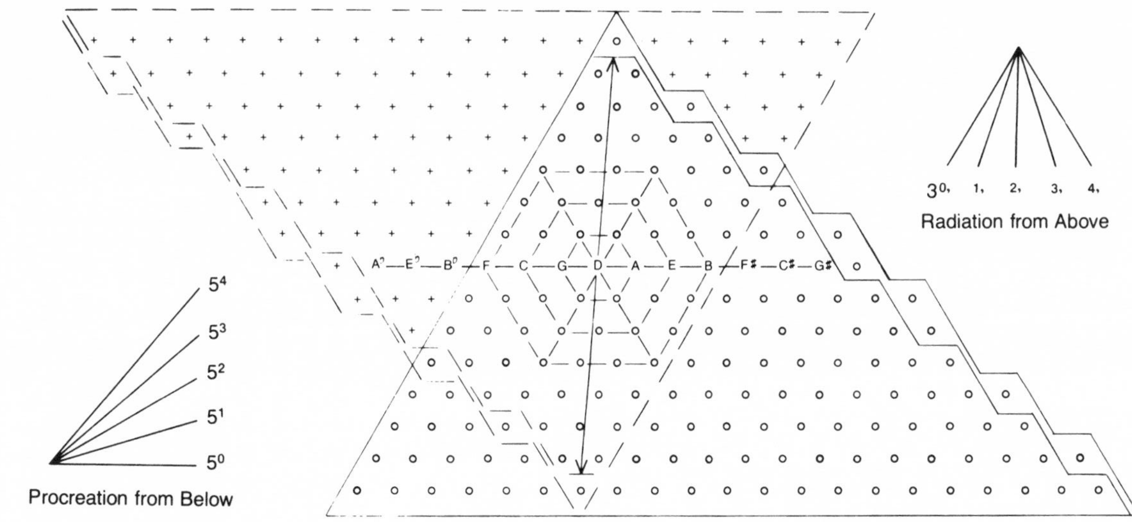

CHART X Early Hindu Cosmology

Algebraic array of integers 3^p5^q within the Kalpa and Brahmā cycles (4,320,000,000 and 8,640,000,000 respectively). The Kalpa array contains 3^6 = G♯ from the "car-pole" of Chart IX, and the Brahmā array contains 5^7 and 5^{-7} (in a context which represents Viṣṇu and Vṛta) from its star-hexagon. All four limits of the central cross are approximations to the square root of two, lying in the middle of the octave and at the bottom of the tone-mandalas. Notice that the Kalpa:Brahmā ratio is 10^7 times the octave module 432:864 in Chart IId, thus several of the primary concerns of the science of mathematical harmonics reach fruition simultaneously in this yantra.

CHART XI

HINDU–GREEK MODULAR EQUIVALENTS

(Any fifths or fourths)	Philolaus and Plato log order	Plato's *Timaeus* circle or scale order	Ṛg Veda order of Gods within Kalpa triangle
F	$3^0 =$	$1 = \times 2^{14} = 16384$	or $\times 2^{15}5^7 =$ 2,560,000,000
C	$3^1 =$	$3 = \times 2^{12} = 12288$	or $\times 2^{14}5^7 =$ 3,840,000,000
G	$3^2 =$	$9 = \times 2^{11} = 18432$	or $\times 2^{12}5^7 =$ 2,880,000,000
D	$3^3 =$	$27 = \times 2^9 = 13824$	or $\times 2^{11}5^7 =$ 4,320,000,000
A	$3^4 =$	$81 = \times 2^8 = 20736$	or $\times 2^9 5^7 =$ 3,240,000,000
E	$3^5 =$	$243 = \times 2^6 = 15552$	or $\times 2^7 5^7 =$ 2,430,000,000
B	$3^6 =$	$729 = \times 2^4 = 11664$	or $= 2^6 5^7 =$ 3,645,000,000
F♯	$3^7 =$	$2187 = \times 2^3 = 17496$	or $\times 2^4 5^7 =$ 2,733,750,000
C♯	$3^8 =$	$6561 = \times 2 = 13122$	or $\times 2^3 5^7 =$ 4,100,625,000
G♯	$3^9 =$	$19683 = \quad = 19683$	or $\times 2 \times 5^3 =$ 3,075,468,750

In order for this series to be extended the first number would have to be divisible by 3, or the last one by 4.

In the Brahmā octave the Kalpa numbers are doubled.

The Kalpa number is given in the Ṛg Veda (4.53.2–3) as follows:

> Four are his horns, three are the feet that
> bear him; his heads are two, his hands
> are seven in number.

4	"horns"
3	"feet"
2	"heads"
0,000,000	"hands" (= 10^7)
4,320,000,000	

The Brahmā number is similarly given (1.126.3–5) in the "poetic" form in which later Indian astronomers "learned an entire table of sines by heart." The occurrences of 432 and 864 multiplied by 10^7 suggests that the Hindus possessed a "place marker" equivalent to zero at least as early as the composition of the poems.

Gītā. It is by this power that Vṛtra's body is dismembered by Indra's thunderbolt piercing "thrice-seven close-pressed ridges of the mountains," a possible allusion to the 21 numbers along the base of the Brahmā triangle. While the exact details of Vedic "mathematical-harmonics" must remain conjectural, the evidence strongly suggests that it constituted a highly developed system of thought comparable in many ways to our modern theory of topological-mathematical groups. At what point in the history of culture the primal forces of nature, probably long deified, were deliberately *rationalized* by the metaphor of number theory no one can say. However, we can at least try to bring out whatever rationality we are able to discover through our intercourse with others. The various symbols (tones, stones, circles, triangles, etc.) were ubiquitous in the ancient world; Vedic poets claimed to have invented nothing, but sought only to *preserve* a tradition. Whatever the origins of this supremely rational poetic logic—of which the Western world has remained largely ignorant—there is no doubt that the text of the *Gītā* is permeated with it. Thus it will be impossible for us to make sense of the *Gītā* unless we are able to account first for its whole body; namely, its context and structure. Furthermore, we must see to it that the *Gītā's* meaning remains embodied, even after we have tampered with it.

For philosophy to be truly humanized, mathematical logic must be viewed from within the body which gave it birth. We must avoid the sin of submerging other people under our own rationality: a single personality. Musical activity validates the conceptual structure of the arithmetic, supplying the *metric* base which leads to our topological subgroups and their content. If music, however, is subtracted from ratio theory, the *metric* element disappears, and the pure ratio theory which remains suffers *disembodiment.* Modern rationality and its imperialistic demands might consider this loss a gain, but from a radical human viewpoint it will remain a loss, an amputation of the human body, of the science of mathematics, for then topology will lose all *metric* sense and will be reduced to mere algebra. It is by such reductionism that the Ancients are shrunk to "primitiveness," other peoples' reasons are discriminated and discarded as irrational, and our own rationality is on the verge of death as a result of its anaemic condition.

As can be seen from the tables and diagrams here

presented, Hindu symbolism demonstrates that even *within* the restricted areas of number theory and geometry a plethora of alternatives confront us. Each one demands a decision from us. To achieve a tuning, we must choose to act in view of our choice. The world is our responsibility. In the West we have tried—and failed—to bury responsibility by a public agreement on equal-temperament, an imposition of one kind of reason over all others. However, the Hindu musician—man—continues to live by the lessons of his tradition, keeping alive all the diversity his culture embodies. His musical scale—on which his model of embodiment and dismemberment is based—contains wholetones, semitones and quarter tones, all *ambiguously* defined from a purely *mathematical* viewpoint; but the *care* he expends on arriving at an *exact* tuning for a particular season, or day, or raga wins the admiration of Western observers whose own tradition, for more than 20 centuries, has ached with a desire to freeze all possibilities into one universal solution, *unambiguously* defined.

Our Western crisis in music is again a paradigm of our own crisis in philosophy. Conversely we offer ample proof that by feeding rationality into our own philosophy through other peoples' reasons, we may save the human circumstance *of* which our present human body is made.

Meaning: Saving the Human Circumstance

Chapter Seven

In whatever way men approach me,
In the same way they receive their reward;

B.G. IV. 11.

Many are my past lives and yours, Arjuna;
I know them all, you do not.

B.G. IV. 5.

We started a journey many pages ago in search of meaning, under the particular theme of Man and Circumstance. We called this journey philosophical, for, we said, only philosophy has the capacity to uncover, therefore know, the radical ground on which man stands every time he takes a human step. Man always acts according to a plan, a radical interpretation of what for him life in general, or a concrete form of life, consists of. We found out that in every case life is an interpretation of itself or a multiplicity of interpretations which man not only encounters but "counts on" in order to act, and to live. These interpretations—realities—which he counts on are more absent than present; they are possibilities the culture, world, people, offer him, which man must realize, seize (know) in order to live with them, in order to act in them, to make his life by going beyond them (by knowing them). This implies that what we call a human life or human circumstance is a multiplicity of interpretations about life surrounding man from everywhere.

Man, we found, is therefore condemned to make himself through others. Others are thus man's own possibilities to become himself. No philosophical activity, therefore, is born out of nothing; it arises in the midst of interpretation, of our own life as it encounters other peoples' lives. No philosophy, therefore, is presuppositionless, but the task of philosophy is primarily to become aware of its presuppositions: to see the world, feel, touch, listen to the world from inside the skin of others, not as others but as interpreting selves. We have no other alternative but to possess other peoples' circumstance as ours, for theirs is also our circumstance as the necessary and sufficient condition for our lives.

Since a culture defines itself, however, according to some arbitrary temporary interpretation of itself, in order to solve some particular pressing problem, to satisfy some communal interests, philosophy must keep itself open to the plurality of its own activity as constituting a plurality of life interpretations within the culture, and not only of the interests defined by a momentary arbitrariness of power, or principles. Philosophy's activity is *anonymous* and cannot be reduced to fashionable, interested or imperialistic manipulations rationalized by criteria alien to the action of philosophy though dressed in philosophical garb. Philosophy is not just giving reasons, reasons are given because there is already a "philosophy."

Philosophy, radically understood, is like the forest with which we open this book. It is *anonymous,* populated through with a multiplicity of perspectives of itself but radically unidentifiable. Yet, like human life, it has no mystery. Its only mystery is the decision to discover it. It is opened and inviting: a continuous challenge to the feet, heart, and imagination of those few men who know not to rest in the same spot twice. To do philosophy radically one has to love not only the trees around him but also love their absence when he has to keep on moving.

It is of this radical emptiness of human life, of philosophy and of the forest that the multiplicity of the worlds of man was born in the first place.

Since the passage through the forest, however, is a passage through particular perspectives on the forest, philosophy has of necessity to travel through a multiplicity of interpretations as its own sustenance for the journey. Philosophy's own rationality can only remain rational if it is capable of feeding itself through rationality. For this, again, it depends on others. As the Eastern saying goes, "If one wants the whole world to be covered with leather, all one needs to do is wear leather shoes." This kind of rationality is not rational, for it can never know itself, but a device to submerge other people under one form of rationality: a single personality, a single perspective. It kills the forest. Man stops being a possibility to become a machine. Man must, of necessity, in order to do philosophy radically stand *no where.* Or at least be ready to stand *no where* as he goes on stepping on other peoples' ground. But this is not possible unless man can take hold of his own presuppositions. Man, therefore, does not really stand nowhere, but amidst decisions about his circumstance and himself. It is only by saving the other that he can save himself. Man must make truth, decide about it and progressively go on executing it. Man must make meaning of his circumstance.

The fact that man must make meaning of his circumstance has made us aware that we needed, in order to proceed in our journey, to abstain from defining philosophy in any sense. We could not put limits on an activity that man must, of necessity, do to remain human. What philosophy is, we found out, can only be discovered as philosophy constitutes itself historically and problematically. Nor can the activity of philosophy be reduced to being one among the many activities men perform. No activity of man is possible without a conscious or unconscious acceptance of a radical interpretation of a life form. This is the activity philosophy performs. Thus, we decided, that our only way out from any form of conceptual colonialism was to proceed historically; that is, by focusing on the activity people in different cultures, or periods of a culture, had to perform to radically orient themselves, or give meaning to their lives. Thus, we were forced to encounter and clarify the "other" as circumstance: what surrounds me, stands against me and I must embody in order to remain free and human.

We were thus forced to identify the constitutive elements of circumstance. We found that these elements, though distinguishable, are inseparable in every human action. We identified them as context, structure and meaning. We have tried to establish that it is only through the recovery of such concrete elements that philosophy constitutes itself radically—necessarily and sufficiently—when interpreting ourselves through others.

Context: In the most general terms we identified context as a latent, all-embracing image which organizes human experience in a certain definite way. That is, it makes it possible for man to act in a world. In its more technical sense context would be the horizon of all horizons within a particular historical, social, scientific or human domain in the sense that the latent image, or ultimate horizon, helps organize and give meaning to all the other ideas, isolated or systematic, within each one of the different cultural fields. Thus, we must be cautious to distinguish context in the above sense from the notions of "leading idea," *(Leitfaden),* "guiding motif," "a horizon to be known," etc., which may at times be arbitrarily assigned the role of absolute context yet differ from our radical context in the sense that our notion of radical context functions always in a way which is latent—it is grounded on a "consciousness I count on" in order to act—while the notion of leading idea, or guiding motif, or horizon is always explicit and grounded on the "consciousness of" in order to act.

Context in our sense is always a radical belief—an idea people count on, believe in, in order to act. Or rather, a system of beliefs, mutually connected, related in a hierarchical order of priorities, with the absolute power of organizing the whole system or systems of conscious ideas within a particular domain of a culture or a period within a culture, a field, a human endeavour. Context is thus the ultimate ground on which man stands in order to act. In this sense it is a world of human possibilities; a heuristic anticipation, a dark, unformed world or worlds to be discovered; worlds of silence not yet formed into language; propositions not yet spoken; myth not yet made knowledge.

Thus we saw how in Greek philosophy *Moira* as Destiny, The Elements, Nature, *Physis, Arkhé,* Being, *Doxa* (Opinion), *Alétheia,* Definition, Wisdom, *Eĩdos,* Ideas, Substance, Principles of Logic, *Ataraxía,* etc., are the organizing images of certain particular human experiences and actions. Whether these images are the ultimate context of our Greek tradition is to say the least problematic. The fact is that men acted on them to organize their lives in a certain definite way, and that these images determined in a certain definite way the paths philosophy followed up to our times.

Structure: In the most general terms structure was identified as "conscious order plus things." In practical terms we find that what we call reality and things *consist in structure*:

a conscious ordering or mapping for the sake of another; i.e., context, in the ultimate, radical sense; or in the particular sense of a horizon, a theory, a leading idea, etc. Thus we find in the history of philosophy—our own—that structure has as many definitions as particular contexts determine it:

- Objects have structure in the sense that they are known to us through concepts.
- Objects have structure in the sense that they have a configuration independent of all knowing minds.
- Two objects have the same structure in the sense in which they participate in the same type.
- Two objects have the same structure in the sense that we speak of them with a word that has a univocal meaning.
- Two objects have the same structure in the sense that there is an image that unifies them.
- Structure is not a function of objects but of facts.

These and other definitions of structure point out the main claim of our method that structure is always for the sake of another. Structure is context dependent. The History of philosophy is a clear example of how philosophers, oblivious of this dependence, have tirelessly tried to freeze structures into absolute contexts, thus freezing rationality into a definite absolute form with the demand that it be applicable to all men. The individual biography of every man is also another example of how this obliviousness of dependence has not only frozen for many their own rationality but has also reduced their possibilities to the act of absolutizing objects, again as ultimate and radical ground of their lives. Structure is the world already formed; horizons known; man within language; propositional worlds.

The most dramatic and radical example in human terms of the dependence of structure on context is our idea of the human body itself. Embodiment and dismemberment, the unification and multiplication of human acting is itself a consequence of the relationship, culturally mediated, between context and structure. For those of us trained to believe that the human body is an organism—even though at the top of the ladder of organisms—we were not given just a belief. Rather, the belief that we are an organism determined for us a whole system of body-sensations-feelings that made us conform in our human actions to the idea of the organism. In short, we turned, through our belief, an idea into flesh.

Meaning: In its radical form meaning can only be identified as an activity of "making truth": the verification of a life form in order to constitute a human world. It is a discovery of the other as one's own possibilities; what people—philosophers included—had to do in order to necessarily and sufficiently act in a world. In every case, meaning is context and structure dependent. It is a capacity and a habit to judge (act) by being able to, at a glance, size up a circumstantial situation—past, present, future—and infuse it with a renewed life. It is the birth of new languages, new worlds, new human grounds. In every case, meaning and the different meanings of meaning have to be discovered circumstantially. In every case, even in the case of the claim of meaning being the meaning of words independent of subjects, meaning is context and structure dependent.

We have seen from the examples of Greek philosophy how the men of those days moved between the demands for philosophy to justify a world which would be universal, i.e., universal principles—unification through method and ideas—which would be universally applied and accepted; and, on the other hand, the demand to reduce knowledge —unification through method and communal though partial agreement—to only that which, in its particular form, knowledge could handle. Once this method and agreement about knowledge was accepted by the part of the population that counted—had the power to execute this vision—then it became an established form of knowledge for the culture to accept. A particular form of knowledge became thus myth, devaluating both knowledge and the world.

Mediaeval philosophy followed the trend by requiring through philosophy that there be only *one* universal world, derived and rationalized through such metaphysical principles. The following period of science exemplified the demands for only one form of knowledge, again in the form of a universal myth, i.e., that the method of science as explanation, prediction and the implied possibilities of the control of phenomena should be necessary and sufficient conditions for the organization of human life. The temptation has always existed for philosophers to elevate structure to the heights of context, demanding simultaneously that their interpretive and *public*—not universal—condition be forgotten. Whichever way the culture and men move philosophy can always open both to their own plurality of interpretations and possibilities, avoiding thus any form of conceptual imperialism and human reductionism.

In our effort to capture our own presuppositions through contemporary philosophy, we were made aware that the biases of interpretation of our own life or of other peoples' rests mostly on the exaggerated inflation of structure to the heights of context, and the reduction of meaning to agreement about generalized structural elements. As we have seen, Aristotle started the trend in Western philosophy by elevating one particular structure (the knowledge of logical causes and reasons) to the heights of context (a universal knowledge for all about all that there is). Thus, a particular model of knowledge was accepted and universalized for a whole culture to follow. Contemporary philosophy, as we have seen, made the same move on the wake of the Kantian critique by identifying philosophy with a particular rationality or by grounding philosophy on logic and rhetoric. In both cases *structure* takes the form of myth—organizes and controls or claims organization of the whole of human life in a total and sufficient way—while *context*—other models of knowledge, other present reasons—and *meaning* are both claimed to be less than the human circumstance demands. When human radical orientations, however, are covered up by methodological coercions, we have instead objective illusion and mass ideology.

As we have seen through our survey of contemporary philosophy, Western philosophy demands that knowledge and self-consciousness go hand in hand; that is, that in order to know, Western philosophy has decided that knowledge ought to be grounded on some form of *consciousness of. Consciousness of,* however, when absolutized in this manner, becomes a coercive human space with the fixed coordinates of space and time bounding human action: this we know as human history. These space-time coordinates, however, are a *logical* space-time substitute condition, but not a human time-space reality. Thus, it is a method. As such this fixed universal *consciousness of* is not self-constituting, but rather it demands that self-constitution be grounded on a universal fixed method, grounded on a particular logic with universal rules of action and communication measurable against the fixed coordinates of space and time of this method. Such a dictatorial method lacks self-awareness of what it does and philosophically contradicts the self-awareness it demands of others and claims for itself. This reduction of human time and space to a particular logic—that of classical physics—is more clearly revealed in the demand, supposition and constitution of society as a universal objective illusion.

Kant helped the theory of knowledge become conscious of itself, but then he identified knowledge with mathematical and physical knowledge, which according to him is prototypical of science. He also identified the self, because in what he names an originary-synthetic unity of transcendental perception, his model of the self is a pure self-identity in which the self relates to the self. He further determined both identifications through the theoretical space of the paradigm of Classical Physics where the value-free sciences of the understanding become the model on which to regulate human life. Kant introduced the terminology and the division between theoretical reason (i.e., able to produce sciences of the understanding) and practical reason (i.e., able to set norms and determine the will). The division in its general terms does not only immunize the sciences from critical philosophy as the positivists will do, but also reduces the human spaces within which man can constitute himself as human. Underlying this divorce of man into the two spaces of knowledge and ignorance, however, there is a further unspoken presupposition that for any knowledge to be had, or be possible, two coordinates must always remain constant: fixed space and time. Only on the condition that space and time remain "fixed" can we have what is transcendentally defined as the realm of the objects of possible knowledge: i.e., the possibility of reliable knowledge.

Hegel too fell into the Kantian error of making a particular concept of science the only authoritative one: at the end of the *Phenomenology* he identifies the critical consciousness of the theory of knowledge with "absolute knowledge."

For Marx, his single, universal science—scientific materialism—has the same function as "absolute knowledge" for Hegel. While in Hegel science turns into philosophy, in Marx philosophy turns into science. The normative validity of this science, however, establishes *a priori* its own identifiable conditions, and these conditions become its own logic and its own boundaries. Thus it breaks the critical claims of epistemology by not being fully aware of its own activity. It is a coercion of history rather than the result of the mediation of history.

These few remarks on the theory of knowledge has made us aware of an easy and vague ready agreement among the sciences and philosophy about the concept of society. It appears in general as a concomitant necessary condition to the previous requirements of identifying consciousness with the *consciousness of,* knowledge with scientific knowledge and a particular *logic* substituting for temporality and history. In more general terms it appears as a fixed and controlled space called historical within which humans make their predictable and controllable logical moves. It will help to clarify our critical remarks to bring out the fact that this situation, again, is the unmediated result of having taken as paradigm of knowledge scientific practice. The relation of theory and practice in empirical-analytic science demands as a fixed presupposition the fixity and otherness of Nature, and on this model, the fixity, continuity and otherness of society, the self and the body.

The possibility of experimental observation would not be possible unless nature, and on its model, society, the self and the body, were not conceived as one variable that remains constant while varying another. It is necessary that a constant variable be conceived as "historically resting," while the subject as "historically moving." Nature, society, the self and the body must remain *objective* and fixed so that explanations of those elements remain always explanations about the *same* elements. They have to remain fixed so that the repeatability of experiments for establishing reliable knowledge remains possible. Only then, and on the basis of these presuppositions, are we able to establish laws which can predict and control nature, society, the self and the body.

This method of empirical-analytical science is the paradigm of science discovering laws not only for the control of nature, but also of social and individual behavior. To the degree, however, that people react to each other through distorted or without communicative understanding of each other; to the degree that people are determined by social processes without understanding them; to the degree that controlling systems may go on behind the backs of the social agents and thus create for themselves a kind of autonomy because of the agents' lack of autonomy; to the degree that education is one more instant of technical manipulation rather than emancipation, the methods of the sciences become also the paradigm of the social. They grasp what the method creates. They concentrate on what through the method is positively given. They sanction for eternity their way of conceiving what actually is. They make history and the change of human conditions superfluous. To conceive of society as a historically resting monolith analogical to scientific nature is to conceive it in an ideological way. To keep society and human history *resting* by means of social technology is to act out of dictatorial coercion.

When we affirm that empirical-analytical science descriptively conceives the facts of nature, we must remember that the facts in question are constituted as empirical facts in a context defined by technique or instrumental action, i.e., instrumental action organizes the kind of experience which empirical-analytical science represents. The basic propositions of empirical-analytical theories are not direct representations of "facts." They express rather the results of our instrumental or technical operations within controlled systems; i.e., they create the "facts." If nature made up her mind to behave in another way, made up her mind to get "historically moving," our experiments would not be repeatable as experiments giving the same results. The concept of experiment and the concept of technique would become very problematic indeed (as they are in social science), as is the case in modern physics, especially quantum mechanics. We had to suppress nature in order to make her react according to the established laws of nature. We had to suppress society so that we could have control of society. Techniques and method change to authoritarian practice and experiments imply only a moment of power and coercion.

The main point here is that technique or instrumental action is not something secondary or external in relation to empirical-analytical science in the sense of being only its practical application. Experimental observation refers to and presupposes technique. Technique is so to speak a presupposition for the possibility of empirical-analytical science. Empirical-analytical theories reveal regularities in nature which we can take advantage of. When we are able systematically to take advantage of regularities in nature, we have technology. With technology the "cunning consciousness" turns the laws of nature against nature herself. By presupposing society we turn the regularities in society into natural laws and turn these laws into a preparation for the elimination of society itself. Society, like the self and knowledge and the body, is neither given nor identifiable. It has to be empirically discovered as it originally and radically constituted itself, i.e., in its plural history and within its historical mobility.

The absolute *falsification* of this methodology, of imposing from the outside a theoretical demand of what society or individual should be, finds its continuous confirmation in the continuous crisis of both society and the individual. Social crisis and individual crisis are both the mediating ground of the falsification of any theory imposed on them from the outside, and simultaneously the mediating ground of their own firm resolve to live in the authenticity of their own radical corporality. Unfortunately neither societies nor individuals move for their own authenticity and corporeal life at this radical level; what we find instead is a 'second hand' and more epidermic, so called, *radicality* where both societies and individuals plant their own theoretical feet for the sake of expedient political survival or expedient therapeutic stupor.

The *decision* about what kind of society one needs to presuppose in order to justify one's theory of self, knowledge and the body has never been transparent to the decision makers. This lack of transparency has been, of course, due to a previous commitment of those decision makers to crypto-orientations towards the substitution of the social for an absolutized and manageable form of the social. It has been a decision historically unmediated and therefore born of coercive impulses rather than emancipating possibilities, but in any case it has always been a *decision* hidden to itself as a radical decision about a radical human condition.

The crisis of philosophy is radically linked to the *decision* that it surrender itself to the disciplinary methods of the *scientistic* disciplines. On this demand and decision the method of the sciences take the place of philosophy and philosophy is manipulated to exorcize and immunize the sciences from philosophy's critical activity. Thus philosophy is identified with a particular form of knowledge, a particular method derived from particular disciplines, which is generalized into a universal form of manipulation of both the individual human being and of the cultures within which these human beings derive their own life. In terms of the individual human being, his only light may be derived from a surrender to the scientistic method, and from the point of view of culture, his richness and rationality is erased in favor of his surrender to the method of the scientistic disciplines. In both cases there is a reductionism to the criteria proposed by the method of the scientistic disciplines. It is obvious that no amount of interdisciplinary dialogue may mediate what can only be mediated culturally and individually. We shall leave until later the cultural dimension of our criticism and concentrate now on what Western philosophy concentrated on more systematically: individual man.

The capital sin of our philosophical past, as exemplified by the method criticized above, has been to submerge a whole people and its diversity into a single vision, a single personality. This problem of identification is central to Ortega's and our theme of "man and circumstance," for unless we can suspend the natural tendency to identify others with ourselves, and vice versa, historic reason cannot emerge.

At a synthetic glance, we have summarized the main attitudes and demands of Western philosophy as:

- a search for universal principles, applicable to man, *universal* man, in general. These universal principles guarantee man everything except to be a man;
- the atomization of man, individual man and woman, through the affirmation and universalization of a particular situation; self-commitment as opposed to self-surrender: authenticity vs. hypocrisy;
- the reduction of man to those momentary approved norms of behavior which are scientifically explainable, predictable and controllable.

These three modes of manipulating philosophy have left contemporary Western man with three corresponding modes of being-in-the-world—possibilities which existentialism has summarized for us in three concrete universal images: the *Democrat and Anti-Semite* (Sartre); the *Underground-Man* (Dostoevsky); and the *Grand Inquisitor* (Dostoevsky).

In every one of these three forms of self-identification, the demand is that man ought to surrender all his multiplicity of selves to only one. In *The Democratic and Anti-Semite* fashion the demand is for a universal self to dissolve all the situational (contextual, structural, ethnic, individual) selves and surrender them to a universal leveling idea of a self which applies equally to all men in all circumstantial situations. Institutions, "Establishments," governments of bodies and souls (Churches and States) work on this hypothesis.

The Underground-Man, on the other hand, elevates a concrete situation to the heights of universality, commits himself to it, and lives thereby on the brink of self-annihilation or incarceration. Radical political groups, the counter culture, the extremist, the self-tortured man, the neurotic, are committed to this kind of self-identification.

The Grand Inquisitor, as we know it, is the demand of the scientific establishment (whatever establishment be in power) to universalize their laws and method to control human behavior. In spite of the demand made upon man to surrender his own freedom, man concedes easily (in many cases, unwittingly) his freedom for the rewards of security, bread and blissful peace. This man, identified with the "herd," still considers himself free; his craving for identification with the "community" is more powerful than his strength to be free.

What is significant about these three modes of being-in-the-world is that they exist simultaneously in every society, and that no one mode is possible without the other two.

Regardless of the merits of this synthetic glance, it is still valid to generalize that these three forms of being-in-the-world for Western man (notwithstanding their drama, anguish, success, glory, ecstasy, despair, value) are made possible for only one simple, philosophic reason. The radical need instilled in Western man for self-identification. However, identity-making decision has no one factual answer, but rather depends on a great variety of criteria for determining personal (or other) identity. Statements about identity in any language are language-bound; it is not merely trivial to say that statements about identities do not always refer to the same subject or object. In truth, such statements do not *necessarily* refer to any subject or object at all, though at times they may do so. Self or other identification terms, in any language, do not prescribe the criteria for their use. It is up to everyone who uses language—and only to him—to choose the type of identification game he is going to play with respect, say, to sensation or any other term, so that he may decide (even while suffering, enjoying, acting) which kind of "candidate" he wishes to have as "sensation-owner."

Plato started his *Timaeus* by asking: "One, two,

three, . . . where is the fourth?" Is self-identification in any of the three forms described above the only alternative for man to be-in-the-world? Is there a fourth? These, of course, are not rhetorical questions. We understand man to be the possibilities of man as actualized by man: man in his circumstantial situations as actualizing and modifying his circumstance through these actualizations. By focusing on the radical activity of philosophy as it constitutes itself culturally, man transcends the limits of his own actualizations (context, structure and meaning) and actualizes his own possibilities. Thus, ontological and ontic detachment are necessary and sufficient conditions of radical philosophy. Therefore the fourth way of man-in-the-world is that which we have implicitly identified as the *activity* of doing philosophy at a radical level: as the saving of the human circumstance, as historic reason, as what philosophy does if it fully (necessarily and sufficiently) justifies itself: guarantees human life. However, our doing of philosophy has also made a very important clarification regarding the doing of philosophy itself, or the modality of man-being-in-the-world in a radical sense: we could not have done it *without* doing it (philosophy) through what others have done. Our method is not a method in opposition to others, a way of being-in-the-world against the others or an alternative (either/or) to the others. Ours is a method, a doing, a path, through the others and it is because of the others, of what others have done that our method is possible. It does not destroy a thread of the human fabric; it leaves rationality opened; it does not close itself in the cocoon of any system; it renews human life through human life on an equality with equals.

This fourth way of being-in-the-world, which we are proposing, would integrate and thus transcend the previously described three modes of being-in-the-world which contemporary Western man seems condemned to follow. This fourth way we identified as the way which the *Bhagavad Gītā* exemplifies. The *Bhagavad Gītā,* we stated, cannot be recovered unless we use what we have specified as the method of radical reason. For the *Gītā* to have meaning, it must appear in its own context and structure; it is not to be identified as something—a book or a doctrine—which is already known to us. We must start with the *Gītā's* own initial situation: the crisis of man through self-identity. This is Arjuna's concrete situation in the *Bhagavad Gītā*—a concrete human situation in which a man, in order to survive as man, must take stock of his own convictions. We must discover how these convictions function in a man's life—a function so important that unless it is recovered man cannot act. Our challenge is not only to save Arjuna but also the culture that gave us Arjuna: the *Bhagavad Gītā*. Our own salvation depends on being able to save them. As Ortega y Gasset put it: I am I and my circumstance, and unless I can save it I cannot save myself.

There is no more dramatic document in Hindu tradition to challenge our own method than the *Bhagavad Gītā* and the crisis and emancipation of Arjuna the warrior as narrated in it. A man, a culture, need be saved so that we, through this activity, come to know our own presuppositions, become our own ground. This document, moreover, is early enough to give us at a glance the multiple perspectives of a single culture; the single note which provided the rhythm to the ear and to the dance of early Hinduism and much of the rhythmic beating that went before and followed this document. Above all, however, the *Bhagavad Gītā* gives us the opportunity of making relevant the obvious and saving the trivial.

Arjuna's crisis as described in chapter I of the *Gītā* is apparently a crisis about Arjuna's decision to fight or not to fight. Which would be fine if indeed Arjuna had a choice of either. Arjuna, the warrior, prince, politician, leader, is no ordinary man: a whole social life hangs on his decisions. Generations of warriors before him and his own thirteen years in exile have made him ready for what is facing him now in the "field of battle," the "field of *dharma*." Or have they? Apparently not. Sin and guilt wrap around the body of Arjuna and threaten to submerge him into a sea of despair. In fact, Arjuna's body is so heavy with sin and guilt that it inevitably sinks into an almost catatonic inaction.

It is methodologically important that we radically focus on Arjuna's and our problem as interpreters. If we are to be faithful to our theme of man and circumstance from a civilizational perspective, we may as well realize from the start that we have as much of a problem in understanding Arjuna's problem as he has from his own bag of skin. Or to be even more direct, Arjuna's problem would have no meaning for us unless we are able to get inside his bag of skin.

Regardless of the merits of war and peace, Arjuna's crisis is radically grounded on three basic presuppositions: (a) There is a body and only one body belonging to Arjuna to which the attributes of crisis—sin, guilt, despair, etc.,—can be ascribed; this body, moreover, remains always constant; (b) It is this radical belief or presupposition that "decides," in fact, for Arjuna his course of action or inaction together with his despair or crisis; (c) This is, in fact, the kind of radical knowledge which grounds Arjuna's crisis, the basic orientation which makes the crisis possible.

These presuppositions, with the host of others they bring along, like language, reality, a metaphysical hierarchy of absolute forms, eternal truths, ideas in the mind, might not make us even blink. This is how we are accustomed to "see" things and ourselves. However, it is such an abstract theory of human acting which catapulted us out of the experienced world by draining it of meaning and into the arms of existentialism, despair and the psychiatric couch. It is these presuppositions appropriated by Arjuna that catapult the self of this appropriation into a crisis.

From a civilizational perspective, however, presuppositions (a), (b) and (c) in Arjuna's crisis are totally out of place, or are at the most a temporary lapse of memory. Arjuna could have known better. Early Hindu tradition, as the *Gītā* shows us, is radically grounded on a complete absence of substances, things, bodies, ontologic and ontic attachments through which properties may be derived or to which properties may be "pinned to." We may pose the problem in general terms by asking two related questions: How can properties be ascribed to *a body* when the tradition holds that there is *no body* to pin them to? Or even more radically, how does the *Bhagavad Gītā* understand the *body* so that Arjuna's initial crisis and its resolution is a basic problem about knowledge rather than about morality?

It is of great importance in cross-cultural studies to understand which field of experience (e.g., audial, tactile, visual) predominates in a given culture or document of a culture, mapping for us spatial and temporal dimensions. Above all, it is radically important that we consider the possibility that underlying all these fields of experience there is a more basic orientation and foundation for them all: the body as lived, as the kinaesthetic background, the structured flesh opening up the senses to the lived context towards which it is itself directed.

Much of the *Gītā* is lost in interpretation by not paying

attention to the first chapter and the clues it provides both for the crisis of Arjuna and for the path of its eventual resolution. We need to focus radically on the movement of the first chapter on the basis of its kinaesthetic orientation. Only thus can we retrieve the oriented context through which its action gains meaning. Thus, from Arjuna's viewpoint, we find that the context towards which he is oriented is the ontological unity between himself and the action confronting him. This decision about "the way things are" makes him dependent on the result of those actions attributable to him.

The setting of the first chapter of the *Gītā* follows the same line of thought by clustering names upon names and adjectives upon adjectives. There are names of warriors, kings, relatives, gurus, men and animals, weapons, musical instruments, bows, rewards and punishments. There is also a concomitant list of adjectives, properties, descriptions, decisions, indecisions attributable to those names. One might even believe that the Sanskrit language has no verbs or that their function has been purposely stopped, at least for the time being. It is towards this cluster of names and properties attributable to them with their permanence or destruction in the battlefield that Arjuna's crisis orients itself. These names and their properties weigh so heavily on Arjuna that he himself cannot "see" himself but as a name with properties: an agent, an actor, a body upon which the weight of all those names and properties heavily lean on until Arjuna's body is crushed into inaction.

It is such an abstract theory of human acting that drains Arjuna's world of all meaning and leads him into crisis. It is such a context that structures Arjuna's body into a body of sadness, sorrow, weakness; a body that trembles, whose hair stands on end, whose mouth dries up, that can barely stand, his mind reeling, his skin burning. The body becomes the structured flesh of a radical context.

It will be most dangerous for us if we forget this initial situation of the *Gītā* and fail to see it within the contextual orientation towards which it is self-oriented. In our search for meaning we must be aware of this initial crisis of Arjuna. If we saddle the interpretation of the *Gītā* with the *names* of Arjuna and Kṛṣṇa, we will be forced to mount it also on the hidden horses the *theory of names* of much of our Western tradition carries with it: the appropriation by names, empirically known by way of quantifiable sense-data, of qualities or characteristics clustered around them; the theory of abstract concepts which the mind applies correctly to things or those names; subjects facing objects; things moving in space and linear time; thinking substances facing matter; fallen bodies facing heaven; what is and what ought to be.

By way of the contextual thinking we have set ourselves to think through, we find ourselves instead facing moving webs, moving structures, each structure a rhythm through which a body-world appears, revealing as it appears a background of living beings together with the glory and terrors of their life. It is against this cultural horizon that the moving bodies of Arjuna and Kṛṣṇa speak out, make present, their world. It would be, therefore, a radical misinterpretation of the *Gītā* to resolve this initial crisis of Arjuna with the same theory of knowledge and epistemology that led him into crisis. We soon learn that Arjuna has radicalized as his ground a knowledge which makes him depend for his own identification on the senses and the objects of the senses as he is able to appropriate those objects and sensations to himself through his linguistic behavior *(ahaṃkāra)* and the *manas* (mind) reinforcing interpretation of the same process. This is how Arjuna "sees" the world, this is how Arjuna's enemies also see the world, and this is how every man who acts through self-identification sees the world. This "seeing" is the ground of human crisis: this is Arjuna's crisis.

Arjuna's search for meaning, together with our own, will have to move through seventeen more chapters. The first chapter of the *Gītā,* however, offers us some clues as to the direction that this search will take. There is first the chariot within which two different perspectives of the present situation appear: Arjuna's and Kṛṣṇa's. The difference between these two perspectives is a turn of the chariot pole of 180°. Chapter XI of the *Gītā* will offer us the consummation of Kṛṣṇa's perspective.

And then there is the world of sound. Beyond Arjuna's crisis, underlying Kṛṣṇa's and Arjuna's moves within the culture there is a whole world of sound and movement which makes those moves possible. This sound-movement-world is what in the words of St. John of the Cross we may call "the sounding silence" *(el silencio sonoro)* in which the world of the *Gītā* is submerged and which we must recover to give the *Gītā* its own meaning.

Chapter I of the *Gītā* gives us the most important clues

for discovering the *sound* setting of the song–poem. Our first clue is to observe how the author of the *Gītā*—whoever he might be—presents the story. The author remains unknown (though it is speculated his name to be Vyāsa, the compiler), thus he avoids identifying himself with his work and does not force the reader to focus on his own limits. Instead, the whole story is narrated by the charioteer *Saṃjaya* to his blind king, *Dhṛtarāṣṭra,* while both get ready to watch the battle which is about to take place from a safe distance. It is from amongst the roars of men, the tumultuous sounds of conch shells blowing, kettledrums, cymbals and horns, amidst the clanging of armour, weapons, chariots and amidst the nervous exultation of animals and men that *Saṃjaya*–and through him the whole tradition and ourselves—is able to *hear* a whispering dialogue, in the distant center of the battlefield, between Arjuna and his charioteer Kṛṣṇa. The *Gītā's* body stretches as far as its voice is heard.

At the end of the *Gītā* in XVIII 75, *Saṃjaya* repeats this same clue by reminding us that this is the story that he has heard, "a marvelous hair-raising dialogue," a dialogue which he recalls again and again.

The reader should remember that Indian literature is of two types: *smṛti,* "remembered" or "commented upon" and *śruti,* literally "what has been heard." Thus the *Gītā,* through Arjuna's crisis, brings together the whole world of the moving *yugas* and the two traditions of *smṛti* and *śruti* and their reconciliation: "Destroyed is my delusion; by your grace, O Unshaken One, I have gained remembrance. I take my stand firmly, with doubt dispelled; I will do your word." The *Gītā* is the body-sound that brings and holds the two world perspectives of Arjuna and Kṛṣṇa together.

It is this model of sound we should keep in mind, for it is only by understanding it that *movement* will appear as a living, embodied movement rather than just a disembodied movement of discursive thought.

As the first line of the *Bhagavad Gītā* says: "*Dharmakṣetre-Kurukṣetre,*" the field of the Kurus, the field of battle is also the field of *dharma,* the manifestation of a radical orientation. Man is bound to fight and question.

Arjuna's surrender of his life to meaninglessness is the result of his decision about a knowledge which is absolute and his decision about a body which is also absolute. The path that Kṛṣṇa will force Arjuna to follow in search of emancipation will be an effort to correct this initial absolute and objective illusion.

Where Arjuna will rely for his identification on the *ahaṃkāra,* I-maker, Kṛṣṇa will propose the *anahaṃvādī*, not the "I" speaking, as the linguistic modality of dwelling in the world. Where Arjuna relies on the *manas* interpretation of sensation, Kṛṣṇa will propose the *buddhi* interpretation with its contextual dependence, rather than the absolutized form of sensation repeated by the *manas* interpretation. Where Arjuna relies for his absolutizing orientation on the movement of his own thought, Kṛṣṇa will show Arjuna the absolute emptiness of these moves by making him realize the circumstantial moves within which thought, knowledge and body are already moving and express their moves within the situation facing them.

The same way we have made the reader aware of the way that the Sanskrit language functions in order to depersonalize action in favor of its emphasis on the activity of the verb, we should also pay note to the possibility that we might misunderstand the moves of the *Gītā* if we do not uncover the presuppositions with which our English language forces us to read them. We have to be aware that our English metaphors to describe a man's memories are linear, covered with words like "river," "stream," "chain," "train." This linear thinking reinforces the belief in a theoretical consciousness which remains constant. It cannot account for "the circumstances" we face in every action without reducing them to a theory which in no way changes our presuppositions about memory, consciousness or the body. This linear thinking is presupposed in all our methods of induction and deduction and distributive logic with their distributive laws of and/or.

Cause and effect are similarly connected and in the same way we trace the *path* of a statistical graph, a historical development, a personal biography, the evolution of man from the ape to the mystic. Motivation and response follow the same linear path, and so does thought, action, life, reason, argument, conversation, and the path of salvation. Our language cannot function without the and/or connections, and this determination of language reinforces our colonialist or reductionist tendencies both in relation to experience and other peoples' cultures. Yet the contemporary quantum logic of modern physics is a nonlinear, nondistributive orthocomplemented lattice of sentences where the distributive laws (and/or) have been dropped. The Boolean logic of our language has not yet made room for the non-Boolean character of experience. However, unless we have this in mind, the moves of the *Gītā* will be difficult to "see." These moves are non-Boolean in character in the sense that each of them is a complete situation in itself: a perspective-body totality oriented towards a cultural origin, aperspectival and bodiless, which becomes perspective and flesh simultaneously with every human move. *Puruṣa* and *Prakṛti*, Kṛṣṇa and Arjuna function in the *Gītā* as the embodiment of these generalizations.

Simultaneous with Arjuna's form of knowledge there is Kṛṣṇa's: a knowledge which not only includes reflection but is a form of reflection which is fed by the multiplicity of social "regional ontologies" and their perspectives as they surround both Kṛṣṇa and Arjuna. It is, moreover, a knowledge intentionally directed towards the recovery of its own original grounding orientation: the absolute present. The "other" becomes for Kṛṣṇa's way of knowledge the possibilities of its own emancipation and radical constitution. This is the kind of knowledge a whole social fabric has been "counting on" in order to live in innovation and continuity. Arjuna's and Kṛṣṇa's consciousnesses plus their radical original orientation form the necessary and sufficient conditions for the culture—the *Gītā*—to be. All three have to be accounted for. Any one of them absolutized would be no culture at all, at least not the culture of the *Gītā*.

The integration, however, of multiple perspectives and their ground is not possible if ultimately knowledge is not mediated through a radical sacrifice of perspectives. It is through this sacrifice that human knowing as an embodied-vision of man's actual body may be opened up; that the multiplicity of actual human empirical spaces for man's interaction and communication may be made possible; and that the originating aperspectival ground which made possible the subsequent multiplicity may be recovered.

Arjuna's crisis and despair can be read in chapters I and XI of the *Gītā,* Kṛṣṇa's resolution of this crisis, his own dependence on Arjuna and their simultaneous moves can be seen through chapters II to X and XII to XVIII. Chapter XI will appear in the *Gītā* as the absolute present mediating and grounding the moves of the past and the future, Arjuna's and Kṛṣṇa's.

When a man is in the midst of a crisis, like Arjuna's, things must first get worse before they get better. The crisis must reach bottom before it is resolved.

If Arjuna had been able, in his moment of crisis, to realize that his body was as large as his *tamasic* condition; if he had been able to realize the dependence of body-feelings on perspective and realize also this ontological unity, then the subsequent journey of the *Gītā* would have been superfluous. But Arjuna settles instead for a crisis, and the *Gītā's* wheel goes on.

The structure of the journey between chapters II and X of the *Gītā* is again a structure to be "seen," in order to understand. It shares the same kind of ontological union-viewpoint dependence as the structure of crisis. Through a mediation of memory—the lived memories of Arjuna's past, the imaginative variations of a life lived and forgotten—Arjuna is able through those chapters to refeel his body as it felt and thought in different contexts: *Sāṃkhya* and *Yoga* (II); *Karmayoga* (III): the yoga of action; *Jñānayoga* (IV): the yoga of knowledge; *Karmasaṃnyāsayoga* (V): the yoga of renunciation of actions; *Dhyānayoga* (VI): the yoga of meditation; *Jñānavijñānayoga* (VII): the yoga of wisdom and understanding; *Akṣarabrahmayoga* (VIII): the yoga of the imperishable Brahman; *Rājavidyārājaguhyayoga* (IX): the yoga of sovereign knowledge and sovereign secret; and *Vibhūtiyoga* (X): the yoga of manifestations. Within each one of these contexts, world-body-feelings are different; the intentionality of the context determines actions and the way these actions world-body-feel. This long journey of lost memories is a journey of re-embodiment. It demands an *ontological reduction* grounded on the realization of nonexistence of reference for language, perception or experience in general, but the conclusion of such journey of re-embodiment shows the futility of trying to grasp to substances or anything permanent. Chapter XI of the *Gītā* shows the finality, dissolution and despair of any world grounded on permanence.

This is the end of Arjuna's moves through the first eleven chapters of the *Gītā*. What we *see* in this journey of Arjuna is that the memories he re-embodies are lived memories. Arjuna himself has gone through them and therefore knows how they world-body-feel. Arjuna is able to body-feel his own body while traveling the corridors of his memories. He is able to body-feel other body-feelings he himself was when those memories were not memories but a living body. He knows of other world–unions which are possible through himself or that he himself has been, but again, as phenomenology reminds us, these body–unions are problematic. One may decide to ascribe all these memories, all these imaginative variations, to the same constant body; that is, one may decide to ascribe them to a body which remains constant through all these variations and to whom memories—imaginative variations—are never recoverable as embodied, but are only possible as embodied attributes from a logical world to a logical subject. This union is a precarious one, a theoretic unity to which different sensations, different body-feelings, may be ascribed, or may be denied. Man can never find himself at home in such a body, and the only way out for man is either to declare himself in crisis—go crazy—or diligently dedicate himself to the task of finding his own emancipation.

Since the *Gītā* goes on, we take it that Arjuna decides for emancipation rather than crisis, but by this decision alone and the concentrated effort of the first eleven chapters, we find that he has already changed. Faith (XII) is no longer any thing or any god, but rather a space beyond any god. Knowledge (XIII) is no longer the absolutized universal knowledge that led him into crisis, but rather: "Know me, O Bhārata, to be the knower of the field in every field; the knowledge of the field and of the knower of the field: This I hold to be (real) knowledge." The body (XIV-XVIII) will appear as a radical embodied unity, a multiplicity of body-feelings-sensations, complete each time it acts, in every action, in every social situation, but to retrain the body to "think itself up" every time it acts, requires not only time but also the constant effort and habit of learning how to shift perspectives, i.e., from the perspective of Chapter I to the perspective of Chapter XI: 180° turn in every action.

The ontological clues of this path of recovery we found in the knowledge (liberating action-knowledge) that action *(karman)* belongs to *dharma*:

> *Dharma* to man's *situation* or *guṇas*;
> The *Guṇas* to *prakṛti* (man's body-interpretations);
> *Prakṛti* to *puruṣa* (embodied vision);

> *Puruṣa* manifests itself through *prakṛti,* which acts through the *guṇas,* which act through *dharma,* which acts through *karman.*

All human actions and their knowledge besides are woven of the larger fabric of the *yugas,* the cosmic *guṇas* of which man creates his world (nonattached action-knowledge) or his crisis (attached action-knowledge). Man's circumstance, to be saved, has to find its creative *situation* in the constantly moving world around it. Man and world are in constant change and movement. Attached thought action either stops man or the world in its actual course.

Kṛṣṇa's mode of action-knowledge in the *Gītā* is the prototype of man's unattached and dedicated path to find his and the world's human creative liberation. Kṛṣṇa's mode of acting in the world is the prototype of an activity of man which lets life pass *through* without breaking its rhythm or its flow through self-made and self-appropriated thought-body-actions.

Liberated man, like Kṛṣṇa, has as a necessary and sufficient condition to save his circumstance, to know the field in every field. Of this knowledge new worlds are made; but Kṛṣṇa could not save any world, any body, if Arjuna—*prakṛti,* the body—could not "think itself up" to the embodied vision every action demands of both: Kṛṣṇa and Arjuna. They are ontological equals and inseparable.

Some have claimed that the *Bhagavad Gītā* is repetitious and could well have ended with chapter XIII. It is easy to understand why such a claim has been made. Faith and knowledge, as presented in chapters XII and XIII, are attributed to a god in whose love, knowledge and faith find their fulfillment, but to the degree that such an interpretation of the *Gītā* emasculates the text of the *Gītā,* it also disembodies the world by denying it its flesh. Neither faith nor knowledge in the *Gītā* rest on such *theoretic solutions* to the human problem. What such theoretic interpretations of the *Gītā* miss is the sophisticated understanding and development of the human body that the *Gītā* presents.

If one sees the *Gītā* only from the viewpoint of Arjuna or the *guṇas* of *prakṛti,* then whatever interpretation of the *Gītā* one undertakes to make, nothing, of necessity, will change in the *Gītā*: Arjuna will remain the same and so will the world and the reader. In more concrete terms, Arjuna's body will remain the same theoretical, individual and continuous body that led him into crisis. His knowledge will be reduced to some form of theoretic syntheses ascribable to the same body, and his liberation will be reduced to a fruitless hope that somebody—someone else besides him—might be able to pull him out from a situation he himself is incapable of understanding, of changing. From this viewpoint Arjuna's way of "seeing" remains as constant as his theory of the body, memory, the world, and his self.

This is the world of *saṃsāra,* birth and death, origin and dissolution, because the knowledge that holds it together is not only disembodied—a demand of what knowledge should be—but it is not even capable of "seeing itself." Or to put it differently, what this knowledge "sees" is not its own movements but rather the crystalized, static, stagnant repetitions of a structure which takes its own ground for granted. This is the reason why, regardless of how many lives a man lives, how many memories a man has, even while he talks of maturity, change, growth and being different, he keeps being reborn again and again into the same kind of body: the world of *saṃsāra.* The round of birth and death is only possible when man systematically lobotomizes his living flesh for a theoretic substitute that remains constant in spite of the multiplicity of body-world-changes through which a man plays out his human life.

However, when a man *sees* as Kṛṣṇa does, neither the world, nor the self, nor man is what Arjuna thinks it to be. All there is, is movement, fleeting, changing, speeding up or slowing down, and unless one learns to see the movement, hear its sound, dance on its rhythmic waves, one has no other alternative than to stop the world and triumphantly call the movements of thought the movements of the world. Of this reduction human pain, human crisis, human despair is born.

Neither we nor the *Gītā* are proposing the substitution of one world for the other, nor proclaiming one better than the other. The human condition is such that both worlds make up human life. Either man learns to live with both or he will remain forever incomplete. Both words are on equal ontological parity and both worlds depend on one another. Their complementarity, however, is radical. What can truly be said in one, the same cannot be truly said in the other. This understanding of complementarity is shared by modern physics and applies not only to two separate, though complementary worlds, but to every action of man if we take it in its circumstantial completeness, i.e., an action-body situation.

Kṛṣṇa's dependence on Arjuna, or the *puruṣa's* dependence on *prakṛti* is the dependence of perspective on the body. Without this dependence and complementarity the moves of the *Gītā* would make no sense. It is the movement of the *puruṣa* through the multiple *prakṛtic* situations in search of its own embodied liberation. In this sense, any statements which can truly be affirmed in one context, or action-body, are only true in relation to those conditions and limited by those same conditions. The same statement cannot be true in any other situation or *prakṛtic* condition, nor can the same statement be true even if the same conditions appear to be identically duplicated: no human situation is repeatable even for the *same* body.

Kṛṣṇa's moves, as can be seen from chapters II through XVIII of the *Gītā,* are intentional moves for a very definite purpose: the emancipation of Arjuna. This emancipation, however, is not possible unless Arjuna is desensitized from the one way of body-feeling-sensing he has reduced himself to by way of the *manas*-interpretation of sensation, or even the *buddhi*-interpretation of the same process.

What Kṛṣṇa is actually performing for Arjuna in chapters II through X of the *Gītā* is the multiplication, the dismemberment, of Arjuna's own body as it really embodied itself through other orientations, other memories, and sensed itself embodied as such distinct bodies. Chapters II through X is the journey of such an embodied movement, a dance of prolonged frequency and low intensity, high and low pitched, but with one conclusion in mind: Arjuna is not the body he believes himself to be in chapter I; he is also the multiplicity of bodies he has through the memories of chapters II to X re-embodied: all those bodies are alive and asking for release from Arjuna's prostrated and depressed body facing the battlefield.

In trying to understand the *Gītā,* especially from chapters XIV to XVIII, one has to bear in mind all the previous action the *Gītā* has forced Arjuna to perform on his own *view* of the circumstance around him and on himself. One has to bear in mind, especially, that in chapter XI Arjuna has touched his own emptiness, the absolute bereavement of what he took to be the solid ground of his body-feelings, and that new lenses have been put before his eyes, new auditory devices before his ears, and that for Arjuna the world cannot be seen or heard in the same old way again: the very structure of Arjuna's meaning has changed forever. The same has happened to the text of the *Gītā*.

The strangeness of the new situation demands a critical change not only in conceptual structures, but also a relearning of the new process of body-feeling, a re-education of the muscular and nervous systems and above all a change in conceptual structure to account for the new situation. This is the change during which a whole new style of embodied interpretation is assembled, but this is not achieved without an intellectual bereavement which can only proceed to relearn its own process of formation step by step, action by action: how to walk, sit, fight, perform rituals, interact with others, talk, sing, dance, even eat leftovers. For a man who knows, who acts on the radical orientation of chapter XI, every action is dangerous, for each one contains the creation and the dissolution of the world.

Every spot in Arjuna's world is now explosive, for in it the whole creation is present. "It is the upturned peepal tree, with its branches below, its roots above. The branches stretch below and above, nourished by the *guṇas,* its sprouts are the sense objects; when this tree reaches the world of men, it spreads out its roots that result in action." But men do not see how their actions are so umbilically joined to the whole world. "They do not comprehend its form, not its end, not its beginning, nor its foundation. Their only way out is to cut their firmly rooted tree with the weapon of nonattachment. Only those who have the eye of wisdom are able to see that it is only a fraction of the grounding self which appears as a living, eternal self and draws into its power the five senses and the mind that comes from *prakṛti,* but taking or leaving a body he takes all these along, like the wind carrying perfume from a home. He enjoys the objects of the senses, using the ear, eye, touch, smell and the mind." But one has to be able to distinguish the *puruṣa* from *prakṛti,* perspective and the body. "This is the vision the yogins see in their own self, but the mindless whose self is not ready yet, even if they strive, they do not see."

Arjuna should not only be a warrior in name but he should learn to live as a warrior, and amongst the plural conditions that make up a warrior the most important one is the patient waiting for the right conditions to act. Take a piece of land and there will be as many perspectives as men passing through it, but for a warrior *every* piece of land is all the life there is. In fact, there is only *every single action* for him to count on as "his life" as a warrior and it is in every action that he will have to throw himself with the full power of his decisions. A warrior's life is a life of a strategy about every action, and amongst those actions he has to discover also the strategy of waiting for the right action. For a warrior everything is mortally dangerous. A trap hides behind every door, every bush, every branch; but in order to be trapped, a warrior must be willing. He must be willing not to be a warrior and to abandon his will to be a warrior to his desires to be less than a warrior.

From chapter XVI to XVIII the journey of Arjuna, the warrior, to recover his will, to "do as you desire," includes also the capacity to wait and stall for the right conditions. "For there are those who, without patience, throw themselves to the pursuit of pleasure on the excuse that there is no truth in the world. These are men lost in themselves, small in mind, cruel in deed, enemies of the world. They surrender to desire, arrogance, and hypocrisy, and they justify themselves with false philosophies. They only cling to what leads to death, they strive for wealth to gratify their desire; and they can only speak in first person: I have won today; that desire I will obtain; this is mine; this wealth will become mine; I am lord and enjoyer; I am perfect, strong and happy; I am wealthy, well-born; I will sacrifice; I will give; I will rejoice; who else is like me?" The destiny of these men is to be born again under the same conditions which perpetuate their delusions in every action. These men do not have enough faith to be able to wait. For one should be able to act in every situation as the situation acts on itself without self-appropriations.

Arjuna's conclusion at the end of his long journey in terms of a philosophy which would give shape to his vision of chapter XI is obviously a coincidence with Kṛṣṇa: to realize his own emancipation through the action facing him. Through that action Kṛṣṇa, Arjuna, *Puruṣa, Prakṛti* and their orienting foundation coincide. For emancipation to be possible, however, Arjuna's will has to coincide with the original *cultural* will of which both Kṛṣṇa and Arjuna are the body. But this realization could not have been mediated had Arjuna not be able "to body-think himself up."

In our search for meaning through the *Bhagavad Gītā*, we would have considered it a great oversight if we had not been able to at least sketch the conditions of possibility for the cultural will of the tradition we are dealing with to be recovered. Once again we may point out that the conditions of possibility are not themselves the experience. It is really up to the reader to embody the circumstance by being able to "hear" what he constantly thinks he "sees."

There are two radical experiences I owe to India and which the writing of this book has forced me to re-embody. One, is the problematic notion itself of the body which through my life in India became so many other bodies, and the other is the model of music I discovered through Indian chant, music and language. It is this latter model of music which allowed me to make sense of a body which was already moving according to a rhythm which only now have I begun to understand. Before I learned any Indian languages or any cultural theories about Indian life, my body was already in its silent way drawing different bodily structures. I chanted before I learned to speak, and somehow, even without my knowing it, my body was silently shedding a multiplicity of perspectives of itself made possible through the constant variation in perspectives induced through the musical activity.

I did not then understand and I am only now beginning to glimpse the relationship between the two experiences: the body and music. It is a great failure of our educational systems that music is no longer a formal part of the curriculum, but it is, nonetheless, clear to me now why in many civilizations, including ours, music was considered the grounding of both training and education. It is also quite clear to me now the role of music in Plato's thought and his need to "let the musicians in and spoil the order of the banquet" after his careful discursive arguments of the *Symposium.* If we could only "see" all that they "hear."

Returning to India, our search for meaning would be incomplete and our recovery of the cultural will impossible if we did not at least point out that the cultural moves we have been observing in the *Gītā* will not gain their full meaning unless the theory of the body as we have developed it here finds its correspondence in the theory of music we have schematically suggested. It is obvious that this theory of music is not fully developed in the *Gītā,* though it is fully presupposed. It goes back to the Ṛg Veda and the Brāhmanas. It is the theory underlying *Ṛta* and *Vṛtra,* Indra and Agni, the *Puruṣa Sūkta* and *Prajāpati,* embodiment and dismemberment. Though the full theory of music here sketched is developed more fully elsewhere, the suggestions made in this book at the end of Chapter Six should be sufficient to clarify some important criteria for recovering the meaning of the *Gītā.*

Contrary to our Cartesian way of understanding the mind-body relationship and problem, the *Gītā* forces us to face the same relationship and problem from a totally opposite perspective: in fact, 180° different. While from a Western perspective we are used to conceive the mind-body relationship as two opposing substances where the mind has the upper hand, control and direction of the body, the *Bhagavad Gītā* offers us instead a body—field or *prakṛti*—which in order to act appropriates in every action a perspective—*puruṣa*—or radical interpretation of itself as it encounters it. Of this body-perspective-appropriation the whole journey of the *Gītā* is undertaken. It is a journey for the body to body-think itself up to that perspective which will make him act in every action with complete emancipation or without attachment to the fruits of action. A height which coincides, in every action, with the embodied vision which created the culture in the first place.

Most of the statements of the *Gītā* and the movement of the *Gītā* itself will remain lost if we are not able to account for the model upon which the emancipation of the body is made possible. As shown in Chapter Six of this book, the model on which the body moves—Arjuna, Kṛṣṇa—is that of music. It is on a mimesis of sound and number, musical tuning or some kind of *mantra–yantra,* that the movements of the *Gītā* with its corresponding statements may be understood.

Every action in the *Bhagavad Gītā* is to be understood as modelled on a sound-point, or tone. As sound-point every action is both a limit and an origin of manifestation—the "male" principle symbolized by an integer "cutting" the undifferentiated pitch continuum, thus opening space itself, the "female" principle, to further differentiation. Much of the "mystery" of Hindu thought and practice could be erased, especially in the later Tantric tradition, if these musical and mathematical ideas and presuppositions would be thoroughly examined. When projecting integer arithmetic into a tone-circle—linking the female matrix with the continuum of real number—it is obvious that the matrix cannot be divided and subdivided into equal parts. Thus one is continually confronted with imperfection and "uncleanliness." This is also the reason no mantra is "chantable" but one can only chant one *kind* of mantra or another. There is no ground for any form of absolutism or dogmatism.

It is on this understanding of sound-point that space and time may be understood as both the occasion and challenge for a complete embodiment in every action. For it is on every sound-point that the whole body-perspective plays out its whole human life: its manifestation and its dissolution.

The complete embodied vision which the *Gītā* proposes to men in every action is not possible unless the body and its appropriated perspective is systematically trained in an activity which would enable the body to shed an appropriated perspective as it moves from sound-point to sound-point in the scale. The body-movement and embodied vision which the *Gītā* proposes is implied in a "tuning-theory" which tries to reconcile a multitude of alternate perspectives of the tone-field and the related number field without reducing it to *one* system. We should be aware that (1) *number,* in its restriction to *integer,* or in the general sense of *rational* number, is inadequate to completely define the continuum of the octave, or more specifically, (2) that any division of the octave cycle into *equal* parts (meaning parts in *proportion,* in the *same* ratio) is arithmetically impossible, requiring the later concept of *real* number, thus (3) *any* system of tuning requires that some ideal value be sacrificed at some point in the cycle. The fact that Hindus do not mathematize their scales in the Greek way suggests that they have always known, from Ṛg Vedic times, this lesson.

The serenity and calmness with which Hindu *maṇḍalas* and *yantras* have appeared to the West have blinded Western eyes to the dynamism within them. Few know of the dynamic, vigorous, passionate and very often explosive power which the beautifully symmetrical *mantras–yantras* of Hindu life requires to reconcile circles, squares, points, lines and on its mimesis, human life. Hindu *mantras–yantras* can only be seen as embodied by the double dynamic process of history and of the viewer; that is, as Socrates yearned to see his own ideal forms: not as "noble creatures in a painting," but "in motion and actively exercising the powers promised by their form."

We have tried to exemplify the above remarks through Table VIII in Chapter Six of this book as it summarizes the power and dynamism of the whole movement of the *Gītā*. It is the chariot of the gods, as mentioned in the Ṛg Veda, the Upaniṣads, etc., and as being the central figure in chapter I of the *Gītā*. It is the chariot on which Arjuna and Kṛṣṇa stand at the beginning of the book. It contains the full cultural body, Arjuna and Kṛṣṇa, and points towards the recovery of the cultural will. It is surrounded by sound-points, possible body-actions, which can only be fully human actions if the full cultural body—Arjuna and Kṛṣṇa—is capable of "body-thinking" itself up to the originating embodied vision of every sound-point. This cannot be achieved, however, if the body-perspective is unable to raise itself up the 180° that separates the body-perspective of Arjuna in chapter I, and the efficient and original body-perspective of chapter XI. The chariot pole exemplifies the dedicated and time-consuming effort and training which the body requires to prepare itself to act free from absolute perspectives and attachment. We suggest that this chart would make full sense once the reader has been able to run up and down the musical scales and observe the effect that the change of perspective has on the singing body. An epistemology centered on the body and not the mind has to overcome the body-inertia of acting—rather than thinking only—in order to become what it understands.

We have on many occasions referred to the "cultural voice," "cultural will" to orient our own search for meaning. We find, again, that music provides for us the model and ground for meaning. In this sense the moves of the *Gītā* are not only descriptive but normative. They agree with the tradition that has proclaimed from the Ṛg Veda down an exact form of acting, *satya, ṛta.* The Hindu musician takes his stand on any pitch: that is, Hindu theory of music is a theory of relative, not absolute, pitch; and what is even more important, it achieves a wide range of modal tunings only because it is acutely sensitive to the precise values of pure octaves, fifths, *and* thirds. These form an inner metric space which make it possible to deviate from them by one or two "quarter-tones," the least perceptively different pitch intervals. Octaves, fifths *and* thirds are true norms, part of every man's psychoacoustical equipment, culturally reinforced in Hinduism and, significantly, culturally repressed (i.e., the "pure third" is repressed) in all countries of the West where "equal-temperament" is imperialistically elevated to the status of "cultural norm."

It is obvious that the notion of cultural norm plays a profound role in the *Gītā,* permeated through norms of diversity. Arjuna is above all a man in search of a full embodiment which implies that he must carry with him into battle, or into any action, the social and cultural norms around him. It is only in this total affirmation of the total cultural norm that structure and context, body and perspective, are possible on the *Bhagavad Gītā's* terms, whatever the outcome of the actions. It is only in this normative sense that Arjuna's action is equally essential to friends and enemies. It is for this same reason that the whole Hindu world of the *Gītā* depends on Arjuna for its survival, on the condition that through Arjuna the cultural norms of the *Gītā* find a living body, an incarnation, to keep its wheel moving.

I would like to conclude these meditations through the *Bhagavad Gītā* with some general reflections on Ortega's cultural theme of Man and Circumstance in view of our democratic American circumstance.

In our search for meaning, the meaning of our own life *through* the meaning other people give to their lives, we decided to follow the principle of economy: to focus radically on an *activity* which man, must, of necessity, perform in order to act. According to this principle of economy the essential element of our inquiry was this human radical activity. Everything else we considered accidental, derived or dependent on this radical activity. What is primary in man we found to be action-movement radically oriented and manifested through a perspective made flesh. The flesh of man is radically made up of perspective, a radical orientation towards which his flesh is opened in continued movement.

In order to grasp the movement of other people's bodies, however, we were forced from the beginning of our journey to systematically get hold of our radical orientations so that we could simultaneously make room for other peoples' orientations, regardless of the outcome. Thus we found that while with all good intentions we were ready to understand others by learning their concepts—a mind facing other minds—at the end of our journey we were forced to become bodies through an embodiment of other people's perspectives. *We could no longer understand without becoming what we understood.* Our theme of Man and Circumstance forced us to bracket our initial model of knowledge and body in order to be able to radically embody the circumstance we set ourselves to face.

The beginning of our journey through the *Gītā* was the ability to focus on the systematic effort of a man, Arjuna, to surrender to nonmovement in a moment of crisis. This impossible effort was mediated by a reflection on the frightening discovery that the soil upon which man stands is never secure. It has to be renewed again and again in every action. Even the appearance of nonmovement is a tension begotten by movement and destined to fall apart in order to give way to new movement which creates new tensions, new worlds. Movement speaks out *of* the body-perspectives of all things. Crisis is in the *Gītā* the triggering mechanism of a man's effort to discover the orienting context which dictates his body movement. The *Gītā* makes it amply clear that it is through the discovery of these body-movement-orientations that a man may create the emancipation of himself and his world and avoid the self-strangulation and desensitization of repeating the same conceptual and absolute body-movement-scheme to death.

Underlying the *Gītā* there is only one reason offered for this eternal cycle of crisis, reflection, embodied vision: faith. This faith, however, is not in any god, person or institution, but in human life: It is the love of life's own body. Gods, persons or institutions are this side of creation, and it is through them that a human life becomes flesh, incarnate, through every renewed human presence. Life is a continuously recurring problem that man must give body through his own body-orientation. Kṛṣṇa and Arjuna are the body-perspective, the embodied vision, of their own cultural body. They are inseparable and incomplete without the cultural will, body, tradition which oriented their moves in the first place and in every place. Their apparent split in the *Gītā* is only for the time being, as long as it takes for the body to think itself up to the original orientation of the culture, but this lift is a gigantic effort of love for the human body around us and our own.

The theme of our journey, Man and Circumstance, has forced us to strew our path with many conceptual corpses. Our systematic effort to make reason through other people's reasons has forced us to sacrifice ideas, models, presuppositions, perspectives all along our path. The most radical sacrifice being that only one kind of reason may be rational. We were unaware that this dehumanizing demand on what reason should be has been determining for centuries our own way of body-feeling-sensing other people and that while we were ready to tolerate their ideas, we could only tolerate them as long as our way of body-feeling-sensing would not have to change. In a radical sense we condemned ourselves to a perpetual wandering along a path of a discursive thought which could only function discursively by in the end reducing our own human body to absolute insensibility and disorientation. Our whole educational system, psychology, the social sciences, philosophy and even religion are guilty of this sin of systematic disembodiment. The *Gītā,* on the other hand, has made us aware that underlying all classification, all definitions, all situations—*sattva, rajas, tamas*—underlying the analytic and the synthetic side of our reason—the two sides of the brain: *manas, buddhi*—that there is a body appropriating perspectives in every situation as it moves along—*prakṛti* and *puruṣa.*

We can no longer be satisfied with dialectical syntheses where body movements are reduced to the thought movements of discursive thought, the body remaining as if unconcerned. If we are to walk on stone, we need stone feet. If we are to know other people, other cultures, we must get under their skin on their own terms. The languages of other people, their criteria for their use, their models of knowledge and ignorance have to become ours as much as theirs. Whatever contributed to their body-orientation must become also ours so that in the process we build our own human body.

What we can no longer tolerate are those programs of comparative studies, religion in particular, where all actions from other cultures are reduced to disembodied ideas any student may carry in the disembodied vaults of his brain. Unless a systematic effort is made to retrain the bodies of the students and faculty through the systematic disciplines—yoga, meditation, music—of the culture they study, what is given as religious studies or comparative philosophy or comparative literature is a systematic effort to reduce man—our own students and the men of other cultures—to bodiless ideas. We may end up knowing everything, understanding less, and embodying nothing. Democracy needs bodies, cultural bodies, to avoid manipulation. Two thousand years of Christianity should be example enough that it is not sufficient to teach the concepts of Christianity to other people and convert them to this cultural onslaught and colonization, but rather that Christianity was radically grounded on one single fact: the incarnation, the word made flesh, the flesh made human language, speaking through a particular body, with particular gestures, particular set of customs, mannerisms as trivial as walking, sitting, standing, eating. This is the way God became flesh for the Christians in a Jewish village, and the challenge of Christianity would be to see that this fact, this incarnation, is repeated again and again in every concrete community it encounters. Buddhism and Hinduism repeated for man the same message of incarnation not by forcing man to perform the impossible and abstract task of being *a human being* but, like Christianity, by preparing the body to embody a perspective "that knows the Father." How God becomes flesh is not a mystery but a systematic effort of orienting the body to become what it knows. It is the effort and gift, in Christian terms, of the Holy Spirit. It is Arjuna, Kṛṣṇa and their orienting ground. This systematic effort, however, is neither religious, philosophical, psychological or faddish: it is the radical will of man in search of his own survival as man. He has, somehow, to continuously transcend his-self, his society, his culture, his body, in and through every action.

In case the reader may think we are meandering into dangerous "mystical" grounds, let us retrace our steps and conclude as we started: within the philosophical path. What we propose is also formalizable and rigorously philosophical. It is a philosophical synthesis of a particular kind.

A philosophical synthesis which has as its model the body-perspective rather than the model of Boolean logic and the mind as the synthesizing activity is obviously a difficult and obscure notion. But philosophical synthesis in general is itself obscure and ambiguous, deriving its sense from a wide variety of contexts. Let me reassure the reader that the notion we propose finds its model in the heart of modern physics as suggested by an analysis of the structure of quantum mechanics and aims at being logically precise and controllable in use. Its value and applicability can be checked within virtually every domain of human experience. According to this notion of philosophical synthesis—the formalization of our embodied vision—a synthetical development takes place when in a particular historical setting traditions which are antithetical—not simultaneously realized by the same person or group of persons—become synthesized in a more comprehensive embodied vision. From the point of view of the later synthesis, the earlier traditions were partial or complementary; from a point of view prior to the synthesis they are said to be dialectically opposed or in tension. A body-dialectic then supposes the kind of relation that the thesis and antithesis have to one another in the light of subsequent synthesis. A synthetic development would then involve not only a manifold of conceptual frameworks ordered in a logical and temporal way but also that the movement of the logical and temporal ordering be oriented towards their original context. In this sense we would have a partial ordering (elements of a set without a unique antecedent and a unique consequent) of a set or sets of elements in a nondistributive, orthocomplemented lattice where both the logical and the temporal aspect of the ordering is preserved. The important aspect of this synthetic development, however, is that there is a transformation of meaning as we go up and down the lattice which would make in every case meaning, context and structure dependent. The aspect of movement preserves the historicity of man and avoids the reduction of those body movements to a logic or an algebra.

If philosophy then is to contribute to man's emancipation it must first emancipate itself. It must stop frequenting the homes of the rich and powerful by rationalizing their ideologies and return to the people. Philosophy is emancipation if it has the ability to settle down anywhere: the circumstance facing us, the American plural life-forms, the little Jewish village, the Arab deserts, the Japanese hamlet, the Hindu ashram, the Chinese commune, the black ghetto, the University, the Government, the man in the street, you and I. We may repeat ideas to one another but we can never repeat a human body. We may demand that people have ideas in order to be educated and we may even reward them for their aetherial collection. But the truth of the matter is that people *do not have* ideas; ideas *have* them. Their theoretical body-sensations-feelings are the result of such systematic desensitizing programs in education. A human body, a cultural body, on the other hand, is all the decisions made about all it has and all it encounters. It does not need to carry in its living path absolutizing ideas that stop the world cold in its trajectory. But it offers instead a living possibility to a multiplicity of perspectives hopelessly looking for a fleeting moment of human life. The human body, the cultural body, is more demanding, however, than the ideas substituting for it. It demands above all a continuous exercise of love for its own living sake: An exercise of love which needs to be repeated through everybody one encounters without obviating the effort of this discovery by presupposing its knowledge. For, after all, life, human and even divine, *counts on* the flesh of man for its own manifestation.

The Avatāra's time is the time when theory gives way to corporality. The "myth of invariance" is about to become body and word as man is able to encounter man flesh to flesh.

Appendixes and Notes

Appendix to Chapter Two

LOGIC AS CONTEXT

G. E. Moore and Russell

Behind the reasons philosophers give there is a philosophy philosophers hide.

In "The Refutation of Idealism" (1903) G. E. Moore maintains that human experience instead of being a product *of,* is the simple juxtaposition of two different sorts of elements: the object of experience (what is experienced) and the act, or activity of experiencing this object. They are also the elements and the only elements, involved in more complex perceptions and cognition. Moore's strategy, in order to bypass the Kantian revolution and avoid the solipsism and skepticism in which Cartesinism, as Hume had shown, ended was to maintain that in an act of awareness there is no intermediary idea at all, for consciousness was transparent and added nothing to experience. Consciousness in its essential nature is consciousness *of.* To be conscious of blue is to be conscious of blue, not of the mental image of blue.

According to Moore the objects of the world are of two classes: items that are "mental" (or physical) and items that are not. Some of the items that are not mental are physical objects; some are not. But, all these items have the characteristic of being in their nature independent of minds. They exist, as what they are, even if they are not for any consciousness at all. Even more, this objective and public world which is thus revealed to view is just the world that common sense believes in. The truth of this world is obvious to anyone who takes the trouble to look carefully at experience.

This is the problem. How do we agree what an object is? Is it a sense datum? If so, how does a sense-datum relate to physical object? Moore opted for defining it as a whole set of sense-data that all possible observers would experience under all possible conditions of observation. Thus the obscure and puzzling relation of "being a property of" could be replaced for the readily understood relation of "being a member of a class." This is the course Russell took, but not Moore, more concerned with vindicating common sense.

When we look closely at this realist interpretation of experience, a whole nest of other problems are created. The only solution was a series of eliminations and reductions which in order to save the realist attitude were necessary. In the first place, consciousness. Since there is no mediating idea between the mind and its object, consciousness could be ignored. Thus they could concentrate in the object uncontaminated by the mind and its constructs. Their contention was later on reinforced by a behaviorism which starting with James, sanctioned by Russell and supported by the Positivists' Verifiability Principle, held that sentences containing assertions about inner states can be eliminated and replaced by sentences about bodily states.

Russell delighted in mathematics, or what he called "the restfulness of mathematical certainty." He looked for a more positive certainty than that of Moore and even that of Descartes. Russell's aim was to find an absolutely secure ground for the world that science describes and that we experience in ordinary perception. Though Russell's views changed more often than the English weather, he still clung throughout these changes to these two main positions: (1) The distinction between those objects about whose existence we are absolutely certain because we are directly aware of them—like Moore, and those which we know about, or believe in, by inference; and (2) The need, in the interest of simplicity and certainty, to reduce as much as possible the numbers of inferred entities.

Initially Russell allowed that the universe contains, in addition to universals, sense-data, minds and physical objects. Later he decided that physical objects could be eliminated, and still later that acts of consciousness and with them the mind in which they occur, could also go. He did not write of these "things" as mere "appearances," for that would have been tantamount to admitting that physics and psychology were not about the real world, but he tried to show that they were a "logical construction" or a "symbolic substitution."

Russell's attempt at a certain grounding of reality on mathematics through symbolic substitution or logical construction remained only programmatic. Russell did not eliminate matter or even less mind, still less did he vindicate the commonsense world of Moore and still less did he make real the neutral, value-free world he had in mind. He ended by admitting that though he wanted, like Descartes, to vindicate the claims of physics, in the end he believed in this world of physics "without good grounds."

Logical Positivism

After World War I a program similar but more radical than Russell's logical construction or reduction was launched by the so-called Vienna Circle and later on known as the logical positivists. Their main goal was to save scientific knowledge. Or to be more accurate, according to this group: (1) It is only in the sciences and especially in physics that we have anything that can properly be called *knowledge*. (2) We should, therefore, extend the use of scientific methods to all domains and by its means test every assertion, eliminating any that do not "measure up." (3) The essential feature of the scientific method for the positivist would become known as the Verifiability Principle: the Method of verifying a proposition and the meaning of the proposition. Propositions for which no means of verification exist are literally meaningless. Thus they became passionately antimetaphysical, in contrast to Moore and Russell. The positivists, in contrast, held that realism and idealism were both nonsense. In positivist parlance that statement is to be translated as: "I don't understand you. What you say asserts nothing at all!"

Underlying logical analysis, was the conviction that, when language has been correctly analysed, it will be isomorphic with the world: the linguistic relational structures that are exposed by analysis exactly mirror the relational structures that characterize the world. Hence, Wittgenstein thought it sufficient to show what follows from the nature of logic about the sort of basic structure the world must have. "The world divides into facts," and each of these facts is completely independent of every other. "Each item can be the case or not the case while everything else remains the same." Accordingly all complex scientific statements had to be reduced to elementary statements and furthermore, elucidations should be provided for these elementary statements. The positivists had trouble with elucidations and settled instead for what they called protocol sentences.

When this method is applied to sentences about God, the Absolute, reality, etc., it was easy to show that, since they are unverifiable, they are meaningless. Equally so are all normative sentences about, for example, the good and beautiful. Some positivists, however, allowed certain normative predicates and even metaphysical statements for as Carnap said: "They serve for the expression of the general attitude of a person towards life."

The positivists believed they could eliminate problems by eliminating meaningless words and answer problems by creating a unified science in terms of protocol sentences in the language of physicalism.

> Doubt can exist only where a question exists, a question only where an answer exists, and an answer only where something

> can be said . . . The solution of the problem of life is seen in the vanishing of the problem.

The Verifiability Principle, however, did not prove as solid as the positivists had hoped. How are protocol sentences to be verified? For after all protocol sentences may change. If so, then do they require verification systems of their own verification? Then we are involved in an infinite regress.

Besides, what is the status of the Verifiability Principle itself? On the positivist view all meaningful sentences are either analytic (tautologies) or are verifiable by empirical means. Clearly the principle is not analytic. It is, then, an empirical generalization, and if so, how can it be verified? If, however, the Verifiability Principle is only a recommendation, or suggestion, that the terms meaningful and meaningless be used in a certain way, then the whole positivist program collapses, for there is no longer an ideal language whose structure is revealed by logical analysis, and which when revealed, exactly mirrors the world, but we have rather a variety of languages, none of which is isomorphic with the world and which can all be equally recommended on different grounds.

Husserl

Like the realism of Moore and Russell, Phenomenology started at the turn of the century from Brentano's assertion that consciousness is consciousness *of*. Contrary to the limited account of the realists in regard to the objects of consciousness, however, Husserl extended the meaning of objects as sense data—like the realists claimed—to a vast variety of inner entities and acts which the realists overlooked.

Furthermore, Husserl had to refute through his philosophy the two main interpretations, current in his day: *psychologism* and *historicism* as the foundations of philosophy. Both claimed validity for themselves on "facts," but, "facts," Husserl claimed, have no absolute validity. Both theories are a contradiction since they are a theory about the absolute non-validity of all theory.

The first move for Husserl was to establish a special attitude which he would call "phenomenological reduction."

The second move was for Husserl to reestablish the claim that once we free ourselves from all presuppositions (or suspend the natural attitudes) we not only have one more view of reality (against the realist, organicists, etc.) but, achieve a face-to-face confrontation with reality itself in all its purity. This would lead to a science which by confronting reality directly would be apodictically certain, and to deny its possibility would be to fall into contradiction: that there is a valid and absolute knowledge that a valid and absolute knowledge is impossible.

As Husserl puts it, what is demanded is

> a scientific critique and in addition a radical science, rising from below, based on sure foundations, and progressing according to the most rigorous methods . . . *Weltanschauung* can engage in controversy; only science can decide.

A quest for certainty was indeed the ruling passion of Husserl's life:

> I have been through enough torments from lack of clarity and from doubt that wavers back and forth . . . I must win clarity, else I cannot live; I cannot bear life unless I can believe that I shall achieve it.

Husserl believed not only that philosophy was possible as a rigorous science but that it was within his grasp if through transcendentally reduced observation he succeeded in stripping away *all* presuppositions. The transcendental reduction, of course, is not done as the starting point of the inquiry but it has to be prepared and achieved progressively. Thus, to begin with, one must start by bracketing the "natural attitude":

> I am aware of a world, spread out in space endlessly, and in time becoming and become, without end . . . (Besides), this world is not there for me as a mere world of facts and affaires, *but, with the same immediacy,* as *a* world of goods, a practical world . . . with value-characters such as beautiful and ugly, agreeable or disagreeable, pleasant or unpleasant. . . To know (this world) more trustworthily, more perfectly than the naïve lore of experience is able to do . . . is the goal of the sciences of the natural attitude.

It would be hard to find any reason for the realists like Moore not to accept the above description of experience as to what they understood experience to be in the world of commonsense, but, while these philosophers saw no reason for moving out of this "natural attitude"—indeed, they saw every reason for remaining in it—Husserl's whole philosophical enterprise will consist in making such a move:

> Instead now of remaining in this attitude, we propose to alter it radically . . . we set it as it were out "of action," we "disconnect it," "bracket it." It still remains there like the bracketed in the bracket, like the disconnected outside the connextional system.

Bracketing, if it succeeds, that is if it can suspend judgment —neither believing nor not believing—in everything that I confront, gives us an awareness of consciousness which is itself beyond doubt and apodictically certain. This reduction or bracketing does not remove illusions of the products of fantasy—things which we very well do doubt—but it makes possible their analysis as accomplishments or intentional acts.

> For what can remain over when the whole world is bracketed? . . . That consciousness in itself has a being of its own which in its absolute uniqueness of nature remains unaffected by the phenomenological disconnection. It, therefore, remains over as a "phenomenological residumm," as a region of Being which is in principle unique, and can become in fact the field of a new science—the science of Phenomenology.

What bracketing has really achieved is to make everything different: a complete shift in attitude:

> Let us suppose that we are looking with pleasure in a garden at a blossoming appletree, at the fresh young green of the laws, and so forth . . . Between . . . the real men or the real perception on the one hand, and the real appletree on the other, there subsist real relations . . . Let us now pass over to the phenomenological standpoint. The transcendent world enters its "bracket" . . . We now ask what there is to discover, on essential lines, in the nexus of noetic experiences of perception and pleasure-valuation. Together with the whole physical and psychical world the real subsistence of the objective relation between perception and perceived (as likewise between the pleasure and that which pleases) is obviously left over, a relation which in its essential nature comes before us in "pure immanence," purely, that is, on the ground of the phenomenologically reduced experience of perception and pleasure, as it fits into the transcendental stream of experience.

Translating the above description we would have that when I "bracket" the apple tree, I not only suspend the belief in its independent existence as an object but I also cease to relate to it as an object. I am now occupied with it in its *meaning*. The reduction situates us within the field of *meaning*. I do not reflect on what to do with the tree, or the apples; bring them to the market, spray the tree, or use it as a conceptual projectile in defense of a realist thesis, and so on. I can now, however, (while still enjoying the tree) concentrate (focus) my attention on its relationship between my experiencing and its contents: a relationship I will overlook if I remain in the natural attitude.

As a result of "bracketing" my attitude has become different:

detached; I observe that which I never observed before: the "meaning" of objects with the nature of "pure" consciousness. In this transcendentally reduced observation I encounter a multitude of mental acts—perceiving, things, imaginings, dreamings, and the like—and a multitude of different objects intended by those different acts. I may now further proceed through a higher level reduction to apprehend the "essence" of the object.

Husserl's next project was to report his observations of "essences" in transcendentally reduced experience. Since in Husserl's view transcendental reduction consists in the "self-appearing, the self-exhibiting, the self-giving" of objects themselves, Husserl avoided the problem of realism which had to infer the existence of objects which are not directly present; we directly intuit the essence of objects:

> . . . continuously as on objective unity in a multiform and changeable multiplicity of manners of appearing, which belong determinately to it. These, in their temporal flow . . . flow away in the unity of a synthesis, such that in them "one and the same," appears now from this "side," now from that; and the "visual Perspectives" change . . . Always we find the feature in question as a unity belonging to a passing flow of "multiplicities."

So much for the objective pole of pure consciousness. Husserl's third move was the most problematic: the transcendental ego. Husserl's followers branded him an idealist and neo-Kantian. But, this was not Husserl's intention. Phenomenology made it salutary clear that in experience we are not dealing with either the mental or the physical, but rather with the subjective and objective poles of pure consciousness. But, while Husserl's followers went along with his analysis and description of the objective pole, they did not find his description of the subjective pole as captivating. Husserl who was resolved not only on establishing a descriptive method for an objectively valid science but was also resolved that this method should yield absolute certainty, decided to guarantee *a priori* knowledge by the activities of a transcendental ego. Where Kant held that his ego and its categorical synthesis are *behind* experience, Husserl held that they are *in* experience: they are "constitutive" of experience. And, where Kant had only to present logical arguments that justify our inferring the existence of these syntheses, Husserl unable or unwilling to abandon his commitment to phenomenological description had to find the syntheses or synthesizing operations of the transcendental ego in experience. This demanded narrower and more rigorous "bracketing" on "pure" consciousness which smacked to many phenomenologists of idealism and very few were prepared to follow. Husserl's insistence of the transcendental ego "constituting" the world appeared to many as close to "constructivism" as they were willing to go along with. Thus phenomenology appeared to many to fall back into what it had tried to get out of, the Kantian paradigm and its subsequent idealist path.

Husserl's phenomenology, however, carried within itself the explosive seeds which would move philosophy from the demands of reducing it to the justification only of logic and rhetoric as contexts, to the more critical task of focusing on its own anonymous and founding activity. The main elements of Husserl's phenomenology which, when developed, would carry through this program for philosophy are: the intentionality of consciousness, the temporality of consciousness—as distinct from the Kantian reduction of the analysis of time to spatial metaphors—and the notions of horizon and World.

According to Aristotle intentionality meant only the referential character of knowledge. For Descartes consciousness was a mere *cogito,* but for Husserl consciousness is a *cogito-cogitatum,* not a mere self-consciousness but a subject open to an environing world of objects given or to be given in experience. The basic structure of this situation is then a human consciousness which is both a subject and a field of objects toward which it is turned intentionally. Intentionality (or noetic-noematic structures) becomes in the hands of Husserl and his followers the study of the way objects are constituted as objects present to and in consciousness by the functioning of the appropriating intention which characterizes the form of life —horizon—in question. It is within this intentional consciousness that meaning is possible. The notion of constituting intention took on more complex meanings in Husserl embracing eventually these elements:

- the objectification of sensory (hyletic) data by unifying them into an empirical object and relating the object so established to one thing;
- the relating of successive sensory data to a permanent object;
- the conjoining to an object of the various profiles *(Abschattungen)* which it would present from different perspectives;
- the projection of an object into an intersubjective field.

Intentional consciousness is for Husserl a concrete cognitive intentionality structure implicit—rarely explicit—in a concrete form of life—or horizon as a concrete form of life. The noetic —subjective—and noematic—objective—aspects make up an intentionality structure. The noetic aspect is the subjective heuristic anticipation as already structured by the method of inquiry—

—rationality—through which the object *(noema)* which fulfills the anticipation is to be attained. The *noema* or object appears to a knowing subject in the light of the heuristic anticipation to which it corresponds. *Noesis,* therefore, is a structured heuristic anticipation. It corresponds to an open field of connected, often implicit, questions addressed by a subject to empirical reality and *implying the acceptance* of a particular interpretation of experience, whether in a common sense framework or in a scientific framework. The domain of reality to which this particular interpretation of experience belongs Husserl calls a *horizon.* A horizon appears then as a set of actual or possible objects revealed or to be revealed by the functioning of a particular empirical noetic intention. The functioning noetic intention constitutes then—and determines to a great extent—a reality-outline to be filled. The intentionality structure of a particular question, then, determines or prefigures the kind of answer it will receive. It does not determine, however, that there should be a meaningful answer, but only that an answer will be given as revealing the *neomata* looked-for within an already ordered set of *noemata* which we call *horizon.*

The *World,* Husserl calls, the totality of all horizons, "the horizon of all horizons." True reality for a subject is the World. A subject could settle for a horizon, but since horizon takes meaning from the World, no horizon can stand on its own isolation from the World. The World is the source of meaning for the set of horizons found in it, and for the noesis-neomata structures of particular horizons with which they appear.

With these notes in mind it will be easier to follow the subsequent steps within phenomenology and existentialism and also—and more importantly—how the preceding steps of the history of philosophy lead us to the method (way) for philosophy we are proposing in this book.

Phenomenology will shift from an emphasis on man as knower, to man as doer and will concentrate, through phenomenological description on two main courses. Some would try to discover "regional" ontologies, while others will focus on the self of man, not as a Deweyan heroe, capable and competent to solve the problems he is confronted with, but as a moral and social agent: man living, acting, suffering in a world which he no longer understands mostly because the reasons given (in history) for the kind of world he had to cope with are reasons imposed on man from above, outside or ignorant of man: they are ignorant of historical man, the great stranger in his own world.

It is obvious that while phenomenology was capable of describing life forms in a rational way, it was not able to discover the rationality of the World. It either presupposed what reason was, or reason was left as problematic as when phenomenology entered the scene.

A. N. Whitehead

Whitehead's philosophy of organicism was philosophy on the same scale as Kant's and Hegel's, but, in contrast to Kant he dislodged the mind from the center of the world, and in contrast to Hegel he shared the realist spirit that guided Moore and Russell and the opponents of idealism.

Whitehead's philosophy was of course a large anachronism in the 20th century, fond of short books and shorter themes and articles. Whitehead's philosophical enterprise was a vast speculative synthesis "allied to [the] mathematical pattern," on which he grounded his belief that the "ultimate natures of things lie together in a harmony which excludes mere arbitrariness." Whitehead relied on the basic concepts of modern physics rather than in the old Newtonian world, with a relational language of mathematics, English being a poor translation of it. He believed these concepts could be generalized to form a "categoreal" scheme providing a unified, instead of a broken image of the world. This scheme is, of course, too complex to even try to summarize: it involves a "category of the infinite," eight "categories of existence," twenty-seven "categories of explanation," and nine "categorical obligations." I will only focus on some suggestions regarding his "hidden context," on which he grounded the activity of philosophy.

The ultimate harmony (paradigm?), Whitehead held to be intelligible to the human mind. The function of philosophy is "to seek the form in the facts," to make explicit the pattern that is otherwise only implicitly present in the social system and so only "ignorantly entertained," but, because "we are finite beings," the grasp of the pattern "in its totality . . . is denied us." Because, philosophy is an "attempt to express the infinity of the universe in terms of the limitations of language," every formulation of the pattern will itself sooner or later descend into the "inactive commonplace." Hence the work of philosophy is never finished, since it relies on ordinary English, a perversion of the perfect relational language of mathematics. This separation between the pure language of mathematics and ordinary English perversion of its relational structure explains the apparent differences between Whitehead's view of language and the view of Russell, the positivists, and the tractarian Wittgenstein that the business of philosophy is to construct an ideal language that is isomorphic with the facts into which the world divides. Since Whitehead's model of logic was not the old Newtonian and Boolean one, nor the fixed coordinates of space and time of Kant, but the new non-Boolean logic and the space-time-continuum of modern physics, Whitehead saw philosophy as akin to poetry and mysticism, rather than to the old logic, and thus could afford to be speculative, where Russell and the positivists could not.

It is thus the poetic, moral, and humanistic view of man and the universe that Whitehead wanted to rehabilitate, and he thought that recent developments in science—especially relativity theory and quantum physics—provided a way of doing so.

The ultimate constituents of the universe, according to the scheme, are neither Russell's "particulars" nor material things nor egos: they are *events,* and each event is the "grasping into unity," or "prehending," of other events. It is easy to understand the notion of "prehending into unity" at the human level, but Whitehead held that an electron is equally a center of prehensive activity; to limit the activity of prehending to the human level of conscious perception and cognition would be to abandon realism and lapse into the idealism that Whitehead wanted to avoid. According to Whitehead every event in the universe is prehending every other of the "simultaneous events throughout the rest of the universe." What makes each event unique is that each event feels all other events from a particular "perspective."

Further, a prehending center is not merely a passive contemplator of all the other manifold "aspects of nature" from its particular point of view. Each center is a life, a process having a beginning and ending in a consummation: this, again, is as true of a human life as of an electron, and for the same reason. Each involves a principle of selection and exclusion; each is "a unit of emergent value." Hence, whereas 19th-century physics had regarded the physical world as inert matter, fundamentally different from man, quantum physics (at least in Whitehead's view) requires us to think of nature as involving processes that, even at the elementary level, are not different in kind from human cognition and volition. The world is alive with related perspectives. Philosophy's task is to prehend them. But, what is to be prehended is not historically mediated. It is an *a priori* universalized "pattern" to which all other historical "patterns" must be reduced in a hopeful harmonization.

No one has understood better Whitehead's thought than Professor Justus Buchler. "On a Strain of Arbitrariness in Whitehead's System," Professor Buchler distinguishes two trends which account for two different ways of bringing together Whitehead's thought. The possibilities of metaphysical articulation present in the first trend are cancelled out by the second trend, where through a gratuitously dogmatic "ontological priority," attributes like "individuality," "efficacy," and "determinateness" raise their ugly heads again to gain the honorific status they always had in the history of Western Philosophy. For this reason Professor Buchler's conclusion to Whitehead's whole system of thought is a most dramatic "cosmological story" which in many ways summarizes the drama of our own Western history of philosophy:

> From the epic or dramatic standpoint it is clear why the 'whole story' must be an account of concrescence; why actual entity must

> play the central role and occupy the central location. A story has a plot. There must be action. And action or activity is nothing apart from actual entity. The other entity-types play their roles, but their roles are defined by the destiny of the central being, the individual that unifies the multifariousness of the world. The note of tragedy is sounded. Actual entity perishes in the fulfillment of its subjective being. But immortal in its objectivity, it contributes itself to endless generations. Without it there is no life and nothing to record or recount. It is the bearer of novelty, which is the measure of direction. As metaphysical hero, it receives the accolades of being: true unity, complete individuality, final reality, pure actuality, concreteness in the highest. These emerge as heavily charged conceptions, mirroring the philosopher's moral reaction to what is. Eternal object, stiff and immobile, gets second billing. But it makes a vivid impact. Whereas actual entity harbors an 'internal principle of unrest,' eternal object undergoes 'adventures' and 'suffers changing relations.' The ways that obtain between the eternal and the actual tuted by the dramatic mediation of God.

And thus, once again, a mediating idea takes the place of human history.

RHETORIC AS CONTEXT

Heidegger

Heidegger's main work *Being and Time* opens with a quotation from Plato:

> For manifestly you have long been aware of what you mean when you use the expression "*being*." We, however, who used to think we understood it, have now become perplexed.

Heidegger viewed the entire development of philosophy since Descartes as a forgetfulness of Being. Descartes' distinction between knower and known had led Kant to abandon Being (which Kant had called "things-in-themselves") and concentrate on the phenomenal world. Philosophy had then wallowed in subjectivism, and though the so-called realists claimed to be talking about the real world, they had not the slightest idea of what Being was—they were merely interested in establishing the objectivity of the physical world in order to vindicate the claims of physics. Nor did the Aristotelian–Scholastic tradition previous to Descartes fare better in relation to Being. For even though this tradition made metaphysics the science of Being, Heidegger held that the philosophers who represented this tradition concentrated their attention on the various species and genera of being, not on Being itself; it seemed to him that Being for these philosophers meant nothing more than the highest genus, the most universal of concepts.

Heidegger's program, however, was to "work out the question of the meaning of *Being* and to do so concretely." To do so concretely would be to discover the "involvement of being in human nature," since it has been the absence of such involvement that has "determined the entire modern age," for it has left us forsaken and "more and more exclusively (abandoned) to beings," from which Heidegger thought we had "to return to the ground of metaphysics." "If our thinking would succeed . . . it might well help bring about a change in human nature." How can we return from being to Being? Obviously through beings, especially through the being of human beings, for after all man is the being who cares about Being.

Heidegger thought that Husserl had made a mistake in concentrating on "pure consciousness" not only because of its dangers of idealism but because of its "purity" which overlooks man's existential and moral involvement in the world. Thus Heidegger characterized consciousness as "Dasein"—presence, in order to force man to think of this involvement and thus "come to understand the nature of Being itself" How does man find the key to pass from being to Being? First by realizing that man lives in a world not of neutral objects but in a world of things ready-to-hand: "The wood is a forest of timber, the mountains a quarry of rock; the river is water-power, the wind is wind in the sails." With this description Heidegger seems to emphasize only what Husserl had called the "environing world of life," as opposed to the "idealized and naïve" world that physics and behaviourist psychology presupposed; but for Heidegger the fact that our environing life world is ready-to-hand is not as important as the fact that we are "thrown" into it and that in it we are strangers.

Our experience of the world as alien and of ourselves as thrown into it generates anxiety, and anxiety from which we seek to escape. "In the face of its thrownness Dasein flees to the relief which comes with the supposed freedom of the they-self." Which means, that instead of living an authentic life in which we courageously confront the loneliness, facticity and alienation of human existence, we retreat into an inauthentic social existence whose daily round is determined by what 'they' (other people) expect of us. But, there is one fact about human existence which nobody can elude—death.

> Dasein cannot outstrip the possibility of death. Death is the possibility of the absolute impossibility of Dasein . . . As such, death is something distinctly impending . . . Thrownness into death reveals itself to Dasein in a more primordial and impressive manner in that state-of-mind we have called 'anxiety.' . . . Anxiety in the face of death must not be confused with fear in the face of one's own demise. This anxiety is not an accidental or random mood of 'weakness' in some individual; but, as a

basic state-of-mind of Dasein, it amounts to the disclosedness of the fact that Dasein exists as thrown Being towards its ends.

Which means that our knowledge that we are inevitably to die makes the being of human beings "impossible" while, by contrast, the Being of Being cannot die. However, though Heidegger believed a formal account of Being could be given through such insights as the ones he gives in the first part of *Being and Time,* by the second half of the book he doubted himself, postponed and then canceled it. Poets, he thought, were better equipped than philosophers to reveal Being, but in the end he concluded that even they must fail.

"Language," he wrote "is the house of Being," and since "there are many languages, Being has many houses." If man by virtue of his language dwells within the claim and call of Being, then we Europeans presumably dwell in an entirely different house than Eastern man . . . And so, "a dialogue from house to house remains nearly impossible." "The course of such a dialogue," Heidegger wrote, "would have to have a character all its own, with more silence than talk. Above all, silence about silence."

So, by the phenomenological route we reach the same conclusion of the positivists: an ideal language isomorphic with reality is an illusion. Furthermore, Heidegger had shown that the pursuit of sheer immediacy would lead to a community of mutual silence. Or would it be that Heidegger who looked for Being gave ultimate reality to beings forgetting that both are held together by philosophy–history–life. Would it be possible that Heidegger had given up not the search of Being, but the search of philosophy as it constitutes itself?

Sartre

Sartre, meanwhile, was subjecting man's role, in a world forgetful of philosophy (philosophy–reason–life), to the discovery of its absurd passion. Heidegger obviously believed that communication is for the sake of agreement (about Being) and not for self-expression (about the radical interpretation which for each house constitutes the Being of beings). Sartre shared the same belief and therefore tried to gather support (agreement) about the absurdity of reality when like Husserl it is conceived as a consciousness-of, and has to justify itself through a transcendental ego. Sartre attacked Husserl because Husserl's need, like Kant's, to suppose a synthesizing activity which would make mine all those consciousness-of that I experience necessary. Since consciousness of an object is also consciousness of self, the transcendental ego is unnecessary. Getting rid of the transcendental ego not only eliminated idealism and reestablished the possibility of ontology, but in Sartre's hand it also eliminated the subjective pole of experience as a self which both is responsible for what it does, and limits human freedom. Instead Sartre proclaimed at the subjective pole pure spontaneity. There are thus no limitations either psychological or ontological, on what I may become.

> This monstrous spontaneity is at the origin of numerous psychasthenic ailments. Consciousness is frightened by its own spontaneity . . . This is clearly seen in an example from Janet. A young bride was in terror, when her husband left her alone, of sitting at the window and summoning the passersby like a prostitute. Nothing in her education, in her past, nor in her character could serve as an explanation of such a fear . . . She found herself monstrously free.

The answer to all our questions are provided by society, so we know of no freedom, no despair; in fact, we flee from freedom and despair by living the roles given to us by others. We never know despair; we never have any real moral problems; and so we are hardly men. "Human life begins," as Orestes says in Sartre's play *The Flies,* "on the other side of despair."

Man, however, is not only free, he is conscious, and "what sort of being is this consciousness-being?" It is "for-itself," he answers. For-itself being is opposed to being-in-itself: an apple tree, an ashtray; they are in-itself: "massive," "solid," "glued to itself," "undivided singleness." It is what it is. Not so man. For being-for-itself, "is what is not and is not what it is." Consciousness is full of imaginative possibilities: a homosexual can imagine himself being straight; a barber can imagine himself a king. This awareness cannot but affect the homosexual playing his role or the barber playing his, as homosexual or barber. Hence man always or almost always must live acting, rather than living. He is in "bad faith." Consciousness thus, for Sartre, introduces divisiveness into man, like freedom and by being aware of it, it introduced despair. Furthermore, God as the contradictory being who is both in-itself-for-itself is a contradiction and therefore impossible. Since even man's hope is absurd, man is doomed to disappointment. He is in fact "a useless passion."

With Sartre we have in retrospect the best critical reading of the absurd demands on man or philosophy as dogmatized by the history of philosophy deprived of its own self-reflection, its own historical constitution. Sartre points out, that for man to be human, he has to isolate himself from the demands of a tradition which has reduced experience to a conceptual-empirical-theological-consciousness, projecting it either, *nontemporally*: to God (Kierkegaard), Logic (early Husserl), Being (Jaspers), Mystery (Marcel), or *temporally,* to Death (Heidegger).

Heidegger's philosophical stand in relation to the philosophical projects of Kierkegaard, Nietzsche, Jaspers, Marcel, Husserl, Bergson, etc., did not imply a fresh ontology. It tried to stimulate man into a sober awareness under the light of *dread*—a general concern for an event, a capital event (death) which is sure to happen though *it is not yet*. By its very presence (ideal) death can confer a right evaluation on one's projects. As long as one is alive one has to stand by a sense of values and be responsible for one's day-to-day occupation; but with death in the horizon one should know that all values or interests are radically devalued and nullified. It is a complex psychological–philosophical stand with responsibility (care) and detachment in order to avoid pessimism or recklessness which might easily come to anyone committed to the conceptual-empirical mode of thinking.

Heidegger, obviously, did not detach himself, or it was impossible for him to do so, from Death: an event which is only the idea of an event; nor rescue man from the commitment of his tradition to find humanization, or salvation, in an absolute surrender to the intellectualization of man's life.

For Sartre all the previous philosophers, and in particular the immediate phenomenologists–existentialists, are a willing prey of the "theoretic consciousness." For Sartre to admit death as unnihilating the human condition is to fall back into some kind of objectivism. Sartre, after World War II, had seen too vividly that the look in some people's eyes was more petrifying than death itself. We could see it again today in any American supermarket. The present can never be replaced by an idea. Sartre's emphasis on the human condition as a total *not* is an effort at reaching the inner core of man before it is touched by any theory. It is a moment of suspension between the notion of God and no-God; between culture and no-culture; between the thoughts-that-were and the thoughts-that-are-not-yet. It is a confrontation with a naked mirror: a naked self who abhors all the superimpositions and presences (against Husserl and Heidegger) forced on him by traditional philosophy and who enjoys himself by negating all projects: in its face even death cannot stand. Sartre's reading of Western philosophy, ends like the classic Orestes: a king without subjects or kingdom, facing his obscene nakedness, yet for an instant moment alive. It happened to Antoine Roquentin in the *Jardin Publique* when he discovers his own existence:

> . . . I can't endure any more, I'm stifling: existence is penetrating into me everywhere, through my eyes, my nose, my mouth . . .
>
> . . . existence had suddenly revealed itself . . . it was the very stuff of things; . . . the diversity of things, their individuality was only an appearance, a varnish. This varnish had dissolved, leaving monstrous, flabby masses, in disorder—naked, with a frightening and obscene nakedness . . .

> This moment was extraordinary; I was there motionless and chilled, plunged into a horrible ecstasy . . . Contingency is the essential thing. I mean that, by definition, existence is not necessity. To exist is simply *to be there*; existing beings appear, may be *met,* but one can never deduce *them*. . .
>
> It (existence) must invade you abruptly, it must sit upon you, it must weigh heavily on your heart like a big motionless beast—or else there is nothing at all anymore.
>
> Everything was complete, everything in action, there was no lax time . . .
>
> I was not surprised, I knew very well that this was the World, a completely naked World which appeared suddenly . . . It did not make sense; the world was everywhere, present, in front, behind. ("Wednesday, 6 p.m.," *La Nausee,* 1938.)

Let the reader read the above quotation against chapter XI of the *Bhagavad Gītā*.

Appendix to Chapter Five

KNOWLEDGE AND CONSCIOUSNESS AS A FIXED LOGICAL TIME-SPACE MATRIX.

We have repeatedly made the point that what Ortega calls vital needs appear in human contexts within certain radical orientations or basic conditions for the self-constitution and self-reproduction of a particular communal human group, as it acts and interacts. When human radical orientations, however, are covered up by methodological coercions, we have instead objective illusion and massive ideology.

As we have seen in Chapters One and Two, Western philosophy demands that knowledge and self-consciousness go hand in hand; that is, that in order to know, Western philosophy has decided that knowledge ought to be grounded on some form of *consciousness of*. *Consciousness of,* however, when absolutized in this manner, becomes a coercive human space with the fixed coordinates of space and time bounding human action: this we know as human history. These space-time coordinates, however, are a *logical* space-time substitute condition, but not a human time-space reality. It is thus a method. As such this fixed universal *consciousness of* is not self-constituting, but rather it demands that self-constitution be grounded on a universal fixed method, grounded on a particular logic with universal rules of action and communication measurable against the fixed coordinates of space and time of this method. Such a dictatorial method lacks self-awareness of what it does and philosophically contradicts the self-awareness it demands of others and claims for itself. This reduction of human time and space to a particular logic—that of classical physics—is more clearly revealed in the demand, supposition and constitution of society as a universal objective illusion. This same reduction is what makes our task as interpreters so difficult.

It all started in Kant however, when he first helped the theory of knowledge become conscious of itself. As we saw earlier in Chapter Two, Kant identified knowledge with mathematical and physical knowledge, which according to him is prototypical of science. He also identified the self, because in what he names an originary–synthetic unity of transcendental perception, his model of the self is a pure self-identity in which the self relates to the self. He further determined both identifications through the theoretical space of the paradigm of classical physics where the value-free sciences of the understanding become the model on which to regulate human life. Kant introduced the terminology and the division between theoretical reason (i.e., able to produce sciences of the understanding) and practical reason (i.e., able to set norms and determine the will). The division in its general terms does not only immunize the sciences from critical philosophy as the positivists will do, but also reduces the human spaces within which man can constitute himself as human. Underlying this divorce of man, however, into the two spaces of knowledge and ignorance there is a further unspoken presupposition that for any knowledge to be had, or be possible, two coordinates must always remain constant: fixed space and time. Only on the condition that space and time remain "fixed" can we have what is transcendentally defined as the realm of the objects of possible knowledge: i.e., the possibility of reliable knowledge.

The normative validity, however, given to knowledge by Kant under such identifiable conditions, has not always been accorded his identifiable mathematical or natural knowledge: its history needs historical mediation. This historical mediation, however, becomes almost impossible because of Kant's substitution of historical time for a logic of space-time. The subsequent moves in the history of Western philosophy will show the determination that this decision to substitute time for logic will have to bind philosophy to the same logical space within which it became conscious of itself.

Hegel in his identification of the self took as originary the complementary relations of two individuals who recognize each other. Hegel's formulation is based on the everyday experience that self-consciousness first forms itself on the basis of mutual recognition. Individuation is simultaneously socialization, and *viceversa.* Hegel understands the mind *(Geist)* as what both surrounds and makes possible both processes, the individual and the general. Its bearer is the family, the culture, the nation, the people. That is the medium in which communicative behavior, interaction, takes place and forms the identity of self-consciousness as a result, but it also establishes the dialectics of opposition.

Hegel's *Phenomenology of the Mind* goes behind the unspoken presuppositions of the Kantian theory of knowledge: the presupposition of a normative concept of science, the equally normative concept of the subject of knowledge and the rigid separation between theoret-

Knowledge and Consciousness as a Fixed Logical Time-Space Matrix

ical and practical reason. Its effort is to reconstruct the formative process of critical philosophy, "the detailed history of the process of training and educating consciousness itself up to the level of science."

Hegel, however, also fell into the Kantian error of making a particular concept of science the only authoritative one: At the end of the *Phenomenology* he identifies the critical consciousness of the theory of knowledge with "absolute knowledge." It would appear, therefore, that the "phenomenological experience" always maintains itself in the medium of an absolute movement of the mind and therefore must necessarily end in "absolute knowledge." This can only mean that he is convinced that he has not radicalized the critical claim of epistemology through phenomenological investigation, but rather made it superfluous. The completion of the formative and educational process demonstrates natural science to be *one* of the forms of "phenomenal knowledge" *(erscheinendes Wissen),* just as the transcendental unity of self-consciousness, which Kant set up as the decisive example in the question of pure rational knowledge, is one of the forms of knowledge of the emerging mind *("Geist").* Thus Hegel's dialectics move within the same logical space-time coordinates fixed by Kant and all his efforts to infuse them with history will not succeed, for the coordinates of space and time are prior to history, they are not the mediation of history.

Marx's formulation of the theory of knowledge may be seen in the first thesis on Feuerbach: the major flaw of all previous materialism is "that the object, reality, sensuousness, is conceived only in the form of an object or perception, but not as concrete human activity, praxis, rather than subjectively." "Concrete human activity" aims at the *constitution* of objects which because they are natural objects share the moment of being-for-themselves but at the same time are objects which have been created through human activity. Human activity, according to Marx, is a transcendental achievement grounded in the process of labor. The subject of the constitution of the world is not a transcendental consciousness in general, but rather the concrete human species which reproduces its life under natural conditions and limitations. That means that "concrete human activity" creates both the real conditions for the reproduction of life and the transcendental conditions for possible objectivity about objects of experience; it regulates the "exchange of matter between men and nature" and thus immediately constitutes a world. To the degree to which the species transparently becomes the bearer of this activity, it posits, and at the same time it shapes itself as the societal subject. In this sense Marx adopted Hegel's critique of Kant materialistically.

The Marxian positing, however, of a self-constitution of the human species *only* through work leads Marx to the identification of knowledge with a particular form of knowledge. Though Marx's theory of society takes into account the wider relationships of production in addition to productive forces, the moments of domination and ideology, where Marx relates to philosophy and the awareness of his philosophical praxis, this side of praxis is not revealed. It will follow, by implication, that the development of productive forces and the progress of science and industry must lead by themselves to the emancipation of a self-conscious general subject which controls the process of production. Yet Marx uncompromisingly fought this over simplicity. History had taught Marx that the social process of production cannot be considered independently from the institutional framework in which it appears. And this framework is not an unmediated result of labor practices; it does not unmediatedly represent a step in technological development, but rather a relationship of social forces: class consciousness as the power of one social class over another.

The identification of the act of self-formation with labor alone led knowledge into the positivistic threshold. As in Kant and Hegel, it leads to the conclusion of establishing a particular category of science as normative: "it is a social movement as a natural-historical process, guided by laws which are not only independent of the will, consciousness and intention of man, but much rather the inverse—they determine man's desires, consciousness and intentions." Thus, Marx never explicitly diverted from his early intentions set down in the *Economic and Philosophic Manuscripts*: "Natural science will in time subsume under itself the science of man, as the science of man will subsume under itself natural science: there will be *one* science." This single, this universal science—scientific materialism—has for Marx the same function as "absolute knowledge" for Hegel. While in Hegel science turns into philosophy, in Marx philosophy turns into science. The normative validity of this science, however, establishes *a priori* its own identifiable conditions, and these conditions become its own logic and its own boundaries. Thus it breaks the critical claims of epistemology by not being fully aware of its own praxis. It is a coercion of history rather than the result of the mediation of history. We hope to make these points clearer in what follows.

THE IDEA OF SOCIETY AS OBJECTIVE ILLUSION

The previous discussion on the theory of knowledge has made us aware of an easy and vague ready agreement among the sciences and philosophy about the concept of society. It appears in general as a concomitant necessary condition to the previous requirements of identifying consciousness with the *consciousness of,* knowledge with scientific knowledge and a particular *logic* substituting for temporality and history. In more general terms it appears as a fixed and controlled space called historical within which humans make their predictable and controllable temporal moves. It will help to clarify our critical remarks to bring out the fact that this situation, again, is the unmediated result of having taken as paradigm of knowledge scientific practice. The relation of theory and practice in empirical analytic science demands as a fixed presupposition the fixity and otherness of Nature. So we presuppose a fixed society. To understand this point let us bring out how it works in the empirical-analytic sciences.

The procedure of a natural scientist is hypothetico-deductive. The scientist forms hypotheses, deduces consequences from the hypotheses and checks that the deduced consequences correspond to the experimental results. A hypothesis confirmed by observation, i.e., observation made under conditions systematically controlled by the observer, assumes the status of a theory. The scientist can continue to deduce consequences from it and present them as predictions. When a class of phenomena is thoretically explained, we are able to predict phenomena belonging to this class. A theory giving no basis for prediction, is not an explanatory theory; it remains an empty hypothesis.

The possibility of experimental observation, e.g., the possibility of keeping one variable constant while varying another, refers to a special kind of relationship between the experimenting observer and the phenomena observed. This relationship we might describe as a subject-instrument-object relation wherein the subject is controlling the object and its condition of behavior through his instrumental practice.

It is necessary, however, that the object be conceived as "historically resting," while the subject as "historically moving." The object or *Nature* has been "resting," let us say, from the time of Aristotle to our time; i.e., Aristotle and the present scientists are facing the *same* Nature, but the scientific approach to this same Nature has changed with the improvement of its instruments. The *unchangeability* of Nature is a presupposition for saying that we in one sense have better explanations of natural processes than Aristotle had. If Aristotle and present-day science explained different Natures, we could not say this. The *unchangeability* of Nature is also a presupposition for establishing experimental techniques giving the same results at the time t_1 as t_n. The *unchangeability* of Nature is also a presupposition for linking the progress in knowledge with the improvement in the instruments of science. The repeatability of experiments is a presupposition for establishing reliable knowledge through the sciences of the understanding. And on the basis of established natural laws we are able to predict and to control. The control is facilitated by our ability to predict what happens under conditions which we are technically able repeatedly to produce.

This method of empirical-analytical science is thus the paradigm of science discovering laws. To the degree, however, that people react to each other through distorted or without communicative understanding of each other; to the degree that people are determined by social processes without understanding them; to the degree that controlling systems may go on behind the backs of the social agents and thus create for themselves a kind of autonomy because of the agents' lack of autonomy; to the degree that education is one more instant of technical manipulation rather than emancipation, the methods of the sciences become also the paradigm of the social. They grasp what the method creates. They concentrate on what through the method is positively given. They sanction for eternity their way of conceiving what actually is. They make history and the change of human conditions superfluous. To conceive of society as a historically resting monolith analogical to scientific nature is to conceive it in an ideological way. To keep society and human history *resting* by means of social technology is to act out of dictatorial coercion.

When we affirm that empirical-analytical science descriptively conceives the facts of nature, we must remember that the facts in question are constituted as empirical facts in a context defined by technique or instrumental action, i.e., instrumental action organizes the kind of experience which empirical-analytical science represents. The basic propositions of empirical-analytical theories are no direct representations of "facts." They express rather the results of our instrumental or technical operations within controlled systems; i.e., they create the "facts." If Nature made up her mind to behave in another way, made up her mind to get "historically moving," our experiments would not be repeatable as experiments giving the same results. The concept of experiment and the concept of technique would become very problematic indeed (as they are in social science). We had to suppress Nature in order to make her react according to the established laws of nature. We had to suppress society so that we could have control of society. Techniques and method change to authoritarian practice and experiments imply only a moment of power and coercion.

The main point here is that technique or instrumental action is not something secondary or external in relation to empirical-analytical science in the sense of being only its practical application. Experimental observation refers to and presupposes technique. Technique is so to speak a presupposition for the possibility of empirical-analytical science. Empirical-analytical theories reveal regularities in Nature which we can take advantage of. When we are able systematically to take advantage of regularities in Nature, we have technology. With technology the "cunning consciousness" turns the laws of Nature against Nature herself. By presupposing society we turn the regularities in society into natural laws and turn these laws into a preparation for the elimination of society itself. Society, like the self and knowledge, is neither given nor identifiable. It has to be empirically discovered as it originally and radically constituted itself, i.e., in its plural history and within its historical mobility.

The *decision* about what kind of society one needs to presuppose in order to justify one's theory of self and knowledge has never been transparent to the decision makers. This lack of transparency has been, of course, due to a previous commitment of those decision makers to crypto-orientations towards the substitution of the social for an absolutized and manageable form of the social. It has been a decision historically unmediated and therefore born of coercive impulses rather than emancipating possibilities, but in any case, it has always been a *decision* hidden to itself as a radical decision about a radical human constitution.

To understand the philosophical moves which would link theories of self, knowledge and society in such a way as to need an absolute form of society, one would have to watch closely the moves of the critical philosophers we have already mentioned: Kant, Fichte, Hegel, Marx and also Freud. They will all ground their presupposition of society on their own understanding of judgment, of decision making. They will thus bring themselves and us to the realization that the freedom of man does not lie in his choices but in his decisions. A decision, however, being a choice of a life-orientation systematically executed on what a man takes life to be. Man's life is radically grounded on his judgements, but then judgements are grounded on a radical orientation about knowledge in the form described above.

The question is, therefore, which consciousness is the decision making consciousness? Which consciousness is the bearer of a man's and a culture's intentionality? In Kant, Fichte and Hegel the synthesis of knowledge is achieved in a transcendental consciousness; the synthesis indicates a logical relationship exemplified by the form of a judgement. Kant has recourse to a particular logic to gain the categories of understanding from the tables of judgement. Fichte and Hegel link up with Kant's transcendental logic—the first in order to reconstruct from pure perception the actual *behavior* of the absolute self, the latter to reconstruct the *dialectical movement* of the absolute concept from the antinomies of pure reason. Marx, however, will jump from the synthesis accomplished in the realm of thought, to that of labor, affirming then that its ground is no longer a relationship between propositions, but a system of social labor, and the synthesis itself is no longer an isolated activity of thought, but rather of material production. Marx recognized that productive forces always develop under specific relationships of production which correspond to current conditions. If the former come to contradict the latter, antagonisms arise which finally burst out in revolutions: the classes which are most strongly oppressed by the relationships of production turn against the dominant classes which determine the social order. In this sense history is a "history of class struggles," and to the extent that the worker who finds himself in "material exchange" with nature is always the product of this history, the social concept of synthesis must necessarily take on a second dimension: in addition to the synthesis through social labor, there is that achieved through class struggle. Reflective knowledge thus constitutes class consciousness and society is the field of this class struggle.

Freud conceives culture as Marx does society: a system by which the human species elevates itself above the animal necessities of existence. Culture serves to make assertions in the face of nature and to organize the relationships of men among one another. The difference between Freud and Marx lies in the fact that the latter explains the power of institutions in terms of the specific distribution of rewards and burdens, distorted along class lines, which are set up over a long period of time and grounded in power—whereas Freud, because of his conviction that everyone's drives are an enemy of culture, understands institutional frameworks generally as necessary to the maintenance of the species (as long as the productive forces are not sufficiently developed). For the individual this framework is an unshakeable reality. Desires which are irreconcilable with this reality cannot really be satisfied, except of course in phantasy. However, to the degree that the level of socially necessary repression and the power of institutions which (reinforced by the cultural repression of desires) stabilize, social domination decreases, and wish fulfillment phantasies which, according to Freud, essentially constitute transmission (religious rites and images of the world, ideals, value systems and artistic products) can be transformed into reality.

Psychoanalysis' intention, however, is also to gain a freedom—mediated by knowledge—from objective illusion, but the individual, again, has already been isolated from the community by being stranded on his fixed and isolated consciousness. Thus there too, it is a question of the reconstruction of a process of formation—individual of course—whose product, the neurotic subject, experiences objectivations of his own history as foreign drives coming from the outside.

Psychoanalytic interpretation does not have to do with meaning relationships in the sphere of something consciously intended; its critical work sets aside no accidental lapses. Mutilations in the text—for example, in the text of a dream—have a meaning in themselves. They can be removed only when this meaning is grasped. The analyst brings the patient to the point of being able to read his own texts, which he himself mutilated and twisted, and of learning to translate symbols from a mode of expression, distorted into a private language, into that of public communication.

In addition to disruptions of individual processes of formation,

Freud also considered those of a collectivity. The "diagnosis of collective neuroses," which cannot be generated, as individual neuroses are, from the contrast between the patient and his "normal" surroundings, is based on an investigation of the cultural history of development of the human species, of "cultural processes." It shows that the renunciation of desires which is the basis of culture is primarily that of economic necessity.

Given the condition that renunciation springs from economic scarcity, however, it is therefore of historically variable magnitude and hence historically mediated. Then the measure of socially necessary repression obviously depends on the development of productive forces and would vary according to historical contexts. Freud, however, generalized on the concept of a universal culture when he emphasized that the more the technical power to dispose of nature is expanded and the pressure of reality is relaxed, the weaker the censorship of drives imposed by the system of self-preservation will become and the stronger the organization of the ego and its capacity rationally to overcome renunciation. Before that time, however, such a mastery is obviously unthinkable for the ego. The ego needs exterior drives to make the individual conform to culture. Institutions take care of that. They produce—and therein consists their similarity to pathological forms—relatively rigid reproductions of uniform attitudes which are shielded from any critique.

By circumscribing the life of man into the *a priori* moves of self, knowledge and society, man has been forced to make all his moves within this reduced space, substituting choice for decision, discovery for conformity. Thus dissension and coercion, the social and antisocial, freedom and determinism, right and left, conformity and escapism form the very fabric of an euphemism called society. As Ortega remarks:

> This is enough to make us realize that giving the name of "society" to a collectivity is a euphemism that falsifies our vision of collective "life." So-called "society" is never what the name promises. It is always at the same time, to one or another degree, *dis-society,* repulsion between individuals. Since on the other hand it claims to be the opposite, we must radically open ourselves to the conviction that society is a reality that is *constitutively* sick, defective—strictly, it is a never-ending struggle between its genuinely social elements and behaviors. For a minimum of sociability to predominate and, thanks to this, for any society to endure as such, it must frequently summon its internal "public power" to intervene in violent form and even—when the society develops and ceases to be primitive—to create a special body charged with making that power function in irresistible form. This is what is commonly called the State."

Societies are still to be discovered, not presupposed.

Appendix to Chapter Five

THE EMPTY HUMAN SPACES OF HISTORY.

The remarks that follow are intended to clarify our theme Man and Circumstance and to help the reader make it possible for himself to witness the miracle of the birth of man, for as Ortega remarked, "It is only by seeing things being born that we really know them." Before we summarize Ortega's programmatic philosophy of liberation or emancipation, we will first summarize Ortega's own understanding of philosophy.

Due to the sheer volume of Ortega's work, there is danger of missing the forest for the trees, that is:

The bare simplicity of his philosophical vision, and his radical way of doing philosophy, demanded by this simplicity, which is not customary in the philosophical tradition of the West, or that this tradition has forgotten.

The simplicity of Ortega's philosophical vision and his radical way of doing philosophy arose in him at the beginning of his life. The task of giving birth to Ortega is to make this explicit, and to show that the whole of his philosophical activity is a systematic application and enlargement of his initial vision. In short, Ortega's vision and his mission meet historically as they encounter each other contextually, in his life as he lived it. Thus, Ortega's prolific writings are only significant insofar as they show us Ortega doing philosophy.

The first step is to clarify the Spanish word *principio,* which is essential to the understanding of the meaning of Man and Circumstance. The word *principio* in Spanish has a double meaning: principle and origin. A confusion of both meanings would make Ortega appear a rationalist or an idealist and would take the punch from his critical philosophy. Ortega's claim is that principles have taken man away from the real *principio*—man's original spaces of his life as contextually lived, the ground from which philosophy must draw its reason and its propositions. As Ortega once remarked, "He who would teach us a truth should situate us so that we will discover it ourselves." Philosophy is basically a radically constituting activity.

Ortega's goal in life can only be understood as a program of education, but it is misleading to think that this can be achieved simply by carrying Ortega's program to others. It is Ortega's own process of education through others that we have to discover. The important word in this connection is *goal.* When used in education, it may lead us to believe that there is something out there—either in the systems of education or in the society which hypostasizes those systems—some thing or ideal to which a man who wishes to be educated must conform. According to Ortega's understanding of education as a radical goal of life, such a program would not be education but indoctrination.

As we know, the word "education" comes from the Latin *e-ducere,* which means "to bring out," in the sense of "uncovering" or "dis-covering" what for oneself is an absolute *need*—an anxious necessity without whose satisfaction or fulfillment life would be unbearable. Life is not only mediated through knowledge but also through anxiety, the radical anxiety which life forces on us for its own constitution as ours. Of course, education as normally understood and forced upon students today does not give the word "education" its original meaning; instead of a program of *e-ducere* it has become a program of *ducere*—"leading," "guiding," "railroading" students of all ages to conform to already established and approved social or educational coercive goals which satisfy approved social or educational interests.

Education has in many ways been reduced to technology. Educational theories are analogical to empirical-analytical theories. Educational theories conceived as analogical to empirical-analytical theories are primarily something which makes prediction and control of educational processes possible. The educational aims indicate for what the ability to predict and to control is going to be used. The concept of aim or end is a technological category and refers to a complete mastery over the factors affecting the aim, safeguarding thus the *status quo*.

The material with which the educationist has to work is human beings, and the laws that apply to this material are "the laws of human nature."

In order to administer effectively, the administrating subjectivity must have complete control over the processes to be administered. Psychological theory structured according to the paradigm of empirical-analytical science facilitates this control. The psychologist and the educationist are conceived as persons able "to play at" the laws of human nature. They represent the "cunning consciousness," able to turn the laws of human nature against human nature herself, thus mastering her. This is a relation of control wherein techniques are involved and through which the educationist behaves authoritarianly reinforcing the authoritarian conditions of society. Scientism, in theory, is authoritarianism in practice. Authoritarianism is determining on behalf of others without justifying this determination rationally and discursively. The objectification of the Other, as Ortega remarks, is necessarily irrational, since rational justification presupposes the recognition of the Other as subject.

It is in the context of individually felt, vital needs as a program, mission or destiny that Ortega understands education; truth thereby becomes the activity that "quiets an anxiety" in our life, and morality becomes the disciplined commitment of carrying out this program of soothing one's vital needs.

Two further steps must be taken to understand Ortega's program of education. One concerns his idea of *judgment,* the other that of *intuition*. The sciences (the worlds already constituted) are the result of some vital needs of man satisfied and executed *(ejecutados),* that is, formed—judged sufficient for the need which originated them. Judgment thus circumscribed to its context is indestructible, since it is the condition of possibility for the world to be what it is—and what it can become. It is in the midst of such a world that the man in search of an education finds himself born, one fine morning. For Ortega, this world in which man finds himself born, precariously at home, with the contextual limitations and richness of nationality, university, profession or hobby, is a world within which he lives through *intuition.* This world of intuition is capable not only of making us function within it; it includes the whole intellectual ladder of possibilities, from "normal perception," "rational numbers," to "justice" or "Minkowsky's principle of relativity."

In Ortega's case, the only world within which and through which he could authentically "make himself" was his circumstance—Spain, and later, Europe. To reveal to himself and to others what was already there, lived, felt in all its implications, he turned to philosophy. In uncovering his own circumstances he was uncovering his whole being, and he never believed that this being could be either exhausted by or reduced to his thought. He realized instead that *through* his thought he could quench his inexhaustible need for self-clarity. Thinking as a mediation between man and circumstance became, for Ortega, a way of life: an historic journey of uncovering and constituting (interpreting) the life which was already there surrounding him and taking a *stand* about the world against his.

In Ortega's efforts to liberate philosophy from its slavery to principles, *perception* became the origin and originality of all his thinking. Ortega was not satisfied with the realism and positivist dogmatism of his Spanish compatriots, nor with the idealistic rationalism and subsequent skepticism and relativism of the Germans. Between these two extremes he was able to find a middle path which saves reason and yet is phenomenological in its own unique sense: ontological reduction.

The point of departure for Ortega's program is an epistemological step: perception. As he describes it,

> since 1914 . . . the intuition of the phenomenon "human life" (is) the base of all my thinking. I formulated it then with the occasion of explaining the phenomenology of Husserl, correcting principally (his) description of the phenomenal "consciousness of . . ." which, as everyone knows, constitutes the basis of his doctrine.

Ortega separates himself from Husserl by positing as the origin of philosophy not the "consciousness of" *(Bewusstsein von)* but "human life," the consciousness man *counts on* in order to live:

> the "primary conscience," "nonreflexive naïve," in which man *believes* that which he thinks; he definitely loves and feels a toothache without any other possible *reduction* than an aspirin or the tooth being pulled out. What is *essential,* therefore, to this "primary conscience" is that for it nothing is a mere object but everything is reality. To *become aware,* this consciousness does not have a contemplative character, but simply encounters things themselves, the world.

In *Some Lessons in Metaphysics,* Ortega describes the basic characteristics of this encounter with life as "self-awareness, self-making, self-decision, and perplexity." Yet life is that *which I count on.*

The first chapter of *Meditaciones Del Quijote,* on love, offers us a clue to Ortega's philosophical search for clarity, for a loving self-presence. The need for this constant clarification commits Ortega to his boldest and most daring epistemological position: *being is living and thinking is only an image.* The only way for me to see my love or my pain is to stop loving and suffering and become a "seeing self." The real I—"the true I, the executive I, the present I"—has stopped being, to become a mere image, an object I have in front of me. Ortega concludes this argument by saying:

> We cannot make an object of our understanding, we cannot make anything exist for ourselves unless we turn it into an image, a concept, an idea, that is, unless (whatever is) stops being what it is, to transform itself in a shadow or a scheme of itself. There is only one thing with which we are in intimate relation: this thing is our individuality, our life, but this, *our* intimacy, when turned into an image, stops being an intimacy . . .

Better than we could do, Ortega sums up the radicality of his philosophy:

> Knowledge . . . is a perspective, therefore neither properly an ingress of the thing in the mind as the Classics believed, nor a being of the "thing itself" in the mind *per modum cognoscentis,* as the Scholastics wanted, nor a copy of the thing . . . , not a construction of the thing as Kant, the Positivists and the Marburg School believed, but (knowledge) is an "interpretation" of one thing itself forced into a translation, as it is done from one language to another; we could say from the language of being, which is silent, to the outspoken language of knowing.

Within the context of Western philosophy, Ortega's radical stance in relation to perception turns philosophy into something different from the philosophy of inertia dictated by others. He shows us that the "first principles of philosophy are in fact propositions, since they cannot be proven." He sets realism and idealism right by going through their epistemological presuppositions and transforming rationality into reason. More significantly, he points out the errors in Western philosophy's obsession with knowing things-in-themselves, by showing that "things" appear in thought, not in life, for life is a clarity of presences with oneself and others in the concrete world in which one lives. A concrete world, however, is a contextual world, wherein "every life is a viewpoint on the universe." The perception of any individual (i.e., person, country, historical period, occupation, etc.) is unique to him, but the concepts by means of which he thinks cannot be found ready-made, but must be extracted from the contextual architecture of his world. If one takes into account this radical beginning of Ortega's philosophy as a mission or destiny, one easily understands his sense of vocation:

> My vocation was thought, the desire for clarity about things. This congenital fervor, perhaps, made me see very soon that one of the characteristic signs of my Spanish circumstance was the lack of precisely that which I had to become out of my own intimate need. Evidently, the personal inclination towards thought and the conviction that this was besides a service to my country become in me one. This is why all my work, the whole of my life, has been a service to Spain. And this is an unmovable truth, even though objectively it might turn out that I had been of no service at all.

It is precisely in this social *present*-to-be-saved that Ortega grounds his philosophical activity, and it is because our contemporary present demands from us its own and our salvation that the ground of philosophy as a self-constituting and self-justifying activity lies. If the *present* did not need its own self-revelation, and through this activity we would not find our own self-revelation and maturity, then philosophy would just be an ideology lacking its own radical ground, its justification to exist as philosophy. Because philosophy, however, is grounded on radical human needs, or radical basic orientations, or radical *present* human possibilities, philosophy is possible and can make our present possibilities actual by realizing those empty spaces of human history.

To conclude this journey through Western philosophy, we will try to summarize the philosophical ground on which our doing of philosophy is radicalized. It is, of course, our hope that this is the way philosophy has always radicalized itself and that, therefore, through this radical recovery philosophy may not only know other cultures as others but radicalize them also as our contemporary ground as it discovers them: they are philosophy's own possibilities.

Philosophy's own justification lies in the fact that it can not only uncover man's radical human constitution but that through this discovery it constitutes contemporary man's ground and vision of himself.

I can find no better way to sum up my position here than to use Ortega's own cryptic *sūtra* (short-hand summary of his philosophy): "I am I and my circumstance." This *sūtra,* by the way, may be focused upon analytically and may be forced to distill for us its human emancipating program, or it may be also turned into a *mantra* and be sung in English or in Spanish *(Yo soy yo y mi circunstancia)* with as much efficacy as a Sanskrit *mantra.*

The key to understanding the phrase "I am I and my circumstance," lies in understanding the three different forms of being in the world represented by the three I's in the sentence. The first I, like the forest, is the executive I, the indivisible I, the unidentifiable I, the ground of possibilities necessary and sufficient for the other I's to be: where man is at home amongst a clarity of presences and possibilities and no questions asked.

The second I is the I which appears in reflection simultaneously with the circumstance. The circumstance is both what surrounds me and what stands opposite me. The temptation has been, in Western philosophy, to radicalize man and philosophy on this reflective confrontation. Either by reducing the I to the circumstance or subjugating the circumstance to the I. In both cases knowledge has been understood as a weapon of coercion rather than a ground of mediation.

Knowledge as mediation is possible if the second I is turned through philosophical activity into the third, where circumstance and I are reconciled through the mediation of knowledge as *my* circumstance. *My* circumstance as mine is no longer a confrontation of two opposing perspectives or objects, but rather the equal interpretation of two I's on the same ontological basis as the first I. Interaction has given way to intra-action whereby mutual reflective perspectives are sacrificed and incorporated as a-perspectival presences in the first I. When the circumstance becomes *my* circumstance, the other has become my possibility and not my limitation or my confrontation. Emancipation or liberation is a philosophical program where the other or circumstance becomes, through the mediation of knowledge, the necessary and sufficient condition for man to transcend any form of coercion. At the root of the security and anxiety of values, lies man, the creator of radical interpretations: I am I and my Circumstance and unless I save It I cannot save myself. The test of this emancipating program is, of course, its own execution.

Critical Notes to Chapter Three

PRONUNCIATION OF SANSKRIT WORDS

The ancient Indian grammarians of the Sanskrit language have identified forty-eight sounds as worthy of notation, and in the script that was developed over the centuries each character represents that one sound unalterably. Hence there can be no confusion about how a particular word was pronounced, though different schools of Veda transmission show slight variations in the articulation; yet compared with the haphazard correspondence of Roman notation and English pronunciation, Sanskrit notation is extremely precise.

The sequence of the alphabet again was completely scientific. The order of letters is not the historical jumble of the Roman alphabet, which imitated the sequence of Semitic scripts, but simply the path of the breath through the hollow of the mouth from the throat to the lips, producing the vowels; through the nose, producing these vowels with nasalization; and the same breath with occlusion of the tongue to points in the hollow of the mouth from the throat to the lips, producing the consonants.

The Alphabet

a ā, i ī, u ū, ṛ ṝ, ḷ, e ai, o au
k kh g gh ṅ
c ch j jh ñ
ṭ ṭh ḍ ḍh ṇ
t th d dh n
p ph b bh m
y r l v

ś ṣ s
h
ṃ
ḥ

Vowels

a—ā in America or o in come
ā—a in far or in father
i—i in pit or in pin
ī—ee in feel or i in machine
u—u in put or pull
ū—u in rule
ṛ—properly *ur,* but by modern Hindus as *ri* in river or in writ. *Ṛta (Rita), Ṛg Veda (Rig Veda), Prakṛti (Prakriti), Kṛṣṇa (Krishna).*
e–ay in say or a̲ in made
ai—i in rite or a̲i̲ in aisle
o—o in go
au—ou in loud

Consonants

Consonants are pronounced approximately as in English, except:

g—g in gun or in get (always "hard")
c—ch in church
sh (ś, ṣ—sh in sheet or in shun)

When *h* is combined with another consonant (e.g., th, bh), it is aspirated: *th* as in boathouse; *ph* as in uphill, etc. The palatal ñ is like the Spanish señor (jña, however, is pronounced most often by modern Hindus as "gyah," with a hard g).

Accent

The rule of thumb is that Sanskrit words are accented in English like Greek and Latin words: stress the penultimate vowel, if that is long. Length is indicated either by a long vowel or a short (or long) vowel followed by more than one consonant, e.g., *rāma, raṅga.* If the penultimate syllable is short, stress the antepenultimate, whether it is long or short: *Mahābhārata, Arjuna* (the antepenultimates are long), and also *Aruṇa* (antepenultimate is short, as in *Herodotus, Thucydides).*

The real stumbling block in the transcription, which

follows international convention, is that of the *c*. The *c* is always pronounced as the English *ch,* never *k*.

The notes I have chosen for consideration are only some proper names to help the reading of the text and some terms, expressions, and critical remarks which bear specific philosophical value in the context of the *Gītā*. Philosophical value does not mean for this author to make the *Gītā* pass a philosophical examination by any of the Western boards of philosophy and see how the *Gītā* fairs in such a test. By philosophical value the author means no more and no less than to point out to the reader, in a critical manner, the philosophical presuppositions of the text so that the text itself brings out its own meaning within its own context or contexts, regardless of how this way of doing philosophy in the *Gītā* compares to any of our Western ways of engaging in the same activity. I purposely omit allusions to any other commentators from East or West, like Śaṃkara, Rāmānuja, Edgerton, etc. Though this comparison may be useful in its proper place, I do not think this to be the place. My critical approach with its contextual emphasis is too far removed in time and method from previous ones. Yet it is my hope that the reader will be able to find by himself how my method depends on the complementarity of previous interpretations. It is this individual activity by the reader that will make him go beyond linguistic similarities to a more comprehensive and radical vision of himself and his circumstance as the *Gītā* suggests. This activity—way—is what I want most to recover traversing the paths of the *Gītā*.

This book is written because of a felt need, and hope, that it will point out what others have overlooked. It is not written to right any wrongs or destroy other people's work. All there is, is interpretation.

> Two birds with fair wings, inseparable companions,
> have found a refuge in the same sheltering tree.
> One of the birds incessantly eats from the peepal tree;
> the other, not eating, just looks on.
>
> *Ṛg Veda 1,164,20*
> *Muṇḍaka Upaniṣad III, i, 1*

> Know the self (ātman) as riding in a chariot,
> The body as the chariot.
> Know the intellect (buddhi) as the chariot-driver,

And the mind as the reins.
The senses, they say, are the horses;
The objects of sense, what they range over.
The self combined with senses and mind
Wise men call "the enjoyer."

Kaṭha Upaniṣad III. 3

INTRODUCTION TO CAUTION THE READER

Historical Setting

Sometime around the twelfth century, B.C., a great war involving a large number of small regional kingdoms occurred in what is now the Karnal district of Hariana State in northern India. Because of the scanty historical records available, the varied and complex issues that precipitated the conflict are, and perhaps always will be, matters for speculation and dispute. Undoubtedly, many legendary accretions have been added to the tenuous historical data, but whatever the particular elements of this complex event may have been, it is in any case fairly certain that a war of major proportions did occur and that it had most serious subsequent political consequences for India. Hindus have for centuries regarded this war as a crisis point in their civilization.

Several centuries later—perhaps somewhere between the fifth and second centuries, B.C.—the author of the *Bhagavad Gītā* utilized this historical event as the setting for what to his view was a basic conflict for man. The final recension of the work was made during the Gupta period (fourth to seventh centuries, A.D.). One of the earliest manuscript sources dates back to Śaṃkara's commentary on the *Gītā* in the ninth century A.D., though a Kashmir text is believed to be somewhat earlier, the difference between the two is minimal.

The *Gītā* forms a small part, seven hundred stanzas, of the epic the *Mahābhārata,* two hundred thousand lines, (chapters 23 to 40 of the Bhīśma–Parvam).

Authorship of the Gītā

When reading the *Gītā* one must be aware that the whole book is about Arjuna's crisis and its resolution. The author of the *Gītā* takes, therefore, a concrete man—a prince, politician, leader, warrior—in a concrete historico-cultural setting—a battle—and identifies as the starting point of the book a crisis, Arjuna's. This crisis arises because Arjuna identifies himself with his actions. He believes himself to be the actor and therefore is caught in the results of those actions. It will take eighteen chapters to resolve this impasse.

With this in mind the reader of the *Gītā* should not try to read the *Gītā's* words literally. To take the *Gītā's* words literally would be to fall into the same misconception of identification that led Arjuna to his crisis and the reader to a possible misunderstanding and/or institutionalization of man's hope, faith, charity, and even crisis and despair.

The first clue to notice as to a possible way of not reading the *Gītā* literally is to observe how the author of the *Gītā* presents the story. The author remains unknown—(though it is speculated his name to be Vyāsa)—thus he does not identify himself with his work; but the whole story is narrated by Saṃjaya, the charioteer, to his *blind* king, Dhṛtarāṣṭra. Saṃjaya hears the story in the battle field, and it consists in a dialogue between Arjuna and his charioteer, Kṛṣṇa. Thus the author—whoever he was—brings within his own narrative form the same message of the *Gītā:* beware of self-identifications. Furthermore, Indian literature is divided into two types: *smṛti,* "remembered" or "interpreted" and *śruti,* literally "what has been heard." The author of the *Gītā,* through Arjuna's crisis, brings together both traditions in a living message: Arjuna's reconciliation between *śruti* and *smṛti* as grounded on Arjuna's crisis and its resolution. Kṛṣṇa is the voice that brings and holds these worlds together. As the story develops, the reader will find that any identification or institutionalization of Kṛṣṇa with his first person speech is sheer idolatry and contrary to the story of the *Gītā.*

To help the reader, at a glance, anticipate in his imagination, the story, I will add here a short index summary of its development.

INDEX

Part I: Man of crisis.

Chapter I. *Arjunaviṣādayoga* Arjuna's *crisis,* man's identification with his own actions.

Part II, The development by Kṛṣṇa of Arjuna's theoretic consciousness: All that he had forgotten.

Chapter II. *Sāṃkhyayoga* The way of memory: clarification of *Karman-Dharma:* action-context. *Manas*-interpretation and *buddhi*-interpretation of sense and sense objects and their orientation to knowledge or absolutization through *manas*—interpretation, etc.

Chapter III. *Karmayoga* Liberation of self-identification. Sacrifice of perspectives as in the Ṛg Veda.

Chapter IV. *Jñānayoga* Knowledge as goal.

Chapter V. *Karmasaṃnyāsayoga* Action without attachment.

Chapter VI. *Dhyānayoga* The best action is mind-control through meditation. (control of thoughts and their fruit anticipation.)

Chapter VII. *Jñānavijñānayoga* Contex determines things. Things do not exhaust the context.

Chapter VIII. *Akṣarabrahmayoga* Liberation and rebirth both depend on knowledge.

Chapter IX. *Rājavidyārājaguhyayoga* Kṛṣṇa's knowledge as the prototype.

Chapter X. *Vibhūtiyoga* Kṛṣṇa's knowledge is the embodiment of all that the culture had to offer up to his own time: the end of the "theoretic consciousness."

Part III: The resolution of Crisis: life's faith.

Chapter XI. *Viśvarūpadarśanayoga* Man is time. Arjuna's crisis reaches its resolution when he confronts reality directly, that is when the theoretic consciousness is pulled from under his feet. Past, present and future stand frighteningly naked in front of Arjuna.

Chapter XII. *Bhaktiyoga* What keeps Arjuna alive is his faith in his own life. The power of life to remake itself as my own, no longer as other people's life.

Part IV: Action for the sake of knowledge. The action of knowledge.

Chapter XIII. *Kṣetrakṣetrajñavibhāgayoga* Liberating knowledge is to know the field in all fields. The orientation to knowledge.

Chapter XIV. *Guṇatrayavibhāgayoga* Man's concrete fields or contexts or circumstance is here described as the *guṇas*.

Chapter XV. *Puruṣottamayoga* Man's path is like the peeple tree with its branches below and its roots above. Through *buddhi* knowledge of perspectives may be transcended into an a-perspectival vision of reality.

Chapter XVI. *Daivāsurasaṃpadvibhāgayoga* Liberation consists in not taking first person discourse *(ahaṃkāra)* literally. This identification of liberation is bound to one's own historical circumstance.

Chapter XVII. *Śraddhātrayavibhāgayoga* When one is free, one acts and remains in the same world. Identification with action changes: it is no longer the I that speaks but one's knowledge.

Chapter XVIII. *Mokṣasaṃnyāsayoga* Man's circumstance is saved when all the *guṇas* are oriented and energized towards the liberating knowledge of which Kṛṣṇa and Arjuna are the prototypes.

NOTES

Figures below refer to stanza and line number, within individual chapters.

Chapter I

1.1 *Dhṛtarāṣṭra:* lit. "one who holds the kingdom." He is the weak and blind king of the Kurus. Though legally disqualified by blindness to be king, he held the throne. Arjuna and his four brothers—the Pāṇḍavas—were brought up in this court with their cousins the Kauravas. The old blind king could not rule, even less hold the balance between his sons and their cousins. In the "great epic," the Mahābhārata, Dhṛtarāṣṭra gave his throne to his nephew Yudhiṣṭhira (one of Arjuna's brothers) instead of to the oldest of his hundred sons, Duryodhana, a cruel and selfish man. Duryodhana conspired nevertheless to gain the kingdom and destroy the Pāṇḍava brothers, and arranged to have Yudhiṣṭhira invited to a series of dice games, Yudhiṣṭhira liked to gamble and lost not only the games but also his entire kingdom. As a result and by the stakes of the final game, he with his brothers and their common wife Draupadī, was exiled for thirteen years. Dhṛtarāṣṭra was displeased with this venture and promised the Pāṇḍavas that after the exile and on certain conditions they could return to their kingdom and reclaim it. When the period of exile was over and the conditions met, however, Duryodhana refused to give up the kingdom. The weak king could not bring about a reconciliation between the cousins, and when both sides appealed to their relatives and friends they found themselves on the brink of a civil and family war. When the battle is about to begin, Arjuna's crisis takes place and the Gītā unfolds to man his own radical condition.

1.2 *Pāṇḍu:* brother of Dhṛtarāṣṭra, and father of Yudhiṣthira, Bhīma, Arjuna, Nakula, and Sahadeva. His wife is Kuntī, mother of the five Pāṇḍavas.

1.3 *Saṃjaya:* the charioteer of Dhṛtarāṣṭra and narrator of the events of the war.

1.4 *Kurukṣetra:* the field of Kuru where the battle is to take place. The significant critical point to make here is how Dhṛtarāṣṭra equates the field of battle with the field of *dharma*. This is significant in the following philosophical sense: to enter the battle field and to be determined by *dharma* are the same thing. In other words, *dharma* stands for the conditions or contextual situation within which certain actions must necessarily occur. In this sense, a man entering the contextual situation of war is as determined to act in that contextual situation as the weapons used in that war. It is also important to notice that the conditions that make such contextual situations or *dharmas* are man made and that together with the objects of the contexts, carry a determination of action and a specific way of looking at the whole, but limited, situation. We shall see later on (37–44) that the crisis of Arjuna arises because of the confusion in his mind between reducing life to conforming to only one kind of *dharma* instead of, as Kṛṣṇa will advise, integrating the different *dharmas* within which he functions in such a way that he becomes the complete man he is capable of becoming, as in Chapter XIII.

2.4 *Droṇa:* the instructor who taught the art of war to both the Pāndava and the Kuru princes.

3.3 *Drupada:* the King of Pāncāla, father-in-law of Arjuna; Dhṛṣtadyumma is his son.

4.2 *Arjuna:* other names used for Arjuna are Bhārata (descended of Bhārata), Dhanaṃjaya (winner of wealth), Guḍākeśa (having the hair in a ball), Pārtha (son of Pṛthā), Paraṃtapa (oppressor of the enemy).

4.2 *Yuduhāna:* a charioteer; also called Sātyaki.

4.3 *Virāta:* King of the Matsyas.

5.1 *Dhṛṣṭaketu:* King of the Cedis.

5.1 *Cekitāna:* a warrior.

5.3 *Purujit:* a warrior.

5.3 *Kuntibhoja:* brother of Purujit.

5.3 *Śaibya:* King of the Śibis.

6.1 *Yudhāmanyu:* a chieftain in the Pāṇḍava army.

6.2 *Uttamaujas:* another chieftain of the Pāṇḍava army.

6.3 *Son of Subhadrā:* Abhimanya, whose father is Arjuna.

6.3 *Draupadī:* wife of the five Pāndava brothers.

8.1 *Bhīṣma:* an old warrior who brought up both Dhṛtarāṣṭra and Pāṇḍu.

8.1 *Karṇa:* half-brother to Arjuna.

8.2 *Kṛpa:* brother-in-law of Droṇa.

8.3 *Aśvatthāman:* son of Droṇa.

8.3 *Vikarṇa:* third of the hundred sons of Dhṛtarāṣṭra.

8.4 *Son of Somadatta:* Somadatti; father is King of the Bāhikas.

21.1 *Kṛṣṇa:* other names used for Kṛṣṇa are Madhusūdana (slayer of the demon Madhu), Arisūdana (slayer of enemies), Govinda (herdsman or giver of enlightenment), Vāsudeva (son of Vasudeva), Yādava (descendent of Yadu), Keśava (having fine hair), Mādhava (the husband of Laksmī, Hṛṣīkeśa (lord of the senses, *hṛṣīka-īśā),* Janārdana (the liberator of men).

40.2 *See 40:* Arjuna does not seem to realize, and hence his crisis, that the human condition requires at times of the individual drastic and painful *aporia* (nonexit) and inaction. Kṛṣṇa will force him by painful analysis to understand this human situation and the role of man in the world. Not conformity but embodied vision. See note 4. The most important philosophical presupposition here regarding the human condition is the following one: human life functions within certain contexts or *dharmas;* these contexts or *dharmas* create not only a definite set of objects but also a definite set of actions;

the objects of a context or the men within the contexts have certain choices, but no freedom. The intention of the *Gītā* seems to indicate from the very beginning that for a man to be a man absolute freedom is necessary, but that this freedom is unattainable unless he realizes in his moments of crisis that he must, in order to remain human, become aware of the full context which led him to the crisis, which somehow will appear as only one of the multiple contexts that he as a man already is. In this activity of integration lies the road to freedom or, in the spirit of the Gītā to an embodied vision of man as the context-maker and the knower of his contexts.

What man must avoid at all costs, and hence exit out of his own crisis, is his own incarceration within a context-dharma. Incarceration means no more and no less than the fact that a one-man-context-dharma has already absolutized this one context-dharma into a fixed perspective and all its relations, possible, actual and future.

Chapter II

1. I translate *Sāṃkhyayoga* as "understanding" to better comprehend the "way" of the *Gītā*. "Under-standing" literally means—and so it functions in Chapter II—as the ground upon which Arjuna stands. Only that he has forgotten. What Kṛṣṇa is going to say is no more than to throw back at Arjuna the *beliefs* which have held him together and acting up to this moment. These are the beliefs of his kind, on which he and all others have been acting without question up to now. Only Arjuna now forgets the ground he stands on: the memories, the promises, the beliefs, the inertia which has made him function to the point of war. Kṛṣṇa's first move is to remind Arjuna of his own ground: his concrete, though general, circumstance: what he has to save, to save himself. And it is because Arjuna has not "saved" his circumstance and has instead reduced it to the small field of battle, identifying himself with his actions that he is in crisis: in-active. If this were the case then Arjuna should not behave *anāryajuṣṭam (an-ārya-juṣṭa)* in a way unbecoming to his role in this context in which he so firmly believes. The first move is "memory," the first step in the path of the *Gītā*.

11.2 *prajñāvādān (prajñā-vāda):* speech of wisdom; in this context, "empty rhetoric," for Arjuna has not yet learned anything.

13.1 *dehin:* embodied. It is important for the reader to notice the relation that holds between context or *dharma,* vision and body. It is easy to see from the very beginning how the fear of Arjuna coincides with the vision of his body and other bodies as just being the small objects of the context created by the battle field. Kṛṣṇa's way from this moment on will be to embrace his concrete human circumstance: present, past, future. In sum, the body is not a bag of skin but a way of looking at the world which has the capacity for making one's body larger or smaller. Kṛṣṇa is the prototype of the embodied vision of his whole culture. See 22, 30, 59, etc.

14.1 *mātrāsparśās (mātrā-sparśā):* contacts with the objects of the senses or "contacts with material elements."

15.4 *amṛtatvāya:* immortality, state of endless continuity.

16.2 *asat:* "that which is nonexistent"; *sat:* "that which is existent." These terms have different philosophical meanings in different historical contexts of Indian philosophy. In the Ṛg Veda, for example, *asat* stands for "all the human possibilities not yet given form," while *sat* means that which has already been given form. For this see my *Four-Dimensional Man* (1971). In Advaita Vedānta *sat* stands for the permanent, eternal and only for Brahman; *asat* stands for nothing because of its lack of empirical data. Similar uses of these terms can be found in the Upaniṣads. In the context of the *Gītā* these terms are not used in a technical sense, but in a more down to earth way. The way of the *Gītā* starts on a concrete situation of man in crisis and this is *sat.*

17.2 *avināśin:* indestructible.

17.4 *avyaya:* immutable.

18.1 *antavat:* perishable.

18.2 *nitya:* eternal.

18.3 *anāśin:* indestructible.

18.3 *aprameya:* immeasurable, incomprehensible.

19.3 See *Kaṭha Upaniṣad,* II, 18, 19.

20.3 *aja:* unborn.

20.3 *śaśvata:* everlasting; constant, eternal.

22.2 *śarīra:* body.

24.2 *sarvagata:* all-pervading, omnipresent, in all the worlds.

24.2 *sthāṇu:* unchanging.

24.2 *acala:* immovable.

25.1 *avyakta:* unmanifest; latent.

25.1 *acintya:* unthinkable as a thought.

25.1 *avikārya:* immutable.

30.2 *avadhya:* indestructible.

33.4 *pāpa:* sin or evil in general; in the Indian context, that which violates social custom rather than the will of a god.

44.1 *buddhi:* "intellect," "reason," "faculty of discrimination." Indian philosophical schools generally distinguish two aspects of mental life, called *manas* and *buddhi. Manas,* or "sense mind," is the instrument which assimilates and synthesizes sense impressions and brings the self into contact with external objects. It lacks discrimination, though, and thus furnishes the self only with precepts which must be transformed and acted upon by a higher mental function, the *buddhi.* This is the faculty of judgment, that which gives rise to intellectual beliefs and makes understanding possible. The *buddhi* can become lost by following the *manas,* thus absolutizing its sense interpretations, or become free by striving for an embodied vision, or firm knowledge. (Read II, 54; XIV, 21).

44.4 *samādhi:* disciplined concentration: meditation.

45.4 *dvandva:* pairs, suggesting various opposites like pleasure and pain, cold and heat, etc. For notes 25, 26, 27 see also Part III, Chapter V: Context.

45.4 *niryogakṣema (nir-yoga-kṣema):* not caring for the possession of property, more literally, "free from acquisition and possession."

47.2 *phala:* fruit. This term is employed extensively in the *Gītā* to connote the results or consequences of one's actions; that which is produced by them.

48.5 *samatva:* serenity or equilibrium, evenness of mind.

49.2 *buddhiyoga:* discipline of understanding; means of attaining correct discrimination or intellectual insight; the concentration of the *buddhi* on liberation, freedom, not in the context of *manas:* sense interpretation.

50.4 *karmasu kauśalam:* skill in action; the perfection which results from concentrated activity carried on without being obsessively concerned with the results of the activity.

54.2 *sthitaprajñasya (sthita-prajñā):* man of steady mind or "one who has firmly established wisdom."

55.2 *kāma:* desire; sensuous delights.

55.4 *ātman:* self. The *Gītā* uses the term *ātman* extensively, sometimes suggesting by it the "universal Self," the real Self of man," etc., and perhaps more often suggesting by it the "individual self," the *jīva,* the *puruṣa.* Although these meanings sometimes shade off into one another in the text, it is usually not too difficult to determine the meaning by the context in which the term appears.

57.1 *anabhisneha:* not attached, disinclined.

57.2 *abhinandati:* be pleased or delighted.

57.2 *dveṣṭi:* upset; dislike, be hostile to.

58.2 *indriyāṇī:* (the) senses: the usual five with *manas* (sense interpretation) sometimes taken as the sixth.

59.1 *viṣayas:* objects (or pleasures) of sense.

59.1 *param:* the Supreme, the highest.

62.2 *saṅga:* attachment.

64.1 *prasāda:* clarity, serenity, calmness of mind.

66.2 *bhāvanā:* concentration, determination, realization.

71.1 *nirvāṇa:* extinction of desires. For early Buddhism, with which the term is usually associated, *nirvāṇa* was taken in its literal meaning of "extinguishing the flame of desire," or that state of being which is attained when all desire is extirpated. See verse 71.

Chapter III

Title,1 What candidate shall we find for action-identification? Is it me, or my vision-knowledge? This chapter tries to point out other ways to act without the slavery of phenomenal-self identification.

6.1 *karmendriyāṇi (karma-indriya):* organs of action; or the five "motor organs"; tongue, feet, hands, the ejective and generative organs.

6.2 *smaran:* remembering. Memory plays an important role in Indian philosophy from the *vajra* of Indra in the Ṛg Veda to the present. It is important here to notice that "to remember objects with one's mind" is not to live experience directly, but rather to *imagine* experience to be like the ghosts of memory. As Plotinus said, "Memory is only for those who have forgotten."

8.1 *niyata:* that action which is prescribed by one's *dharma.*

9.1 *yajña:* sacrifice. See *Four-Dimensional Man,* Chapter 8.

10.1 *Prajāpati:* father of creatures; appears in the Ṛg Veda and becomes most important in the Brāhmaṇas.

10.4 *kāmadhuk:* the wish-granting cow; a Ṛg Vedic allusion.

15.2 *akṣara:* the term was used in Ṛg Veda I.164 and later on in Brahmanism as a prime syllable, the indestructible unit of sound with full meaning.

18.1 *artha:* interest; purpose, motive.

20.2 *Janaka:* king of Mithilā, father of Sītā, wife of Rāma. Though a king, he worked to inspire the people.

20.2 *siddhi:* state of arrival at perfection; determination to arrive at freedom.

20.5 *lokasaṃgraham (loka-saṃ-graha):* the term implies the maintenance of a human quality of human life rather than any kind of physical creation.

21.3 *pramāṇa:* standard, measure.

27.3 *ahaṃkāra:* literally, the I-maker. It refers to those people who take first person speech and themselves literally. The Sanskrit language provides ways of making sure that the subject appears more or less involved in the action which the verb represents. See *Four-Dimensional Man,* Chapter 5.

28.1 *tattvavit (tattva-vid):* he who knows the true essence.

28.2 *guṇakarmavibhāgayos (guna-karma-vi-bhāga):* there is ontological unity between vision and action but not between the doer and the action.

29.4 *akṛtsnavidas (a-kṛtsna-vida):* knows only a part.

30.1 *adhyātmacetasā (adhi-ātma-cetasā):* with your mind fixed on the supreme self.

31.1 *mata:* doctrine

31.2 *śraddhā:* the term comes from the Ṛg Veda and rather than suggesting adherence to a creed, it means the disposition and discipline to make one's life.

36.5 *niyojita (ni-yuj):* compelled, constrained.

40.2 *adhiṣṭhāna:* basis or seat, foundation, etc.

41.4 *jñāna:* knowledge, wisdom; *vijñāna:* understanding. The distinction between the two terms in the Gītā appears more a distinction of quality. *Jñāna* is closer to vision than *vijñāna*.

Chapter IV

1. All ways of action are enveloped by a context of knowledge. Discover that knowledge and you will liberate yourself by your own self. This is the path of this chapter.

1.4 Vivasvān, Manu, Ikṣvāku: *rājarṣayaḥ:* sage-kings who knew and ruled with this same wisdom.

8.4 *yuga:* the cyclic history of man. See *infra.* note to Chapter VIII, 17.4

10.4 *tapas:* austerity. In the *Gītā* the term seems to signify simply "practice," "hard-work," "effort," or "disciplined concentration."

13.1 *cāturvarṇa (cātur-varṇa):* four-class system; cf. *jāti,* "caste."

16.4 *aśubha:* evil or disagreeable.

18.4 *yukta* (from *yuj):* disciplined.

19.1 *kāmasaṃkalpavarjitās (kāma-sam-kalpa-varjita):* free from desire *(kāma)* and compulsion *(sam-kalpa).*

21.4 *kilbiṣa:* "sin," "guilt"—as with *pāpa,* violation of social order.

25.3 As with Śaṃkara I take it to mean the offering of oneself as a perspective in "sacrifice."

30.4 *kalmaṣa:* sin, guilt.

33.3 *parisamāpyate (pari-sam-āp):* is completed, culminated, terminated.

38.1 *pavitra:* purifier.

40.2 *saṃśaya:* doubting; incapable of making decisions.

Chapter V

Action done without attachment, is better than to renounce to action. For even renouncing action is an action. Both paths, however, share the same goal of knowledge.

1.1 *saṃnyāsa:* renunciation; the giving up of actions prescribed by one's social *dharma* in contrast to performing these actions without attachment to their results (*karmayoga*).

3.2 *nityasaṃnyāsī (nitya-saṃnyāsin):* the eternal renouncer; man unattached in the midst of action.

10.1 *ādhāya (gerund of ā-dhā):* sharing Brahman's viewpoint.

13.3 The "nine gates" refer to the eyes, ears, nostrils, the mouth, the anus and the sex organs.

14.3 *prabhu:* the sovereign Self, or "the Lord."

15.1 *vibhu:* the all-pervading spirit, or "the Lord."

18.1 *samadarśinaḥ: (sama-darśina):* look equally or "see the same"; "see with an eye of equality."

21.3 *brahmayogayuktātmā (brahma-yoga-yukta-ātman):* "being joined by *yoga* to Brahman"; vision or to share in the way of viewing the world of Brahman.

28.2 *mokṣa:* liberation; freedom, release.

Chapter VI

No union in knowledge is possible without mind-control. Therefore learn meditation as a way to get rid of what distracts your self from your self: your thoughts aiming for results of actions.

3.1 *kāraṇa:* means or "the cause."

4.1 *sarvasaṃkalpasaṃnyāsī (sarva-saṃ-kalpa-saṃnyāsin):* renounced all desires or "renouncing all compulsions."

10.2 *yatacittātmā (yata-citta-ātman):* with mind and self controlled or "restraining his thought and his self."

12.3 The *Gītā is describing here some of the essential characteristics of rāja yoga,* the physical and psychological disciplines.

24.2 *saṃkalpaprabhavān (sam-kalpa-pra-bhava):* born of I-making; "arising from compulsion" and identification with the I-maker.

27.4 *brahmabhūtam (brahma-bhūta):* become one with Brahman or "become Brahman."

28.5 *brahmasaṃsparśam (brahma-saṃ-sparśa):* sharing Brahman's vision, (unity of touch).

32.2 *ātmaupamyena (ātma-aupamya):* the same for himself or "equally in himself."

33.2 *sāmya:* equality or "non-difference," "sameness." The

state of evenness of mind which follows from a strict controlling of the sense interpretation by the mind etc.

44.5 *śabdabhraman (śabda-brahman):* rules of the Brāhmaṇas; the word set forth in the Brāhmaṇas and ritual traditions.

47.3 The reader should or could at this point look back at the last three chapters and try to discover by himself the didactic moves that Kṛṣṇa is making in his teaching to Arjuna. For this we suggest that he reads back the following verses: IV. 11, 35, 39, V. 24, 25; and VI. 5-8, 28, 30. We may suggest as a hint only that there is a progressive suggestiveness in Kṛṣṇa that tries to lead Arjuna away from a vision of himself and his world which is narrow and circular to another vision like Kṛṣṇa's. This vision will not be made fully clear until Chapter XIII.

Chapter VII

Things do not exhaust the context. Context determines things. To know both is another step in the path.

4.2 Though the *Gītā* uses the categories of the Sāṃkhya system, one must not take them in any technical sense, and wait to see what the *Gītā* tries to accomplish with them.

5.2 *aparā:* lower condition or *prakṛti;* parā: higher condition or *puruṣa* or *parā-prakṛti.*

5.3 *jīvabhūtām (jīva-bhūta)*

6.1 *etadyonīni (etat-yoni)*

30.2 *sādhibhūtādhidaivam (sa-adhi-bhūta-adhi-daiva)*

Chapter VIII

The path of vision and the path of rebirth. Both depend on knowledge.

1.2 *adhyātman (adhi-ātman).*

3.3 *svabhāva:* essence; lit. "own-being."

3.5 *bhūtabhāvodbhāvakaras (bhūta-bhāva-ud-bhāva-kara).*

6.2 *tadbhāvabhāvitas (tad-bhāva-bhāvita).*

11.4 *brahmacarya:* celibacy.

17.4 To understand the history of Hinduism is not to chain together a string of disconnected events that some scholar decides are important. Hindu history is the uncovering of man's conceptual schemes within which facts gain meaning. With this in mind, it will be easy to understand the *yugas*. There are four *yugas* which divide a world period consisting of 4,320,000 years into four ages: 1. *kṛta,* the "golden age" which lasts for 1,728,000 years; 2. *tretā yuga* which lasts 1,296,000 years; 3. *dvāpara yuga* of 864,000 years; and 4. *kali yuga,* the "dark age," which lasts for 432,000 years. These *yugas* mark the eternal creation of man and his world by himself. The difference between the "golden age" and the "dark age" is just one of decline in man's self-critical attitude toward his own conceptual schemes. Brahmā, the god, not Brahman, the ground of all possible creations, has as one of his life-days a rotation of a thousand times of the four cycles. This is called *kalpa.* Manifestations appear during the day of Brahmā; the dissolution of these manifestations constitute the night of Brahmā: the appearance of the *avatāra,* like Kṛṣna.

24.4 There are two paths to follow after death: the path to the sun and the path to the moon. From the first there is no return; from the second follows rebirth. *Chāndogya Upaniṣad,* IV. 15, 5.

Chapter IX

To be a true path, the path must have that knowledge (like Kṛṣṇa's) alone as its goal.

2.2 *pratyakṣāvagamam (pratyakṣa-avagama).*

3.2 *saṃsāra.*

6.2 *ākāśa.*

7.4 *kalpa:* see note 17.4, chapter VIII.

15.2 *ekatvena.*

20.2 *Soma:* an hallucinogenic drink used in Vedic ritual which is extracted from a kind of mushroom.

21.1 *svargaloka (svarga-loka).*

24.1 *bhoktā.*

32.2 *pāpayonayas (pāpa-yoni).*

Chapter X

The path is endless if undertaken only intellectually. The repetitions and endless descriptions contrast vividly with next chapter's manifestation of reality. Thus this chapter ends: (42) "But of what use is this (factual) detailed knowledge to you, Arjuna?"

5.1 *ahiṃsā.*

6.2 The progenitors of Hindu culture.

8.1 *bhāva.*

10.2 *buddhiyoga.*

21.2 *Ādityas:* from the Ṛg Veda the gods that "unbind."

21.2 *Maruts:* from the Ṛg Veda, the storms

23.2 *Yakṣas and Rakṣasas:* from the Ṛg Veda, powerful binding creatures.

23.2 *Kubera:* lord of wealth.

24.3 *Skanda:* chief of the heavenly armies.

26.1 *Aśvattha:* holy fig tree.

26.3 *Gandharvas:* divine musicians.

27.1 *Uccaiḥśravas:* Indra's horse.

27.3 *Airāvata:* Indra's elephant.

28.2 *Kandarpa:* the god of love.

29.1 *Nāgas:* snakes.

29.1 *Varuṇa:* god of the waters; important in the Ṛg Veda as the custodian of law *(ṛta).*

29,2 *Yama:* from Ṛg Veda, god of death.

30,2 *Vinatā:* Viṣṇu's bird.

31.1 *Rāma:* the hero of the *Rāmāyana.*

33.1 *dvandva:* the dual compound in Sanskrit that strings words together with equal status.

35.1 *Bṛhatsāman:* a portion of hymns dedicated to Indra.

35.2 *Gāyatrī:* meter of twenty-four syllables.

35.3 *Mārgaśīrṣa:* the first month of the ancient Hindu calendar; includes parts of the winter months of November and December.

Chapter XI

This chapter is one of the most important in the Gītā and has been easily institutionalized through pious interpretations. This is the chapter in which Arjuna's crisis "resolves" itself. In this chapter past, present, and future come together and appear to Arjuna as a frightening presence. The identification Arjuna made of himself and his actions in Chapter I is here "resolved" as being groundless. Arjuna's theoretic journey, from Chapter II through X, is here also completely denied. All Arjuna faces is the throbbing presence of life without any crutches. Arjuna will have to make it anew from here on. His first judgements, in his fear, are about the kind of knowledge he will need to start taking this awesome moment of despair in faith: the faith of life which life bestows when its presence is so immediately felt. The only thing left to Arjuna, without his theoretic consciousness, is his own fullness of despair. Let no man institutionalize it. *Kalo 'smi:* I am time. Man is not *in* time. Man is time: his own time, which needs to be remade anew constantly and eternally.

1.4 *madanugrahāya (mad-anu-graha).*

32.1 *kāla.*

39.1 *Vāyu:* the wind, cf. Ṛg Veda.

39.1 *Agni:* fire; god of sacrifice, cf. Ṛg Veda.

39.1 *Śaśāṅka:* the moon.

Chapter XII

1. *Bhakti* is here translated as devotion. One should note, however, that devotion in this chapter *functions* as faith since it is by this faith that Arjuna hangs on by his nails to life. The life he knew has been removed from under his feet. It is by faith in the throbbing excitement of life itself that Chapters XI and XIII are connected. Without understanding this faith, the journey of the Gītā collapses. And so does the model of knowing the Gītā offer to save the human circumstance, from Chapters XIII through XVIII.

6.1 *matparā.*

9.4 *abhyāsayogena (abhi-āsa-yoga).*

19.3 *aniketa.*

Chapter XIII

The kind of knowledge needed to make life anew (authentic, my own) is to know the field in all fields. This chapter describes both the field and the knower of the field. The first step in saving the human circumstance is being oriented as to knowledge, what a man needs to know to be fully human.

1.2 *śarīra*.

1.2 *kṣetra*.

1.4 *kṣetrajña*.

4.4 *brahmasūtrapadais (brahma-sūtra-pada)*.

5.3 The categories of the Sāṃkhya system are as follows: the "gross elements," *(mahābhutas)*, the sense of I *(ahaṃkāra)*, understanding *(buddhi)*, the unmanifested *(avyakta)*, the ten senses, the five usual senses and the five organs of action, and the *manas*. The *tanmātras* or "subtle elements" are not here included.

5.3 *doṣa*.

11.2 *tattvajñānārthadarśanam (tattva-jñāna-artha-darśana)*.

14.1 *ābhāsa*.

20.4 *kārya:* acts or effects; *karaṇa:* causes; *kartṛtva:* agency; *hetu:* causes.

22.2 *upadraṣṭṛ:* witness.

22.2 *anumantṛ*.

22.2 *bhartṛ*.

22.3 *bhoktṛ*.

Chapter XIV

The orientation of knowledge of Chapter XIII becomes more circumstantialized in Chapter XIV. Knowledge is not desembodied but appears in man's own concrete circumstance. This circumstance of man is concretized in the Gītā, in this chapter, through the three *guṇas:* three elemental and dynamic human "systems" within and through which knowledge is made possible. According to the Gītā there is no actor, only the *guṇas* act. All phenomena in human life are the result of the relations and variations of the *guṇas*. There is no ontological priority among the *guṇas:* they are a simultaneous triumvirate of ontologies which require organization and they are also the required energy for such organization. The three *guṇas* as inertia or resistance *(tamas)*, energization *(rajas)*, and resolution towards the fully organized system *(sattva)* are the condition of possibility for knowledge to be liberated from its dependence on the *manas*—interpretation. Thus transcendence into the *buddhi*—interpretation of sense objects or impressions is possible. The knowledge of Chapter XIII becomes in Chapter XIV concretized thus:

Arjuna said:

21. Lord, by what marks is he who has gone beyond these three *guṇas,* distinguished?
What is his conduct?
How does he pass beyond these three *guṇas?*

22. The Blessed One said:
He does not dislike clarity *(sattva)* and activity *(rajas)* nor delusion *(tamas)* when they arise, O Son of Pāṇḍu,
Nor desire them when they cease.
(See from 23 to end).

6.5 *jñāna.*

18.3 *jaghanyaguṇavṛttisthā (jaghanya-guṇa-vṛtti-sthā).*

20.2 *dehasamudbhavān (deha-sam-ut-bhava).*

Chapter XV

The concretization of the human circumstance is further described here on the metaphor of the peepal tree with its branches below and its roots above. It is by sharing an a-perspectival vision of the whole of human life and human acting that the perspectival vision of parts, senses, mind, *buddhi,* etc., can be not only comprehended but oriented towards their eventual resolution and efficacy.

7.2 *jīvabhūtah (jīva-bhūta).*

15.2 *smṛti.*

15.2 *apohana.*

17.2 *paramātman.*

Chapter XVI

The human circumstance is concretized further in this chapter by describing kinds of men: those bound by the desires of the "I" maker *(ahaṃkāra)* and those free from those desires because of their orientation towards the highest knowledge. The important point to note, however, is that one's orientation to knowledge depends to a great extent on the concrete historical "situation" of one's own birth. The surrounding circumstance could determine one's life for ever and for ever be reborn into the same surrounding in-activity and absence of knowledge. Rebirth and knowledge are here equated, and one's circumstance includes all that affects me: my birth, family, etc. To save it I have to acknowledge it first so that I may transcend them—not be them—but become me, oriented towards my own human fulfillment.

1. *daiva-āsura:* lit. those "wishing to know," and those bound: they are translated normally as divine and demonic qualities. They function in the text as freeing or binding perspectives.

8.4 *aparasparasaṃbhūtaṃ kim anyat kāmahaitukam.*

24.1 *śāstra:* scripture. One must remember that the scripture in this context stands for whatever one has been taught or has heard in relation to Brahman. In many ways it was their formal education.

Chapter XVII

What happens when one knows, or one is oriented towards knowledge? Actions remain the same ones. What changes, however, once one knows or is oriented to wards knowledge is the *candidate* one chooses for identification of these actions. It is no longer the "I" or self of speech, but "knowledge": the faith a man has and determines his actions.

3.2 *sattvānurūpā (sattva-anu-rūpa).*

24.3 *brahmavādinām.*

28.2 *sat* and *asat:* this understanding of the *sat* and *asat* is as old as the Ṛg Veda. The *asat* (see Ṛg Veda 7, 104, and *Four-Dimensional Man,* Chapter 6) refers not only to possibilities, always present, not yet formed, but also to the dogmatic attitude people take in regards to their faith which makes the "sacrifice" (or change and integration of perspectives) possible.

Chapter XVIII

This final chapter brings the path of the Gītā to its end. Arjuna's orientation to knowledge has been regained in such a way that now he knows his intellect *(buddhi)* should lift up from the *sattvic* condition the *manas*—interpretation of sense and sense objects of the *rajasic* and *tamasic* conditions. He must, therefore, avoid to be trapped in any one state—*sattvic, tamasic* or *rajasic*—and absolutize them through the self identification of the *ahaṃkāra,* the I maker. See, 14, 16, 18, 22, 26, 30, 38, 39, 49, 57, etc. Only this activity will make it possible for Arjuna to recover his "memory"—all that he had forgotten and led him to crisis—thus, will Arjuna be able to recover his own desire: *yathā icchasi tathā kuru:* do as you desire (63).

14.4 *adhiṣṭhāna:* the body; *kartā:* the agent; *karaṇa:* instrument; *ceṣṭā:* activity; *daivam:* intention.

26.2 *anahaṃvādī:* not taking first person discourse literally. Not "I" speaking.

52.3 *dhyānayoga.*

63.3 *yathā icchasi tathā kuru;* do as you desire. Desire is the fountain of creation in Indian Philosophy from the Ṛg Veda, 10, 129 through the Upaniṣads to the Gītā. See Gītā, Chapters V and VIII.

Notes

The Forest

p. 4

line 27 . . . Forest. The quotations are selections translated by me from Ortega y Gasset's *Meditaciones del Quijote.* I have of course edited Ortega in some parts. I have tried to be faithful to him, making my translation from his *Obras Completas* Vol. I. (Madrid: Revista de Occidente; 1966). The entire *Meditaciones del Quijote* is available translated into English as *Meditations on Quixote* by Evelyn Rugg and Diego Marín, with introduction and notes by Julián Marias (New York: W. W. Norton & Co., Inc., 1961), pp. 57–69. Selections translated by Antonio T. de Nicolãs from *Meditaciones del Quijote* are copyright © 1976 by W. W. Norton & Co., Inc., New York, N.Y.

As a point of philosophical interest, the reader should compare Ortega's *lived* forest to Husserl's *imaginations* or imaginative variations in *Ideas,* 4, and to Heidegger's: "let the tree be" in *What is Called Thinking,* a translation of *Was Heisst Denkey?* with intr. by Glenn Gray. (New York: Harper & Row, 1968), pp. 41–44.

Husserl writes in *Ideas,* 4:

> The *eidos,* the *pure essence,* can be intuitively exemplified in empirical data, in data of perception, memory, etc., but equally well *in mere data of fancy.* We can, therefore, in order to apprehend an essence in itself and *originally,* start off from corresponding empirical intuitions, *but equally well from intuitions that are nonempirical*—which do not seize upon something which is in existence—but rather merely imaginative.

I direct the reader to Julián Marías comparative points between Husserl and Ortega on this subject in: *Ortega: Circumstance and Vocation,* trans. Frances M. López-Morillas (Oklahoma: University of Oklahoma Press, 1970), pp. 413–433. See also Marías Julián Manás notes to *Meditations on Quixote*.

The fundamental idea of *circumstance (circum-stance:* what surrounds me) as a constitutive and radical condition of human life Ortega discovered and initially developed independently of and previous to the *idea* of *stimuli* of Uexhull and Husserl. See "Adán en el Paraiso," (1910) (*O.C.* I,470) and "Vejamen del Orador," (January, 1911), (*O.C.* I,557). The use of these ideas in *Meditaciones del Quijote* is more systematic than in the earlier works and makes even more deliberate Ortega's method of doing philosophy. I do not see as great a distinction as Julián Marías wants to make between Ortega's "lived circumstance" and Husserl's "imaginative variations." Both are tremendously rich in their effective methodological possibilities. I do not think this is the level at which Ortega and Husserl part company. I do think Ortega's *circumstance* is more concrete and functional in dealing with the noetic side of the transcendental ego than Husserl's method of consciousness; especially since instead of the "consciousness of" of Husserl one focuses on the activity itself of doing philosophy as it radically constitutes itself circumstantially, i.e., as lived, historically. This is what Ortega calls the consciousness "I count on." This led Ortega, who so greatly influenced Sarte on this point, to criticize Husserl's description and need to posit the "consciousness of" as the ground for doing philosophy. In this sense Ortega had to depend more effectively and develop further the phenomenological method of "imaginative variations" than Husserl did, though Ortega called it "circumstance"; life as lived. There is a very real sense though in which both, Husserl's "imaginative variations" and Ortega's "circumstance" can only be taken as "imaginations" and in no way as reality itself. The forest, of course, would be reality in its proper sense, undivided, a-perspectival, whole, while the rest is interpretation: imagination. This does not entail that reality and interpretation are two separate realities. Both are given in experience simultaneously but discovered and distinguished as "what they are not"—separable.

What one cannot do is start philosophy by presupposing what reality ought to be, like Husserl, i.e. an image of logic, lived or fancied. Ortega did not commit this original reduction and therefore his method is still functional and an open path. In fact, Husserl's consciousness of, is just one case of the consciousness-I-count-on of Ortega and not vice-versa.

Heidegger, of course, is later than Ortega and never had as clear an idea of what he was doing philosophically as Ortega and

Husserl did. Ortega was shocked to hear people quote Heidegger and ignore him. This is the irony of certain times, of philosophy's winds and the fact that the Spaniard Ortega, unlike his French and German contemporary philosophers, was too much ahead of his contemporary Spain.

There is a sense in which no other philosopher is recoverable. One has to jump on him as on a spring board and thus go beyond him. This happened in Ortega's case with Marías and Zubiri and in Husserl's case with Heidegger and Sarte principally.

One practical lesson of reading Western philosophy from Ortega's prespective and a consequence of his method is to read in the philosophies of irrationalism, existentialism and life, not so much what they claimed life to be: irrational, meaningless, etc., but rather that the philosophy immediate to them had forgotten life, or the meaning of life, or the reason of life. Ortega's "circumstance" brings out the meaning, not only of my life, but of other people's, and the meanings and reasons other cultures counted-on for their living.

CHAPTER ONE

p. 23

l. 18 . . . done. Julián Marías; *Obras* Vol. I. "Epîlogo de José Ortega y Gasset" (Madrid: Revista de Occidente, 1969) p. 475.

l. 23 . . . different, José Ortega y Gasset, *Qué es Filosofía?* (Madrid, Colección El Arquero: Revista de Occidente, 1966) p. 19.

l. 26 . . . analysis. Julián Marías, *Obras* Vol, I. "Epîlogo de José Ortega y Gasset" (Madrid: Revista de Occidente, 1969) p. 475.

l. 33 . . . come . . . *Ibid.* p. 478.

p. 24

l. 32 . . . needs" The word "need" has been so misused by the psychological tradition that we should understand clearly what Ortega has in mind when he uses this word. I will keep the word "need" for the first chapter of this book and change it to the word "interests" in the second one in order to keep pace with the tradition. Ortega understands "need" in the following sense:

> The disciplines—whether they be metaphysics or geometry—exist. They are here because men created them by brute force, and if they used that force, it was because they needed those disciplines so badly that they had to have them.

> The truths that these disciplines might contain were found in the first place by one man, and were then rethought or rediscovered by others who added their own efforts to that of the first man. But if they found these truths, it is because they sought them, and if they sought them, it is because men had need of them, because for one reason or another they could not do without them. (José Ortega y Gasset, *Unas lecciones de metafísica* (Madrid: Alianza Editorial, 1966), trans. as *Some Lessons in Metaphysics,* by Mildred Adams (New York: W. W. Norton & Company, Inc., 1969) p. 15.

What the student, on the other hand, finds in what is called the world of education is:

> . . . himself with the science already made, as with a mountain range that rises in front of him and cuts off his vital road. In the best of cases, I repeat, the mountain range of science pleases him, attracts him, seems good to him, promises him victories in life. But none of this has aynthing to do with the genuine need which led originally to the creation of this science. (*Ibid.* pp. 17–18.)

Ortega further contrasts the two approaches:

> It is enough to compare the approach of a man who is going to study an already-existing science with the approach of a man who feels a real, sincere and genuine need for it. The former will tend not to question the content of the science, not to criticize it. . . . What he seeks is simply to assimilate it as it already is. On the other hand, the man who is needful of a science . . . will approach this bit of ready-made knowledge with caution, full of suspicion and prejudice, submitting it to criticism, even assuming in advance that what the book says is not true. In short, for the very reason that he needs, with such deep anguish, to know, he will think that this knowledge does not exist, and he will manage to unmake what is presented as already made. It is men like these who are constantly correcting, renewing, recreating science. (*Ibid.* p. 18.)

p. 32

l. 9 . . . way History and Reason in their constitutive relationship are two of the most problematic themes of Philosophy. I follow, by design and inclination, the guidelines to interpreting history as historical reason suggested by Ortega y Gasset. See his *Obras Completas:* Revista de Occidente; Madrid, 11 Volumes, 1966. See in English *History as a System* and *Man and Crisis* both published by W. W. Norton and Company, Inc., 1962. See Antonio T. de Nicolas, "The Americanization of Ortega y Gasset"; *Main Current in Modern Thought,* Vol. 28, No. 5, May–June 1972. Since the problem of History and Reason is urgent for the understanding of this book, I will add here a summary of its problematic theme as interpreted by Julián Marías and can be seen in his *Introducción a la Filosofía: Obras* II, Revista de Occidente, Madrid, 1962. An English version can be found in *Reason and Life,* Yale, 1958, though this book is out of print. The quotations which follow are taken mostly from this text.

History: Reason and History.

> Descartes and Malebranche in the seventeenth century established that Reason had nothing to do with History, and it is even opposed to it; what reason produces, i.e., a city constructed according to a unified plan is the contrary of what history accumulates as it goes along, which appears to be the work of *chance.* (*Discourse de la méthode,* 2nd part.) Reason proceeds *more geometrico;* history by fortuitous accumulation, irrational caprice.
>
> In the eighteenth century people like Bayle, Vico, Voltaire, Turgot, and Condorcet approach history with nothing more than pure reason, naturalistic or physicomathematical reason. Cassirer writes: "From the beginning, eighteenth-century philosophy treats the problem of nature and the historical problem as a unity which does not permit of arbitrary division or separation. It tries to deal with both by using the same intellectual approach; it attempts to apply the same manner of posing the problem and the same universal method of *reason* to nature and history." (*Philosophie der Aufklárung.*) The principle of historical explanation is an appeal to *nature,* which according to traditional explanation and according to Voltaire voicing the common belief is always the same. Human reality is determined by human nature; the only thing which allows variation is custom, regarded as the superficial manifestation of an identical and unchanging reality. History, in so far as it applies to reason, tries to discover the hidden and constant root of unchanging nature; that is, it gives up what is properly historical and falls back into the natural as an explanation. History is an appearance, hiding a *real* substratum incapable of change, *given* once and for all; reason's task is to reduce that variability of history to its principle, in recognizing beneath the multiplicity of historical forms, the a-historical unvarying and ever identical human nature in which man consists and which is the

source of changes. The triumph of reason is the elimination of history, by resting in the permanent and immutable, the fixed consistency, that which is already made and is always the same; nature.

The deliberate intention of Hegel's *Philosophy of Universal History* is to introduce, for the first time in Western tradition, reason into history. In *Lectures on the Philosophy of Universal History* I, 6–7 and 122 he writes: "Philosophy is first of all reproached for coming to History with certain thoughts, and then considering it in accordance with these thoughts. But the only thought which philosophy brings is the simple one of *reason:* the thought that reason governs the world, and that consequently universal history, like everything else, must have happened rationally. This conviction and evidentness is an *assumption,* with regards to history as such. In philosophy, however, it is not an assumption."

"It is necessary to bring to history the idea and the belief that the world of the will is not given over to pure chance. We assume it to be a truth that the history of nations is governed by an ultimate end, that in universal history there dwells a Reason—not that of an individual thinker, but devine and absolute Reason. The demonstration of this truth is the image and act of reason. But the true demonstration is found rather in the knowledge of reason itself. Reason is revealed in Universal history. Universal history is only the manifestation of this ultimate reason; it is one of the particular forms in which reason is revealed; it is a copy of that model which presents itself in a special element, in the nations . . . Universal history is the development, the explication of the spirit in time; just as the idea unfolds itself in space as nature."

Hegel then brings reason to history but with the prior assumption that this reason will have to be logical reason. But logical reason is not historical. Hegel's logicalism conceals besides a disguised naturalism: historical temporality is 'eternalized' as a logical dialectic, and interpreted as the actualization of something already existing; thus the radical innovation in which history and human life consist is suppressed. Hegel's titanic effort to join reason and history fails because instead of taking history as a reality, he starts from an interpretation of it and applies extra-historical concepts to it. Hegel *uses* reason to understand history, but this reason being prior to history and independent of it does not take into account its particular contexts, nor adapts itself to its structures and still less is *meaningful* in a historical sense for it does not emerge from history. It would have been a different matter if Hegel, instead of *knowing already* that reason in its determination, is the thing, had inversely, directed his attention to the *things themselves,* and the structures and contexts within which they appear and had found their *reason* in *them.* Then it would have been possible for us to speak of a reason in history; *historical reason.*

August Comte, the father of positivism, through his *Discours sur l'esprit positif,* his *Systeme de politique positive* etc., brings the demand for history a step further. "The doctrine which succeeds in adequately explaining the *ensemble* of the past will inevitably obtain, as a result of that unique test, the mental presidency of the future." As he states in Chapter VII of the second volume of his *Systeme de politique positive,* his task is to determine: "the positive theory of the general limits of variation proper to the human order." In sum, for Comte *fundamental reality* of man consists not in being a body, nor in being a mind but in something else, and precisely in that thing the being of which is *historical;* and that is the most important reason why he had to begin his positive philosophy with a philosophy of history. This history is grounded on the principles which govern "social moldifiability." Therefore one must study the duration of life, as "the living are essentially governed by the dead, and the interval between generations since they regulate human change." (*System* . . . II, pp. 447–448). Therefore, the past must be made present in the form of history to avoid *estrangement* and *alienation,* as was the situation of his period which he says "is brutally ignorant of the noble yoke of the past, even while it dreams of the future." (*Ibid.* p. 458). According to Comte the 19th century will be characterized (3rd Vol. of his *System*) by an irrevocable preponderance of history in philosophy, in politics and even in poetry. Positivistic relativism must extend regulated variability to the object and then to the subject as well. Reason must restore speculation to its place in the totality of historical life—action, imagination, feeling—in order to attain thus to that reality. The Anarchy of the West, in his own words, consists in the *disturbance of human continuity,* in the revolt of the living against the totaliterianism of the dead.

Comte's methodological assumption however does not allow him to reach history proper. He stops short of it. All phenomena, he presumes are subject to unvarying laws (*Cours de philosophie positive* I, p. 14); it is thus essential to make homogeneous all human conceptions, until they are reduced to a definite state of possitivity. Unity of method is necessary, therefore. This method is the *natural* one, his reason physico-mathematical. (*System* III, p. 1) History, Sociology, what he calls 'social statics and dynamics' can only be saved when all progress is shown to be the development of order. (*Ibid.* p. 3) All dangers are avoided by reducing or *subordinating movement to existence.* This can only be done by understanding the dynamic laws in a *deductive* manner, and not in the inductive and primitive way it was understood before. That is, *operari sequitur esse:* Progress is not an innovation but a development; laws are acquired, or arrived at by deduction, not induction from historico-social reality itself; and only at this price do they acquire rationality.

The reaction against Comte is of course a move towards "irrationalism" in order to understand the fundamental character of history and so we have the thinkers of "vitalist" or "historicists" tendencies like Spengler and Rickert; Unamuno and Bergson.

Spengler writes (in *Die Grenzen der naturwissenschaftlichen begriffsbildung,* 4th ed.): "We can count, measure, dissect only the lifeless and so much of the living as can be dissociated from livingness. Pure becoming, pure life, is in this sense incapable of being bounded. It lies beyond the domain of cause and effect, law and measure." Reason, system and comprehension kill as they 'cognize.' "The reality which is irrational for theoretical cognition must also remain irrational with respect to its relationship with *values.*" (*Ibid.* pp. 7, 102, 507.)

Dilthey belongs to the second generation after Comte. He takes two ideas from Comte: that the whole of previous philosophy is *partial,* has not taken reality integrally as it is; and secondly that metaphysics is impossible; by metaphysics he understands "absolute" and universal valid knowledge; consequently he will attempt to ground philosophy on complete and entire reality *(Zur Weltanschauunslebre)* and thus overcome the 'absolutism of the intellect.' Both attempts will necessarily lead him to history.

Dilthey did not create a system, nor a theory of life in the strict sense of the word, nor even a historical doctrine: he did less and more; he made direct contact with the reality of life, and therefore history; and he brought us *historicism,* a mode of being: historical consciousness. Life is in its own substance history; history is life itself from the point of view of the whole of humanity (*Gesammelte Schriften,* VII, p.

256); this vital reality is not a "world" of things and people, but a complex of vital relationships. Our life presents itself as an enigma which demands it be understood by us; death, which is the incomprehensible, sets this demand inescapably for us; but life can be understood only from itself; cognition cannot get back behind life; and for this reason, over and against causal explanation which the method of the natural sciences demanded, Dilthey will make *descriptive understanding* the method of the "sciences of the mind," of the knowledge of life.

In *Zur Weltanschauungslebre* Dilthey writes: "What Philosophy is is a question which cannot be answered according to each man's taste; its function must be empirically discovered in history. This history, of course, will have to be understood from the standpoint of the spiritual validity which is our own starting point, and in which we 'live philosophy." Furthermore, "intelligence is not the unfolding within the isolated individual, comprehensible in relation to him, but a process in the evolution of the human race, and this latter is the subject in which the will to knowledge exists . . . only by means of a historical process of abstraction are abstract thoughts and knowledge in general constituted." And he adds that "Philosophy, understood in this way, is the science of the real." In other words, intelligence is historical; must be derived from life itself; reality, in the last analysis, cannot be logically explained, but only understood: "What is given to us is irrational; the elements by means of which we represent are irreducible to one another, knowledge never gives the *whole* of reality."

For Dilthey the foundation of philosophy (history being its propaedeutic) is *Selbstbesinnung,* self-awareness; from this one progresses towards hermeneutics, that is, the understanding of other peoples' lives, and therefore history; finally one arrives at the knowledge of *nature*. From what is nearest to us we progress to what is furthest. For this journey Dilthey postulates a *critique of historical reason;* a reason which is broader than naturalistic reason, by not excluding the peculiar character of the historical, by giving up the 'absolutism of the intellect' and which would consider historically existing systems as constitutive facts of human consciousness, as conceptions of the world or *Weltanschauungen* which are ultimately rooted not in something intellectual, but in life itself, and are therefore imperishable and irrefutable. "None of these ideas of the world can be erected by metaphysics into a universally valid science. Nor can they be destroyed by any kind of criticism.

They have their roots in a relationship which is not susceptible of demonstration or refutation; they are imperishable; only metaphysics is perishable." (*Ibid.*)

Dilthey's demand for 'historical reason' falls short of historic reason because in his case history qualifies or colours reason, it does not constitute it. History is postulated, but reason remains the same kind of reason as traditionally understood, not only applied to history but interpreted as a function of it; we are left with a sort of historicized reason. It is no doubt a great advance on the previous tradition but Dilthey did not leave us with the reason of history, the reason which history itself is. Only this could properly be called historical reason. In the first place a 'typology' of ideas is not enough. One is in a world and one is forced to discover the reason of this world; one finds himself in a world which presupposes a choice. Secondly, ideas of the world, even historical ideas of the world are not enough. One must find the reason for these ideas; one must give account historically of these ideas, as others had to do it for themselves historically, but Dilthey does not do that and leaves the ideas 'absolutized' to such an extent that there is nothing more to do with them except to classify them in types. Dilthey's postulate of history falls short of both history and reason: neither discover each other in the same method, they run in parallel roads. Only when life itself functions as reason do we succeed in understanding anything human. Every vital act—not only intellectual acts—is an interpretation: eating, drinking, making love, thinking, living. The same reason which is vital is also historical. It is life itself which gives us knowledge and by virtue of it apprehends reality in its connectedness. This is reason, this is human life. That is why to live means to give an account of what one does in each moment, which is always in view of the totality of one's life. The whole of life acts on each and every point of it, and this fundamental reference is the most profound—root sense—of the word system. Life itself is reason, and reason is systematic: Interpretation and its radical constituents, context, structure, and meaning.

p. 35

l. 9 . . . way Greek philosophy as a field to question the radical activity of doing philosophy has been focused upon most effectively by two of Ortega's disciples: Julián Marías and Xavier Zubiri. In the following pages I have tried to follow them closely, though only to a point. See their works:

Marías, Julián, *Obras,* Revista de Occidente, (Madrid. Vols. 8., 1958).

Generations. A Historical Method, trans. Harold C. Raley (University: Alabama University Press, 1971).

History of Philosophy, trans. Stanley Appelbaum and Clarence C. Stowbridge. (New York: Dover Pub., Inc., 1966).

José Ortega y Gassets Circumstance and Vocation, trans. Frances M. Lopez-Morillas (Norman: University Oklahoma Press, 1970).

Miguel de Unamuno, trans. Frances M. Lopez-Morillas (Cambridge, Mass.: Harvard University Press, 1966).

Philosophy as Dramatic Theory, trans. James D. Parsons, (Univ. Park: The Pennsylvania State University Press, 1971).

Reason and Life: The Introduction to Philosophy, trans. Kenneth S. Reid and Edward Sarmiento (New Haven: Yale University Press, 1956).

Upcoming translations in English: The Social Structure and *The Biography of Philosophy.* (Norman: University of Oklahoma Press Publications).

Zubiri, Xavier; *Cinco Lecciones De Filosofia.* (Editorial Moneda y Credito, Madrid, 1970).

Zubiri, Xavier; *Sobre La Esencia.* (Sociedad De Estudios Y Publicaciones, Madrid, 1963).

l. 35 . . . (Koinoníai). *Sophist,* 253, c–e

l. 37 . . . logon). *Parmenides,* 137a

p. 36

l. 23 . . . be. I dare to suggest that Plato's way of doing philosophy is a systematic "ontological reduction." His dialogues light up concrete but discreet areas of the culture and Plato cancels them as he moves on to others. The result of this method would be a human embodiment of concrete possibilities. But by reducing the method of Plato to Aristotle's interpretation of him we have only half of Plato and no Platonic method. The search for ideas is reduced to a search for ideas as conforming to a particular model of rational principles and reasons, while Plato's Ideas, as a human ground to reveal human possibilities, is thus obscured and canceled. As a consequence, much of Plato remains unknown and much of what is known remains trivialized. A good effort in recovering Plato through his own method and its human possibilities may be seen in Ernest McClain, who is seeking to interpret Plato's mathematical/musical cosmology and metaphors. See his article, "Plato's Musical Cosmology," *Main Currents,* 30, 1 (Sept.–Oct. 1973), pp. 34–42.

p. 37

l. 40 . . . physei)." *Metaphysics,* 980a

p. 38

l. 1 . . . exercise. *Ibid.*

l. 22 . . . say Iliad II, 204

l. 23 . . . repeat *Metaphysics XII, 10, 1076–4*

l. 25 . . . ésto). The Model of knowledge accepted mostly by academic tradition as its own, has been that of explanation, or the belief, that *to know* was to *explain.* To explain means literally *ex-plicare,* to unfold what is folded or im-plicit. Explanation consists in appealing from the immediate and "given" to the mediate and latent, which is supposed to be "implicit" in the former; explanation thus replaces what can be questioned by something else which claims to be more intelligible; a process of reduction is thereby involved from the problematical and unknown to the comprehensible and known. In general, this reduction takes the form of a reduction of effects to causes. The rainbow is reduced to the physical phenomenon of refraction (of light waves from air to water), and sight itself to electramagnetic vibrations in the sense organs, nervous system and brain structures. True knowledge has been equated under the rubric of explanation with the knowledge of the "causes and origin" of things; where cause and origin have been taken as synonimous since Aristotle increasing thus the problematic question of knowledge. Explanation is therefore not a primary mode of knowledge but, a reduction of the real to an interpretation of the real. Since the real does not allow itself to be so reduced it follows that all explanatory knowledge must be preceeded by a prior apprehension of the real exactly as I encounter it in its pure circumstantial concreteness: This is what we call *description.* Historically, this tradition can be traced to two main sources: Maine de Biran in France reacting against the sensualism of Condillac and his followers discovers that physical life can only be considered on an analysis of intimacy or introspection and grounds his method on an *inner sense* which uncovers reality as the *resistence to effort.* The second source comes from Auguste Comte reacting to German idealism and its demand for "the constructivism of knowledge." Comte demands a return to *facts* and the substitution of imagination and ratiocination for *observation.* Postivism claims the need for facts and phenomena but it soon falls back on the mechanism of explanation by looking for the laws which govern phenomena and facts: furthermore, it introduces a metaphysics which arbitrarily identifies the real with the given and the given with what is the object of sensory perception; like explanation, description in the hands of positivism replaces what it is actually observed by a mental construction or theory.

Description comes into its own at the hands of Dilthey who opposing the explanatory and casual psychology of his day demands a descriptive and analytical psychology closely connected with his studies in Hermeneutics. Brentano, a believer in natural science as the proper method for philosophy, affirms nonetheless the need for an "empiricism" more radical than the positivists since it appeals to the evidence of phenomena in their selfhood. Husserl is of course the central figure and greatest theorist of *description*. He has made description the central method of phenomenology: the return to things themselves: "absolute possitivism as opposed to partial positivism," says Husserl.

p. 39

l. 18 . . . ousīa) *Met.* 1028 b 2

p. 40

l. 5 . . . wisdom. See Arnim: *Stoicorum veterum Fragmenta,* II, 35.

l. 10 . . . contemplation. See Plutarch: *De Stoicorum repugnantiis* 2,3 p. i. 033; also, Ritter–Preller: *Historia Philosophiae Graecae,* 481a.

l. 37 . . . certi." Cicero's: *De Finibus* II, 14.

p. 41

l. 24 . . . anything. Sextus Empiricus: *Outline Sketches of Pyrrhonism* I, 4,12.

l. 36 . . . tranquillity. Seneca: *De Tranquillitatae Animi,* II.

l. 39 . . . (philosophía). The etymologies of the Greek and Latin uses of reason show also their context and structure dependence. Aristotle considered Logos as a declarative utterance *(logos apophantikós)* or reason, that is meanings in connection *(katá simplokén)*. This is the primary meaning of *légein (Iliad* XXIII, 239) "to collect together some bones." Reason in Greek comes from *nous* and *logos,* or the verbs *noein* or *legein. Noein, Nous,* in Greek, means all these things: to see; to perceive with the mind, apprehend; and therefore its derived meanings of selecting, considering, and conceiving. The noun *nous,* signifies mind, perception, intellectual apprehension, reason, intellect and meaning. Also design and intention. What the terms really try to indicate is the experience of the apprehension of reality, founded on the metaphor of vision on which the Hellenic conception of knowledge rests, as light, aspect and manifestation (*phos,* whence *Phainómenon: eĩdos* or *idéa; alétheia*). The primary meaning of *legein* (verb) is collecting or assembling. Derivates are, selecting or choosing, from which come counting or enumerating and therefore "giving an account." From this is derived 'saying' but, appears relatively late, not in Homer but in Hesiod for the first time. *Legein* means also calling or naming and by analogy meaning or signifying.

Logos means primarily calculation or count, and so designates a department of the treasure, a public office (like ratio); by analogy it means measure and more generally relation or correspondence. This meaning retains all through Greek tradition a quantitative tinge so that *logos* is the name for the ratio or mathematical proportion between certain magnitudes. From here, it passes to a qualitative designation as rule and norm, i.e. for conduct; this norm which is the measure or relationship of acts functions simultaneously as explanation of them and as justification or motive for them; then comes the sense of argument used in explanation and correlatively that of foundation or reason; from a formal viewpoint, *logos* stands for formula, or more accurately definition and at the same time the act in which the definition is seized, i.e. reason as a faculty. *Logos* is also 'utterance': as narrative or story, fable, legend, tale or else historical narrative, as opposed to *mythos;* it also means stories in the plural as opposed to history; prose as opposed to poetry, or works of the historians. What it does not mean originally is word but, a sentence hence a 'saying' rumor, oracle, or proverb, or section or treatice very close to that of 'book.' From what is said we pass to what is spoken about the *logos,* then it means subject or theme. Lastly, in a more formal way *logos* means utterance or speech—*dzõon logon exon*—'rational animal' as Aristotle defined man, meaning animal having speech and so language. *Lógon didónai,* to give account, *Herodotus* III 142 in ref. to money. In the Hellenic view to apprehend fully is to give an account of what is seen. Noetic vision achieves its fullness in the logos which says what things are; and what they are—*ón,* being—only manifests itself to the *nous.* In the poem of Parmenides which signifies the discovery of being by the way of truth, there is a passage in which the goddess orders the philosopher to "judge by reason" *(krĩnai de logõ)* in the matter of what is, of what the noetic vision contains (Diels, Fr. I). And, in

Plato, the mode of possession of seen reality—the ideas or aspects—is *dialectic,* the movement of the logos itself, and consequently its expression in dialogue.

In Latin we consider *mens, intellectus* and *ratio,* the three complementing and not exhausting our term reason. *Mens* refers to direct acts of memory and imagination, *memini: commentum, commentor, commentarius, mention, mentior* lying. Intellectus from *lego (legere)* is equivalent to the Greek *legein:* collect or choose. *Legere* to read understood as collecting together words or letters to extract their meaning. *Intellectus* alludes not to reading the inside but, to collecting or gathering into the mind, that is, seizing or apprehending something interiorly.

Ratio, is very close to *logos.* From *reor (reri)* to calculate. Ratio is primarily account and hence its use in finance; calculation as in forsight and also the faculty of calculation or forseeing, of apprehending the order and connection of things. *Lógon didónai* equals *rationem redere.* While in Greek possession of reality equals *theoría,* vision, in Latin contemplation is limited to a space *templum* within which the omens were observed; a movement from the *outside* vision to the *inside* contemplation.

Besides Baily's dictionary one may consult the *Greek–English Lexicon* of Liddell and Scott (Oxford, 1940) or the *Dictionnaire Etymologique de la Langue Grecque* of E. Boisacq (2nd ed. Paris–Heildelberg, 1923).

Cfr. Breal et et Bailly: *Dictionnaire Etymologique Latin* 5th ed. (Paris 1902).

Ernout et Meillet: *Dictionnaire Etymologique de la Langue Latine,* (Paris 1939).

Marías, Julián: "Introducción a la Filosofía," *Obras* Vol. 2 pp. 147–152.

CHAPTER TWO

p. 53

l. 38 . . . relativism," Quotation by Nietzsche in "Schopenhauer as Educator" in *Existentialism from Dostoevsky to Sartre,* trans. and ed. W. Kaufmann (New York: Meridian Books, 1956) p. 102.

l. 43 . . . clarification." Nietzsche, *Beyond Good and Evil,* trans. M. Cowan (Chicago: Henry Regnery Co., 1955) pp. 102,3,6,15.

p. 54

l. 12 . . . features." F. H. Bradley, *Appearance and Reality* (Oxford: Oxford University Press, Clarendon Press, 1930) p. 140.

p. 55

l. 12 . . . variations. Gilbert Ryle describes and classifies this situation by dividing philosophers into three groups:

> There were philosophers like Frege, Husserl, and Russel who wanted "to save mathematics from the combined empiricism and psychologism of the school of John Stuart Mill," by proving that besides the material and the mental realms there was 'a realm of nonmaterial and also nonmental logical objects' such as concepts, truths, falsehoods, classes, numbers, and implications. (Ryle, Gilbert: "The Theory of Meaning," in *The Importance of Language,* ed. Max Black (Englewood Cliffs, New Jersey: Prentice-Hall, Inc., 1962) p. 164.)

The second group Ryle calls "armchair mental science or introspective psychology practitioners" who were in danger of losing their jobs because of the scientific psychologists, like James. Finally, the third group consisted of Brentano's disciples, Meinong and Husserl, who though Brentano's principal of intentionality separated:

> . . . the intellectual as distinct from the sensitive volitional or affective acts of consciousness. (*Ibid.*)

Husserl and Meinong named these intellectual objects Meanings (Bedeutungen). In Ryle's own words: Their aim was,

> to recitify the Locke–Hume–Mill accounts of abstraction, conception, memory, judgment, supposal, inference and the rest, by distinguishing in each case, the various private, momentary and repeatable acts of conceiving, remembering, judging, supposing and inferring from their public non-momentary accusatives; namely, the concepts, the propositions and the implications which constituted their objective correlates (*Ibid.*)

p. 59

l. 33 . . . world?" Ludwig Wittgenstein, *Tractatus Logico–Philosophicus,* trans. D. F. Pears and B. F. McGuiness (New York: Humanities Press, 1961), sec. 5.552, 5.5521.

p. 62

l. 16 . . . ignored. Antonio T. de Nicolás, "The Americanization of Ortega y Gasset," *Main Currents in Modern Thought,* (Vol. 28. No. 5, May–June, 1972).

Max Black, *A Companion to Wittgenstein's 'Tractatus'* (Ithica: Cornell Univer. Press, 1964) p. 136.

p. 63

l. 13 . . . ground. Ludwig Wittgenstein, *Philosophical Investigations,* trans. G. E. M. Anscombe (New York: Macmillan, 1973) sec. 107.

l. 22 . . . analysis.” Tractatus . . . sec. 4.5; 3.5.

l. 27 . . . it. Investigations . . . sec. 114.

p. 64

l. 11 . . . expressions. Ibid., sec. 11–14.

p. 65

l. 4 like. Ibid., sec. 81.

p. 67

l. 8 . . . possess.” J. Wisdom, "Philosophy and Psycho-Analysis," in *Philosophy and Psycho–Analysis.* "Philosophy, Metaphysics and Psycho–Analysis," in *Philosophy and Psycho–Analysis.* "Philosophy, Anxiety and Novelty," in *Philosophy and Psycho–Analysis,* (Oxford: Basil Blackwell, 1953).

J. L. Austin, *Sense and Sensibilia,* ed. G. J. Warnock (New York: Oxford University Press, 1964).

G. Ryle, *The Concept of Mind,* (New York: Barnes and Noble, 1971).

l. 35 . . . time.” W. Van, O. Quine, *Word and Object,* (Cambridge, Mass.: M.I.T. Press, 1960) p. 22.

p. 68

l. 7 . . . itself. See for example, Arthur C. Danto, *Mysticism and Morality: Oriental Thought and Moral Philosophy,* (New York: Basic Books, Inc., 1972).

p. 71

l. 14 . . . rests. Teaching philosophy shares in many ways the general biases about knowledge of the natural sciences. Th main source of bia es in interpretation is the belief that to know is to explain. This belief is so ingrained in our historical natural sciences, that our interpretations of ourselves and others still labor under the following main presuppositions:

- That Western rationality was best served by absolute objectivism; that is, the dogmatic assumption that objectivated knowledge of any kind, represents the world, its objects as they exist in themselves independently of human intentionality-structures. The world, in this view, is an objective world picture already-out-there-now-real. (In criticism we may add that the ontological dimension of ontic beings is systematically thus concealed, the historicity of the world and man lost; knowledge is conceived as a mental copy of what is antecedently out-there.)

- That Western rationality, as above understood, was to be the measuring rod to which others had to conform to have meaning, giving thus no possibility for other historic reasons to appear, or ours to increase.
- That "scientism" or the methodology of the positive sciences is in principle capable of answering all meaningful questions. Speculation and philosophy, being only prescientific (or Indian literature for that matter) will disappear in a scientific future.
- That "technicism" is the only philosophy of the future, in the sense that it is the best tool for manipulating and controlling social behaviour.

That our ordinary language—English with its Classical Physics viewpoint—is capable of translating in a one-to-one correspondence any concept or word from any other language, like Sanskrit, for example, as long as the finished product is objective, scientific and technical.

Let me, however; add immediately that even in our own culture we must distinguish *science* as an element of our total contemporary science: as "historical science," and science as the professionals *do* it, or "experimental science." Objectivism, scientism and technicism are among the biases to be found in historical sciences, not in experimental science, where experimental science, especially physics, has all the hermeneutical, ontological, historical and dialectical dimensions negated by historical science and used in interpretations of ourselves and others. It is also my contention that these biases of interpretation are overcome and the qualifications of experimental science are met in the interpretations of texts from other cultures, in particular the text of this book: the *Bhagavad Gītā*. The need, however, to interpret the *Gītā* is not a distant need out-there, but a compelling need of now-here since this text and its life is part of our present socio-cultural life.

l. 18 . . . reasonable. The program of philosophy as a critical, constitutive activity to turn man from a natural man to a cultural man was started, in our tradition, with the Greeks. Socrates started the trend to elevate man from a state of simple natural growth into a cultural achievement. Plato continued this insight showing that the disciplining of thinking and willing must begin with a disciplining—critical awareness—of one's own speaking. He further enlarged the Socratic method to cover every area of the culture known to him. This activity, however, of the Platonic dialectic was lost in the tradition, as we have shown, starting with Aristotle. Not until modern science and modern philosophy with Kant and Hegel has reason, in its practical exercise, come into its own. German Idealism bypassed reflection on language as part of one's own speech. Ortega y Gasset, reinforced by Kant and Hegel, takes up the Platonic challenge and turns the project of philosophy into this emancipatory self-reflection and constitution. It is in this sense that the teaching of philosophy is lacking self-critical awareness. Philosophers are not aware of what they do when they say what philosophy is.

The examples I have in mind as exception to this custom of teaching philosophy in the dark are many in Europe—Germany, France, and Spain—but few in America. To mention just two, see the works of:

> Patrick A. Heelan, *Quantum Mechanics and Objectivity* (Nijhoff: The Hague, 1965). "Horizon, Objectivity and reality in the Physical Sciences," *International Philosophical Quarterly,* Vol. 7 1967. (pp. 372–412.) "Quantum and Classical Logic: Their Respective Roles," *Synthese* 21, 1970.
>
> Richard M. Zaner, *The Problem of Embodiment* (Nijhoff: The Hague, 1964). *The Way of Phenomenology* (New York: Pegasus, Western Publishing Company, Inc., 1970) "An Approach to Philosophical Anthropology," *Philosophy and Phenomenological Research,* Vol. XXVII, N. 1, Sept., 1966. (pp. 55–68.)
>
> In this connection see my: *Four-Dimensional Man: The Philosophical Methodology of the Ṛgveda* (Bangalore, India: Dharmaram College, 1971.)

CHAPTER FOUR

p. 164

l. 34 . . . (Sartre); Sartre, *Antisemite and Jew,* trans. by George J. Becker (New York: Schocken Books, Inc., 1948).

l. 35 . . . (Dostoevsky), Fyodor Dosteovsky, *Notes from Underground,* trans. by Ralph E. Matlaw (New York: E. P. Dutton & Co., Inc., 1960).

l. 35 . . . (Dostoevsky). Fyodor Dostoevsky, *The Grand Inquisitor,* trans. by Ralph E. Matlaw (New York: E. P. Dutton & Co., Inc., 1960). In every one of these three forms of self-identification, the demand is that man surrenders all his multiplicity of selves to only one. In the Democratic-Anti-Semite fashion the demand is for a universal self to dissolve all the situational (contextual, structural, ethnic, individual) selves and surrender them to a universal leveling idea of a self which applies equally to all men in all circumstantial situations. Institutions, "Establishments," Governments of bodies and souls (Churches and States) work on this hypothesis.

The Underground-Man, on the other hand, elevates a concrete situation to the heights of universality, commits himself to it, and lives thereby on the brink of self-annihilation or incarceration. Radical political groups, the counter-culture, the extremist, the self-tortured man, the neurotic, are all committed to this kind of self-identification.

The Grand Inquisitor we know it as the demand of the scientific establishment (whatever establishment be in power) to universalize their laws and method to control human behaviour. Inspite of the demand made upon man to surrender his own freedom, man concedes easily, in many cases, unwittingly, his freedom for the rewards of security, bread, and blissful peace. This man, identified with the "herd" still considers himself free with empty words of "mystery," "miracle," and "authority." His craving for identification with the "community" is more powerful in the "herd-man" than his strength to be free.

What is significant about these three modes of being in the world is that they exist simultaneously in every society and that no one mode is possible without the other two.

p. 165

l. 17 . . . "sensation-owner." See Wittengenstein, *Philosophical Investigations,* op. cit. 404, 405.

p. 167

l. 42 . . . methods I have in mind principally philosophers like Radhakrishnan (*The Bhagavad Gītā,* London: George Allen & Unwin, Ltd., 1948), Surendranath Dasgupta (*A History of Indian Philosophy,* Vols I and II, London: Cambridge University Press, 1932), and K. N. Upadhyaya (*Early Buddhism and the Bhagavad Gītā,* Delhi: Motilal Banarsidass, 1971). They prove the point that interpretation is done within interpretation. Although it is obvious that these and other Indian Scholars are not in agreement with the general interpretations of Western Scholars of the *Bhagavad Gītā,* still it is this audience they have in mind—in fact, they are unable to escape this audience—when writing about the *Bhagavad Gītā.* The truth is they have to satisfy this audience in order to be heard in the first place. Indian Scholars, in fact, have been so busy answering and correcting Western Scholars and themselves that they have not yet had time to dedicate themselves to saying what they really want and need to say. To better understand this impasse, let me show with some suggestive examples the difficulties of interpretation the exegesis of the *Bhagavad Gītā* had to survive up to this point.

Chronology: Both Eastern and Western scholars have centered their research on establishing a date for the *Bhagavad Gītā.* They, of course, have not been able to come to a definite conclusion, with differences of opinion ranging from dating the *Bhagavad Gītā* from about A.D. 500 to around the 5th century B.C. Indian scholars are in more general agreement about the early date of the B.G. while Western scholars, in general, settle for a compromise data of the second century B.C. On this point see : Upadhyaya's *Early Buddhism and the Bhagavad Gītā,* pp. 1–29. The conclusion of his study is certainly not conclusive, yet it shows theee emphasis of scholars on historicity as a system of revelation. It does not really matter very much to know the exact date of the B.G. (in fact, nobody does know) if we just rest our case there. The important point is to show how the text itself is for the tradition a "positional" document able to bring back the culture to its original intentionality and how it goes about doing it. It is significant, however, that some Western and Indian people have made the text so close to a Christian document that any differences between the B.G. and the New Testament are hardly noticeable. Our position shares the Indian inclination to date the B.G. around the 5th century B.C. as a "positional" document taking a stand against the other unorthodox, puzzling, forcing, constraining, narrower tendencies emerging in the midst of the social life of those—or other similar—times. Our thesis will not be destroyed if the date of the B.G. was found to be a different one.

Sources of the Bhagavad Gītā: If the *Bhagavad Gītā* is as early as the 5th century B.C., then the different schools of Hindu thought it mentions are posterior developments of this earlier synthesis of Hindu thought and action. If on the other hand the B.G. is posterior to this date, then the B.G. is a synthesis of those schools of Hindu thought it mentions. In any case, the *Bhagavad Gītā's* main sources are to be traced to the Upaniṣads and not to Buddhism since in fact the B.G. is the Hindu position against the extremist and unorthodox Buddhist criticism of Brahmanism. This argument has been used by practically all scholars dealing with the interpretation of the B.G. See Upadhyaya's *Early Buddhism and the Bhagavad Gītā,* pp. 106–150. Since the knowledge of the date of the B.G., however is problematic, the above argument in its first or second form is speculative and ineffective. This analytic approach to the text of the *Gītā* is in many ways necessary but certainly insufficient, for it obviates the obvious *action* of what the text itself of the B.G. does. Words do not make a poem, nor Sāṃkhya, Vedānta, Yoga, the Upaniṣads make the *Bhagavad Gītā*. What the *Bhagavad Gītā*. is, the *Bhagavad Gītā* does; and no external document can substitute for this activity. In fact, the *Bhagavad Gītā's* own rationality has, under these two arguments, been obscured as we shall see in chapters Five and Six principally.

Linguistic Problems: Interpreters of the *Bhagavad Gītā* have also fallen into the scientistic habit of equating Sanskrit grammar and word structure with ordinary English, forgetting that these words belong to different intentionality structures. Thus we find even in the most scholarly efforts definitions and translations of the *Bhagavad Gītā* equated with Western religious and ethical language on a one to one correspondence. This, to say the least, is misleading and most problematic. Names like God, egotism, ethics, nature, spirit, soul, etc., etc., have no equal function in Hindu tradition, Sanskrit language, or Hindu norms of behaviour as they do in Western texts. No wonder works like *The Bhagavad Gītā As It Is,* author A. C. Bhaktivedanta Swami Prabhupāda, (New York: Collier Books, 1972) are even possible inspite of the complete disregard for the Sanskrit language the author says he translates from. Example: *dharmakṣetre, kurukṣetre* is translated as "place of Pilgrimage??"

p. 168

l. 3 . . . size. There is no English equivalent of such Sanskrit words as *Prakṛti, Puruṣa, ātman, dharma, guṇa, ahaṃkāra,* etc. To translate them as Nature, Spirit, soul, duty, evolutes, egotism is to say nothing, for these words in English are loaded with different meanings derived from different Western contexts in no way equal to the *Bhagavad Gītā's* intentionality—as we have seen in chapters two and three of this book. Until such time as people understand what these words mean in their Hindu context, it is better to leave them in Sanskrit and explain their function. After all, not only scholars but a large part of the American population, educated or "pop," are familiar with these words, use them and make sentences with them. The function of language is communication not just translation. We need new words and new sentences to communicate new and different rationalities.

l. 8 . . . fate. Original texts of the *Bhagavad Gītā:* Gītā Press, (Gorakhapur: 126), tr. Radhakrishnan, Allen & Unwin (London: 6th ed., 1960); With Śaṃkara's Commentary, Gītā Press, (Gorakhapur: 10th ed., 1961); With Rāmānuja's Commentary,

Gītā Press, (Gorakhapur: 3rd ed., 1960). There is also a version of the *Gītā* found in Kashimir discovered by Professor F. Otto Schrader with some minor divergences from the above text. This, however, does not alter the meaning of even a single proposition much less of the whole text. F. Edgerton, moreover, believes this edition to be a later and secondary edition. (*Journal of the American Oriental Society*. New Haven: Vol. 52, pp. 68–75).

Other translations that may be consulted: Arnold, Sir Edwin, *The Song Celestial; or Bhagavad Gītā,* (Philadelphia: D. Mckay Co., 1934). Deutsch, Eliot, *The Bhagavad Gītā,* (New York: Holt, Rinehart & Winston, 1968). Edgerton, Franklin, *The Bhagavad Gītā Translated and Interpreted,* (Harvard Oriental Series: 38–39, 1944); and (New York: Harper & Row, 1944). Van Buitenen, J. A. B., *Rāmānuja on the Bhagavad Gītā, a Condensed Rendering of his Gītābhāshya with Copious Notes and an Introduction,* (Leiden: 's-Gravenhage, 1954).

p. 173

l. 8 . . . wish. *Bhagavad Gītā* (B.G.) XVIII, 63; "*yathā icchasi tathā kuru.*"

l. 23 . . . (pratirūpa) For the story of Indra see *Four-Dimensional Man, esp. Chapter VII. For the translation of the* Ṛg Veda see: Griffith, Ralph, *The Hymns of the Ṛg Veda* (Varanasi, India: Chowkhamba Sanskrit Series, 1963) Vols. I and II. See also: *A Philosophy in Song-Poems,* by J. B. Chethimattam and Antonio T. de Nicolás (Bangalore, India: Dharmaram College, 1971).

> His form is to be seen everywhere for of every form He is the Prototype. Indra, by his power (māyā) appears in many forms, indeed, his bay steeds are yoked a thousand times.
>
> *Ṛg Veda* 6.47.18
>
> He whom we follow bows not to the firm or the strong, or to the challenger incited by the restless foe; To Indra the lofty mountains are as plains and in the deeps there is a foot-hold for him.
>
> *Ṛg Veda* 6.24.8

l. 24 . . . Indra. This is the ancient, accepted path by which all the gods have come into existence. Through this is one born stepping its very widest. Let him not do otherwise, and destroy his mother.

I do not go forth this way: hard is the passage. I will step out obliquely from the side. Much that has not yet been done must I accomplish: I must both fight and question.

Ṛg Veda 4.18.1-2

l. 31 . . . creation Ṛg Veda (Abr. R.V.) 10.129.6; cfr. *Four-Dimensional Man,* esp. Chapters six through nine.

l. 34 . . . society For translations of the Upaniṣads see: Radhakrishnan, S., *The Principal Upaniṣads,* London, 1953; Hume, Robert Ernest, *The Thirteen Principal Upanishads,* 2nd ed. Oxford, 1931.

For examples of the warrior's position in the Upaniṣads and Gītā see: *Bṛhād.* II. 1 and *Kausītaki* IV; *Chāndogya.* V. 2; *Bṛhād.* VI. 2 and *Chāndogya.* V. 3.7; *Chāndogya.* VII. 26.2; *Bṛhād. VI. 2.8 and Chāndogya.* V. 3.7; *Bṛhād.* II. 1.15; *Kausītaki* IV. 19; *Bṛhād.* VI. 2.7–8; *Chāndogya* V. 11.7; Bhagavad Gītā (Abr. B.G.) IV. 1–2; B.G. IX. 2; B.G. VIII. 25–26; B.G. X. 24–26;

p. 174

l. 25 . . . Dharma." Dharmakṣetre-Kurukṣetre, B.G. I. 1.

p. 175

l. 19 . . . condition sve-sve karmaṇy abhirataḥ saṃsiddhiṃ labhate naraḥ, B.G. XVIII. 45.

l. 20 . . . doubt B.G. IV. 40; VI. 39; VIII. 7.

l. 22 . . . judgment asaktabuddhiḥ, B.G. XVIII. 49.

p. 176

l. 26 . . . field; B.G. XIII.

l. 41 . . . tradition. para*ṃparāprāptam,* B.G. IV. 2; of the royal sages *rājarṣayo, Ibid.*

p. 177

l. 2 . . . dharma, dharmyād dhi yuddhāc chreyo 'nyat kṣatriyasya no vidyate, B.G. II. 31.

l. 2 . . . heaven." svargadvāram apāvṛtam, B.G. II. 32.

l. 7 . . . goal niḥśreysakarāv ubhau, B.G. V. 2; *yat sāṃkhyaiḥ prāpyate sthānaṃ tad yogair api gamyate,* B.G. V. 5.

l. 12 . . . battlefield." Dvāv imau puruṣavyāghra sūryamaṇḍalabhedinau; parivrāḍ yogayuktas ca raṇe cā'bhimukho hataḥ, 32, 65. *Mahābhārata (MB) Udyoga.*

l. 14 . . . head." daṇḍa eva hi rājendra kṣatradharmo no mundanam, MB, *Śānti* .23.46.

l. 15 . . . destruction." kṣatād yo vai trāyatī'ti sa tasmāt kṣatriyaḥ smṛtaḥ, MB. XII. 29.138.

l. 18 . . . death." *saṃbhāvitasya cā 'kīrtir maraṇād atiricyate,* B.G. II. 34.

l. 19 . . . glory." *anāryajuṣṭam asvargyam akīrtikaram arjuna,* B.G. II. 2.

l. 22 . . . sin." *atha cet tvam imaṃ dharmyaṁ saṃgrāmaṃ no kariṣyasi tataḥ svadharmaṃ kīrtiṃ ca hitvā pāpam avāpsyasi,* B.G. II. 33.

l. 25 . . . earth." *hato vā prāpsyasi svargaṃ jityā vā bhokṣyase mahīm,* B.G. II. 37.

l. 28 . . . glance. *Vedā'haṃ samatītāni vartamānāni cā 'rjuna bhaviṣyāni ca bhūtāni,* B.G. VII. 26.

l. 35 . . . sin, See next section on the *guṇas.*

l. 41 . . . (Arguna)." *ṛte 'pi tvāṃ na bhaviṣyanti sarve ve 'vasthitāḥ pratyanīk ṣu yodhāḥ tasmāt tvam uttiṣṭha yaśo labhasva jitvā śatrūn bluṇkṣva rājyaṃ samṛddham mayai 'vai 'te nihataḥ pūrvam eva nimittamātraṃ bhava savyasācin,* B.G. XI. 32–33.

p. 178

l. 2 . . . him. *nirmamo bhūtvā yudhyasva vigatajvaraḥ,* B.G. III. 30.

l. 13 . . . you" *yad ahaṃkāram āśrita na yotsya iti manyase mithyai' ṣa vyavasāyas te prakṛtis tvām niyokṣyati,* B.G. XVIII. 59.

l. 18 . . . fear." *svalpam apy asya dharmasya trāyate mahato bhayāt,* B.G. II. 40.

l. 20 . . . lordliness . . . " B.G. XVIII. 43.

l. 26 . . . knowledge-wisdom), B.G. XVIII. 49 and II. 41.

l. 28 . . . sit?" B.G. II. 54;

l. 29 . . . less; B.G. II. 67, 71, 73; XII. 8; IX. 34; IX. 1; III. 32; IV. 40; VI. 39; VII. 21 and VIII. 7.

p. 179 . . .

l. 17 . . . on This may be seen from B.G. I. 40–44. See especially 43, "*janmakarmaphalapradām;* they only gather rebirth as the fruit of their action." Karmic viewing and rebirth go together. *Saṃsāra* commonly used in Indian tradition for rebirth, means as a noun, "a going, a wandering through," etymologically derived from the root *sṛ,* which like *śru* means to flow; *sam-sṛ* is thus the verbal form for "to flow together with, to go about with, wander with, walk, or roam with." It is never a liberated free wandering, but an attached, crisis-inducing wandering.

p. 180

l. 3 . . . creatures).” B.G. VIII. 3. The same idea in other contexts can be deduced from the following passages: II. 42–43; II. 47–57; III. 4–9; III. 14–15; III. 19–20; III. 22–25; IV. 14–24; IV. 32–33; V. 1–14 and XVIII. 2–25.

l. 9 . . . agent; B.G. III. 27; *kartā 'ham iti manyate,* "yet he who is deluded by the sense of I thinks 'I am the doer." In contrast XIII. 29; *prakṛtyai 'va ca karmaṇi kriyamāṇāni sarvaśaḥ yaḥ paśyati tathā 'tmānam akartāraṃ sa paśyati,* He who sees that actions are everywhere done by *prakṛti* and who likewise sees his self not to be the doer, he sees indeed."

l. 14 . . . wrong.” B.G. XVIII. 16.

l. 15 . . . action B.G. XVIII. 15.

l. 16 . . . action. B.G. XVIII. 59.

l. 30 . . . him B.G. II. 3.

l. 31 . . . dharma, dharmasaṃmūḍhacetāḥ, B.G. II. 7.

l. 33 . . . (niścitaṃ), B.G. II. 7.

p. 181

l. 12 . . . dharma. B.G. V. 15; XVI. 19 and IX. 16, 24.

l. 33 . . . maker. B.G. X. 42.

l. 35 . . . speaking. B.G. XVIII. 19, 26, 40.

l. 38 . . . else See: *Four-Dimensional Man,* Chapter 5.

CHAPTER FIVE

p. 189

l. 22 . . . therapy.” When a whole society surrenders or legimitizes the surrender to "therapy" as a correction of neurotic and obsessive behavior rather than the search for the radical orientation man needs to recover and behave humanly, then we have what Rollo May calls the "age of therapy," or Nietzsche prophesized as a "general hospital" condition. See in this respect: Rollo May, *Love and Will* (New York: Dell Publishing Co., A Laurel Edition, 1974), p. 20.

> One of the values of living in a transitional age—an "age of therapy"—is that it forces upon us this opportunity, even as we try to resolve our individual problems, to uncover new

meaning in perennial man and to see more deeply into those qualities which constitute the human being as human.

But even "therapy" is culturally mediated.

The magazine's September 23, 1974 issue says in respect to this that in Japan it is not just creative people who avoid the couch. Everybody does. Tokyo, with a population of 11 million, has only three psychoanalysts in private practice. New York City (pop. 9 million) has nearly 1,000.

Seriously disturbed patients in Japanese mental hospitals generally receive similar kinds of treatment to those offered in the U.S. The 3,000 Japanese who are qualified psychiatrists usually prescribe tranquilizers for patients who display neurotic or obsessive behavior, instead of probing for the root of the trouble.

Why the near total rejection of psychoanalysis? After all, Freud's works had been translated into Japanese by 1930, and after World War II many Japanese medical students and doctors went to the U. S. to study psychoanalysis. Tokyo analyst Soichi Hakozaki offers one answer: the "softened ego" of the Japanese, produced by a clannish and group-oriented culture that ignores the individualism that is essential to the success of analytic techniques.

Individualism may be on the rise, however, now that more and more Japanese corporations are discarding their traditional paternalism. Tensions and anxiety are certainly increasing among the Japanese. But instead of setting up psychiatric care for their executives and workers, the corporations have begun subsidizing group trips to Zen temples for sessions of meditation.

p. 190

l. 28 . . . on" On methodological grounds it would be important to bear in mind the distinction we introduce in this book between the "consciousness of . . . ," or reflective consciousness and the consciousness we "count on," or the radical human ground. This radical ground though mediated through reflective consciousness can never be absolutized or identified.

As we have seen from Chapters one, two and three, the reflective consciousness is the predominant form—academically a monopoly—of our systems of explanation, prediction, description and control. We shall see later its demands and limitations.

The consciousness I "count on," on which reflective consciousness is grounded was first introduced in philosophy by Ortega y Gasset in this systematic way. At the epistemological level it is the "other" as my possibility; as my possible life; what surrounds me and through which I make and save myself. At the theoretical level it is a possible theory of man-knowledge-society by which the determinations of the reflective consciousness are embodied; through which one feels at home, or one's multiple social surroundings become home, but where neither man—I—, knowledge or society are fixed or identified. Their living process of innovation through integration and continuity are made thus possible. We shall clarify these points as we go along.

p. 195

l. 15 . . . knowledge. The reader may like to compare the different approaches we are suggesting by reading, besides the books already mentioned in the previous chapters, the following:

R.C. Zaehner, *The Bhagavad-Gītā,* (Oxford University Press, 1969).

Franklin Edgerton, *The Bhagavad Gītā,* (New York: Harper Torchbooks, 1964).

Sri Krishna Prem, *The Yoga of the Bhagavat Gita,* (Baltimore, Maryland: Penguin Books, Inc., 1973).

Eliot Deutsch, *The Bhagavad Gītā,* (Holt, Rinehart and Winston, 1968).

Richard Garbe, *Die Bhagavadgītā,* 2nd ed., Leipzig, H. Haessel, 1921.

Douglas P. Hill, *The Bhagavadgītā,* (London, Oxford University Press, 1928), 2d, abridged ed. (lacking Sanskrit text), Madras, Oxford University Press, 1953.

Swami Nikhilananda, *The Bhagavad Gītā,* (New York: Ramakrishna-Vivekananda Center, 1944).

Rudolf Otto, *The Original Gītā: The Song of the Supreme Exalted One,* trans. from the German by J. E. Turner (London: Allen and Unwin, 1939).

Sri Aurobindo, *The Original Gītā: The Song of the Supreme Exalted One,* trans. from the German by J. E. Turner (London: Allen and Unwin, 1939).

Sri Aurobindo, *Essays on the Gītā,* (New York: Dutton, 1950).

J.A.B. van Buitenen, *Rāmānuja on the Bhagavadgītā: A Condensed Rendering of his Gītā bhāṣya,* (The Hague: H. L. Smits, 1953).

Mahadev Desai, *The Gospel of Selfless Action, or, The Gita According to Gandhi (Ahmedabad: Navjivan Publishing House, 1956).*

Satis Chandra Roy, *The Bhagavad-Gītā and Modern Scholarship,* (London: Luzac, 1941).

B.G. Tilak, *Srīmad Bhagavadgītā Rahasya,* 2 vols. (Poona: R.B. Tilak, 1935–36).

p. 199

l. 13 . . . enemies I. 38: Those "whose minds are afflicted by greed," i.e., by appropriation and identification. II. 43: "Whose selves are made of desire, whose highest goal is heaven, who are full of ritual acts for the sake of enjoyment and power, they only gather rebirth as the fruit of these actions."

l. 23 . . . (Kṛṣṇa)." I. 39.

l. 27 . . . crisis. I. 32; II. 8.

l. 29 . . . dharma, *dharmasaṃmūḍha-cetāḥ,* II. 7.

l. 31 . . . battle. I. 25–30.

l. 34 . . . victory I. 32 and II. 5, 8.

l. 39 . . . identification. II. 10–11.

p. 200

l. 1 . . . knowing. *. . . ete na paśyanti lobhopahatacetasaḥ,* I. 38.

l. 2 . . . delusion *moha,* II. 52; VII. 13.

l. 2 . . . desire *kāma,* II. 55; III. 37.

l. 3 . . . anger *rāga, bhaya* and *krodha,* II. 56; VI. 10.

l. 3 . . . hatred *dveṣa,* XVIII. 51.

l. 6 . . . appropriation. II. 62; III. 37, 38.

l. 9 . . . ignorance, II. 14–15.

l. 9 . . . evil, II. 57.

l. 13 . . . (ajñānenā), *ajñānenā 'vṛtaṃ jñānaṃ tena muhyanti jantavaḥ,* V. 15.

l. 15 . . . action XVIII. 17: "He who is free from the sense of I, whose understanding is not tainted, though he slay these people, he slays nor nor is he bound." III. 27: "Actions are engaged in by way of the *guṇas* of *prakṛti* alone: Yet he who is deluded by the sense of I thinks 'I am the doer.' "

l. 16 . . . pleasure, *samaduḥkasukhaḥ,* II. 15, 56; XII. 13, 18, XIV. 24.

l. 17 . . . dishonor, *sama* or *tulyamānāpamānayoḥ,* XII. 18; XIV. 25.

l. 17 . . . praise, *tuly nindā stutiḥ,* XII. 19; XIV. 24.

l. 18 . . . foes *tulyo mitrāripakṣayoḥ,* XIV. 25; XII. 18.

l. 19 . . . judgement. *sthitaprajña,* II. 58.

l. 29 . . . life. XIV–XVIII.

l. 32 . . . cured XVIII. 32.

l. 32 . . . divided. bhedam, III. 26. See Chapter Six of this book.

p. 202

l. 4 . . . see, na ca śreyo 'nupaśyāmi, I. 31; *na cai 'tad vidmaḥ kataran no garīyo,* II. 6.

l. 5 . . . Kṙsña. yac chreyaḥ syan niścitaṃ brūhti tan me, II. 7; *tad ekaṃ vada niścitya yena sreyo 'ham āpnuyām,* III. 2; V. 1.

l. 19 . . . tradition. II. 11.

l. 21 . . . self. II. 11–25.

l. 22 . . . grief, II. 25: *tasmād evaṃ viditvai' naṃ nā' nuśocitum arhasi;* also in VI. 35: *yaj jñātvā na punar moham evaṃ yāsyasi pāṇdava.*

l. 24 . . . dualities dvandvas, II. 14–15.

l. 25 . . . amṛtatva). II. 14–15.

l. 27 . . . possible. na hi jhnānena sadṛśaṃ pavitram iha vidyate, VI. 38; savrvaṃ *jñ9anaplavenai 'va uṛjinaṃ saṃtariṣyasi,* IV. 36; *jñānaṃ labdhvā parāṃ śāntim acireṇā 'dhigacchati,* IV. 39.

l. 30 . . . whatsoever. asakta buddhiḥ sarvatra, XVIII. 49.

l. 35 . . . killed. ubhau tau na vijānīto nā 'yaṃ hanti na hanyate, II. 19.

l. 36 . . . imperishable; II. 17 ff.

l. 37 . . . indestructible; VIII. 3 ff.

l. 38 . . . field, XIII. 1 ff.

l. 41 . . . Reality, jñāninaḥ tattvadarśinaḥ, IV. 34.

l. 41 . . . yogins. yatantaḥ yoginaḥ, XV. 11.

p. 203

l. 2 . . . see." vimūdhā nā 'napaśyanti paśyanti jñānacakṣuṣaḥ, XV. 10.

l. 7 . . . known. yaj jñātvā ne 'he bhūyo 'nyaj jñātavyam avaśiṣyate, VII. 2.

l. 10 . . . marvel," āścaryavat paśyati kaścid enam, II. 29.

l. 10 . . . knowledge," guhyatamaṃ jñānam, IX. 1.

l. 11 . . . secrets," *guhyād guhyataram,* XVIII. 63.

p. 204

l. 9 . . . men, IV. 37–41.

l. 10 . . . life," III. 4, 20; VI. 43; VIII. 3; VII. 15, etc.

l. 11 . . . creatures," V. 25 and XII. 4.

l. 15 . . . Bhārata." IV. 42.

l. 16 . . . knowledge," IV. 37.

l. 17 . . . multiplicity XVIII. 20.

l. 18 . . . kind XVIII. 21.

l. 22 . . . manifestation. X. 42.

l. 27 . . . (nirahaṃkāra), II. 71 and XII. 13.

l. 28 . . . not-I-speaking. See Chapter IV of this book.

l. 29 . . . stand. *sarvabhūtāśayasthitaḥ,* X. 20; *hṛdi sarvasya dhiṣṭhitam,* XIII. 17; *sarvagataḥ,* II. 24; XIII. 32; *samaṃ sarveṣe bhūtesu tiṣṭhantaṃ parameśvaram,* XIII. 27; *sarvasya cā 'haṃ hṛdi saṃniviṣṭo,* XV. 15; cf. XIII. 2, 22; XVIII. 61.

l. 31 . . . beings." *avibhataṃ ca bhūteṣu vibhaktam iva ca sthitam,* XIII. 16.

l. 33 . . . affected." XIII. 32.

l. 37 . . . Brahman." XIII. 30.

l. 42 . . . form. XI. 8.

l. 43 . . . cakṣu) *paśyanti jñānacakṣuṣaḥ,* XV. 10; *. . . evam . . . ye vidur yānti te param,* XIII. 34.

p. 205

l. 3 . . . discerned, *sūkṣmatvāt tad avijñeyaṃ,* XIII. 15.

l. 4 . . . qualities. *nirguṇatvāt,* XIII. 31.

l. 5 . . . self, *yatanto yoginaś cai 'naṃ paśyanty ātmany avasthitam,* XV. 11; *dhyānenā 'tmani paśyanti,* XIII. 24; *īkṣate yogayuktātmā,* VI. 29.

l. 6 . . . It. *vimūḍhā nā 'nupaśyanti,* XV. 10; *nai 'naṃ paśyanty acetasaḥ,* XV. 11.

l. 7 . . . terms, II. 12–30.

l. 7 . . . incomprehensible, aprameya, II. 18.

l. 8 . . . unthinkable, acintya, II. 25; VIII. 9.

l. 8 . . . undefinable anirdeśya, XII. 3.

l. 9 . . . condition, II. 29; XIII. 3; XIII. 15.

l. 13 . . . doer,'" III. 27.

l. 15 . . . bound," XVIII. 17.

l. 17 . . . slain." II. 19.

l. 18 . . . ancient, II. 20.

l. 19 . . . reality, X. 20; XIII. 17, 22, 27, 31; XVIII. 61.

l. 21 . . . emancipation. XIII. 32.

l. 23 . . . beings. bahir antaś ca bhūtānām, XIII. 15.

l. 24 . . . embodied." XIII. 31.

l. 26 . . . world." lokasaṃgraham evā 'pi saṃpaśyan kartum arhasi, III. 20.

l. 30 . . . ne ti), Bṛhadā. II. 3.6; IV. 4.22; Tait. II. 7; Kaṭha. III. 15.

l. 30 . . . paradoxically, Kena. II. 1–3; kaṭha. II. 21; Iśa. 4; Śvetā. III. 19.

l. 30 . . . analogically; Bṛhadā. IV. 3.7.

l. 31 . . . contradictions, Bṛhadā. IV. 9.22 ff; IV. 4.5; Tait. II. 6; Kaṭha. II. 20; Iśa. 5.

l. 31 . . . opposites. Bṛhadā. III. 8.8; Kena. I. 3; Kaṭha. II. 14; Iśa. 10, 13; Śvetā. IV. 18; Māṇḍūkya 7.

l. 33 . . . expression. Kena. I. 3; *Tait.* II. 9; *Kaṭha.* II. 8; *Muṇḍaka* III. 1.7; *Māṇḍūkya.*

l. 34 . . . Brahman. Kaṭha. II. 16; IV. 5–9.

p. 206

l. 3 . . . done. tasya kāryaṃ na vidyate, III. 17.

l. 7 . . . advantage. kaścid arthavyapāśrayaḥ, III. 18.

l. 12 . . . perfection. III. 4.

l. 17 . . . prakṛti. III. 5.

l. 21 . . . vain. evaṃ pravartitaṃ cakraṃ na 'nuvartayatī 'ha yaḥ aghāyur indriyārāmo moghaṃ pārtha sa jīvati, III. 16.

l. 26 . . . world. lokasaṃgraham evā 'pi saṃpaśyan kartum arhasi, III. 20.

l. 30 . . . action. III. 22.

l. 33 . . . people. utsīdeyur ime lokā na kuryāṃ karma ced aham samkarasya ca kartā syām upahayāmimāḥ prajāḥ, III. 24.

p. 207

l. 1 . . . together. kuryād vidvāṃs tathā 'saktaś cikīrṣur lokasaṃgraham, III. 25.

l. 4 . . . IV. 36.

l. 7 . . . action. XVIII. 45.

l. 10 . . . vaded. XVIII. 46.

l. 15 . . . thing). XVIII. 47.

l. 19 . . . kuntī. XVIII. 48.

l. 24 . . . sacrifice yajñārthat karmano 'nyatra loko 'yam karmabandhanaḥ tadarthaṃ karma kaunteya muktasaṅgaḥ samācara, III. 9.

*l. 28 . . . desires. sahayaj*hn*aḥ prajāḥ sṛṣṭvā puro 'vāca prajāpatiḥ anena prasaviṣyadhvam eṣa vo 'sṭv iṣṭakamadhuk,* III. 10.

l. 31 . . . good. III. 11.

l. 36 . . . thief. III. 12.

p. 208

l. 2 . . . sacrifice. sarvagata*ṃ brahma nityaṃ yajñe pratiṣṭhitam,* III. 15.

p. 209

l. 4 . . . (sthitadhīr). II. 41–56.

p. 210

l. 7 . . . buddhiyoga. II. 39. See in this connection: Sri Aurobindo, *On Yoga I: The Synthesis of Yoga,* (Madras: Sri Aurobindo Library, 1st ed., 1948), pp. 351–373, 734–770. Also: *Essays on the Gītā,* (Calcutta: Arya Publishing House, 4th ed., 1944), First Series, Chapters VII–X.

See also one of the few Western scholars aware of this problem: David White, "The Yoga of Knowledge in the *Gītā* according to Sri Aurobindo," in *International Philosophical Quarterly,* Vol. XII, No. 2, June, 72; pp. 243–250.

l. 12 . . . fear. II. 40.

l. 17 . . . happiness." VI. 21.

l. 20 . . . earth." II. 50.

l. 21 . . . (samatva); II. 48.

l. 23 . . . sarvatra); XVIII. 49.

l. 24 . . . (buddhimān); IV. 18.

l. 25 . . . judgment, II. 65.

l. 26 . . . (muni). II. 69, 71.

l. 28 . . . action, Nirvāṇa, II. 72.

l. 30 . . . himself XII. 8.

l. 31 . . . is. XVIII. 57.

l. 34 . . . creatures." V. 25; XII. 4.

l. 41 . . . resolute." II. 41.

p. 212

l. 11 . . . "wheel," XVIII. 61.

l. 12 . . . string," VII. 7.

l. 13 . . . feet. IX. 6.

l. 15 . . . tree," XV. 1.

p. 213

l. 3 . . . varuṇa, R.V. 7.61.4.

l. 4 . . . sacrifice R.V. 10.61.11.

l. 8 . . . (varivas) R.V. 1.46.11.

l. 10 . . . (vīdvamhas). R.V., 4.3.14.

l. 13 . . . effective. Further examples of this insight may be seen in R.V. 9.113.3; 9.1.6; and principally in 10.151. See also *Four-Dimensional Man,* Chapter IX.

p. 214

l. 1 . . . (citta-vṛtti-nirodha). See: Surendranath Dasgupta, *A History of Indian Philosophy,* Vol. II., pp. 443–444.

p. 215

l. 1 . . . dependence See: XI. 33.

l. 16 . . . word. *naṣṭo mohaḥ:* delusion destroyed. *smṛtir labdhā:* memory restored. *sthito 'smi:* I stand firmly. *gatasammṃdehaḥ:* without doubt. *kariṣye vacanṃ tava* I will do your word.

l. 21 . . . self, II. 17, 18, 20, 23, 24.

l. 22 . . . kṣatrīya, II. 31.

l. 26 . . . sensations. II. 14.

l. 28 . . . immortality. II. 15, *amṛtatvāya:* immortality or continuity is the ground of the dualities of the senses.

p. 216

l. 2 . . . goals. II. 43.

l. 4 . . . (karman)." II. 49, 50.

l. 31 . . . yogins. III. 1, 3.

l. 33 . . . together." III. 25.

l. 34 . . . sacrifice, yajña, III. 9.

l. 36 . . . (saḥ). III. 42.

l. 38 . . . action, III. 9.

l. 38 . . . Janaka III. 20.

l. 40 . . . action. III. 22.

l. 41 . . . Brahman, III. 15.

l. 41 . . . Prajāpati. III. 10.

p. 217

l. 3 . . . alone. III. 27.

l. 4 . . . action. III. 33.

l. 5 . . . lost. III. 32.

l. 5 . . . condition, III. 33.

l. 7 . . . wise. III. 39.

l. 9 . . . womb. III. 38.

l. 21 . . . desire. III. 43.

l. 34 . . . time. IV. 1, 2, 3.

l. 35 . . . secret. rahasyaṃ hy etad uttaman, IV. 3.

l. 37 . . . Brahman," IV. 32.

l. 38 . . . next?" IV. 32.

p. 218

l. 1 . . . things." IV. 33.

l. 3 . . . me." IV. 34, 35.

l. 8 . . . dissolved." IV. 23.

l. 10 . . . self, IV. 6.

l. 11 . . . lives, IV. 5.

l. 12 . . . decreases; IV. 7.

l. 16 . . . cycles. IV. 8.

l. 18 . . . divine. IV. 9, 10.

l. 22 . . . them. IV. 11.

l. 23 . . . Brahman," IV. 24.

l. 25 . . . itself." IV. 25.

l. 29 . . . castes IV. 13.

l. 31 . . . ashes, IV. 37.

l. 34 . . . ignorance IV. 37.

l. 37 . . . vindati). IV. 38.

l. 39 . . . me." IV. 35.

p. 219

l. 12 . . . Veda See *Four-Dimensional Man,* especially Chapter VII and "Religious Experience and Religious Languages," in *Main Currents in Modern Thought,* Vol. 28, No. 2 Nov–Dec., 1971, by the same author of this book.

l. 19 . . . sacrifice-knowledge. This *Yajña* can be *daiva-yajña, brahma-yajña, dravya-yajña, topo-yajña, yoga-yajña, svādhyāya-yajña* and *jñāna-yajña* in IV. 24, 25, 26–28, 29 and 30. Even when the *Gītā* speaks of the yoga practice and conduct of yogins, as in Chapter IV. 27, *prāṇāyāma* and *prāṇa-karmāni*–breath activity—they are called not actions of yoga practice but of *yajña-vidaḥ.*

l. 20 . . . rebirth, VIII. 28; IX. 4.

l. 22 . . . circumstances, III. 15.

l. 23 . . . possible. III. 16.

p. 220

l. 2 . . . decisively.” V. 1.

l. 5 . . . good. V. 2.

l. 8 . . . both. V. 4.

l. 9 . . . sacrifice. V. 7.

l. 12 . . . fruit. V. 13, 14.

l. 14 . . . know V. 19.

l. 17 . . . beings.” V. 28, 29.

l. 29 . . . himself.” VI. 5.

l. 34 . . . same.” VI. 7–8.

l. 39 . . . himself,” VI. 20.

l. 41 . . . tion.” VI. 19, 20.

p. 221

l. 2 . . . from. VI. 21.

l. 4 . . . little,” VI. 25.

l. 6 . . . restrain, VI. 35.

l. 7 . . . faith?” VI. 37.

l. 9 . . . deeds. VI. 40.

l. 13 . . . better. VI. 41.

l. 17 . . . tion. VI 42–47.

l. 30 . . . doubt. VII. 1.

l.32 . . . known. VII. 2.

l. 34 . . . reaches. VII. 3.

l. 37 . . . (nityayukta), *nitya* is derived from the two particles *ni-* in, en, and the suffix *-tya,* meaning that which is found in the place illustrated by the adverb or preverg: etymologically it means ‘found inside of,’ or the ‘source of.’

l. 37 . . . (ekabhaktir), VII. 17.

l. 39 . . . (yuktātmā). VII. 18.

l. 40 . . . wisdom. VII. 19.

p. 222

l. 1 . . . higher VII. 4, 5.

l. 5 . . . man. VII. 6,7,8.

l. 5 . . . life VII. 5.

l. 6 . . . gunas VII. 12.

l. 8 . . . ground VII. 14.

l. 9 . . . them. VII. 20.

l. 11 . . . me." VII. 23.

l. 14 . . . generator. VII. 24, 25.

l. 18 . . . action VII. 29, 30.

l. 22 . . . . to. VIII. 21.

l. 25 . . . perspective VIII. 1, 2.

l. 31 . . . coincide. VIII. 4.

l. 34 . . . becomes. VIII. 6.

l. 35 . . . stand. VIII. 22.

l. 37 . . . place VIII. 27, 28.

l. 38 . . . apparent; VIII. 18.

l. 40 . . . night Ibid.

l. 41 . . . into. Ibid.

l. 41 . . . action, VIII. 12–17.

l. 43 . . . yugas. VIII. 3, 4, 10, 17.

p. 223

l. 22 . . . (aśradhādhānāh), IX. 3.

l. 24 . . . rebirth. IX. 3.

l. 27 . . . beings"; IX. 5. The reader should be very conscious not to read mystical escapes in verses 4 and 5 of this Chapter IX. It is obvious that these verses are diffeicult to translate, for whatever translation we offer will be trapped within our own coordinates of space and time on a visual model synthesizing the sensorium. We will have to wait for the next chapter in this book to see how the "sound" model implicit in the *Gītā* would make sense of these two verses. In the meantime, *"matsthāni sarvabhūtāni na cā 'haṃ teṣv avasthitaḥ,"* in verse 4 could be better translated as

"Though all beings are *fixed* in me, I am not *fixed* in them." While, *"bhūtabhṛn na ca bhūtas ho mamā 'tmā bhūtabhāvanaḥ"* could be better translated as "Generating beings, yet not being generated by them, my very self is the source of beings." No idea, god, thing, being or whatever may coincide, erase, cover up the original "sound-point" originating the whole cosmic dance. See next chapter on Structure.

l. 28 . . . again"; IX. 8.

l. 30 . . . revolves, IX. 10.

l. 32 . . . wisdom. IX. 15.

l. 35 . . . sacrifice. IX. 25.

l. 36 . . . undividedly, IX. 30.

l. 37 . . . castes. IX. 32.

l. 39 . . . dharma, IX. 31.

l. 40 . . . goal. IX. 32.

l. 44 . . . action. IX. 34.

p. 224

l. 3 . . . path, IX. 23.

l. 3 . . . on." II. 16; VIII. 18, 19; IX. 7, 10.

l. 6 . . . interest. X. 1.

l. 8 . . . chapter. Ibid.

l. 13 . . . generated. X. 2–11.

l. 16 . . . ground. X. 12–18.

l. 19 . . . meditation. X. 17.

l. 22 . . . case." IV. 11.

p. 227

l. 2 . . . delusion. XI. 1.

l. 2 . . . see. XI. 4.

l. 4 . . . yoga." XI. 8.

l. 9 . . . seen. XI. 9–14.

l. 16 . . . crumble. XI. 23.

l. 19 . . . me." XI. 31.

l. 22 . . . world." XI. 32.

l. 25 . . . bhava)." XI. 33.

l. 28 . . . altogether. XI. 41, 42.

l. 29 . . . vision. XI. 45.

l. 30 . . . fear. Ibid.

l. 32 . . . living. Ibid.

l. 36 . . . into, XI. 54.

l. 37 . . . action. XI. 55.

p. 229

l. 13 . . . unmanifest." XII. 1, 5.

l. 16 . . . devotion: XII. 2, 8, 20. It would be interesting for the reader to see in relation to this distinction we made here, the understanding of faith the people of the ṛgveda legated to the culture. See for example, *Four-Dimensional Man,* p. 167, 170. In *Ṛg Veda* 10.151 we read:

> 1. By Faith is Agni Kindled, by Faith his oblation offered. Full of happiness we rejoice in Faith.
>
> 3. Just as the gods had faith even in the powerful *asuras* (demons) Make this wish of mine come true to those Who are generous in the Sacrifice.
>
> 4. Protected by Vāyu, both men and gods increase In Faith by Sacrificing. Men gain Faith through the instilled desires of the heart And become richer through Faith.
>
> 5. Faith in the early morning, Faith at noon we implore. Faith at the setting of the Sun. Faith increase our Faith.

Implied in the Ṛg Veda, however, there is the idea, later on embodied through the *avatāra,* of the "son becoming his father's father." 1.164.16; 18; 22.

p. 230

l. 34 . . . Kṣetra-jñanin. XIII. 1.

l. 36 . . . knowledge." XIII. 2.

l. 37 . . . tradition XIII. 4.

p. 231

l. 4 . . . madbhāvāya." XIII. 18.

l. 8 . . . indeed XIII. 29.

l. 15 . . . it XIII. 30.

l. 16 . . . it, XIII. 32.

l. 19 . . . field. XIII. 34.

l. 24 . . . prakṛti. XIII. 34.

l. 35 . . . prakṛti XIV.

l. 37 . . . One. XV.

p. 232

l. 33 . . . word. XVIII. 73.

l. 38 . . . all. sarvam, VII. 19.

l. 40 . . . knowledge." IV. 37.

p. 233

l. 12 . . . kind. XVIII. 21.

l. 13 . . . things. XVIII. 20.

l. 14 . . . life." III. 4, 20; VI. 43; VIII. 3; VIII. 15. etc.

CHAPTER SIX

p. 237

l. 5 . . . order. The reader will remember that this formulation is part of Ortega's larger thesis "I am I and my circumstance," which he formulated in 1914.

l. 8 . . . Marías, See Julián Marías, *Metaphysical Anthropology: The Empirical Structure of Human Life,* trans., by Frances M. López–Morillas (The Pennsylvania State University Press, 1971), especially pp. 70–79.

To guide the reader and help him place this thesis historically, I will note in Marías' fashion the difference between what I propose and what he and Heidegger propose under resembling titles:

- Heidegger speaks of *Daseinsanalytik,* or more specifically, existenziale Analytik des Daseins. This coincides with the level at which Heidegger's theory meets with Julián Marías' and mine.
- Heidegger and Marías use phenomenological description. But while Marías does not resort to the epokhé or reduction through bracketing, I consider that phenomenological description is *radically* impossible unless one resorts to the form of "ontologi-

cal reduction" we resort to in this book. It is only through this reduction that historical man can be recovered historically. Thus we also think insufficient *phenomenological* reduction.

- Heidegger, of course, does not use vital reason nor has any idea of it. In this Julián Marías and I are in full agreement. We also both agree that the *Dasein* (existing), in Heidegger's sense, is not "human life" but the mode of being *(Seinsweise)* of that being which we are.
- Where we differ from both Marías and Heidegger is in our interpretation of the body. For this we refer the reader to the text.

l. 32 . . . construction. The fact that structure is both analytical and empirical accounts also for what Ortega called *"leere Stellen,"* the empty spaces of human history. As a formula it is not yet knowledge, nor is knowledge possible without the formula, which means that analytical theory is not yet *real* knowledge—in fact, it is only knowledge of an unreal structure—but empirical reality is graspable only by means of that theory. The important point, however, is that both analytic and empirical structure are given within a cultural context which need first be identified.

p. 241

l. 38 . . . age." R.V. 10.72.1

p. 242

l. 4 . . . yugas. B.G. VIII. 17, 18, 19.

l. 7 . . . word. B.G. XVIII. 73.

p. 243

l. 9 . . . reeling. B.G. I. 28, 29, 30.

l. 14 . . . end, XI. 14.

l. 17 . . . tremble, XI. 20.

l. 18 . . . I XI. 23.

l. 20 . . . peace, XI. 24.

l. 21 . . . refuge. XI. 25.

l. 23 . . . afraid. XI. 35.

l. 24 . . . you, XI. 42.

l. 28 . . . Lord; XI. 45.

l. 31 . . . (am I). XI. 51.

p. 245

l. 4 . . . Gītā. See Surendranath Dasgupta, *A History of Indian Philosophy,* Vol. II, pp. 455–479.

p. 247

l. 11 . . . again. IX. 8.

l. 14 . . . maker). VII. 4.

l. 25 . . . puruṣa. XIII. 26.

l. 26 . . . prakṛti; XIII. 19.

l. 31 . . . guṇas. XVIII. 19.

l. 33 . . . themselves. III. 27, 28.

l. 38 . . . beginningless. XIII. 19.

p. 248

l. 2 . . . action XIII. 20.

l. 3 . . . moves. IX. 10.

l. 6 . . . kṣtra. XIII. 2.

l. 7 . . . kṣetra. XIII. 34.

l. 12 . . . guṇas. XIII. 14.

l. 25 . . . beings. XIV. 14, 15, 16.

l. 27 . . . puruṣottama; II. 15, 21, 60; III. 4, etc.

l. 28 . . . perspective; XV. 16, 17.

l. 29 . . . (unchangeable.) XV. 15, 18.

l. 30 . . . puruṣottama, XIII. 20.

l. 38 . . . field: See XIII. 14, quoted above.

p. 249

l. 2 . . . Self. XIII. 22.

l. 25 . . . prakṛti. III. 5.

l. 28 . . . action. III. 8.

l. 31 . . . mind. XVIII. 33.

p. 250

l. 38 . . . self" XIII. 24.

l. 38 . . . self" IV. 42.
See the insightful article of Malcolm Macfarlane, "Structure and Function: Complementarity in the Phenomenon of Life," in *Main Currents in Modern Thought,* May–June, 1973, Vol. 29, n.5 pp. 172–178. This article was written under the guidance of David White, Dept. of Philosophy, Macalester College, Minnoesota.

p. 260

l. 3 . . . Body, The Hague: Martinus Nijhoff, 1964.

l. 10 . . . own.'" *Ibid.,* pp. 260–261.

l. 17 . . . on." *Ibid.,* p. 260. Underlining mine.

p. 264

l. 23 . . . occasion" XI. 33.

l. 26 . . . field. XIII. 1.

l. 28 . . . fields; XIII. 2.

l. 31 . . . world. XIII. 13.

l. 35 . . . guṇas. XIII. 14.

l. 37 . . . beings. XIII. 16.

l. 39 . . . knowledge XIII. 17.

p. 265

l. 2 . . . takes. XIII. 23.

l. 7 . . . prakṛti. XIII. 34.

p. 266

l. 24 . . . interpreted. For readings on these points and appropriate bibliography, I refer the reader to a special issue of *Main Currents in Modern Thought,* September–October, 1974, Vol. 31, No. 1. This issue is devoted to the consideration, from a number of different perspectives, of one central theme: the critical significance of movement in our present understanding of the world.

p. 273

l. 15 . . . being." XIV. 2.

l. 17 . . . dissolution." Ibid.

l. 18 . . . prakṛti. XIV. 19, 20.

l. 22 . . . body . . . XIV. 5.

l. 24 . . . actions. XIV. 7.

l. 26 . . . sloth . . . XIV. 8.

l. 27 . . . caring). XIV. 9.

l. 33 . . . knowledge. XIV. 6.

p. 274

l. 2 . . . guṇas? XIV. 21.

l. 9 . . . guṇas. XIV. 25.

l. 13 . . . doubt. XIV. 23, 24.

l. 19 . . . action. XV. 1, 2.

l. 24 . . . attachment. XV. 3.

l. 25 . . . see XV. 10.

l. 27 . . . prakṛti XV. 7.

l. 30 . . . mind. XV. 8, 9.

l. 36 . . . puruṣa. XV. 16–19.

l. 38 . . . see. XV. 11.

p. 275

l. 9 . . . me.") XVIII. 65.

l. 25 . . . desire," XVIII. 63.

l. 28 . . . pleasure XVI. 8.

l. 29 . . . world. Ibid.

l. 30 . . . world. XVI. 9.

l. 32 . . . philosophies. XVI. 10.

l. 33 . . . desire; XVI. 12.

l. 38 . . . me? XVI. 13–15.

l. 40 . . . action. XVI. 19–20.

l. 41 . . . wait. XVII.

l. 43 . . . appropriations. XVIII.

p. 276

l. 3 . . . performed; XVIII. 47.

l. 5 . . . fulfillment. XVIII. 45.

l. 9 . . . smoke. XVIII. 48.

l. 13 . . . you. XVIII. 59.

l. 28 . . . word. XVIII. 73.

p. 277

l. 7 . . . killed," II. 19.

l. 8 . . . dualities, II. 14–15.

l. 8 . . . eternal, II. 11–25.

l. 9 . . . grief, II. 25.

l. 10 . . . (amṛtatva), II. 14–15.

l. 12 . . . imperishable, II. 17 f.

l. 13 . . . undistractible, Ibid. **p. 278**

l. 12 . . . (non-action). See: *Four-Dimensional Man,* especially Chapter Six.

p. 279

l. 13 . . . sound. See: Ṛg Veda 1.164,39, 41, 42; see also J.A.B. Van Buitenen in *Journal of the American Oriental Society,* 79, 176–187; also W. Norman Borwn in the same journal, 88,199–218.

l. 15 . . . syllables. R.V. 1.164.41–42.

l. 19 . . . change. Mānd. Up. I.2.

l. 19 . . . end. Mund. Up. I.6–7.

l. 21 . . . made. Bṛhadā. III. 8.3–10; IV. 4.16–IV. 5.14.

l. 31 . . . universe Cfr. Chan. U. II. 23.3.4; Mund. U. II. 2.2; Praśna U. IV. 9.11 and 10.

p. 281

l. 14 . . . (pratiṣṭhita)." Bṛhadā IV. 1.7. See also the *Bhagavad Gītā* in VIII. 12, "He who controls all the gates of the body and confines the mind to the heart."

l. 23 . . . body. See for its historical development: *Instant et Cause,* by Lilian Silburn, (Paris: Librairie Philosophique J. Vrin, 1955), pp. 112–118.

l. 27 . . . victory R.V. 10.55.1.

l. 29 . . . planted. R.V. 10.61.6. See *Four-Dimensional Man,* pp. 54, 90, 137, 160, and 165.

p. 284

l. 39 . . . McClain. See Ernest McClain, "Musical Marriages in Plato's Republic," in *Journal of Music Theory,* Fall 1974. See also Ernest McClain, "Plato's Musical Cosmology," in *Main Currents in Modern Thought,* 30, 1 (Sept.–Oct. 1973). pp. 34–42. See also: Siegmund Levarie and Ernst Levy, "The Pythagorean Table," in *Main Currents in Modern Thought,* 30, 4 (March–April 1974), pp. 117–129.

p. 286

l. 14 . . . number. The great moral of Greek Pythagoreanism as it applies to music was drawn by Aristotle and his pupil Aristoxenus when they denied that *number* determined the relations between the tones. Christian mythology had such deep roots in the same "Protopythagorean arithmology"—such a fervent commitment to integer relations—that Europe could not face the musical truth with equanimity until the time of Galileo, or later. See *Tuning and Temperament* by J. Murray Barbour and the role of Vincenzo Galilei, p. 57. (East Lansing, Michigan State College Press, 1953).

l. 30 . . . form." *Timaeus,* 19b.

p. 288

l. 4 . . . "equal-temperament." Ancient zodiac constellations were not of equal size, and the rational numbers available could not define equal-temperament. Furthermore, the discrepancy of about 5¼ days between solar year and 360 day schematic calendar is the same order of magnitude as the discrepancy between Ab and G# in both "Just" and "Pythagorean" tuning (the first falling short of a complete cycle, and the latter exceeding it). Thus the musician's problem parrallels the astonomer's at the level of pure number theory and its geometrical graphs.

l. 5 . . . reciprocal. The rising scale is our Western *Phrygian* mode, the ancient Greek *Dorian* mode, and can be tentatively identified with the North-Indian Bhairavī mode. The following scale, Western major mode, correllates with the North-Indian Bilāvala and Tilak-Kāmoda modes. (Alain Daniélou, *Indian Music,* Paris, UNESCO, 1952; pp. 18–19.)
Indian Music, Paris, UNESCO, 1952; pp. 18–19.)

l. 13 . . . symmetry. Western *Dorian* mode, North-Indian Bāgéshrī mode.

l. 15 . . . Ṛg Veda). The rising scale correlates with North-Indian

Malhāra mode and, under our assumption of octave-equivalence, the same five tones (with a change in tonic) recur in the Bhūpali mode.

p. 291

l. 18 . . . possibilities." Musical cosmology develops from the logical assumption that patterns are invariances describable by "smallest integer" sequences. Thus the Just diatonic scale (30:60 in Chart Ib) is the logical starting point because no smaller integers can define a scale with two similar tetrachords, but the same integers define both a rising and a falling sequence whose eleven tones can only be coalesced within the double defined by 6! = 720 (or one of its multiples). The 360 devisions within this cycle (360:720) bring us automatically into near correlation with the calendar year. Hence it is the logic of arithmetic, not the whimsy of poets, which unifies music and astronomy at this *radical* or *primitive* level. The contradiction between the linear, *arithmetic* time intervals and the *logarithmic* musical intervals intrigued the ancient mind as much as it does any modern one when introduced to a slide-rule.

p. 292

l. 8 . . . interpretation. In *Hindu Polytheism,* (Bollingen Series LXXIII, Pantheon Books, 1964), Alain Daniélou discusses the yantras shown here with attention to their wider symbolic implications (See especially, pp. 360–356.) The numbers in the star-hexagon are those from which Plato constructed his "marriage allegory" in Book VIII of the *Republic* (546) and were discussed extensively in the ancient literature of Platonism, at least until the time of Proclus (5th c. A.D.). (See Robert Brumbaugh, *Plato's Mathematical Imagination,* Bloomington, Indiana University Press, 1954—New York, Kraus Reprint Corporation, 1968, pp. 136–137; and James Adam, *The Republic of Plato,* Vol. II, Cambridge, University Press, 1902, 2nd ed. 1963, pp. 201–208 and 264–312.)

l. 12 . . . Śiva. The "drum of Śiva" is the model for Plato's Chi (X) in the creation myth of *Timaeus* (35–39). A musical interpretation was offered a century ago by Albert von Thimus, and is extended further in "A New Look At Plato's *Timaeus,*" by Ernest McClain (In *Music and Man,* vol. 4, pp. 341–360). The drum would appear to be the Cretan "double-axe," widely diffused in the ancient world, and found as far west as Stonehenge. The "drum" played an interesting geometric function in Ptolemy's *Almagest.* We suggest that the *multiplication* symbolized in this abstract "pebble" pattern brings the *increase in insight* which Vedic poets paean in their hymns to Soma, the Moon, whose waxing and waning correlates metaphorically with the *reciprocal* implications of integers (as multiples and submultiples). Soma is "secured by sheltering rules, guarded by hymns," achieved by "listening to the stones," and is never "tasted" by true Brāhmans. (R.V. 10.85.3–4.)

p. 295

l. 16 . . . pole. In Ṛg Vedic metaphor, the Sun is born in the east (as "8th hero" along the "transevering" horizontal axis = *horizon* of our table), and then rises high in the heaven where he looks down on Vṛtra, his reciprocal, with whom he encloses the *irrational* number $\sqrt{2}$ = Ab = G# within a very narrow interval. It is the problem of the square root of two, then, which apparently motivates the Hindu search for algebraic yantras of sufficient size to bring all aspects of that problem within some comprehensive perspective. (See Chart IX.)

p. 296

l. 7 . . . yantra. Count upwards along the left side of the yantra to find Viṣṇu = 5^{14}. Count to the right along the base of the yantra to find Vṛtra = 3^6, and multiply by 2 until he falls *within* the Kalpa-Brahmā "double" where he confronts Viṣṇu face-to-face. Compare both values with the Kalpa-Brahmā limits to test approximations to $\sqrt{2}$.

$$\text{Vṛta} = 3^6 \times 2^{23} = \frac{6{,}115{,}295{,}232}{4{,}320{,}000{,}000} = 1.415+$$

$$\text{Viṣṇu} = 5^{14} = \frac{8{,}640{,}000{,}000}{6{,}103{,}515{,}625} = 1.415+$$

The direct ratio of Vṭra/Viṣṇu is about 1.0019, an acoustically negligible difference of about 2 parts in a thousand (about 3 *cents* or one degree in a tone maṇḍala. Since Vedic imagery links tones, numbers, maṇḍalas and the reciprocal forces of gods and demons with the elaborate rites of sacrifice, it would appear that the poets possessed a full understanding of what we in the West understand as a need for "tempering" the ideal scale. *Whatever* tuning we decide to use involves an "error" from one perspective or another, an "original sin" among both numbers and tones.

The "ten heroes" along the "transevering axis" within the "Kalpa" triangle (F to G#) (ignoring reciprocals) correlate with the cosmology of Philolaus and Plato in the ways shown in table 1. (They recur doubled in the Brahmā triangle.)

p. 297

l. 29 . . . heart." See B. L. van der Waerden, *Science Awakening,* p. 54. (New York, John Wiley and Sons, 1963). This author provides a detailed description of sexagesimal arithmetic in Chapters 1–3.

For a thoughtful summary of ancient mathematics, including Bayblonian virtuosity with reciprocals in a sexagesimal system and Egyptian skill with "unit fractions," see Carl B. Boyer, *A History of Mathematics,* chapters 1–3, (New York, John Wiley and Sons, 1968). Boyer suggests that ancient pottery, weaving, and basketry "show instances of congruence and symmetry, which suggest a sort of applied group theory, as well as propositions in geometry and arithmetic." (p. 6)

Appendix to Chapter Two

p. 341

l. 3 . . . "Idealism" Philosophical studies, (Patterson, N.J.; Littlefield, Adams & Co. 1959.)

p. 342

l. 18 . . . certainty." B. Russell, "My Mental Development" in *The Philosophy of Bertrand Russell,* ed. P. A. Schlipp (Evanston, Ill.: Library of Living Philosophers, 1946), p. 7.

l. 38 . . . substitution." See for example, B. Russell, *The Analysis of Mind,* (London: George Allen & Unwin, 1921) pp. 141–2, etc.

p. 343

l. 18 . . . all!" M. Schlick, "Positivism and Realism," *Logical Positivism,* edl. A. J. Ayer (Glencoe, Ill." The Free Press, 1959) p. 107.

l. 27 . . . same." Ludwig Wittgenstein, *Tractatus Logico-Philosophicus,* trans. D. F. Pears and B. F. McGuiness (New York: Humanities Press, 1961) sec. 1.2; 1.21.

l. 30 . . . statements. Ibid, sec. 2. 0201; 4.221; 3.26; 3.144.

l. 32 . . . sentences. Analysis begins from a sentence in the "system language" in which scientific assertions are formulated: say, "the ether does not exist." From this, one deduces a sentence in the protocol language, say: "If the ether does not exist, then no time difference is observed by Michelson and Morley." One then compares this sentence with the actual protocols of Michelson And Morley. Michelson: "No time difference observed." Morley: "No time difference observed." Accordingly the sentence in the system language, "The ether does not exist, *means,* No time difference observed." That is, it means the protocol sentences that verify it. See: O. Neurath "Protocol Sentences" in *Logical Positivism,* (p. 202).

p. 344

l. 2 . . . problem. L. Wittengstein, *Tractatus,* sec. 6.5; 6.521.

l. 13 . . . suggestion, Cfr. A. J. Ayer, "Editor's Introduction," *Logical Positivism,* p. 15.

l. 19 . . . grounds. R. Carnap, "Empiricism, Semantics, and Ontology," *Meaning and Necessity,* 2nd ed., (Chicago: Univ. of Chicago Press, Phoenix Books, 1958) pp. 208, 221.

p. 345

l. 4 . . . decide, See Husserl, "Philosophy as Rigorous Science," in *Phenomenology and the Crisis of Philosophy,* trans., notes & int. Quentin Lauer (NewYork: Harper Torchbooks, Harper and Row, 1965) pp. 141–2.

l. 10 . . . it. From Husserl's Diary in 1906 and quoted by H. Spiegelberg, *The Phenomenological Movement,* 2nd ed. (The Hague: Martinus Nijhoff, 1956) sec. 1:82.
This reminds us of Descartes:

> But this task is a laborious one, and insensibly a certain lassitude leads me into the course of my ordinary life. And just as a captive . . . I fall into my former opinions, and I dread awakening from this slumber . . . *Meditations, Philosophical Works,* I, pp. 149–9.

l. 26 . . . attitude E. Husserl, Ideas: *A General Introduction to Pure Phenomenology,* trans. W. R. Boyce-Gibson (New York: The Macmillan Co., 1931) sec. 27, 30.

l. 38 . . . system. *Ibid.,* sec. 31.

p. 346

l. 12 . . . Phenomenology. *Ibid.,* sec. 33.

l. 30 . . . experience. *Ibid.,* sec. 88.

p. 347

l. 22 . . . multiplicities." E. Husserl *Cartesian Meditations,* trans. D. Cairns (The Hague: Martinus Nijhoff, 1960) pp. 39–40.

p. 348

l. 38 . . . field. Husserl's earlier position may be seen in the *Ideen su einer reiner phānmenologischen Philosophie,* known as *Ideen* I

Tape: F Job No.: 482
Ms/c pages: Footnotes

Pub. Title: Humanization
Operator: Cynthia

(1913), or *Ideas*. Husserl's later position may be found in the *Cartesianischen Meditationen,* or *Cartesian Meditations*. See especially the Second Meditation, sections 19–22, or pp. 44–45 of the English translation.

Not all those inspired by Husserl agree with Husserl on the Methodological value of some aspects of his practice of transcendental reduction, i.e., of the epoché of phenomena, his search for apodicticity, of the possibility of uncovering a universal *a priori* in the transcendental subject unconditioned by factual experience.

In relation to this writer's reservations his position is definitely post-Husserlian in the sense that (a) he conceives the epoché as being insufficient if applied only to phenomena and not also to the structures and contexts within which they appear (ontological indifference, besides ontic indifference); (b) he conceives philosophy not as a search for an "absolutely grounded science" but rather for the *a priori* conditions of possibility, ontological and ontic, subjective and objective, of actual, present human experience; (c) that the demands for a universal *a priori* of the transcendental subject does not consist of eidetic essenses, but rather in the polymorphic structure of human and systematic self-reflection in which data, understanding of data and judgment about the understanding of data succeed one another according to certain principles determined by such polymorphic human structures and its polymorphic contexts. Philosophy's rationality consists in its own formative activity.

p. 349

l. 10 . . . horizon. Husserl's account of the noetic-noematic polarity of human consciousness is to be found in *Ideen* I, especially sec. 3, chapt. 3 (pp. 260–350 of *Ideas*). Also in the *Cartesian Meditations* especially the Second Meditation. For Husserl's further development of this theme in relation to the historicity of man and science, see: *The Crisis of European Sciences and Transcendental Phenomenology,* trans. David Cairns (North Western University Press, 1970) pp. 158; 237; 162; 243; 358–59; 168; 149.

l. 21 . . . horizons." Husserl's notion of World may be found in *Ideen* I, sec. 1, chap. 1; and sec. 2, chap. 1 (pp. 91–96; 133–136 in Ideas). See also in the *Crisis,* as horizon, p. 143; social, 164; as totality and unity, p. 31.

p. 350

l. 10 . . . pattern," A. N. Whitehead, *Modes of Thought* (N.Y.: The Macmillan Co., Free Press Paperback, 1968), p. 174.

l. 12 . . . arbitrariness." A. N. Whitehead, *Science and the Modern World* (N. Y.: The Macmillan Co., 1925) p. 27.

l. 28 . . . us." A. N. Whitehead, *Modes of Thought,* p. 42.

l. 30 . . . language," A. N. Whitehead, *Essays in Science and Philosophy* (N.Y.: Philosophical Library, 1948) p. 15.

l. 45 . . . not. A. N. Whitehead, *Modes of Thought,* p. 174.

p. 351

l. 32 . . . "Whitehead's System" *The Journal of Philosophy,* LXVI, 19, Oct. 2, 1969, pp. 589–600.

p. 352

l. 19 . . . mediation of *God* *Ibid.,* pp. 600–601.

p. 353

l. 4 . . . concretely." M. Heidegger, *Being and Time,* trans. J. Macquarrie and E. Robinson (London: SCM Press, 1962) p. 19.

l. 11 . . . nature." M. Heidegger, "The Way Back into the Ground of Metaphysics," *Existentialism from Dostoevsky to Sartre,* pp. 209–211.

l. 20 . . . itself." *Ibid.,* p. 213.

l. 24 . . . sails." M. Heidegger, *Being and Time,* p. 100.

l. 33 . . . -self." *Ibid.,* p. 321.

p. 354

l. 2 . . . ends. *Ibid.,* p. 294–95.

l. 16 . . . impossible." M. Heidegger, "A Dialogue on Language," *On the Way to Language,* trans. P. D. Hertz (New York: Harper & Row, 1971), p. 5.

l. 18 . . . silence." *Ibid.,* p. 52.

p. 355

l. 2 . . . spontaneity. J. P. Sartre, *The Transcendence of the Ego,* trans. F. Williams and R. Kirkpatrick (New York: Farrar, Straus & Giroux Noonday Press, 1957) p. 79.

l. 11 . . . free. *Ibid.,* pp. 99–100.

l. 34 . . . passion." J. P. Sartre, *Being and Nothingness,* trans. H. Barnes (New York: Philosophical Library, 1956) p. 615.

Appendix to Chapter Five

p. 360

l. 1 . . . itself The acknowledgable reader will immediately notice we are following in this historical criticism Jurgen Habermas. We refer the reader to him for a more detailed analysis and also for bibliography on these points. I will try to avoid more footnotes here so as not to drown the reader in them. Cfr. Jurgen Habermas, *Knowledge and Human Interests,* trans. by Jeremy J Shapiro (Boston: Beacon Press, 1972). Seealso *Toward a Rational Society* (Boston: Beacon Press, 1971).

It is a curious myopia of philosophers, even of those dedicated to critical philosophy, to ignore other philosophers who preceeded them in the history of their own activity. It is incomprehensible to me that modern philosophers doing critical philosophy ignore Ortega y Gasset who first enunciated many of the principles they are using. It is even more incomprehensible with German philosophers since Ortega's works, especially those dealing with critical philosophy, were translated into German and enunciated for German philosophers first. The reader will be able to follow the paths of critical philosophy from Kant, Hegel, Marx and Habermas not from them but through them on Ortega's program of philosophy.

p. 361

l. 4 . . . science." G. W. F. Hegel, *Phenomenology of the Mind,* trans. by Baillie, 2nd ed. (N.Y., 1949), p. 136.

l. 28 . . . subjectively." Karl Marx, *Fruhschriften,* ed., S. Landshut (Stuttgart, 1953), p. 339.

p. 362

l. 24 . . . intentions." Karl Marx, *Okonomische Scriften,* Vol. I, ed. J-J. Lieber and B Kautsky (Darmstadt, 1962), p. xxix.

l. 28 . . . science." Karl Marx, *Economic and Philosophic Manuscripts of 1844,* (Moscow, 1961), p. 111.

p. 367

l. 46 . . . State." Ortega y Gasset, *Obras Completas* (Abbr. O.C.), Vol. VII pp. 268–69. In English it may be seen in *Man and People,* trans. by Willard R. Trask (W. W. Norton & Company, Inc., New York, 1957), pp. 271–272.

E. Husserl, *Ideen zu einer Reinen Phaenomenologie und Phaenomenologischen Philosophie* (Haag, Martinus Nijhoff, 1952), p. 55ff.

E. Fink, *Zur Ontologischen Freuhegeschichte von Raum-Zeit-Bewegung,* (Haag, Martinus Nijhoff, 1957).

"Sensación Construcción e Intuición," in *Apuntes sobre el pensamiento,* in *O.C.,* Vol. V, pp. 517–545. The reader may clearly see in these notes of Ortega his critical position regarding Husserl and phenomenology.

O.C., VIII, p. 273.

Prólogo para alemanes, in *O.C.,* Vol. VI, 48–49.

O.C., pp. 252–253.

Ibid., p. 254.

Origen y Epílogo De la Filosofía, O.C., IX, p. 372.

O.C., VIII, p. 273.

Index

human possibilities 193